THE SOUTH CHINA SEA ARBITRATION

On 22 January 2013, the Republic of the Philippines instituted arbitral proceedings against the People's Republic of China (PRC) under the United Nations Convention on the Law of the Sea (UNCLOS) with regard to disputes between the two countries in the South China Sea (South China Sea Arbitration). On 19 February 2013, the PRC formally expressed its opposition to the institution of proceedings, making it clear from the outset that it will not have any part in these arbitral proceedings and that this position will not change. It is thus to be expected that over the next year and a half, the Tribunal will receive written memorials and hear oral submissions from the Philippines only. The Chinese position will go unheard. However, the Tribunal is under an obligation, before making its award, to satisfy itself not only that it has jurisdiction over the dispute, but also that the claims brought by the Philippines are well founded in fact and law (UNCLOS Annex VII, Article 9).

The book aims to offer a (not *the*) Chinese perspective on some of the issues to be decided by the Tribunal and thus to assist the Tribunal in meeting its obligations under the Convention. The book does not set out the official position of the Chinese government, but is rather to serve as a kind of *amicus curiae* brief advancing possible legal arguments on behalf of the absent respondent. The book does not deal with the merits of the disputes between the Philippines and the PRC, but focuses on the questions of jurisdiction, admissibility and other objections which the tribunal will have to decide as a preliminary matter. The book will show that there are insurmountable preliminary objections to the Tribunal deciding the case on the merits and that the Tribunal would be well advised to refer the dispute back to the parties in order for them to reach a negotiated settlement.

The book brings together scholars of public international law from mainland China, Taiwan and Europe united by a common interest in the law of the sea and disputes in the South China Sea.

The South China Sea Arbitration

A Chinese Perspective

Edited by

Stefan Talmon
and
Bing Bing Jia

·HART·
PUBLISHING

OXFORD AND PORTLAND, OREGON
2014

Published in the United Kingdom by Hart Publishing Ltd
16C Worcester Place, Oxford, OX1 2JW
Telephone: +44 (0)1865 517530
Fax: +44 (0)1865 510710
E-mail: mail@hartpub.co.uk
Website: http://www.hartpub.co.uk

Published in North America (US and Canada) by
Hart Publishing
c/o International Specialized Book Services
920 NE 58th Avenue, Suite 300
Portland, OR 97213-3786
USA
Tel: +1 503 287 3093 or toll-free: (1) 800 944 6190
Fax: +1 503 280 8832
E-mail: orders@isbs.com
Website: http://www.isbs.com

Hart Publishing is an Imprint of Bloomsbury Publishing plc.

British Library Cataloguing in Publication Data
Data Available

ISBN: 978-1-84946-547-2

Typeset by Criteria International Ltd
Printed and bound in Great Britain by
TJ International Ltd, Padstow, Cornwall

Preface

Books on important international law cases are normally written only after the parties have submitted their memorials and presented their oral arguments, and the court or tribunal has finally rendered its judgment. The *South China Sea Arbitration* will, in our view, be one of the landmark cases in international law because of the parties involved, the legal questions to be decided and the absence of one of the parties. In a situation not dissimilar to the famous *Nicaragua* case before the International Court of Justice in the 1980s, China, one of the world's major powers and a permanent member of the United Nations Security Council, has decided not to participate in arbitral proceedings instituted by the Philippines under the United Nations Convention on the Law of the Sea (UNCLOS) with regard to the disputes between the two countries in the South China Sea.

China has made it clear from the outset that it will not have any part in the arbitral proceedings because it considers the Tribunal seized with the case to be evidently without jurisdiction and the claims made to be clearly inadmissible and manifestly unfounded. The Arbitral Tribunal will thus receive written memorials and hear oral submissions from the Philippines only. It seems unlikely that China will follow the example of the United States in the *Nicaragua* case and set out its position in an official publication that will be submitted to the Tribunal in an informal manner 'to be made available to anyone at the [Tribunal] interested in the subject',[1] or that it will set out its legal position in letters or other informal communications to the Tribunal. The Chinese position will thus most likely go unheard. China's default of appearance will make the task of the Arbitral Tribunal more than difficult as the factual and legal situation in the South China Sea is 'highly complex'.[2] However, the Arbitral Tribunal is under an obligation, before making its award, to satisfy itself not only that it has jurisdiction over the dispute, but also that the claims brought by the Philippines are well founded in fact and law.[3]

The book aims to offer a specifically Chinese perspective on some of the legal issues before the Arbitral Tribunal, to present the Tribunal with a fuller picture of the facts underlying the Philippines' claims, and thus to assist the Tribunal in meeting its obligations under UNCLOS. The

---

[1] See *Military and Paramilitary Activities in and against Nicaragua (Nicaragua v United States of America)* (Merits) [1986] ICJ Rep 14, 44 [73].
[2] United Nations General Assembly, Law of the Sea: Report of the Secretary-General, UN Doc A/47/623 (24 November 1992) 14 [33].
[3] UNCLOS Annex VII, art 9.

book does not, however, deal with the merits of the disputes between the Philippines and China, but focuses on the questions of jurisdiction, admissibility and other objections, which the Arbitral Tribunal will have to decide as a preliminary matter. The book hopes to show that there are considerable obstacles to the Tribunal deciding the case on the merits and that it would be well advised to refer the disputes back to the parties in order for them to reach a negotiated settlement.

The book does not intend to set out or represent in any way the official position of the Chinese Government but endeavours to serve as a kind of *amicus curiae* brief of interested academics acting in their capacity as independent experts of international law. As pointed out by Salmon LJ, 'the role of an *amicus curiae* [is] to help the court by expounding the law impartially, or if one of the parties [is] unrepresented, by advancing the legal arguments on his behalf'.[4] By advancing possible legal arguments on behalf of the absent respondent, the book hopes to serve the administration of justice and to strengthen the rule of law.

The editors would like to express their gratitude for editorial assistance to Holly Wesener JD and Steven Reinhold MJur who were ably assisted by Franca Maurer, Kathrin Wiesche, Katja Breucker and David Bieger, student assistants at the Institute for Public International Law at the University of Bonn.

Stefan Talmon
Institute for Public International Law
University of Bonn

Bing Bing Jia
School of Law
Tsinghua University, Beijing

---

[4] *Allen v Sir Alfred McAlpine & Sons Ltd* [1968] 2 QB 229, 266.

Contents

List of Abbreviations

AFP	Armed Forces of the Philippines
ARF	ASEAN Regional Forum
ASEAN	Association of Southeast Asian Nations
AUSMIN	Australia-United States Ministerial Consultations
BBC	British Broadcasting Corporation
Bevans	Treaties and Other International Agreements of the United States of America 1776–1949, compiled under the direction of Charles I Bevans
CBM	Confidence Building Measures Mechanism
CERD	Committee on the Elimination of Racial Discrimination
CLCS	Commission on the Limits of the Continental Shelf
COC	Code of Conduct
CS	Continental Shelf
DFA	Department of Foreign Affairs
diss op	dissenting opinion
DOALOS	Division for Ocean Affairs and the Law of the Sea
DOC	Declaration on the Conduct of Parties in the South China Sea
DOC Guidelines	Guidelines for the Implementation of the Declaration on the Conduct of Parties in the South China Sea
DRC	Democratic Republic of Congo
EEZ	Exclusive Economic Zone
EJIL	European Journal of International Law
EU	European Union
GSEC	Geophysical Survey and Exploration Contract
ICAO	International Civil Aviation Organization
ICJ	International Court of Justice
ICSID	International Centre for Settlement of Investment Disputes
IGN	Institut Géographique National
IIL	Institute of International Law
ILR	International Law Reports
ITLOS	International Tribunal for the Law of the Sea
JCBC	Joint Commission for Bilateral Cooperation
JWG	Joint Working Group
KIG	Kalayaan Island Group
km	kilometres
m	meter
MFA	Ministry of Foreign Affairs

MN	Margin Note
NIAS	Nordic Institute of Asian Studies
nm/M	nautical mile
OAS	Organization of American States
OUP	Oxford University Press
PCA	Permanent Court of Arbitration
PCIJ	Permanent Court of International Justice
PHL/Ph	Philippines
PLA	People's Liberation Army
PLC	Public Limited Company
PMC	Post-Ministerial Conferences
PRC	People's Republic of China
Rep	Report
Res	Resolution
RIAA	Reports on International Arbitral Awards
RP	Republic of the Philippines
Sec	Section
sep op	separate opinion
SFA	Secretary of Foreign Affairs
SOM	Senior Officials Meetings
Stat	United States Statutes at Large
TAC	Treaty of Amity and Cooperation in Southeast Asia
TIAS	Treaties and other International Acts Series, issued singly in pamphlets by the United States Department of State
TS	Treaty Series, issued singly in pamphlets by the United States Department of State
UA&P	University of Asia and the Pacific
UK	United Kingdom
UN	United Nations
UNCLOS III	Third United Nations Conference on the Law of the Sea
UNCLOS	United Nations Convention on the Law of the Sea
UNGA	United Nations General Assembly
UNTS	United Nations Treaty Series
US	United States
UST	United States Treaties and Other International Agreements
VN	Vietnam
WPS	West Philippine Sea

Contributors

Michael Sheng-ti GAU, LLB (National Taiwan University), LLM (Cambridge University), LLM (King's College, London), PhD (Leiden University) is Professor of Public International Law at the Institute of Law of the Sea, National Taiwan Ocean University in Keelung. He has acted as legal adviser and consultant on matters of international law and the law of the sea and was also involved in negotiations in Regional Fisheries Management Organizations as well as WTO fishery subsidies negotiations.

Bing Bing JIA, DPhil (Oxford University) is Professor of International Law, Law School, Tsinghua University, Beijing. Prior to taking up his post at Tsinghua he served as Legal Officer at the ICTY and, temporarily, the ICTR (1998–2004), and previously served as Law Clerk at the ICTY (1996–1998). He also acts as a consultant on matters of international law and serves on the editorial boards of *Ocean Development and International Law*, *International Review of the Red Cross* and the *Chinese Journal of International Law*.

Chenxi MI, BA (China University of Political Science and Law, Beijing), LLM (Essex University) is a PhD candidate in maritime law at the Law School, Dalian Maritime University, Dalian. Her research covers questions of public international law and, specifically, the law of the sea. Since 2007, she has been a research fellow with the China Institute for Marine Affairs focusing on the law of marine environmental protection and the dispute resolution mechanisms of the UNCLOS.

Stefan TALMON, DPhil MA (Oxford University), LLM (Cambridge University) is Professor of Public International Law and Director at the Institute for Public International Law at the University of Bonn. He is also a Supernumerary Fellow of St Anne's College, Oxford. Prior to taking up the chair at Bonn he was Professor of Public International Law at the University of Oxford. He practises in the field of international law as a Barrister from 20 Essex Street Chambers, London.

Haiwen ZHANG, PhD (Peking University) is one of the Vice Presidents of the Chinese Society of International Law and the Secretary-General of the Chinese Society on the Law of the Sea. She is a Senior Research Fellow of the China Institute for Marine Affairs. She has acted as legal adviser and consultant on bilateral negotiations on maritime disputes between China and its neighbouring countries and participated in the work of the UN Open-ended Informal Consultative Process on Oceans and the Law of the Sea.

Table of Cases

Permanent Court of International Justice

International Court of Justice

International Tribunal for the Law of the Sea

Arbitral Tribunals

Domestic Courts

Table of Treaties

Table of National Instruments

People's Republic of China

Taiwan Authorities

Republic of the Philippines

Socialist Republic of Viet Nam

1

Introduction

BING BING JIA AND STEFAN TALMON

I. THE DISPUTES BETWEEN THE PHILIPPINES AND CHINA IN THE SOUTH CHINA SEA

IN GEOGRAPHICAL TERMS, the South China Sea covers a sea area of some 3.5 million square kilometres (km) which is semi-enclosed by Brunei, China, Indonesia, Malaysia, the Philippines and Vietnam.[1] It is part of the Pacific Ocean, dotted by numerous islands, islets, shoals, cays, reefs and rocks that are gathered into four groups. These four island groups, or archipelagos, are known to both Chinese and foreign sources as the Xisha [Paracel] Islands; Dongsha [Pratas] Islands; Zhongsha Islands, including Huangyan Island [Macclesfield Bank, including Scarborough Shoal]; and Nansha [Spratly] Islands.[2] The groups fall within an area with the coordinates of 3°57' to 21°N and 109°30' to 117°50'E, stretching for a distance of approximately 1,800 km from the north to the south, and about 900 km from the east to the

---

[1] International Hydrographic Organisation, *Limits of Oceans and Seas*, Special Publication No 23, 3rd edn (Monte-Carlo, Imp Monégasque, 1953) 30–31; China Institute of Marine Affairs, State Oceanic Administration, *Zhong Guo Hai Yang Fa Zhan Bao Gao [China's Ocean Development Report]* (Beijing, Hai Yang Chu Ban She [Oceans Press], 2011) 19–20. The publication by the International Hydrographic Organisation is in the course of revision: Chris Rahman and Martin Tsamenyi, 'A Strategic Perspective on Security and Naval Issues in the South China Sea' (2010) 41 *Ocean Development and International Law* 315, 316.

[2] China Institute of Marine Affairs, *Zhong Guo Hai Yang Fa Zhan Bao Gao [China's Ocean Development Report]* 20. The Report also provides the following details: the Xisha Islands comprise 32 islands and islets, each possessing a surface area larger than five hundred square meters; the Zhongsha Islands are composed of rocks, sandbanks, and reefs among which, by virtue of two rocks, only Huangyan Island (or Scarborough Shoal or Reef) rises above sea level at high tide; the Nansha Islands consist of over 230 islands, islets, rocks, banks, and shoals, among which 25 are islands (ibid, 24). Another Chinese publication describes the Dongsha Islands as comprising Dongsha [Pratas] Island, the Dongsha [Pratas] Reef, and two banks; see Guang Dong Provincial Commission of Toponymy, *Nan Hai Zhu Dao Di Ming Zi Liao Hui Bian [Collection of Materials Regarding the Geographical Names of the Islands in the South China Sea]* (Guangzhou, Guang Dong Di Tu Chu Ban She [Provincial Press of Maps and Atlases], 1987) 164–68. Useful references with regard to the geography and names of those islands may also be found in Marvyn S Samuels, *Contest for the South China Sea* (New York, Methuen, 1982) 183–94.

west.[3] By virtue of its geographic position, the South China Sea forms part of the vital route for maritime trade and transport for East Asian and Southeast Asian States and their trading partners in Asia, Africa and beyond.[4] More than half of the annual global merchant fleet tonnage sails through the South China Sea, with over 70,000 ships entering or exiting the South China Sea through the Malacca and Singapore Straits annually.[5] There are rich fisheries in the South China Sea, ranking fourth in terms of annual marine production.[6] For example, China's marine fishery production in the South China Sea in 2011 was more than 7 million tons, with 3.39 million tons from catch production and the rest from aquaculture production.[7] That accounted for more than 25 per cent of the country's total catch production in 2011. That year capture fisheries in the South China Sea supported over 27,430 Chinese fishing vessels, although the majority of them seem to operate in waters off the mainland coast.[8] Fisheries resources are especially rich in the abyssal region of the Nansha [Spratly] Islands and their adjacent waters. In addition, there are expanding prospects for the exploitation of oil and natural gas reserves in the seabed and subsoil.[9]

The proximity of the littoral States of the South China Sea means that disputes over regional control and influence are bound to arise almost automatically. Such disputes have manifested themselves in a complex and intractable web of territorial and maritime jurisdictional disputes. Five countries (China, both the mainland and Taiwan; Vietnam; the Philippines; Malaysia and Brunei) claim territorial sovereignty over land features in the South China Sea and six countries (China, both the mainland and Taiwan; Vietnam; the Philippines; Malaysia; Brunei and Indonesia) have overlapping claims to various maritime zones in the area. However, disputes between the coastal States became more intense only in the post-1970 era. In the long history of the South China Sea, dating back to at least the third century AD,[10] China has been a major player in the area. This is evidenced not least by the fact of the name given to this sea area, which comprises numerous

---

[3] China Institute of Marine Affairs, *Zhong Guo Hai Yang Fa Zhan Bao Gao [China's Ocean Development Report]* (2011) 20.

[4] Rahman and Tsamenyi, 'A Strategic Perspective on Security and Naval Issues in the South China Sea' 316–18.

[5] ibid, 317.

[6] Tom Naess, 'Dangers to the Environment' in Timo Kovomäki (ed), *War or Peace in the South China Sea?* (Copenhagen, NIAS Press, 2002) 43, 44.

[7] PRC Ministry of Agriculture, Fisheries Bureau, *Zhong Guo Yu Ye Tong Ji Nian Jian 2013 [China Fisheries Statistics Yearbook 2013]* (Beijing, Zhong Guo Nong Ye Chu Ban She [China Agriculture Press], 2013) 46.

[8] PRC Ministry of Agriculture, Fisheries Bureau, *Zhong Guo Yu Ye Nian Jian 2012 [China Fisheries Yearbook 2012]* (Beijing, Zhong Guo Nong Ye Chu Ban She [China Agriculture Press], 2012) 174 (that figure is for fishing vessels subject to the annual fishing ban in the South China Sea).

[9] Lee Lai To, *China and the South China Sea Dialogues* (Westport, Praeger, 1999) 10–12.

[10] Jianming Shen, 'China's Sovereignty over the South China Sea Islands: A Historical Perspective' (2002) 1 *Chinese Journal of International Law* 94, 102–05.

islands and other insular features. The involvement of other littoral States in the South China Sea has been much more recent. The Philippines, for example, only gained independence in 1946. The issues that prompted the present arbitration have an even more recent history and date back to the beginning of the 1970s. The purpose of this brief introduction is not to elaborate on the long history of the South China Sea,[11] but rather to focus on the very facts that gave rise, or are relevant to the Philippines' filing of the Notification and Statement of Claim against China in January 2013.[12]

In June 1933, the then Chinese Government appointed a Commission that was tasked with reviewing maps and atlases produced by private sources in China. This Review Commission of Maps for Land and Water published in January 1935 a list of 132 names, both in English and Chinese, for Chinese islands and other insular features in the South China Sea, which included the Xisha [Paracel] Islands; Dongsha [Pratas] Islands; Zhongsha Islands, including Huangyan Island [Macclesfield Bank, including Scarborough Shoal]; and Nansha [Spratly] Islands.[13] A month later, the Commission's Gazette published a map of the Chinese islands of the South China Sea.[14] In 1946, China recovered from Japan the Xisha [Paracel] and Nansha [Spratly] Islands.[15] There was no reaction from Vietnam or any other State, and the Chinese naval contingent which was sent to the islands erected stone markers on Yong Xing [Woody] Island in the Xisha [Paracel] Islands and Taiping [Itu Aba] Island in the Nansha [Spratly] Islands.[16]

Following further inspections and surveys, the then Chinese Government internally circulated an atlas in 1947, drawing an eleven-dash line to indicate the geographical scope of its authority over the South China Sea, right down to the Zengmu Ansha [James Shoal], at 3°58'N 112°17'E.[17] In the same year, the Ministry of the Interior published a list

---

[11] For a detailed account, see Samuels, *Contest for the South China Sea* (1982). For a brief overview, see Stein Tønnesson, 'The History of the Dispute' in Timo Kovomäki (ed), *War or Peace in the South China Sea?* (Copenhagen, NIAS Press, 2002) 6–23. For an official account of the history, see Position Paper of the People's Republic of China on the Issue of the South China Sea (17 November 2000) Annex I, Doc A.27.

[12] Republic of the Philippines (RP), Department of Foreign Affairs (DFA), Notification and Statement of Claim (22 January 2013) Annex I, Doc B.2 (Notification and Statement of Claim).

[13] The Review Commission of Maps for Land and Water, *Shui Lu Di Tu Shen Cha Wei Yuan Hui Hui Kan [Gazette of the Review Commission of Maps for Land and Water]*, vol 1 (Nanjing, the Commission, January 1935) 61–65.

[14] See the Review Commission of Maps for Land and Water, *Shui Lu Di Tu Shen Cha Wei Yuan Hui Hui Kan [Gazette of the Review Commission of Maps for Land and Water]*, vol 2 (Nanjing, the Commission, April 1935) 68–69.

[15] See Hungdah Chiu and Choon-Ho Park, 'Legal Status of the Paracel and Spratly Islands' (1975) 32 *Ocean Development and International Law* 1, 12–13.

[16] Zhenhua Han, Jinzhi Lin, and Fengbin Wu (eds), *Wo Guo Nan Hai Zhu Dao Shi Liao Hui Bian [Collection of Historical Materials Concerning Our Country's Islands in the South China Sea]* (Beijing, Dong Fang Chu Ban She [Orient Press], 1988) 180–81 (reproducing a publication of May 1948, which contained an account by the Chinese naval command of the Chinese navy's action on the islands).

[17] ibid.

of 172 geographical names, in both Chinese and English, for the islands in the South China Sea.[18] In February 1948, China published an atlas of national administrative districts through the Commerce Press, Beijing, reflecting the 1947 atlas.[19] In May 1949, the four island groups in the South China Sea and other attached islands were placed under the authority of the Hainan District of Guang Dong Province.[20]

China has maintained its position since 1949 with only relatively minor changes over the years.[21] China's position has been gradually clarified and strengthened by national legislation and official documents. Four such documents are of particular importance. Firstly, on 4 September 1958 China promulgated its Declaration on the Territorial Sea.[22] Article 1 not only provided for a 12 nautical mile (nm) territorial sea, but also applied that breadth to China's mainland coast, coastal islands, and such off-lying islands as the Penghu Islands [Pescadores], the Dongsha [Pratas] Islands, the Xisha [Paracel] Islands, the Zhongsha Islands [Macclesfield Bank, including Scarborough Shoal (Huangyan Island)] and the Nansha [Spratly] Islands. Secondly, Article 2 of the 1992 Law on the Territorial Sea and the Contiguous Zone of the People's Republic of China reiterated the above provision.[23] Thirdly, in a Note Verbale addressed to the United Nations Secretary-General dated 7 May 2009, China stated that it 'has indisputable sovereignty over the islands in the South China Sea and the adjacent waters, and enjoys sovereign rights and jurisdiction over the relevant waters as well as the seabed and subsoil thereof'.[24] Attached to that Note was a map illustrating the well-known Chinese position showing the islands and waters in the South China Sea enclosed by a nine-dash line, which has since been made the main bone of contention by the Philippines.[25] Fourthly, on 14 April 2011 China addressed another Note Verbale to the United Nations Secretary-General in which it reiterated its earlier statement of May 2009.[26]

---

[18] Shicun Wu and others (eds), *Nan Hai Wen Ti Wen Xian Hui Bian [Collection of Documents on the Issue of the South China Sea]* (Hai Kou City, Hai Nan Chu Ban She [Hainan Press], 2001) 28–36.

[19] Guang Dong Provincial Commission of Toponymy (n 2) 212.

[20] Wu and others, *Nan Hai Wen Ti Wen Xian Hui Bian [Collection of Documents on the Issue of the South China Sea]* 37–38.

[21] Zhiguo Gao and Bing Bing Jia, 'The Nine-Dash Line in the South China Sea: History, Status, and Implications' (2013) 107 *American Journal of International Law* 98, 102–08.

[22] Declaration of the Government of the People's Republic of China on China's Territorial Sea (4 September 1958) Annex I, Doc A.33. The declaration was approved by the Standing Committee of the People's Congress on 4 September 1958, thus making it part of Chinese law.

[23] Law of the People's Republic of China on the Territorial Sea and the Contiguous Zone (25 February 1992) Annex I, Doc A.31.

[24] Note Verbale CML/17/2009 from the Permanent Mission of the People's Republic of China to the UN Secretary-General with regard to the joint submission made by Malaysia and Viet Nam to the Commission on the Limits of the Continental Shelf (7 May 2009) Annex I, Doc A.24.

[25] See Notification and Statement of Claim, paras 2, 3, 5, 6, 11–14, 20, 27, 31, 39, 41.

[26] Note Verbale CML/8/2011 from the Permanent Mission of the People's Republic of China to the UN Secretary-General with regard to the joint submission made by Malaysia and Viet Nam to the Commission on the Limits of the Continental Shelf (14 April 2011), Annex I Doc A.23 (Note Verbale CML/8/2011 (14 April 2011)).

These documents have been accompanied by significant administrative acts performed by China during the same period. In 1959, Hainan District established an administrative office on Yong Xing [Woody] Island to administer the affairs of the Xisha [Paracel], Zhongsha [Macclesfield Bank, including Scarborough Shoal (Huangyan Island)] and Nansha [Spratly] Islands. The office was transferred to the authority of the provincial government of Guang Dong Province in 1969.[27] In 1984, the Chinese National People's Congress included within the territorial scope of the newly established Hainan Administrative Region, and later Hainan Province, 'the islets, reefs and sea areas of Xisha, Nansha, and Zhongsha islands'.[28] No protest was lodged against any of these measures by other States. In June 2012, the Ministry of Civil Affairs announced the decision of the State Council to establish Sansha City, to replace the existing administrative office for the affairs of the Xisha, Zhongsha and Nansha Islands and adjacent waters.[29] There was no reference to any nine-dash line in that decision. The municipal government of the new city, like the previous administrative office established in 1959, was headquartered on Yong Xing [Woody] Island. It is subject to the authority of the provincial government of Hainan Province. On 27 November 2012, the People's Congress of Hainan Province adopted a set of amended local regulations on border control and security in the coastal areas of the province.[30] The regulations are applicable to the coastal areas of the province and sea areas under its jurisdiction (Article 2). The enforcement of these regulations is entrusted to the public security authorities of the province at all levels (Article 5). Article 31 prohibits foreign ships and their crew from illegally anchoring in the territorial sea of the province, disembarking at local ports without permission, illegally landing on islands subject to the jurisdiction of the province, damaging buildings and other facilities on those islands, illegal broadcasting and other acts in violation of the regulations. Foreign ships and their crew found in breach of this provision can be stopped, boarded, inspected, arrested, expelled or diverted (Article 47). The territorial scope of application of

[27] Guang Dong Provincial Commission of Toponymy (n 2) 163. The Dongsha Islands were already part of Guangdong Province at the time.

[28] Decision of the Second Session of the Sixth National People's Congress on the Establishment of the Hainan Administrative Region (31 May 1984), reproduced in Legislative Affairs Commission of the Standing Committee of the National People's Congress of the People's Republic of China, *The Laws of the People's Republic of China (1983–1986)* (Beijing, Ke Xue Chu Ban She [Science Press], 1987) 146. The islands remained so administered when Hainan became a province in April 1988, ibid, *The Laws of the People's Republic of China (1987–1989)* (Beijing, Ke Xue Chu Ban She [Science Press], 1990) 249.

[29] *cf* 'Min Zheng Bu Guan Yu Guo Wu Yuan Pi Zhun Di Ji San Sha Shi De Gong Gao' [Notice by the Ministry of Civil Affairs on the Approval by the State Council of the Establishment of Sansha City] (21 June 2012) www.gov.cn.

[30] *cf* 'Hai Nan Sheng Yan Hai Bian Fang Zhi An Guan Li Tiao Li' [Regulations on Border Control and Security of the Coastal Areas of Hainan Province] (adopted by the Provincial People's Congress on 27 November 2012, effective as of 1 January 2013) www.hainan.gov.cn. The original regulations were adopted by the Congress in November 1999.

these regulations is determined by, among others, the 1992 Law on the Territorial Sea and the Contiguous Zone.

In contrast, the Philippines emerged as a player in the South China Sea rather late in the day. In 1956, Philippine businessman Thomas Cloma and his associates landed on some features in the Nansha [Spratly] Islands and asserted ownership over them. However, this private act did not gain any official recognition from the Philippine Government.[31] It remained an isolated incident and has little relevance to the present case. It was only in 1971 that the Philippine Government suddenly claimed the 53 maritime features occupied by Cloma in 1956 as the Kalayaan Island Group (KIG). In 1978, the Philippine President, in Decree No 1596, declared that the KIG as well as its seabed, subsoil, continental margin and air space belong, and are subject to 'the sovereignty of the Philippines'.[32] However, all of these acts, as well as the 2009 Republic Act No 9522 revising the Philippine archipelagic baselines and reiterating the claim to sovereignty over the KIG and Scarborough Shoal,[33] and the 2012 Administrative Order by President Aquino unilaterally renaming 'the waters around, within and adjacent to' the KIG and Scarborough Shoal as 'the West Philippine Sea',[34] met with a consistent line of protests and challenges from China.[35] In addition, the military occupation of some insular features in the Nansha Islands by the Philippines could not affect China's territorial sovereignty over these features.[36] It is well-established that the illegal use of force does not produce any legal effect in international law.[37]

---

[31] Samuels (n 2) 81–86; Diane Drigot, 'Oil Interests and the Law of the Sea: The Case of the Philippines' (1982) 12 *Ocean Development and International Law* 23, 44; Benito O Lim, 'Tempest over the South China Sea: The Chinese Perspective on the Spratlys' (2000) 36 *Asian Studies* 69, 77.

[32] Presidential Decree No 1596 — Declaring Certain Areas Part of the Philippine Territory and Providing for their Government and Administration (11 June 1978), reprinted in Aileen San Pablo-Baviera (ed), *The South China Sea Disputes: Philippine Perspectives* (Quezon City, Philippine China Development Resource Center & Philippine Association for Chinese Studies, 1992) 55.

[33] Republic Act No 9522 — An Act to Amend Certain Provisions of Republic Act No 3046, as Amended by Republic Act No 5446, to Define the Archipelagic Baselines of the Philippines, and for Other Purposes (10 March 2009), reprinted in United Nations, Division for Ocean Affairs and the Law of the Sea, *Law of the Sea Bulletin* No 70 (2009) 32.

[34] Administrative Order No 29, s 2012 (5 September 2012) www.gov.ph.

[35] See eg Note Verbale CML/12/2009 from the Permanent Mission of the People's Republic of China to the UN Secretary-General (13 April 2009), Annex I, Doc A.25; Note Verbale CML/8/2011 (14 April 2011) (n 26).

[36] For the islands and maritime features occupied by the Philippines, see PRC Ministry of Foreign Affairs (MFA), 'Foreign Ministry Spokesperson Hua Chunying's Remarks on the Philippines' Efforts in Pushing for the Establishment of the Arbitral Tribunal in Relation to the Disputes between China and the Philippines in the South China Sea' (26 April 2013) Annex I, Doc A.14.

[37] *cf* Charter of the United Nations (adopted 26 June 1945, entered into force 24 October 1945) 892 UNTS 119, arts 2 (3) and 33 (1) (UN Charter), art 2(4) which states that '[a]ll Members shall refrain in their international relations from the threat or use of force against the territorial integrity or political independence of any state, or in any other manner inconsistent with the Purposes of the United Nations'. See also Declaration on Principles of International Law Concerning Friendly Relations and Co-operation Among States, UNGA Res 2625 (XXV) (24 October 1970) UN Doc A/RES/2625 (XXV), Annex, principle I: 'The

With the United Nations Convention on the Law of the Sea (UNCLOS or the Convention) entering into force for China in June 1996, the parties to the disputes in the South China Sea have increasingly based their claims, policies and legal arguments on relevant provisions of the Convention.[38] There has thus always been a temptation for the coastal States of the South China Sea to have recourse to the compulsory dispute settlement procedures of Part XV of UNCLOS when they are frustrated by the slow pace of other means of peaceful dispute settlement. It must, however, be recalled that there are two unique regional mechanisms for the peaceful settlement of disputes in the South China Sea within the Association of Southeast Asian Nations (ASEAN) framework: the ASEAN-China Declaration on the Conduct of Parties in the South China Sea (DOC)[39] and the Treaty of Amity and Cooperation in Southeast Asia.[40] Both provide for the settlement of disputes through friendly consultations and negotiations between the States directly concerned. Neither of these mechanisms is incompatible with the provisions of UNCLOS. On the contrary, both qualify as 'peaceful means of [the parties'] own choice' in terms of UNCLOS, Part XV, section 1. The DOC for one specifically refers to 'the 1982 UN Convention on the Law of the Sea' as part of the legal basis for resolving territorial and jurisdictional disputes in the South China Sea. The two regional mechanisms embody and epitomise the regional approach to the peaceful settlement of maritime disputes in the South China Sea. UNCLOS is part of the legal fabric of this regional mechanism, but by no means the only thread in that fabric. Consultations and negotiations continue to offer the best prospect for the peaceful settlement of the territorial and jurisdictional disputes in the South China Sea, which is shown by the constant reaffirmation of the commitments in the DOC and the continued and persistent efforts of all sides to work for a Code of Conduct (COC) in the South China Sea that will further promote peace and stability in the region.[41] It is against this background of constructive and on-going efforts

territory of a State shall not be the object of military occupation resulting from the use of force in contravention of the provisions of the Charter. The territory of a State shall not be the object of acquisition by another State resulting from the threat or use of force. No territorial acquisition resulting from the threat or use of force shall be recognized as legal'.

[38] Nguyen Hong Thao and Ramses Amer, 'A New Legal Arrangement for the South China Sea?' (2009) 40 *Ocean Development and International Law* 333, 333–49.

[39] ASEAN-China Declaration on the Conduct of Parties in the South China Sea (signed during the 8th ASEAN Summit in Phnom Penh, 4 November 2002) (DOC), reproduced in Vaughan Lowe and Stefan Talmon (eds), *The Legal Order of the Oceans: Basic Documents on the Law of the Sea* (Oxford, Hart, 2009) Doc 69, 771–72.

[40] Treaty of Amity and Cooperation in Southeast Asia (signed on 24 February 1976; entry into force 21 June 1976) 1025 UNTS 15063. China acceded to the Treaty on 8 October 2003.

[41] See eg 'Guidelines for the Implementation of the Declaration on the Conduct of Parties in the South China Sea' (20 July 2012), 'ASEAN-China Joint Statement on 10th Anniversary of DOC in South China Sea' (19 November 2012), ASEAN's 'Six Point Principles on the South China Sea' (20 July 2013) www.asean.org. At the ASEAN-China Sixth Senior Officials' Meeting and the Ninth Joint Working Group (JWG) Meeting on the Implementation of the DOC in Suzhou, China, on 14–15 September 2013 the participants decided to authorize the JWG to

within the ASEAN-China framework to resolve the disputes in the South China Sea in a spirit of friendship and cooperation that the Philippines' unilateral institution of arbitral proceedings must be seen.

II. THE SOUTH CHINA SEA ARBITRATION

The States Parties to UNCLOS, including China and the Philippines,[42] are obliged to submit any dispute concerning the interpretation or application of the Convention, where no settlement has been reached by peaceful means of their own choosing, to a judicial settlement procedure that leads to a binding decision. This obligation constitutes one of the great novelties and achievements of UNCLOS. States are free to choose one or more of the following means for the settlement of their disputes: (i) the International Tribunal for the Law of the Sea (ITLOS); (ii) the International Court of Justice (ICJ); (iii) an arbitral tribunal constituted in accordance with UNCLOS Annex VII or (iv) a special arbitral tribunal constituted in accordance with UNCLOS Annex VIII.[43] In case the States have made no choice, or if States have not chosen the same means of dispute settlement, disputes are to be submitted to arbitration in accordance with Annex VII of UNCLOS.[44] As neither China nor the Philippines have chosen any particular means for the settlement of their disputes, any dispute is to be submitted to an Annex VII arbitral tribunal.[45]

At around one o'clock on 22 January 2013, the Chinese Ambassador to the Philippines HE Ma Keqing was summoned to the Department of Foreign Affairs (DFA) and was handed a Note Verbale by Assistant Secretary Teresa Lazaro.[46] The Note Verbale contained the written Notification under Article 287 and Article 1 of UNCLOS Annex VII, and the Statement of Claim on the grounds on which the Notification is based, in order to initiate arbitral proceedings to challenge, before an UNCLOS Annex VII arbitral tribunal, China's claims to sovereignty and sovereign rights over areas of the South China Sea and the underlying seabed within the so-called 'nine-dash line', and to clearly establish the sovereign rights and jurisdiction of the Philippines over its maritime entitlements

---

have detailed consultations over the COC; see PRC MFA, 'Foreign Ministry Spokesperson Hong Lei's Regular Press Conference' (16 September 2013) www.fmprc.gov.cn.

[42] The Philippines is a party since 8 May 1983 and the People's Republic of China since 7 June 1996.

[43] UNCLOS, art 287(1).

[44] UNCLOS, art 287(3) and (5).

[45] See United Nations, Division for Ocean Affairs and the Law of the Sea, 'Settlement of disputes mechanism — 1. Settlement of disputes mechanism under the Convention: Choice of procedure under article 287 and optional exceptions to applicability of Part XV, Section 2, of the Convention under article 298 of the Convention', www.un.org/depts/los.

[46] Note Verbale No 13-0211 from the Department of Foreign Affairs of the Republic of the Philippines to the Embassy of the People's Republic of China in Manila (22 January 2013) Annex I, Doc B.1.

in the West Philippine Sea under UNCLOS.[47] The Philippines contends that China's nine-dash line 'is, to put it plainly, illegal. It is arbitrary and bereft of any basis or validity under international law, specifically the United Nations Convention on the Law of the Sea or UNCLOS'.[48]

On 19 February 2013, two days before the expiry of the time-limit to appoint an arbitrator, China formally expressed its opposition to the institution of proceedings. The Ambassador of China to the Philippines, Ma Keqing, presented a Note Verbale to the Department of Foreign Affairs of the Philippines, which set out 'the Position of China on the South China Sea issues',[49] and returned the Philippines' Note Verbale of 22 January 2013, as well as the attached Notification and Statement of Claim.[50]

The reasons of China for rejecting the arbitration are threefold. First, the dispute submitted to arbitration by the Philippines is essentially concerned with maritime delimitation between the two countries in parts of the South China Sea, and thus inevitably involves the question of territorial sovereignty over certain relevant islands and reefs, including the Nansha [Spratly] Islands and Huangyan Island [Scarborough Shoal].[51] The Convention

> makes it clear right at the beginning that it aims at 'establishing a legal order for the seas and oceans with due regard for sovereignty of all states'. The Convention is not an international treaty to regulate disputes of territorial sovereignty between states, nor can it serve as the basis to arbitrate such disputes.[52]

Indeed, disputes concerning territorial sovereignty are not the disputes 'concerning the interpretation or application of this Convention'. Moreover, in 2006, the Chinese Government made a declaration pursuant to Article 298 of UNCLOS excluding disputes concerning maritime delimitation from the compulsory dispute settlement procedures, including arbitration.[53]

Second, the Philippines is bound by its solemn commitment in the 2002 ASEAN-China DOC to resolve its territorial and jurisdictional disputes with China by peaceful means through friendly consultations

[47] See RP DFA, 'SFA Statement on the UNCLOS Arbitral Proceedings against China' (22 January 2013) www.dfa.gov.ph.
[48] '"Philippine Policy Response and Action" by Hon. Albert F del Rosario, Secretary of Foreign Affairs' (5 August 2011) www.philippine-embassy.org.il.
[49] The Chinese Note Verbale is not in the public domain.
[50] See PRC MFA, 'Foreign Ministry Spokesperson Hong Lei's Regular Press Conference' (19 February 2013) Annex I, Doc A.17. See also PCA 'Arbitration between the Philippines and China, Arbitral Tribunal, First Press Release' (27 August 2013) www.pca-cpa.org.
[51] PRC MFA, 'Foreign Ministry Spokesperson Hua Chunying's Remarks on the Philippines' Efforts in Pushing for the Establishment of the Arbitral Tribunal in Relation to the Disputes between China and the Philippines in the South China Sea' (26 April 2013) Annex I, Doc A.14.
[52] PRC MFA, 'Foreign Ministry Spokesperson Hong Lei's Remarks on ASEAN Foreign Ministers' Statement on the Six-Point Principles on the South China Sea Issue' (21 July 2012) www.fmprc.gov.cn.
[53] Declaration by the People's Republic of China under Article 298 UNCLOS (25 August 2006) Annex I, Doc A.26. See also 'China's refusal of arbitration request by Philippines meets international law: Senior diplomat' (30 August 2013) english.peopledaily.com.cn.

and negotiations.[54] The Note Verbale of 22 January 2013 and the attached Notification and Statement of Claim 'violate the consensus' reached by ASEAN countries and China in the DOC.[55] The Foreign Ministry spokesperson declared: 'it is regrettable that over recent years, the Philippines has changed its attitude and approach in handling the issue, gone back on its consensus with China, [and] broken its commitment in the DOC'.[56] China was especially disappointed by the institution of arbitral proceedings because the Philippines had previously repeatedly reaffirmed its commitment to the DOC and to addressing the disputes through 'peaceful negotiations' or 'peaceful dialogue'.[57]

Third, the Note Verbale and the Notification and Statement of Claim 'contain serious errors in fact and law as well as false accusations against China'.[58]

UNCLOS Annex VII, Article 3 provides rules for the constitution of an Annex VII arbitral tribunal. The appointment of the five arbitrators and the election of the president of the tribunal go through several stages. The party instituting the proceedings appoints one member, preferably chosen from a list of arbitrators drawn up and maintained by the Secretary-General of the United Nations, who may be its national. Every State Party to UNCLOS is entitled to nominate four arbitrators to that list. Nominees shall be experienced in maritime affairs and enjoy the highest reputation of fairness, competence and integrity,[59] and must not necessarily possess the nationality of the nominating country. Neither China nor the Philippines has nominated any person to the list of arbitrators.[60] The other party to the proceedings shall, within 30 days of receipt of the notification under UNCLOS Annex VII, Article 1, also appoint one member of the tribunal to be chosen preferably from the list of arbitrators, who may be its national. If the appointment is not made within that period, the party instituting the proceedings may, within two weeks of the expiration of the 30-day period, request the President of the ITLOS to make the necessary appointment.[61] The ITLOS President shall

[54] DOC (n 39) para 4.

[55] PRC MFA, 'Foreign Ministry Spokesperson Hong Lei's Regular Press Conference' (19 February 2013) Annex I, Doc A.17.

[56] PRC MFA, 'Foreign Ministry Spokesperson Hua Chunying's Remarks on the Philippines' Statement on the South China Sea' (16 July 2013) Annex I, Doc A.4.

[57] See eg RP DFA, 'AFP Chief of Staff, Chinese Military Officials Reaffirm Peaceful Resolution of South China Sea Disputes' (9 December 2010) and 'Joint Statement of the Republic of the Philippines and the People's Republic of China' (1 September 2011) www. dfa.gov.ph.

[58] Embassy of the PRC in the Republic of the Philippines, 'Chinese Spokesperson Hong Lei's remarks on China returned the Philippines' Notification on the submission of South China Sea issue to international Arbitration' (19 February 2013) Annex I, Doc A.17.

[59] UNCLOS Annex VII, art 1.

[60] Only 31 of the 166 Parties to UNCLOS have nominated one or more persons to the List of Arbitrators; see United Nations Treaty Collection, Multilateral Treaties Deposited with the Secretary-General, Chapter XXI: Law of the Sea, 6. United Nations Convention on the Law of the Sea, treaties.un.org.

[61] UNCLOS Annex VII, art 3(c).

appoint a person from the list of arbitrators within a period of 30 days of the receipt of the request and in consultation with the parties.[62] The three other members of the tribunal shall be appointed by agreement between the parties. They shall be chosen preferably from the list of arbitrators and shall be nationals of third States, unless the parties agree otherwise. The parties to the proceedings shall also appoint the President of the arbitral tribunal from among those three members. If, within 60 days of receipt of the arbitration notification, the parties are unable to reach agreement on the appointment of one or more of the arbitrators, or on the appointment of the President of the tribunal, the remaining appointment or appointments shall be made by the President of the ITLOS at the request of a party to the dispute.[63] Such a request must be made within two weeks of the expiration of the aforementioned 60-day period. The President of the ITLOS shall appoint the remaining arbitrators and the President of the arbitral tribunal from the list of arbitrators within a period of 30 days of the receipt of the request and in consultation with the parties. The constitution of the Annex VII arbitral tribunal thus takes at most 104 days from the receipt of the arbitration notification.[64]

Upon instituting proceedings, the Philippines appointed Rüdiger Wolfrum of Germany as a member of the Arbitral Tribunal.[65] When China failed to appoint an arbitrator within 30 days of receipt of the arbitration notification, the Philippines, at the earliest possible moment, on 22 February 2013, requested the President of ITLOS, Judge Shunji Yani of Japan, to act on behalf of China and appoint another member of the Arbitral Tribunal in accordance with UNCLOS Annex VII, Article 3(c) and (e). This led to the appointment of Stanisław Pawlak of Poland as the second arbitrator.[66] Due to China's non-participation in the proceedings, the three remaining arbitrators and the President of the Arbitral Tribunal could not be appointed 'by agreement between the parties'. Again, at the earliest possible moment, the Philippines in a letter

---

[62] ibid, art 3(e). The ITLOS President 'shall' make the appointment of the arbitrator from the list. The parties, on the other hand, only have to choose their arbitrators 'preferably' from the list.

[63] It is not unusual that the parties cannot agree on the appointment of one or more arbitrators or on the appointment of the president of the tribunal; see *Bangladesh v India*, ITLOS/Press 143 (8 March 2010) and ITLOS/Press 198 (19 July 2013); *Argentina v Ghana (ARA Libertad Arbitration)* ITLOS/Press 189 (5 February 2013); and *Mauritius v United Kingdom*, ITLOS/Press 164 (25 March 2011). See also *Guyana v Suriname* (2007) 139 ILR 566, 578 [12] where a substitute arbitrator was appointed by the Tribunal in accordance with its Rules of Procedure.

[64] In the present case, the final date for the constitution of the Tribunal would have been 6 May 2013.

[65] UNCLOS Annex VII, art 3(b). Rüdiger Wolfrum is a judge of the ITLOS and was its president from 2005 to 2008. Judge Wolfrum was nominated to the list of arbitrators by Mongolia on 22 February 2005; see United Nations, Division for Ocean Affairs and the Law of the Sea, *Law of the Sea Bulletin* No 58 (2005) 30.

[66] Stanisław Pawlak was appointed to the list of arbitrators by Poland on 14 May 2004, see United Nations, Division for Ocean Affairs and the Law of the Sea, *Law of the Sea Bulletin* No 58 (2005) 28.

dated 25 March 2013,[67] requested the President of the ITLOS to appoint the three additional members of the Arbitral Tribunal and name one among them to serve as the President of the Tribunal. On 24 April 2013, the ITLOS President appointed Jean-Pierre Cot (France),[68] Chris Pinto (Sri Lanka)[69] and Alfred Soons (the Netherlands)[70] as arbitrators, and named Chris Pinto as President of the Arbitral Tribunal.[71] In May 2013, Chris Pinto resigned from the Arbitral Tribunal because his marriage to a Filipino national might have raised questions of impartiality.[72] In a letter dated 27 May 2013, the Philippines requested the ITLOS President to appoint another arbitrator and President for the Tribunal 'to ensure the impartiality of the arbitral proceeding' and 'assure that any award that might be rendered in these proceedings is accorded the full degree of respect to which it is entitled, and is as safe as possible from attack by anyone who might be motivated to undermine it'.[73] On 21 June 2013, within the 30-day period, the ITLOS President filled the vacancy by appointing Thomas A Mensah (Ghana) to serve as a member and President of the Arbitral Tribunal.[74] It is of interest to note in this context that President Mensah was nominated to the list of arbitrators by Ghana only a couple of days before his appointment on 30 May 2013, which suggests that this might have been a 'nomination with a view' of being appointed to the Tribunal.[75]

On 11 July 2013, the members of the Arbitral Tribunal held their first constitutive meeting at The Peace Palace in The Hague at which the Tribunal designated The Hague as the seat of the arbitration and the Permanent Court of Arbitration (PCA) as the Registry for the proceedings.

---

[67] The 60-day period for the appointment of the remaining arbitrators and the President of the Tribunal ended on 23 March 2013 which fell on a Saturday. The Philippines submitted its request to the ITLOS President on Monday, 25 March 2013.

[68] Jean-Pierre Cot, who has been a judge of the ITLOS since 2002, was nominated to the list of arbitrators by Mongolia on 22 February 2005, together with Rüdiger Wolfrum; see United Nations, Division for Ocean Affairs and the Law of the Sea, *Law of the Sea Bulletin* No 58 (2005) 30.

[69] Former Secretary-General of the Iran-United States Claims Tribunal Chris Pinto was nominated by Sri Lanka on 8 April 2002, ibid, 31.

[70] Alfred HA Soons, Professor of Public International Law and Director of the Netherlands Institute for the Law of the Sea, was nominated by the Netherlands on 9 February 1998; see ibid, 30.

[71] See ITLOS/Press 191 (25 April 2013) www.itlos.org.

[72] In a letter dated 6 May 2013, Judge Pinto informed the Agent of the Philippines, Solicitor General Francis H Jardeleza, that his wife is a Filipino national; see 'Tribunal to Hear PH Territorial Case vs China Now Complete' (29 June 2013) www.panaynewsphilippines.com. See also 'Lankan Judge in the UN Panel Resigns' (7 June 2013) www.dailymirror.lk.

[73] Michaela del Callar, 'For Having Pinay Wife, Sri Lankan Judge in PHL Arbitral Proceedings vs China Resigns' (7 June 2013) www.gmanetwork.com.

[74] See ITLOS/Press 197 (24 June 2013) www.itlos.org.

[75] Dr Thomas A Mensah is a former Judge and the First President of the ITLOS. See United Nations Treaty Collection, Multilateral Treaties Deposited with the Secretary-General, Chapter XXI: Law of the Sea, 6. United Nations Convention on the Law of the Sea, 'Notifications made under article 2 of annexes V and VII (List of conciliators and arbitrators)' treaties.un.org.

The parties had previously been requested to submit their views on these two matters, and the Philippines had consented to both. At the meeting, the Tribunal adopted a set of draft Rules of Procedure and invited the parties to comment on the Rules by 5 August 2013. It also requested the parties to propose a schedule for the submission of their written pleadings.[76] On 31 July 2013, the Philippines submitted comments on the draft Rules. China, on the other hand, on 1 August 2013 addressed a Note Verbale to the PCA in which it reiterated its position that 'it does not accept the arbitration initiated by the Philippines' and stated that it would not be participating in the proceedings.[77]

In its first Procedural Order on 26 August 2013, the Arbitral Tribunal formally adopted the Rules of Procedure and fixed 30 March 2014 as the date by which the Philippines should submit its Memorial. The Rules of Procedure which, at the time of writing, have not yet been released to the public, set out, inter alia, the course of action to be taken by the Tribunal in the event that one of the parties does not appear in the proceedings.[78]

---

[76] RP DFA, 'Phl Arbitral Proceedings Against China Now Officially Under Way' (16 July 2013) www.dfa.gov.ph.

[77] PCA Press Release (27 August 2013) www.pca-cpa.org. The Chinese Note Verbale is not in the public domain.

[78] ibid.

2

The South China Sea Arbitration: Is There a Case to Answer?

STEFAN TALMON

I. INTRODUCTION

T HE PEOPLE'S REPUBLIC of China (PRC or China) has made it clear from the outset that it will not have any part in the arbitral proceedings instituted by the Republic of the Philippines under the United Nations Convention on the Law of the Sea (UNCLOS or the Convention)[1] with regard to disputes between the two countries in the South China Sea (South China Sea Arbitration) and that this position will not change. On 26 April 2013, the spokesperson of the Chinese Ministry of Foreign Affairs (MFA) explained that the claims for arbitration raised by the Philippines were 'essentially concerned with maritime delimitation between the two countries in parts of the South China Sea' and thus inevitably involved the 'territorial sovereignty over certain relevant islands and reefs'. Such issues of territorial sovereignty, however, were 'not the ones concerning the interpretation or application of the UN Convention on the Law of the Sea'. Considering 'that the Sino-Philippine territorial disputes still remain unresolved, the compulsory dispute settlement procedures as contained in UNCLOS should not apply to the claims for arbitration as raised by the Philippines'. Therefore, it was said, 'the request for arbitration by the Philippines is manifestly unfounded. China's rejection of the Philippines' request for arbitration, consequently, has a solid basis in international law'.[2] This point was reiterated on 29 August 2013 by Huang Huikang,

---

[1] United Nations Convention on the Law of the Sea (adopted 10 December 1982, entered into force 16 November 1994) 1834 UNTS 387 (UNCLOS). The Philippines is a party since 8 May 1983 and the People's Republic of China since 7 June 1996.

[2] Ministry of Foreign Affairs of the People's Republic of China (PRC MFA), 'Foreign Ministry Spokesperson Hua Chunying's Remarks on the Philippines' Efforts in Pushing for the Establishment of the Arbitral Tribunal in Relation to the Disputes between China and the Philippines in the South China Sea' (26 April 2013) and PRC MFA, 'Foreign Ministry Spokesperson Hua Chunying's Regular Press Conference' (12 July 2013); Annex I, Docs A.14 and A.5, respectively.

the Director-General of the Treaty and Law Department of the Chinese Foreign Ministry, who stated in an interview with China's largest news agency, Xinhua, that 'China's refusal has full legal ground' and added: 'By refusing the Philippines' arbitration request, China is exercising its legitimate right, as an embodiment of the rule of law'.[3]

Default of appearance is nothing unusual in international adjudication.[4] The more politically sensitive and sovereignty-charged a dispute is, the more likely the non-appearance of the respondent becomes. Default of appearance will usually make the task of the arbitral tribunal more difficult and thus may cause some inconvenience to the tribunal and the other party. But, while tribunals may express their regret over a party's failure to appear, they may not use a party's non-appearance against it or draw any negative conclusions from it. In particular, the absence of a State cannot be taken as an admission of the facts or the legal views of the applicant, or as showing that the absent party has no, or no convincing, counter-arguments to the applicant's case. Modern procedural law 'does not treat a party in default as guilty, and is far from regarding failure to appear as a *ficta confessio*'.[5] On the contrary, a State may choose not to appear before an arbitral tribunal in order to avoid anything that might upgrade or give credibility to a claim which it considers clearly inadmissible or manifestly unfounded, or where it considers the tribunal seized to be evidently without jurisdiction. Thus, while a party, by not appearing, cannot deny the other party its 'day in court',[6] it can forcefully challenge the jurisdiction of the tribunal. This seems to be the reason for China's non-appearance.[7]

Non-appearance is one of several procedural strategies available to a State to defend its rights and vital interests before a tribunal and does not necessarily imply disrespect for the tribunal.[8] It has been said that

---

[3] 'China's Refusal of Arbitration Request by Philippines Meets International Law: Senior Diplomat' (30 August 2013) english.peopledaily.com.cn.

[4] The Institute of International Law (IIL) noted in its 1991 Basel resolution on 'Non-appearance before the International Court of Justice' (Basel Resolution) the 'frequent cases of non-appearance which have occurred before the International Court of Justice' ((1991) 64-II *Annuaire de l'Institut de Droit International* 377). For examples of non-appearance before the PCIJ and ICJ, see eg Hans von Mangoldt and Andreas Zimmermann, 'Article 53' in Andreas Zimmermann and others (eds), *The Statute of the International Court of Justice: A Commentary*, Oxford Commentaries on International Law, 2nd edn (Oxford, OUP, 2012) 1334–36; Matthias Goldmann, 'International Courts and Tribunals, Non-Appearance' in Rüdiger Wolfrum (ed), *Max Planck Encyclopedia of Public International Law*, vol V (Oxford, OUP, 2012) 607–08 MN 4–7.

[5] *Fisheries Jurisdiction (United Kingdom v Iceland)* (Merits) [1974] ICJ Rep 3, 94 [4] (sep op de Castro).

[6] *cf* UNCLOS Annex VII, art 9, second sentence.

[7] See PRC MFA, 'Foreign Ministry Spokesperson Hua Chunying's Remarks on the Philippines' Efforts in Pushing for the Establishment of the Arbitral Tribunal in Relation to the Disputes between China and the Philippines in the South China Sea' (26 April 2013) Annex I, Doc A.14.

[8] *cf* Gudmundur Eiriksson, *The International Tribunal for the Law of the Sea* (The Hague, Martinus Nijhoff, 2000) 161. See also Hugh WA Thirlway, *Nonappearance before the International Court of Justice*, Cambridge Studies in International and Comparative Law (Cambridge, CUP, 1985) 64–67; Shabtai Rosenne (with the assistance of Yaël Ronen), *The Law and Practice of the International Court, 1920–2005*, vol III (Leiden, Martinus Nijhoff, 2006) 1360.

'[l]itigating States are free to argue their case before the Court as they think best; this is regarded as one of their sovereign attributes, in which the Court should not in normal circumstances interfere'.[9] The freedom of a State to argue the case as it thinks best must also include the freedom not to argue the case at all. There is no general duty under the Convention for a party to appear in arbitral proceedings brought against it. No such duty can be derived from the duty of the parties to a dispute to 'facilitate the work of the arbitral tribunal' (UNCLOS Annex VII, Article 6).[10] An obligation to facilitate the work of the tribunal and an obligation to appear are two different things.[11] The provision stipulates a duty for appearing parties and, in any case, subjects that duty to 'their law'. Non-appearance is expressly recognised in UNCLOS Annex VII, Article 9 which provides special rules for default of appearance.[12] Considering that the litigants before Annex VII arbitral tribunals are sovereign States, the presence of the Article indicates consent to proceedings in default while, at the same time, preserving the sovereign 'right' not to appear.[13] A duty to appear also cannot be deduced from the general duty to settle disputes by peaceful means.[14] States are not under a duty to appear but to abide by the decisions rendered by the tribunal provided that it has jurisdiction under section 2 of Part XV of UNCLOS.[15] Non-appearance cannot, in any circumstances, affect the validity of a judgment. While a party is free not to appear it must accept the consequences of its decision.[16]

This chapter puts China's non-appearance in historic perspective, examines whether its rejection of the arbitral proceedings is justified in international law and asks about the Philippines' ulterior political motives for instituting these arbitral proceedings.

[9] *Certain Property (Liechtenstein v Germany)* (Preliminary Objections) [2005] ICJ Rep 6, 71 [3] (diss op Berman).

[10] See also the Basel Resolution (n 4) which accepts that a State may not appear before the ICJ. In considering whether to appear before the Court, a State should (only) have regard to its duty to co-operate in the fulfilment of the Court's judicial function (art 2 of the Basel Resolution).

[11] *cf* Thirlway, *Nonappearance* (1985) 70.

[12] With regard to non-appearance before the ICJ, see the Basel Resolution (n 4) and von Mangoldt and Zimmermann, 'Article 53' 1326 MN 4; Thirlway (n 8) 65. Both base their finding on art 53 of the Statute of the ICJ, www.icj-cij.org (ICJ Statute), which is largely identical with UNCLOS Annex VII, art 9.

[13] Contra Thirlway (n 8) 80–81 and Goldmann 'International Courts' 610 MN 14, who speak of a 'privilege', rather than a 'right'. But see also *M/V 'Louisa' (Saint Vincent and the Grenadines v Kingdom of Spain)* (Merits, Counter-Memorial of the Kingdom of Spain, 12 December 2011) para 187, www.itlos.org ('Spain decided to appear before the honourable Tribunal').

[14] See Charter of the United Nations (adopted 26 June 1945, entered into force 24 October 1945) 892 UNTS 119, arts 2 (3) and 33 (1) (UN Charter) and UNCLOS, art 279. However, Hermann Mosler, 'Nichtteilnahme einer Partei am Verfahren vor dem Internationalen Gerichtshof' in Ingo von Münch (ed), *Staatsrecht, Völkerrecht, Europarecht: Festschrift für Hans-Jürgen Schlochauer zum 75. Geburtstag am 28. März 1981* (Berlin, Walter de Gruyter & Co, 1981) 442, suggested that, while not being a breach of the law, it may be contrary to the spirit of the UN Charter and the ICJ Statute.

[15] See UNCLOS, art 296(1) and Annex VII, art 11.

[16] *cf Military and Paramilitary Activities in and against Nicaragua (Nicaragua v United States of America)* (Merits) [1986] ICJ Rep 14, 24 [28]. See also ibid, 143 [284].

II. DEFAULT OF APPEARANCE IN HISTORICAL PERSPECTIVE

This is not the first time that China has chosen not to appear before an international tribunal. In the case concerning the *Denunciation of the Treaty of November 2nd, 1865, between China and Belgium (Belgium v China)*,[17] the only case ever brought against China before either the Permanent Court of International Justice (PCIJ) or the International Court of Justice (ICJ), the Chinese Government did not take any steps in the proceedings. The case arose out of China's unilateral denunciation of the Treaty of Amity, Commerce and Navigation between China and Belgium (Treaty of Tiensin), a treaty considered by the then Chinese Government to belong to the category of 'unequal treaties' imposed upon China against her free will in the early years of her foreign relations.[18] The Chinese Government indicated that it would be prepared to discuss the possibility of invoking jointly with the Belgian Government the services of the PCIJ if the Belgian Government indicated a willingness to seek a solution on the broad basis of the universally recognised principle of equality in international intercourse and that of *ex aequo et bono*. It made clear, however, that it would oppose any proceedings initiated unilaterally by Belgium asking the Court for a technical interpretation of an unequal treaty provision.[19] Both Belgium and China had made declarations under Article 36(2) of the PCIJ Statute recognizing as compulsory *ipso facto* and without special agreement the jurisdiction of the Court. On 25 November 1926 Belgium unilaterally instituted proceedings against China by filing a written application with the Court's Registrar.[20] During the two and a half years the case was pending before the PCIJ, before it was eventually withdrawn by Belgium, China never took any action in the proceedings or even communicated with the Court.[21] However, this did not prevent the Court from indicating provisional measures and making several orders for the conduct of the case.[22]

---

[17] *Denunciation of the Treaty of 2 November 1865 between China and Belgium (Belgium v China)* PCIJ Rep Series A Nos 8, 14, 16, 18 and Series C No 16-1.

[18] See 'Statement of the Chinese Government Explaining the Termination of the Sino-Belgian Treaty of November 2nd, 1865' (6 November 1926), reproduced in *Denunciation of the Treaty of 2 November 1865 between China and Belgium (Belgium v China)* (Request Eventually Withdrawn) PCIJ Rep Series C No 16-1, 271–76.

[19] See 'Memorandum of the Chinese Government' (16 November 1926), reproduced ibid, No 16-1, 78–79.

[20] See *Denunciation of the Treaty of 2 November 1865 between China and Belgium (Belgium v China)* (Application Instituting Proceedings of 25 November 1926) PCIJ Rep Series A No 8, 4–5.

[21] *Denunciation of the Treaty of 2 November 1865 between China and Belgium (Belgium v China)* (Order of 25 May 1929) PCIJ Rep Series A No 18, 7 ('Considering that the Chinese Government, the Respondent in the suit in question, has never taken any proceeding in the suit before the Court').

[22] *Denunciation of the Treaty of 2 November 1865 between China and Belgium (Belgium v China)* (Orders of 8 January 1927, 15 February 1927, 18 June 1927, 21 February 1928, 13 August 1928 and 25 May 1929) PCIJ Rep Series A Nos 8, 14, 16, 18.

China is not the first State which has chosen not to appear in a law of the sea dispute. Iceland, for example, did not take part in proceedings concerning the unilateral extension of its exclusive fisheries jurisdiction to a zone of 50 nautical miles around Iceland.[23] Turkey was also absent throughout the proceedings concerning the delimitation of the continental shelf appertaining to Greece and Turkey in the Aegean Sea and the rights of the parties thereover.[24] Both cases concerned proceedings before the ICJ. A default of appearance has not occurred in any of the eight other cases submitted to arbitration under Annex VII of UNCLOS. Indeed, China's default of appearance is the first one under the compulsory dispute settlement system established by UNCLOS.[25]

III. THE CONSEQUENCES OF DEFAULT OF APPEARANCE

UNCLOS Annex VII, Article 9 expressly deals with default of appearance of a party in arbitral proceedings under the Convention. It provides:

> If one of the parties to the dispute does not appear before the arbitral tribunal or fails to defend its case, the other party may request the tribunal to continue the proceedings and to make its award. Absence of a party or failure of a party to defend its case shall not constitute a bar to the proceedings. Before making its award, the arbitral tribunal must satisfy itself not only that it has jurisdiction over the dispute but also that the claim is well founded in fact and law.[26]

A party thus cannot frustrate the proceedings simply by not appearing before the tribunal. On the other hand, non-appearance of a party does not automatically result in a judgment against it.[27] Annex VII arbitrations do not know of a 'default judgment' in favour of the applicant simply on the procedural ground of absence of the respondent. The intention of Annex VII, Article 9 is to protect both parties: the appearing party against any attempts at frustrating the arbitral proceedings and the non-appearing party against any unjustified and frivolous claims. The rights of the non-appearing party, both with regard to any preliminary objections, whether of jurisdiction or of admissibility,[28] and the merits of the case, are safeguarded by the arbitral tribunal's obligation to 'satisfy itself' *proprio*

---

[23] See *Fisheries Jurisdiction (United Kingdom v Iceland)* (Jurisdiction) [1973] ICJ Rep 3, 7 [12], and ibid, (Merits) [1974] ICJ Rep 3, 8–9. There were parallel proceedings brought by the Federal Republic of Germany against Iceland in which Iceland also did not appear.

[24] See *Aegean Sea Continental Shelf (Greece v Turkey)* (Jurisdiction) [1978] ICJ Rep 3, 7 [14], [15].

[25] For a list of UNCLOS Annex VII arbitrations see the 'UNCLOS' tab at www.pca-cpa.org. To this list of eight cases the *Southern Bluefin Tuna Case* must be added. See also n 48 below.

[26] For other provisions dealing with default of appearance, see UNCLOS Annex VI, art 28; UNCLOS Annex VIII, art 4; ICJ Statute, art 53.

[27] *cf Military and Paramilitary Activities in and against Nicaragua (Nicaragua v United States of America)* (Merits) [1986] ICJ Rep 14, 24 [28].

[28] *cf United States Diplomatic and Consular Staff in Tehran (United States of America v Iran)* (Merits) [1980] ICJ Rep 3, 18 [33].

motu that it has jurisdiction over the dispute and that the claim is well founded in fact and law.

UNCLOS Annex VII, Article 9 is an expression of the general obligation of international courts and tribunals to satisfy themselves that they have jurisdiction. In the *M/V 'SAIGA' (No 2)* case, the International Tribunal for the Law of the Sea (ITLOS) observed that, even where there is no disagreement between the parties regarding the jurisdiction of the tribunal, 'the Tribunal must satisfy itself that it has jurisdiction to deal with the case as submitted'.[29] Likewise, in the *Grand Prince* case, the ITLOS stressed that according to

> the settled jurisprudence in international adjudication, a tribunal must at all times be satisfied that it has jurisdiction to entertain the case submitted to it. For this purpose, it has the power to examine *proprio motu* the basis of its jurisdiction. ... As a consequence, the Tribunal possesses the right to deal with all aspects of the question of jurisdiction, whether or not they have been expressly raised by the parties.[30]

The use of the term 'satisfy itself' in Article 9 implies that the Annex VII arbitral tribunal must attain the same degree of certainty as in a case with both parties present that it has jurisdiction over the dispute and that the claim of the party appearing is sound in law, and, so far as the nature of the case permits, that the facts on which it is based are supported by convincing evidence. A finding of *prima facie* jurisdiction or plausibility of the applicant's claim does not suffice.

For the purpose of deciding legal questions, the principle *jura novit curia* signifies that a tribunal is not solely dependent on the argument of the parties before it with respect to the applicable law. This lessens the impact of the absence of one party. As international judicial organs, Annex VII arbitral tribunals are deemed to take judicial notice of international law and are therefore required in a case falling under UNCLOS Annex VII, Article 9, as in any other case, to consider on their own initiative all rules of international law which may be relevant to the settlement of the dispute. In particular, it is for the tribunal and not the party present to establish the jurisdiction of the tribunal. There is no burden of proof to be discharged in the matter of jurisdiction.[31] Given that it is the duty of an Annex VII arbitral tribunal to ascertain and apply the relevant law in the given circumstances of the case, the burden of establishing or proving rules of international law cannot be imposed upon any of the parties, for the law lies within the judicial knowledge of the tribunal.[32] However, this does

---

[29] *M/V 'SAIGA' (No 2) (Saint Vincent and the Grenadines v Guinea)* (Judgment) [1999] ITLOS Rep 10, 30 [40].

[30] *'Grand Prince' (Belize v France)* (Prompt Release, Judgment) [2001] ITLOS Rep 17, 41 [77], [79]. See also *Appeal Relating to the Jurisdiction of the ICAO Council (India v Pakistan)* (Merits) [1972] ICJ Rep 46, 52 [13].

[31] *Fisheries Jurisdiction (Spain v Canada)* (Jurisdiction) [1998] ICJ Rep 432, 450 [37], [38].

[32] cf *Fisheries Jurisdiction (United Kingdom v Iceland)* (Merits) [1974] ICJ Rep 3, 9 [17].

not necessarily ensure that the arbitral tribunal actively searches for and investigates all possible objections to its jurisdiction, the admissibility of the claim or any other objection of a preliminary character which a legally well-advised and creative party may raise.[33] In case of non-appearance of a party, the tribunal could accept or even solicit *amicus curiae* briefs in order to obtain a more complete picture of the procedural or substantive legal issues involved in the dispute.[34] Such a practice would be consistent with UNCLOS Annex VII, Article 5 which allows an arbitral tribunal to determine its own procedure, assuring to each party a full opportunity to be heard and to present its case.[35] Jurisdictional and other objections which require that they be invoked, however, can only be taken into account by the tribunal if the non-appearing party has relied upon them, either directly or indirectly, in its extra-procedural communications with the tribunal or in publications or statements which are in the public domain.[36]

As to determining the facts of a case, an Annex VII arbitral tribunal is, in principle, not bound to confine its consideration to the material formally submitted to it by the appearing party. When one party does not appear it is especially incumbent upon the tribunal to satisfy itself that it is in possession of all the available facts.[37] Nevertheless, the tribunal cannot by its own enquiries entirely make up for the absence of one of the parties; that absence, in a case involving extensive questions of fact, must necessarily limit the extent to which the tribunal is informed of the facts. The ICJ acknowledged that it would be

> an over-simplification to conclude that the only detrimental consequence of the absence of a party is the lack of opportunity to submit argument and evidence in support of its own case. Proceedings before the Court call for vigilance by all. The absent party also forfeits the opportunity to counter the factual allegations of its opponent.[38]

It is, of course, for the party appearing to prove the factual allegations it makes. As was pointed out by the ICJ, 'the burden of proof in respect of these [facts and contentions] will of course lie on the Party asserting them'.[39]

While UNCLOS Annex VII, Article 9 obliges the tribunal to consider the submissions of the party which appears, it does not compel the

---

[33] *cf* von Mangoldt and Zimmermann (n 4) 1344–45.

[34] Duncan EJ Currie, 'The Experience of Greenpeace International' in Tullio Treves and others (eds), *Civil Society, International Courts and Compliance Bodies* (The Hague, TMC Asser Press, 2004) 161.

[35] The power to solicit *amicus curiae* briefs will usually be laid down in the Rules of Procedure which, in the present case, have not yet been made public.

[36] *cf Aegean Sea Continental Shelf (Greece v Turkey)* (Jurisdiction) [1978] ICJ Rep 3, 20 [47].

[37] *cf Nuclear Tests (Australia v France)* (Merits) [1974] ICJ Rep 253, 263 [31] and *Nuclear Tests (New Zealand v France)* (Merits) [1974] ICJ Rep 457, 468 [32].

[38] *Military and Paramilitary Activities in and against Nicaragua (Nicaragua v United States of America)* (Merits) [1986] ICJ Rep 14, 25 [30].

[39] *Temple of Preah Vihear (Cambodia v Thailand)* (Merits) [1962] ICJ Rep 6, 16. See also *Fisheries Jurisdiction (Spain v Canada)* (Jurisdiction) [1998] ICJ Rep 432, 450 [37].

tribunal 'to examine their accuracy in all their details; for this might in certain unopposed cases prove impossible in practice'.[40] It is sufficient for the arbitral tribunal 'to convince itself by such methods as it considers suitable that the submissions are well founded'.[41] In case of doubt about the accuracy of facts, the tribunal may consult information available in the public domain or ask experts to verify that the submissions of the appearing party are well founded in fact.[42] A general declaration by the non-appearing party that it does not accept any of the statements of fact in the statement of claim of the other party 'cannot suffice to bring into question facts which appear to be established by documentary evidence'.[43] The Chinese statement that 'the Philippines' note and its attached notice … contain serious errors in fact and law as well as false accusations against China, which we firmly oppose',[44] may thus not be enough to challenge the Philippines' submissions on the facts or trigger the tribunal to examine the facts in greater detail.

Although UNCLOS Annex VII, Article 9 requires the arbitral tribunal to satisfy itself *proprio motu* that it has jurisdiction over the dispute, the provision does not address the question of whether the tribunal should rule on preliminary objections in incidental proceedings or in the principal proceedings on the merits. This is usually determined by the tribunal's rules of procedure. For example, the Rules of Court of the ICJ and the Rules of the ITLOS provide that upon receipt by the Registry of a preliminary objection, the proceedings on the merits are suspended and incidental proceedings on the objections are triggered.[45] The ICJ followed this procedure even in cases where the respondent did not appear and objections to the jurisdiction of the Court and the admissibility of the application were raised only in extra-procedural communications with the Court.[46]

---

[40] *Corfu Channel (United Kingdom v Albania)* (Merits) [1949] ICJ Rep 244, 248.

[41] ibid.

[42] *cf* UNCLOS Annex VII, art 5.

[43] *Fisheries Jurisdiction (United Kingdom v Iceland)* (Merits) [1974] ICJ Rep 3, 9 [16].

[44] PRC MFA, 'Foreign Ministry Spokesperson Hong Lei's Regular Press Conference' (26 March 2013) and PRC MFA, 'Chinese Spokesperson Hong Lei's Remarks on China Returned the Philippines' Notification on the Submission of South China Sea Issue to International Arbitration' (19 February 2013); Annex I, Docs A.15 and A.17, respectively.

[45] ICJ Rules of Court, art 79(5), www.icj-cij.org; Rules of the ITLOS, art 97(3), www.itlos. org.

[46] See *Fisheries Jurisdiction (United Kingdom v Iceland)* (Interim Protection: Order of 18 August 1972) [1972] ICJ Rep 181; *Nuclear Tests (Australia v France)* (Interim Protection: Order of 22 June 1973) [1973] ICJ Rep 99, 105 [32]–[35]; *Trial of Pakistani Prisoners of War (Pakistan v India)* (Interim Protection: Order of 13 July 1973) [1973] ICJ Rep 328, 330; *Aegean Sea Continental Shelf (Greece v Turkey)* (Interim Protection: Order of 11 September 1976) [1976] ICJ Rep 3, 13 [45]. In the *United States Diplomatic and Consular Staff in Tehran* case, the Court did not consider the question of jurisdiction and admissibility separately. This may be explained by the fact that the non-appearing party (Iran) did not raise any particular preliminary objections, but simply stated in a telegram that the Court 'cannot and should not take cognizance of the case'; see *United States Diplomatic and Consular Staff in Tehran (United States of America v Iran)* (Provisional Measures: Order of 15 December 1979) [1979] ICJ Rep 7, 10–11 [8].

Annex VII arbitral tribunals may determine their own procedure, unless the parties to the dispute agree otherwise.[47] All but one of the Annex VII arbitrations so far has been conducted using the services of the Permanent Court of Arbitration (PCA).[48] The PCA Optional Rules for Arbitrating Disputes between Two States provide in Article 21(4) that,

> [i]n general, the arbitral tribunal should rule on a plea concerning its jurisdiction as a preliminary question. However, the arbitral tribunal may proceed with the arbitration and rule on such a plea in its final award.[49]

These rules are, however, optional. Arbitral tribunals using the facilities of the PCA are free to devise their own rules of procedure. For example, the rules of procedure of the Tribunal in the arbitration under UNCLOS Annex VII between Mauritius and the United Kingdom (Chagos Islands Arbitration) provide that the 'Arbitral Tribunal may, after ascertaining the views of the Parties, determine whether objections to jurisdiction or admissibility shall be addressed as a preliminary matter or deferred to the Tribunal's final award'.[50] In its Procedural Order No 2 the Arbitral Tribunal rejected the United Kingdom's request that its preliminary objections be dealt with in a separate jurisdictional phase as a preliminary matter and, instead, decided that the preliminary objections would be considered with the proceedings on the merits.[51] If a non-appearing party raises preliminary objections in extra-procedural communications with the tribunal or in public statements, the arbitral tribunal should first satisfy itself that it has jurisdiction over the dispute before considering the merits of the case. This conforms with both the ICJ's practice and the intention of UNCLOS Annex VII, Article 9 to protect the non-appearing party against vexatious and frivolous claims. The Tribunal in the South China Sea Arbitration should thus order that the parties address their first pleadings to the questions of jurisdiction, admissibility and other objections of a preliminary character.

Though formally absent from the proceedings, the non-appearing party may decide to submit to the arbitral tribunal letters and documents in ways and by means not contemplated by the tribunal's rules of procedure.[52] It

---

[47] UNCLOS Annex VII, art 5.

[48] Only the *Southern Bluefin Tuna Case* was arbitrated using the services of the Secretariat of the International Centre for Settlement of Investment Disputes (ICSID); see *Southern Bluefin Tuna Case (Australia and New Zealand v Japan)* (Award on Jurisdiction and Admissibility) (2000) 119 ILR 508. The ICSID Arbitration Rules, icsid.worldbank.org, provide in art 41(3): 'Upon the formal raising of an objection relating to the dispute, the Tribunal may decide to suspend the proceeding on the merits'.

[49] Compare this to the PCA Arbitration Rules 2012, www.pca-cpa.org, which are for use in arbitrating disputes involving at least one State, State-controlled entity, or intergovernmental organization. Art 23(3) provides: 'The arbitral tribunal may rule on a plea referred to in paragraph 2 either as a preliminary question or in an award on the merits'.

[50] Rules of Procedure, art 11(3), reproduced in *Mauritius v United Kingdom* (Procedural Order No 2, Application to Bifurcate Proceedings) (15 January 2013) www.pca-cpa.org.

[51] ibid, paras 1, 2.

[52] See *Aegean Sea Continental Shelf (Greece v Turkey)* (Jurisdiction) [1978] ICJ Rep 3, 18–19.

has been said that these informal communications are often so detailed as to be 'pleadings travelling incognito'.[53] In such a case, the tribunal has to strike a balance. On the one hand, it is valuable for the tribunal to know the views of both parties in whatever form those views may have been expressed. On the other hand, the tribunal must ensure the equality of the parties to the dispute and the proper administration of justice. In particular, non-appearance should not be an excuse for entirely side-stepping the time-limits for the raising of preliminary objections set by the tribunal.[54] The intention of UNCLOS Annex VII, Article 9 is that in a case of non-appearance, neither party should be placed at a disadvantage; therefore, the party which declines to appear cannot be permitted to profit from its absence, since this would amount to placing the party appearing at a disadvantage. The rules of procedure concerning the presentation of pleadings and evidence are designed to secure a proper administration of justice, and a fair and equal opportunity for each party to comment on its opponent's contentions. The treatment to be given by the arbitral tribunal to extra-procedural communications or material emanating from the absent party must be determined by balancing these different considerations, and is not susceptible to rigid definition in the form of a precise general rule. The vigilance which the tribunal can exercise when aided by the presence of both parties to the proceedings has a counterpart in the special care it has to devote to the proper administration of justice in a case in which only one party is present.[55]

Despite its non-appearance, the absent State is and remains a party to the dispute and as such may decide at any moment to exercise its procedural rights,[56] provided that they are not time-barred. A party, for example, can no longer exercise its right to appoint a member of the arbitral tribunal once that member has been appointed by the ITLOS President in accordance with UNCLOS Annex VII, Article 3(e). It may, however, exercise that right if the member of the tribunal so appointed resigns or the seat becomes vacant for other reasons.[57] The principle of equality of the parties requires that the absent party is given the opportunity to participate in the proceedings if it so desires.[58] This means, inter alia, that copies of pleadings, documents or correspondence submitted to the

[53] Christopher Greenwood, 'Review of Nonappearance before the International Court of Justice by H. W. A. Thirlway' (1985) 44 *Cambridge Law Journal* 311, 311.

[54] *cf* Goldmann (n 4) 610 MN 16.

[55] *cf Military and Paramilitary Activities in and against Nicaragua (Nicaragua v United States of America)* (Merits) [1986] ICJ Rep 14, 25–26 [31].

[56] *cf* UNCLOS Annex VII, art 9 ('if one of the *parties* to the dispute does not appear' (emphasis added)).

[57] See UNCLOS Annex VII, art 3(f). In case the party ends its non-appearance, the arbitrators appointed by the ITLOS President may, depending on the circumstances, want to consider resigning in order to allow the party to exercise its rights under UNCLOS Annex VII, art 3.

[58] *Military and Paramilitary Activities in and against Nicaragua (Nicaragua v United States of America)* (Merits) [1986] ICJ Rep 14, 143 [284].

arbitral tribunal by the other party must be immediately forwarded to the absent party. The tribunal must address orders for the conduct of the case as well as any other correspondence concerning the case to both parties. It must also fix time-limits and extensions of time for both of them. The schedule for the oral hearing must allocate equal time to each. The tribunal must make arrangements for keeping verbatim transcripts of the oral hearings and ensure that those transcripts, including any corrections, are distributed to the absent party; preferably in electronic form on each day of the hearings. The tribunal must also forward to the absent party copies of any materials submitted for assistance of the members of the tribunal during the oral hearings. Questions addressed to the appearing party by the tribunal at the end of the oral hearings must be transmitted to the non-appearing party as well as any answers received in writing from the appearing party.

As long as the non-appearing party has not taken any steps in the proceedings, the other party may unilaterally ask the arbitral tribunal at any time to make an order officially recording the discontinuance of the proceedings.[59] Communications of the non-appearing party addressed to the tribunal are not considered steps in the proceedings.[60] A copy of the order is to be sent to both parties.

IV. POSSIBLE PRELIMINARY OBJECTIONS TO THE PHILIPPINES' CLAIMS

China has argued that its rejection of the Philippines' request for arbitration has 'a solid basis in international law'.[61] Such rejection may be based on three different grounds: lack of jurisdiction of the Arbitral Tribunal, inadmissibility of the claims or other objections of a preliminary character.

1. Lack of Jurisdiction of the Arbitral Tribunal

The international legal system is based on the sovereign equality of States.[62] One of the consequences of this fundamental principle is that international courts and tribunals can exercise jurisdiction over States only with their consent. As aptly put by the President of the ICJ in an address to the General Assembly of the United Nations:

> Respect for the sovereignty of States is echoed in the cardinal principle of consensualism. No State can be made subject to the verdicts of courts unless it

---

[59] *cf* ICJ Rules of Court, art 89(1); Rules of the ITLOS, art 106(1).

[60] See *Trial of Pakistani Prisoners of War (Pakistan v India)* (Removal: Order of 15 December 1973) [1973] ICJ Rep 347, 348.

[61] See n 2 above.

[62] See UN Charter, art 2(1). In the *Norwegian Shipowners' Claims (Norway v United States of America)* (1922) 1 RIAA 307, 338, the Arbitral Tribunal held that 'international law and justice are based upon the principle of equality between States'.

has already agreed to do so. ... The Court can intervene only at the request of and with the consent of the interested parties.[63]

In case of doubt, such consent must be interpreted restrictively.[64] Both the Philippines and China gave general consent to the compulsory dispute settlement system under section 2 of Part XV of UNCLOS when they became parties to the Convention in 1984 and 1996, respectively.[65] As neither State has made a declaration under Article 287 UNCLOS choosing a particular means for the settlement of disputes concerning the interpretation or application of the Convention, they are both deemed to have accepted arbitration in accordance with Annex VII to UNCLOS.[66] UNCLOS Annex VII, Article 1 expressly subjects the exercise of jurisdiction by an Annex VII arbitral tribunal to 'the provisions of Part XV' of the Convention. It is thus for the arbitral tribunal to satisfy itself that it has jurisdiction over the subject-matter of the dispute. As the scope of the arbitral award is defined by 'the subject-matter of the dispute',[67] the tribunal's jurisdiction must extend to the subject-matter of the dispute in its entirety. The subject-matter of the dispute is defined by 'The Philippines' Claims' and its 'Relief Sought' as set out in its 20-page 'Notification and Statement of Claim'.[68] The Philippines respectfully requests that the Arbitral Tribunal issue an award that addresses 13 different points. Each of these 13 points must be covered by the Tribunal's compulsory jurisdiction under UNCLOS.[69]

a. Limited Subject-Matter Jurisdiction

The compulsory jurisdiction of arbitral tribunals instituted under Annex VII to UNCLOS is not unlimited.[70] It is instead restricted to 'any dispute concerning the interpretation or application of this Convention'.[71] Matters

---

[63] Statement by Judge Mohammed Bedjaoui, President of the International Court of Justice, made in plenary meeting of the General Assembly at its 51st session, on 15 October 1996 (15 October 1996) UN Doc A/51/PV.34, 4. See also *Military and Paramilitary Activities in and against Nicaragua (Nicaragua v United States of America)* (Merits) [1986] ICJ Rep 14, 32 [44] ('The Court's jurisdiction, as it has frequently recalled is based on the consent of the States').

[64] *cf Nuclear Tests (New Zealand v France)* (Merits) [1974] ICJ Rep 457, 472–73 [47] ('When States make statements by which their freedom of action is to be limited, a restrictive interpretation is called for').

[65] *cf* Republic of the Philippines (RP), Department of Foreign Affairs (DFA), Notification and Statement of Claim (22 January 2013), para 32, reproduced in Annex I, Doc B.2 (Notification and Statement of Claim).

[66] UNCLOS, art 287(3). See also Notification and Statement of Claim, paras 35, 36.

[67] *cf* UNCLOS Annex VII, art 10.

[68] *cf Fisheries Jurisdiction (Spain v Canada)* (Jurisdiction) [1998] ICJ Rep 432, 447–48 [29].

[69] While the 'Philippines' Claims' comprises 10 bullet points, its 'Relief Sought' is divided into 13 different bullet points; *cf* Notification and Statement of Claim, paras 31 and 41. In the following reference is made to the bullet points in the 'Relief Sought' and the 'Claims'.

[70] Shigeru Oda, 'Dispute Settlement Prospects in the Law of the Sea' (1995) 44 *International and Comparative Law Quarterly* 863, 863; Kirsten Schmalenbach, 'Dispute settlement' in Jan Klabbers and Åsa Wallendahl (eds), *Research Handbook on the Law of International Organizations* (Cheltenham, Edward Elgar, 2011) 253.

[71] UNCLOS, arts 286, 288(1).

which neither constitute a 'dispute' nor are dealt with in the Convention are beyond the compulsory jurisdiction *ratione materiae* of UNCLOS arbitral tribunals. Jurisdiction *ratione materiae* of a tribunal can be wider in cases of optional jurisdiction, ie jurisdiction established by agreement of the parties. This should be borne in mind when drawing on case-law with regard to the question of jurisdiction.

(1) Lack of Dispute between the Parties

It is a fundamental requirement of international law that there must be a real dispute between the parties to arbitral proceedings.[72] The Permanent Court of International Justice, in its classic statement in the *Mavrommatis* case, defined a dispute as 'a disagreement on a point of law or fact, a conflict of legal views or of interests between two persons'.[73] A mere assertion is not sufficient to prove the existence of a dispute any more than a mere denial of the existence of the dispute proves its non-existence.[74] Thus, whether there exists a dispute or not does not depend on the views of the parties, but is a matter for 'objective determination' by the Tribunal.[75] The Tribunal's determination must turn on an examination of the facts. The matter is one of substance, not of form. In order to establish the existence of a dispute, it must be shown that the claim of one party is 'positively opposed by the other',[76] or, in other words, that 'the two sides hold clearly opposite views' concerning the application or interpretation of UNCLOS.[77] That the Philippines maintains, and China would probably deny, that the dispute involves the interpretation and application of UNCLOS does not in and of itself constitute a dispute over the interpretation or application of the Convention over which the Tribunal has jurisdiction.[78]

The existence of a dispute concerning the interpretation or application of the Convention is problematic with regard to at least three of the points set out in the 'Relief Sought' by the Philippines. The Philippines asks the Tribunal to declare

---

[72] See *Larsen v Hawaiian Kingdom* (2001) 119 ILR 566, 594 [12.6].

[73] *Mavrommatis Palestine Concessions (Greece v United Kingdom)* (Objection to the Jurisdiction of the Court) 1924 PCIJ Rep Series A No 2, 11. See also *Southern Bluefin Tuna (New Zealand v Japan; Australia v Japan)* (Provisional Measures, Order of 27 August 1999) [1999] ITLOS Rep 280, 293 [44].

[74] *South West Africa (Ethiopia v South Africa; Liberia v South Africa)* (Preliminary Objections) [1962] ICJ Rep 319, 328.

[75] *Interpretation of Peace Treaties with Bulgaria, Hungary and Romania* (First Phase: Advisory Opinion) [1950] ICJ Rep 65, 74.

[76] *South West Africa (Ethiopia v South Africa; Liberia v South Africa)* (Preliminary Objections) [1962] ICJ Rep 319, 328. See also *Southern Bluefin Tuna (New Zealand v Japan; Australia v Japan)* (Provisional Measures, Order of 27 August 1999) [1999] ITLOS Rep 280, 293 [44].

[77] *Interpretation of Peace Treaties with Bulgaria, Hungary and Romania* (First Phase: Advisory Opinion) [1950] ICJ Rep 65, 74.

[78] *Southern Bluefin Tuna Case (Australia and New Zealand v Japan)* (Award on Jurisdiction and Admissibility) (2000) 119 ILR 508, 525 [48].

that China's rights in regard to maritime areas in the South China Sea, like those of the Philippines, are those that are established by UNCLOS, and consist of a Territorial Sea and Contiguous Zone under Part II of the Convention, to an Exclusive Economic Zone under Part V, and to a Continental Shelf under Part VI.[79]

This request is basically restating principles from the Convention. Considering that China is a party to UNCLOS, it would probably not be positively opposed to such a general declaration, unless it was to imply that the question of maritime areas in the South China Sea was governed *exclusively* by the Convention. However, UNCLOS, like any other treaty, cannot be interpreted or applied in a legal vacuum, or in the abstract, without reference to the other rules of international law with which it may interact. This rule finds expression in Article 31(3)(c) of the Vienna Convention on the Law of Treaties (VCLT) which permits 'any relevant rules of international law applicable in the relations between the parties' to be taken into account for the purpose of the interpretation of treaties.[80] Thus, any treaty must be read not only in its own context, but also in the wider context of general international law, whether conventional or customary.[81] The Tribunal could not make such an exclusionary declaration, positively excluding or denying the application of all other relevant rules of international law (including those on the acquisition of sovereignty over land territory or historic title and rights over land and marine areas) which could have a bearing on China's rights in regard to maritime zones in the South China Sea, without going well beyond its jurisdiction to decide disputes concerning the interpretation and application of the Convention. A dispute over whether or not UNCLOS applies *exclusively* is not a dispute concerning the interpretation or application of UNCLOS. If, on the other hand, the declaration was to mean that China's rights to maritime zones are governed by UNCLOS as interpreted in accordance with other relevant rules of international law applicable between the Philippines and China, there would be no dispute.

The Philippines also asks the Tribunal to declare that it 'is entitled under UNCLOS to a 12 M Territorial Sea, a 200 M Exclusive Economic Zone, and a Continental Shelf under Parts II, V and VI of UNCLOS, measured from its archipelagic baselines'.[82] Who would question that under UNCLOS the Philippines is, *in principle*, entitled to the various maritime areas? Such a general declaration, however, has no bearing upon the Philippines' *actual* entitlement vis-à-vis Malaysia, Indonesia, Brunei, Vietnam or China (including both the Chinese mainland and Taiwan).[83] In many cases, the

---

[79] Relief Sought, bullet point 1, identical with Claims, bullet point 1. See also Notification and Statement of Claim, para 6.

[80] Vienna Convention on the Law of Treaties (adopted 22 May 1969, entered into force 27 January 1980) 1155 UNTS 331.

[81] See Ian Sinclair, *The Vienna Convention on the Law of Treaties*, 2nd edn (Manchester, Manchester University Press, 1984) 139.

[82] Relief Sought, bullet point 10, identical with Claims, bullet point 8.

[83] The Philippines adheres to the 'one China policy', respecting the position of the PRC Government 'that there is but one China and that Taiwan is an integral part of Chinese

distance between the opposite or adjacent coasts of these countries will be less than 400nm, thus inevitably creating overlapping claims. Even where a declaratory judgment is sought, the usual conditions for legal proceedings must be present, including 'the assertion against an interested party of rights capable of judicial protection'.[84] What the Philippines asks for is a purely abstract declaration which is removed entirely from any factual or legal context. But, as Judge Fitzmaurice put it in the *Northern Cameroons* case: 'courts of law are not there to make legal pronouncements *in abstracto*'.[85] This was confirmed by the arbitral tribunal in *Larsen v Hawaiian Kingdom*, which stated that 'the function of international arbitral tribunals in contentious proceedings is to determine disputes between the parties, not to make abstract rulings. It follows that if there is no dispute between the parties, the tribunal cannot proceed to a ruling'.[86] The breadth of maritime areas cannot be decided in the abstract, but only by reference to the factual circumstances of each individual case. Whether or not the Philippines is actually entitled to a 200nm Exclusive Economic Zone (EEZ) or a continental shelf in a certain sea area will depend on the existence or absence of overlapping claims by other States in the South China Sea. While an abstract question may lend itself to a request for an advisory opinion, it cannot be the subject of contentious proceedings.[87] The function of an UNCLOS arbitral tribunal is to settle existing disputes, not to develop or restate the law. Such a dispute, however, is lacking with regard to the abstract declaration sought.

The same applies to the request that the Tribunal require that China refrain 'from undertaking other activities inconsistent with the Convention at or in the vicinity' of Scarborough Shoal and Johnson Reef.[88] Again, as a party to UNCLOS China will not positively claim that it is entitled to undertake

territory' and that the PRC Government is 'the sole legal government of China'. See 'Joint Communique of the Government of the People's Republic of China and the Government of the Republic of the Philippines' (9 June 1975) para 6, www.fmprc.gov.cn. That position was recently reaffirmed in the 'Joint statement of the Republic of the Philippines and the People's Republic of China' (Beijing, 1 September 2011) www.gov.ph (2011 Joint Statement). For this reason, China will be taken to include Taiwan.

[84] Edwin Borchard, *Declaratory Judgments*, 2nd edn (Cleveland, Banks-Baldwin Law Publishing, 1941) 26. See also *Northern Cameroons (Cameroon v United Kingdom)* ICJ Pleadings 307 (Counsel for the United Kingdom).

[85] *Northern Cameroons (Cameroon v United Kingdom)* (Preliminary Objections) [1963] ICJ Rep 15, 98 (sep op Fitzmaurice). See also *Interpretation of the Statute of the Memel Territory (United Kingdom, France, Italy and Japan v Lithuania)* (Judgment of 11 August 1932) PCIJ Rep Series A/B No 49, 352 (diss op Anzilotti) who stated: 'what they [the claimants] ask for therefore is a decision on an abstract question of interpretation. ... No plea, however, was formulated ... I do not therefore see upon what the Court could give a ruling'.

[86] *Larsen v Hawaiian Kingdom* (2001) 119 ILR 566, 587 [11.3]. The Tribunal comprised James Crawford, Gavan Griffith, and Christopher Greenwood.

[87] *cf Legality of the Threat or Use of Nuclear Weapons* (Advisory Opinion) [1996] ICJ Rep 226, 236 [15].

[88] Relief Sought, bullet point 9. These 'other activities inconsistent with the Convention' seem to include the 'harvesting of endangered species'; see Notification and Statement of Claim, para 21.

'activities inconsistent with the Convention', either in the vicinity of these two features or elsewhere.[89] The Philippines in its Notification and Statement of Claim does not specify what these 'inconsistent' activities are or where they take place. It is thus seeking a mere abstract statement of the obvious.[90] Such a statement bears no relation to the actual legal rights and obligations of the parties and is mainly of symbolic significance. Any decision on the matter would be devoid of legal purpose.

(2) Subject-Matter outside the Jurisdiction of the Tribunal

UNCLOS, Article 286(1) limits the compulsory jurisdiction of Annex VII arbitral tribunals to 'disputes concerning the interpretation or application of this Convention'. An applicant simply claiming that the dispute falls within the Convention does not make it so. Similarly, the rejection of such a claim does not give rise to a dispute concerning the interpretation or application of the Convention. It is for the Tribunal, while giving particular attention to the formulation of the dispute chosen by the applicant, to determine on an objective basis whether the claims made, reasonably (and not just remotely) relate to, and are capable of being decided on the basis of the legal rules and standards of the Convention. In particular, the relief sought must be the result of the application or interpretation of the Convention.

For the Arbitral Tribunal to assume jurisdiction in the present case, it must establish a link between the facts advanced by the Philippines and the provisions of UNCLOS referred to in the Notification and Statement of Claim and show that such facts and provisions can sustain the relief sought.[91] The Philippines submitted in rather general terms that the rights and obligations of the parties to the dispute 'are governed by the provisions of UNCLOS, including but not limited to Articles 3-14 of Part II, Articles 55 and 57 of Part V, Article 76 of Part VI, Article 121 of Part VIII and Article 300 of Part XVI'.[92] The only substantive provision that is referred to more than once in the Notification and Statement of Claim is Article 121.[93] It is these provisions on which any award must hinge in order for the Tribunal to have jurisdiction. In the following it will be shown that the Philippines has artificially, if not forcibly, extracted individual legal issues from a

---

[89] See eg the statement of the spokesperson of the MFA: 'As a signatory to the UN Convention on the Law of the Sea (UNCLOS), China attaches great importance to upholding the principles and purposes of the UNCLOS', (PRC MFA, 'Foreign Ministry Spokesperson Hong Lei's Remarks on ASEAN Foreign Ministers' Statement on the Six-Point Principles on the South China Sea Issue' (21 July 2012) www.fmprc.gov.cn).

[90] It is also difficult to see how the parties could have fulfilled their obligation under UNCLOS, art 283 to exchange views regarding the settlement by negotiations of such abstract questions. On this requirement, see text at section III.2.a.

[91] cf *M/V 'Louisa' (Saint Vincent and the Grenadines v Kingdom of Spain)* (Judgment) [2013] ITLOS Rep [99].

[92] Notification and Statement of Claim, para 39.

[93] See ibid, paras 4, 6, 14, 20, 22, 24, 31, 39 and 41.

complex and inseparable whole which cannot be decided on their own. In particular, several of the points in the 'Relief Sought' by the Philippines concern the questions of sovereignty and other rights over land territory, as well as historic titles and rights, both of which are not dealt with in the Convention and thus fall outside the jurisdiction of the Tribunal.

(a) Sovereignty and Other Rights over Land Territory

It is generally acknowledged that the Convention does not deal with questions of sovereignty and other rights over land territory, and that disputes concerning these questions are not subject to the jurisdiction *ratione materiae* of UNCLOS arbitral tribunals.[94] For example, the Chinese Government summarised the position in July 2012 as follows:

> The Convention is not an international treaty to regulate disputes of territorial sovereignty between states, nor can it serve as the basis to arbitrate such disputes. Countries concerned should settle the demarcation disputes in the South China Sea on the basis of solving disputes of territorial sovereignty over the Nansha Islands [Spratly Islands], in accordance with historical facts and International Law including the UNCLOS.[95]

This position seems to have been accepted by the Philippines which states in its Notification and Statement of Claim that it 'does not seek in this arbitration a determination of which Party enjoys sovereignty over the islands claimed by both of them'.[96]

The Philippines nevertheless asks the Tribunal to declare that 'Mischief Reef and McKennan Reef are submerged features that form part of the Continental Shelf of the Philippines under Part VI of the Convention, and that China's occupation and construction activities on them violate the sovereign rights of the Philippines'.[97] Similarly, it requests the Tribunal

---

[94] See eg Alex G Oude Elferink, 'The Islands in the South China Sea: How Does their Presence Limit the Extent of the High Seas and the Area and the Maritime Zones of the Mainland Coasts?' (2001) 32 *Ocean Development & International Law* 169, 172 ('In any case, disputes concurrently involving a dispute concerning sovereignty or other rights over territory appear to be excluded from the reach of the compulsory dispute settlement provisions of the convention'); Paul C Irwin, 'Settlement of Maritime Boundary Disputes: An Analysis of the Law of the Sea Negotiations' (1980) 8 *Ocean Development and International Law* 105, 114; Henry Bensurto, 'Role of International Law in Managing Disputes in the South China Sea' (CSIS Conference, Managing Tensions in the South China Sea, 5–6 June 2013), 15, csis.org.

[95] PRC MFA, 'Foreign Ministry Spokesperson Hong Lei's Remarks on ASEAN Foreign Ministers' Statement on the Six-Point Principles on the South China Sea Issue' (21 July 2012) (n 89). See also the statement with regard to Scarborough Shoal (Huangyan Island): 'The UN Convention on the Law of the Sea (UNCLOS) is not the legal basis to determine the territorial sovereignty of the Huangyan Island and cannot change the fact that the island belongs to China' (PRC MFA, 'Foreign Ministry Spokesperson Hong Lei's Remarks on Philippine President's Speaking of the Huangyan Island Incident in His State of the Nation Address' (25 July 2012) www.fmprc.gov.cn).

[96] Notification and Statement of Claim, para 7.

[97] Relief Sought, bullet point 4; see also Claims, bullet points 3 and 5. See also Notification and Statement of Claim, paras 3, 15, 16, 28.

to declare that 'Gaven Reef and Subi Reef are submerged features in the South China Sea that are not above sea level at high tide, are not islands under the Convention, and are not located on China's Continental Shelf, and that China's occupation of and construction activities on these features are unlawful'.[98] In both cases, the Philippines asks the Tribunal to request China to terminate or end 'its occupation of and activities on' these features.[99]

These points of the 'Relief Sought' call for several general comments at the outset. First, they are based on the assumption that the continental shelf in the South China Sea of both the Philippines and China is clearly defined and delineated, and that neither the Philippines, China, Vietnam, Brunei nor Malaysia have any overlapping continental shelf claims in the South China Sea which call for delimitation — an assumption that flies in the face of reality.[100] As aptly put by Michael Strupp:

> No land area of the South China Sea, Spratlys included, lies more than 200 nautical miles ('nm') from the nearest national baseline. Hence no outer limit of any Exclusive Economic Zone can be delineated without infringing upon a possible claim raised by the respective adjoining or opposite neighbour.[101]

The whole Notification and Statement of Claim is infused with the misleading assumption that the Philippines 'is entitled to an exclusive economic zone and continental shelf of 200 M from its archipelagic baselines'.[102] It seems that for the Philippines, other States' claims to the Spratly Islands do not exist. The rules on the breadth of the EEZ and continental shelf in UNCLOS are taken at face value without regard for the geographical realities in the area.[103] However, the question of whether the Philippines can indeed enjoy a 200nm EEZ and continental shelf in the South China Sea depends, not least, on the question of territorial sovereignty of other States, including China, over the islands, rocks and low-tide elevations of the Spratly Islands and the ensuing maritime entitlements of those States. As pointed out by Dapo Akande: 'most of its [the Philippines'] claims would seem to require the tribunal to determine

---

[98] Relief Sought, bullet point 6; see also Claims, bullet points 3 and 4. See also Notification and Statement of Claim, paras 18, 19.

[99] Relief Sought, bullet points 5 and 7; see also Claims, bullet point 4.

[100] See eg the Note Verbale No 000819 from the Philippine Mission to the United Nations to the UN Secretary-General (4 August 2009) www.un.org/Depts/los, protesting against the Joint Submission by Malaysia and Vietnam to the Commission on the Limits of the Continental Shelf concerning the outer limits of the continental shelf beyond 200nm in the South China Sea and pointing out that the submission lays claim on contested shelf areas 'that are disputed ... because they overlap with that of the Philippines'. For an overview of the conflicting claims, see eg Nong Hong, *UNCLOS and Ocean Dispute Settlement: Law and Politics in the South China Sea* (Milton Park, Routledge, 2012) 16–20.

[101] Michael Strupp, 'Spratly Islands' in Rüdiger Wolfrum (ed), *Max Planck Encyclopedia of International Law*, vol IX (Oxford, OUP, 2012) 448 MN 1. For an overview of the various claims, see also ibid, 449 MN 2.

[102] Notification and Statement of Claim, para 27. See also ibid, paras 12; 24; 31, bullet point 8; 41, bullet point 8.

[103] See UNCLOS, arts 57, 76(1).

whether particular features or areas are within the maritime zones of the Philippines or those of China'.[104] It is apparent that the Philippines tries to avoid the question of maritime entitlements, both its own and those of other States, and the ensuing question of maritime delimitation, as the former depends on sovereignty over land territory and the latter has been removed from the Tribunal's jurisdiction by China's declaration under Article 298(1)(a)(i) UNCLOS.[105]

Second, even if Mischief Reef and McKennan Reef formed part of the continental shelf of the Philippines, China's occupation of and construction activities on them would alone not violate the 'sovereign rights' of the Philippines.[106] A coastal State under UNCLOS exercises 'sovereign rights' over the continental shelf 'for the purpose of exploring it and exploiting its natural resources'.[107] With regard to artificial islands, installations and structures on its continental shelf, the coastal State has only the 'exclusive right' to authorise and regulate construction activities.[108] Moreover, to the extent that the occupation and construction activities have been carried out by the People's Liberation Army (PLA) they are subject to the optional exception from the jurisdiction of the Tribunal of 'disputes concerning military activities' under Article 298(1)(b) UNCLOS.[109]

Third, adopting for the sake of argument the Philippines' position that low-tide elevations that are not located in a coastal State's territorial sea are either part of a coastal State's continental shelf or of the international seabed,[110] it is difficult to understand how China's occupation of and construction activities on Gaven Reef and Subi Reef can be 'unlawful', unless these reefs are located on the continental shelf of a third State. The Philippines does not claim the two reefs to be part of its continental shelf and denies their location on China's continental shelf (without, however, addressing the questions of maritime entitlements and delimitation).[111] The Convention regulates only installations used for carrying out activities in the Area, that is, all activities of exploration for, and exploitation of, the resources of the sea-bed and ocean floor and subsoil thereof, beyond the limits of national jurisdiction or, in other words, beyond the continental shelf areas of coastal States.[112] The erection and emplacement of those installations is subject to the authority of the International Seabed

---

[104] Dapo Akande, 'Philippines Initiates Arbitration Against China over South China Sea Dispute' (22 January 2013) *EJIL: Talk!*, www.ejiltalk.org.

[105] On the optional exceptions to jurisdiction, see text at section III.1.c.

[106] Relief Sought, bullet point 4.

[107] UNCLOS, art 77(1).

[108] UNCLOS, arts 80, 60(1). With regard to installations and structures, the exclusive right is limited to installations and structures used for the economic exploitation and exploration of the continental shelf; see UNCLOS, art 60(1)(a).

[109] On the optional exceptions to jurisdiction, see text at section III.1.c.

[110] See Notification and Statement of Claim, paras 3, 14.

[111] ibid, para 31, bullet points 3–5. The two reefs are located 205nm and 230nm, respectively, off the coast of the Philippines and thus outside the 200nm continental shelf claimed by the Philippines; see ibid, paras 18 and 19.

[112] UNCLOS, arts 147(2), 1(3), 1(1).

Authority.[113] Otherwise, States are free to construct artificial islands, installations and structures on the seabed in the area of the high seas.[114] The Philippines does not claim that the structures built by China are used for activities in the Area. Thus, the unlawfulness of the occupation of and construction activities on these features can only result from these features being located on the continental shelf of a third State who does not consent to these activities. Whoever that State may be, it would be an indispensable third party for the determination of the lawfulness of the Chinese activities by the Tribunal.[115]

The main obstacle to the Tribunal ruling on the Philippines' claims that China's occupation of and construction activities on Mischief Reef, McKennan Reef, Gaven Reef and Subi Reef are unlawful is that these claims cannot be addressed without dealing with the question of sovereignty or other rights over these reefs and any other insular land territory within 200nm of these reefs. If the reefs are subject to Chinese territorial sovereignty, their occupation by China and the construction activities on them will not be unlawful. Similarly, even if there is only one Chinese island in the vicinity of these reefs which brings them within the area of the Chinese continental shelf, the reefs, according to the position of the Philippines set out above, will form part of the Chinese continental shelf and will be subject to the sovereign rights or, more correctly, exclusive rights of China with regard to the construction of artificial islands, installations and structures. China claims sovereignty, for example, over Itu Aba, Thitu, Sin Cowe, Namyit, Flat, Nanshan and West York which qualify as proper islands in terms of Article 121(2) UNCLOS with their own continental shelf.[116] Each of these islands is located at a distance of between 13nm and 100nm from the four reefs.

It has been argued that in light of the ICJ's decision in *Romania v Ukraine* all the islands in the South China Sea should be treated as 'rocks' in terms of Article 121(3) UNCLOS with a 12nm territorial sea only.[117] This view is

---

[113] UNCLOS, arts 147(2)(a), 1(2).

[114] UNCLOS, art 87(1)(d). See also Albertus Heijmans, 'Artificial Islands and the Law of Nations' (1974) 21 *Netherlands International Law Review* 139, 150.

[115] On the indispensable third party rule, see text at section III.3.a.

[116] The question of whether insular features in the Spratly Islands qualify as islands in terms of UNCLOS, art 121(2) and generate a 200nm EEZ and continental shelf is disputed in the literature. For the view that at least some of the features are proper islands which generate EEZ and continental shelf entitlements, see eg Yann-huei Song, 'Article 121(3) of the Law of the Sea Convention and the Disputed Offshore Islands in East Asia: A Tribute to Judge Choon-Ho Park' in Jon M Van Dyke and others (eds), *Governing Ocean Resources: New Challenges and Emerging Regimes: A Tribute to Judge Choon-Ho Park* (Leiden, Martinus Nijhoff, 2013) 61, 90–93 who treats Thitu, Itu Aba, and Spratly Island as proper islands; Nong Hong, *UNCLOS and Ocean Dispute Settlement* (2012) 59, 60 ('at least some of the islands ... such as Itu Aba'). See also Robert C Beckman, 'International Law, UNCLOS and the South China Sea' in Robert C Beckman and others (eds), *Beyond Territorial Disputes in the South China Sea: Legal Framework for the Joint Development of Hydrocarbon Resources* (Cheltenham, Edward Elgar, 2013) 47, 61.

[117] Jon M Van Dyke, 'The Romania-Ukraine Decision and Its Effect on East Asian Maritime Delimitations' in Jon M Van Dyke and others (eds), Governing Ocean Resources: New

based on a misconception of the decision which was concerned with the delimitation of maritime entitlements generated by the mainland coasts of the parties. The Court did not rule that Ukraine's Serpents' Island, which is above water at high tide, uninhabited and has a surface area of approximately 0.17 sq km, is not a proper island in terms of Article 121(2) UNCLOS.[118] What the Court did say was that Serpents' Island, which lays some 20nm off the mainland coast of Ukraine and 'is not one of a cluster of fringe islands constituting "the coast" of Ukraine ... cannot serve as a base point for the construction of the provisional equidistance line between the coasts of the Parties'.[119] The Court also concluded that 'the presence of Serpents' Island does not call for an adjustment of the provisional equidistance line'. This conclusion was based on the factors that:

> [T]he areas subject to delimitation in this case are located in the exclusive economic zone and the continental shelf generated by the mainland coasts of the Parties and are moreover within 200 nautical miles of Ukraine's mainland coast ... Given this geographical configuration and in the context of the delimitation with Romania, *any continental shelf and exclusive economic zone entitlements possibly generated by Serpents' Island* could not project further than the entitlements generated by Ukraine's mainland coast because of the southern limit of the delimitation area as identified by the Court... Further, *any possible entitlements generated by Serpents' Island* in an eastward direction are fully subsumed by the entitlements generated by the western and eastern mainland coasts of Ukraine itself.[120]

The Court thus did not rule on the question of maritime 'entitlements generated by Serpents' Island' because such entitlements would have had no effect on the delimitation of the maritime spaces belonging to the mainland coasts of the parties. The situation in the South China Sea is different. The islands in question are not located in the exclusive economic zone and the continental shelf generated by the mainland coasts of the parties, and are not within 200nm of the mainland coast of China. Thus, any maritime entitlements generated by these islands would project further than the entitlements generated by China's mainland coast and would not be subsumed by such entitlements.[121] In addition, maritime

---

Challenges and Emerging Regimes: A Tribute to Judge Choon-Ho Park (Leiden, Martinus Nijhoff, 2013) 43, 57–58. For a similar view, see also Marius Gjetnes, 'The Spratlys: Are They Rocks or Islands?' (2001) 32 *Ocean Development and International Law* 191, 199–202.

[118] *Maritime Delimitation in the Black Sea (Romania v Ukraine)* (Merits) [2009] ICJ Rep 61, 123 [187] ('the Court does not need to consider whether Serpents' Island falls under paragraphs 2 or 3 of Article 121 of UNCLOS').

[119] ibid, 110 [149] and 122 [186].

[120] ibid, 122 [187].

[121] Several of the islands in question are larger than Serpents' Island and are inhabited. For example, Itu Aba Island is 0.46 sq km in area, has fresh water resources and is inhabited throughout the year; see Mark J Valencia, Jon M Van Dyke and Noel A Ludwig, *Sharing the Resources of the South China Sea* (The Hague, Martinus Nijhoff, 1997) 230. Itu Aba is also larger than, for example, the two Alburquerque Cays which in *Territorial and Maritime Dispute (Nicaragua v Colombia)* (Merits) [2012] ICJ Rep [27], [103] were treated by the ICJ as islands in terms of UNCLOS, art 121(2) with their own continental shelf.

entitlements do not depend on the size of the island. As the ICJ recently confirmed, 'islands, regardless of their size...generate the same maritime rights as other land territory... It inevitably follows that a comparative small island may give an entitlement to a considerable maritime [ie EEZ and continental shelf] area'.[122]

The fact that some of the islands claimed by China are situated within 200nm from the archipelagic baselines of the Philippines does not mean that they cannot generate maritime zones or that boundary delimitations would automatically give the Philippines maximum extension of its claim to continental shelf and EEZ.[123] In the *Territorial and Maritime Dispute* case which concerned the question of whether several small Columbian islands located off the coast of Nicaragua were entitled to their own continental shelf and EEZ, the ICJ stated that

> no weight should be given to Nicaragua's contention that the Colombian islands are located on 'Nicaragua's continental shelf'. It has repeatedly made clear that geological and geomorphological considerations are not relevant to the delimitation of overlapping entitlements within 200 nautical miles of the coasts of States ... The reality is that the Nicaraguan mainland and fringing islands, and the Colombian islands, are located on the same continental shelf. That fact cannot, in and of itself, give one State's entitlements priority over those of the other in respect of the area where their claims overlap.[124]

The situation is further complicated by the fact that all the islands in the vicinity of these reefs are located within less than 100nm of each other and are claimed by more than one State, namely the Philippines, China (both the mainland and Taiwan) and Vietnam. In addition, all the relevant islands are situated less than 400nm from the main Philippine archipelago. This raises not just the question of allocation of sovereignty over these islands but, in case of conflicting sovereignties, also the question of delimitation of continental shelf boundaries.[125] Questions of boundary delimitation have been excluded from the jurisdiction of the Tribunal by China's declaration under Article 298(1)(a)(i) UNCLOS.[126]

The same problem arises with regard to the Philippines' claims that Johnson Reef, Cuarteron Reef and Fiery Cross Reef are 'rocks' in terms

---

[122] *Territorial and Maritime Dispute (Nicaragua v Colombia)* (Merits) [2012] ICJ Rep [176].

[123] See *Maritime Delimitation in the Area between Greenland and Jan Mayen (Denmark v Norway)* (Merits) [1993] ICJ Rep 38, 69 [70]. On overlapping claims in the South China Sea, see generally Oude Elferink 'The Islands in the South China Sea' 178–82.

[124] *Territorial and Maritime Dispute (Nicaragua v Colombia)* (Merits) [2012] ICJ Rep [216].

[125] *cf* Gjetnes, 'The Spratlys: Are They Rocks or Islands?' 192.

[126] On the optional exceptions to jurisdiction, see text at section III.1.c. See also Robert C Beckman, 'The Philippines v. China Case and the South China Sea Disputes' (Asia Society/ LKY SPP Conference, South China Sea: Central to Asia-Pacific Peace and Security, New York, 13–15 March 2013) 10, cil.nus.edu.sg/wp ('if the Tribunal leaves open the question of whether any of the islands in the Spratlys are entitled to an EEZ and continental shelf of their own, the Tribunal could rule that it cannot decide whose continental shelf such features are part of without engaging in maritime boundary delimitation, which is outside its jurisdiction').

of Article 121(3) UNCLOS and, as such, entitled 'only to a territorial sea no broader than 12 M; and that China has unlawfully claimed maritime entitlements beyond 12 M from these features',[127] and that China must 'refrain from preventing Philippine vessels from exploiting in a sustainable manner the living resources in the waters adjacent to … Johnson Reef'.[128] Johnson Reef, Cuarteron Reef and Fiery Cross Reef are each located within a distance of less than 200nm from one or more proper islands which are claimed by the Philippines, China (both the mainland and Taiwan) and Vietnam.[129] All these islands have their own EEZ and continental shelf. The question of whether China may claim an EEZ (or any other maritime entitlement) in the area of these reefs with the ensuing sovereign rights over the natural living resources thus does not depend simply and solely on their status as 'rocks' or 'islands' (proper) in terms of Article 121(2) UNCLOS,[130] but on territorial sovereignty over the islands in their vicinity and, in case of conflicting sovereignties, maritime boundary delimitation. While the Tribunal can decide on the abstract question of the status of these reefs as rocks or islands,[131] it is without jurisdiction over the matters underlying the question of maritime entitlements in the vicinity of these reefs.

The Philippines tries to circumvent the question of sovereignty and other rights over land territory by arguing that Mischief Reef, McKennan Reef, Gaven Reef and Subi Reef are 'all at best low tide elevations'.[132] It further asserts that such low-tide elevations located outside a coastal State's territorial sea 'are part of the seabed and cannot be acquired by a State, or subjected to its sovereignty, unless they form part of that State's Continental Shelf under Part VII of the Convention'.[133] As a matter of course, the Philippines assumes that the reefs are located on its continental

---

[127] Relief Sought, bullet point 8, and Claims, bullet point 6. See also Notification and Statement of Claim, paras 4, 22–24. It is not at all clear that China claims maritime entitlements 'from these features'. The maritime entitlements may also be generated by other insular features or may be based on historical rights.

[128] Relief Sought, bullet point 9.

[129] The islands in question are Spratly, Itu Aba, Thitu, Sin Cowe, Namyit, Flat, Nanshan and West York. Spratly Island (proper) is not claimed by the Philippines.

[130] Professor Alan Boyle, one of the Philippines' counsel, suggested in his writings that even a territorial or boundary dispute could be brought before the UNCLOS dispute settlement procedures if it were only phrased as 'a dispute about entitlement to an EEZ under Part V and Article 121(3) of the Convention … everything turns in practice not on what each case involves but on how the issues are formulated' (Alan E Boyle, 'Dispute Settlement and the Law of the Sea Convention: Problems of Fragmentation and Jurisdiction' (1997) 46 *International and Comparative Law Quarterly* 37, 44–45).

[131] This still leaves the question of whether there is a 'dispute' between the parties over the status of these reefs as rocks or islands. Johnson Reef, Cuarteron Reef and Fiery Cross Reef are known in Chinese as Chigua Jiao, Huanyang Jiao and Yongshu Jiao. The word 'jiao' in Chinese means 'rock'.

[132] See Notification and Statement of Claim, paras 14, 16, 18 and 19.

[133] ibid, para 31, bullet point 3. But *cf* also Note Verbale No 000228 from the Philippine Mission to the United Nations to the UN Secretary-General responding to two notes from the PRC to the UN Secretary-General (5 April 2011) www.un.org/Depts/los/, which distinguishes between 'Islands and other Geological Features' and claims 'sovereignty and jurisdiction over the geological features' without making any reference to the continental shelf.

shelf and are thus subject to its sovereignty. The argument itself is contradictory in that, on the one hand, it denies that States can acquire sovereignty over low-tide elevations through appropriation and, on the other hand, it subjects low-tide elevations located on the continental shelf to the sovereignty of the coastal State. The sovereignty of the coastal State, however, ends at the outer limit of its territorial sea.[134] Under UNCLOS, the coastal State exercises over the continental shelf only 'sovereign rights for the purpose of exploring it and exploiting its natural resources'.[135] The continental shelf concept does not confer sovereignty over the seabed. In any case, the determination of Philippines' sovereignty or other rights over low-tide elevations would first require the Tribunal to decide on the extent and limits of the Philippines' continental shelf.

The questions of whether low-tide elevations are land territory or part of the seabed and whether sovereignty over them can be acquired by appropriation are disputed. The ICJ held on several occasions that low-tide elevations are not territory and cannot be appropriated in conformity with the rules and principles of territorial acquisition. However, a coastal State has sovereignty over low-tide elevations which are situated within its territorial sea since it has sovereignty over the territorial sea itself.[136] Robert Kolb referred to the Court's denial of acquisition of sovereignty over low-tide elevations as '"legislative" activity'.[137] The Tribunal in the *Eritrea v Yemen* arbitration, on the other hand, seems to have made no distinction with regard to the location of low-tide elevations when it found that 'the islands, islets, rocks and low-tide elevations' of a certain island group 'are subject to the territorial sovereignty' of Eritrea and Yemen, respectively.[138] Judge Oda stated in his separate opinion in *Qatar v Bahrain* that 'the question of whether sovereignty over an islet or a low-tide elevation may be acquired through appropriation by a State ... remain open matters'.[139] Although the ICJ stated in *Qatar v Bahrain* that it was not 'aware of a uniform and widespread State practice which might have given rise to a customary rule which unequivocally permits or excludes appropriation of low-tide elevations',[140] the practice of States seems to point predominantly in one direction. In judicial or arbitral proceedings,

---

[134] See UNCLOS, art 2(1).

[135] UNCLOS, art 77(1).

[136] *Maritime Delimitation and Territorial Questions between Qatar and Bahrain (Qatar v Bahrain)* (Merits) [2001] ICJ Rep 40, 101–02 [204]–[206]; *Sovereignty over Pedra Branca/Pulau Batu Puteh, Middle Rocks and South Ledge (Malaysia/Singapore)* (Merits) [2008] ICJ Rep 12, 100–01 [295]–[299]; *Territorial and Maritime Dispute (Nicaragua v Colombia)* (Merits) [2012] ICJ Rep [26].

[137] Robert Kolb, *Case Law on Equitable Maritime Delimitation: Digest and Commentaries* (The Hague, Martinus Nijhoff, 2003) 544. For support of the ICJ's ruling in *Qatar v Bahrain*, see Yoshifumi Tanaka, 'Low-Tide Elevations in International Law of the Sea: Selected Issues' (2006) 20 *Ocean Yearbook* 189, 203–07.

[138] *Eritrea v Yemen* (First Stage – Territorial Sovereignty and Scope of the Dispute) (1998) 22 RIAA 209, 330 [527].

[139] *Maritime Delimitation and Territorial Questions between Qatar and Bahrain (Qatar v Bahrain)* (Merits) [2001] ICJ Rep 40, 124 [7] (sep op Oda).

[140] ibid, 101–02 [205].

States have generally claimed sovereignty over low-tide elevations irrespective of their location.[141] States have also adopted laws applicable to low-tide elevations.[142] In particular, the States laying claim to the Spratly Islands have claimed territorial sovereignty over the island group as a whole, including all islands, islets, rocks, reefs, shoals, cays and low-tide elevations.[143] Other States also seem to acknowledge that the 'territorial disputes' over the Spratly Islands are not limited to 'islands' in terms of Article 121 UNCLOS but extend to 'land features in the South China Sea' in general.[144]

In *Qatar v Bahrain*, the first case in which the ICJ ruled that low-tide elevations are not land territory, the Court was concerned with the special situation of low-tide elevations in a zone of overlapping territorial sea claims.[145] One may wonder whether the Court's ruling is of general application; especially considering the careful wording employed in the judgment.[146] Article 298(1)(a)(i) UNCLOS speaks of 'sovereignty or other rights over continental or *insular land territory*'.[147] In the literature, low-tide elevations, together with islands, are regularly referred to as 'insular features' or 'insular formations'.[148] It could thus be argued that

---

[141] See eg *Eritrea v Yemen* (First Stage – Territorial Sovereignty and Scope of the Dispute) (1998) 22 RIAA 209, 222 [30]; *Territorial and Maritime Dispute (Nicaragua v Colombia)* (Counter-Memorial of the Republic of Colombia, vol I, 11 November 2008) paras 10.10, 8.19–8.26, 2.26–2.29 (two of the low-tide elevations were outside Columbia's territorial sea); see ibid, (Judgment of 19 November 2012) [2012] ICJ Rep [183]; *Continental Shelf (Tunisia/Libyan Arab Jamahiriya)* (Memorial of Tunisia, 27 May 1980) paras 3.18–3.23 and, in particular, fn 14 ('territoire tunisien') .

[142] See eg Law of the People's Republic of China on the Protection of Offshore Islands (26 December 2009) 56, reproduced in Department of Policy, Legislation and Planning, State Oceanic Administration (ed), *Collection of the Sea Laws and Regulations of the People's Republic of China*, 4th edn (Beijing, Ocean Press, 2012) 364.

[143] For example, Vietnam, like China, claims sovereignty over the 'Truong Sa (Spratly) Archipelago' as a whole and considers it an 'integral part of Viet Nam's territory'; see Law of the Sea of Viet Nam (adopted 21 June 2012) arts 1, 19(2), reprinted at vietnamnews.vn.

[144] See eg US Department of State, 'Remarks at Press Availability, Hillary Rodham Clinton, Secretary of State' (National Convention Center, Hanoi, Vietnam, 23 July 2010) www.state.gov. See also Congressional Research Service, 'Maritime Territorial Disputes in East Asia: Issues for Congress', R42930 (30 January 2013) 6, www.fas.org ('islands and other landmasses').

[145] See *Maritime Delimitation and Territorial Questions between Qatar and Bahrain (Qatar v Bahrain)* (Merits) [2001] ICJ Rep 40, 101 [204].

[146] The ICJ stated that the 'few existing rules do not justify a *general assumption* that low-tide elevations are territory in the same sense as islands' and that it 'is thus not established that *in the absence of other rules and legal principles*, low-tide elevations can, from the viewpoint of the acquisition of sovereignty, be *fully* assimilated with islands or other land territory' (ibid, 102 [206]). See also *Territorial and Maritime Dispute between Nicaragua and Honduras in the Caribbean Sea (Nicaragua v Honduras)* (Merits) [2007] ICJ Rep 659, 703–04 [141]–[144] where the Court elected to decline to make a determinative finding on the question of sovereignty over low-tide elevations due to lack of information rather than decide that there can be no sovereignty over low-tide elevations.

[147] Emphasis added.

[148] See eg Hiran W Jayewardene, *The Regime of Islands in International Law*, Publications on Ocean Development (Dordrecht, Martinus Nijhoff, 1990) 7, 26, 373; Clive R Symmons, *Some Problems Relating to the Definition of Insular Formations in International Law - Islands and Low-Tide Elevations*, Maritime Briefing vol 1, no 5, Clive Schofield and Peter Hocknell (eds) (Durham,

they qualify as 'insular land territory'. Another argument for the quality of low-tide elevations as land territory can be derived from Articles 7(4) and 47(4) UNCLOS which provide for the drawing of straight baselines to and from low-tide elevations located outside a State's territorial sea where 'lighthouses or similar installations which are permanently above sea level have been built on them' or 'where the drawing of baselines to and from such elevations has received general international recognition'. In the case of archipelagic baselines the low-tide elevation may be up to 100nm, and in certain circumstances even up to 125nm, away from the nearest island. Vietnam, the Philippines and China (both the mainland and Taiwan) have referred to the Spratly Islands as an 'archipelago'.[149] According to the principle that 'the land dominates the sea', maritime entitlements flow from, and are determined by, reference to State sovereignty over land territory.[150] As the ICJ pointed out in *Qatar v Bahrain*, it is 'the terrestrial territorial situation that must be taken as starting point for the determination of the maritime rights of a coastal State'.[151] If low-tide elevations were not sovereign territory, it would be difficult to explain how they can generate maritime entitlements. That they can affect maritime entitlements was confirmed by the ICJ in the *Tunisia/Libya Continental Shelf* case where the Court said with regard to a belt of low-tide elevations surrounding islands off the coast of Tunisia at a seaward distance of 9 to 27 kilometres, ie low-tide elevations located partly outside Tunisia's territorial sea: 'In these geographical circumstances, the Court has to take into account not only the islands, but also the low-tide

International Boundaries Research Unit, 1995) 1; Nuno Sérgio Marques Antunes, *Towards the Conceptualisation of Maritime Delimitation: Legal and Technical Aspects of a Political Process* (Leiden, Martinus Nijhoff, 2003) 610; José Luís Jesus, 'Rocks, New-born Islands, Sea Level Rise and Maritime Space' in Jochen A Frowein and others (eds), *Verhandeln für den Frieden/Negotiating for Peace: Liber Amicorum Tono Eitel* (Berlin, Springer, 2003) 579, 580; Clive Schofield, 'The Trouble with Islands: The Definition and Role of Islands and Rocks in Maritime Boundary Delimitation' in Seoung Yong Hong and Jon M Van Dyke (eds), *Maritime Boundary Disputes, Settlement Processes, and the Law of the Sea* (Leiden, Martinus Nijhoff, 2009) 24; Haritini Dipla, 'Islands' in Rüdiger Wolfrum (ed), *Max Planck Encyclopedia of Public International Law*, vol VI (Oxford, OUP, 2012) 407 MN 10. The Philippines itself regards the South China Sea as containing 'many small insular features', Notification and Statement of Claim, para 10.

[149] See eg PRC Ministry of National Defense, 'Remote medical station opens in South China Sea' (12 October 2011) eng.mod.gov.cn ('The Nansha Archipelago is the southernmost part of China's territory'); 'Ministry of Foreign Affairs of the Republic of China (Taiwan) Press Release' (29 July 2010) (2010) 28 *Chinese (Taiwan) Yearbook of International Law and Affairs* 303. The term 'archipelago' is used here in a geographical and a legal sense, within the meaning of the term in the UNCLOS.

[150] See *Fisheries (United Kingdom v Norway)* (Merits) [1951] ICJ Rep 116, 133; *North Sea Continental Shelf (Germany v Denmark)* (Merits) [1969] ICJ Rep 3, 51 [96]; *Aegean Sea Continental Shelf (Greece v Turkey)* (Jurisdiction) [1978] ICJ Rep 3, 36 [86]. The PRC relied on the principle of 'la terre domine la mer' eg in its Note Verbale CML/8/2011 to the UN Secretary-General with regard to the joint submission made by Malaysia and Viet Nam to the Commission on the Limits of the Continental Shelf (14 April 2011), Annex I, Doc A.23 (Note Verbale CML/8/2011 (14 April 2011)).

[151] *Maritime Delimitation and Territorial Questions between Qatar and Bahrain (Qatar v Bahrain)* (Merits) [2001] ICJ Rep 40, 97 [185].

elevations which ... do enjoy some recognition in international law for certain purposes'.[152] The problem with low-tide elevations is, however, that because of their geographical condition of being submerged at high tide the acquisition and preservation of territorial sovereignty will be difficult to establish. The question seems more one of proof than of legal status in general. The PCIJ held that:

> [A] claim to sovereignty based not upon some particular act or title such as a treaty of cession but merely upon continued display of authority, involves two elements each of which must be shown to exist: the intention and will to act as sovereign, and some actual exercise or display of such authority.[153]

Depending on the geographical circumstances, courts and tribunals have been satisfied with very little in the way of actual exercise of sovereign rights, provided that other States could not make out a superior claim.[154] This is particularly true in the case of very small islands which are uninhabited or not permanently inhabited.[155] While the construction and operation of lighthouses and navigational aids are not normally considered manifestations of State authority,[156] the ICJ found that the construction of navigational aids 'can be legally relevant in the case of very small islands'.[157] The same could be argued in the case of low-tide elevations. It is therefore suggested that low-tide elevations are land territory that can be appropriated in conformity with the rules and principles of territorial acquisition.[158] Sovereignty could thus be based either on historic title

---

[152] *Continental Shelf (Tunisia/Libyan Arab Jamahiriya)* (Merits) [1982] ICJ Rep 18, 89 [128] and [129] ('Taking into account ... the low-tide elevations'). Tunisia claimed sovereignty over the banks and shoals on historical grounds (ibid, 72 [99]). In the case concerning *Delimitation of the Maritime Boundary in the Gulf of Maine Area (Canada v United States of America)* (Merits) [1984] ICJ Rep 246, 329–30 [201], a Chamber of the ICJ did not rule out that 'tiny islands, uninhabited rocks or low-tide elevations, sometimes lying at a considerable distance from terra firma' may have a 'limited corrective effect' on maritime delimitation.

[153] *Legal Status of Eastern Greenland (Denmark v Norway)* (Judgment of 5 April 1933) PCIJ Rep Series A / B No 53, 45–46.

[154] ibid, 46. See also *Territorial and Maritime Dispute between Nicaragua and Honduras in the Caribbean Sea (Nicaragua v Honduras)* (Merits) [2007] ICJ Rep 659, 712 [174]; *Territorial and Maritime Dispute (Nicaragua v Colombia)* (Merits) [2012] ICJ Rep [80] ('sovereignty over minor maritime features ... may be established on the basis of a relatively modest display of State powers').

[155] *cf Sovereignty over Pulau Ligitan and Pulau Sipadan (Indonesia/Malaysia)* (Merits) [2002] ICJ Rep 625, 682 [134].

[156] ibid, 685 [147]. See also *Minquiers and Ecrehos (France/United Kingdom)* (Merits) [1953] ICJ Rep 47, 70–71; *Eritrea v Yemen* (First Stage – Territorial Sovereignty and Scope of the Dispute) (1998) 22 RIAA 209, 330 [328]. But see *Territorial and Maritime Dispute (Nicaragua v Colombia)* (Merits) [2012] ICJ Rep [83], where the Court considered the maintenance of lighthouses an act *à titre de souverain*.

[157] *Maritime Delimitation and Territorial Questions between Qatar and Bahrain (Qatar v Bahrain)* (Merits) [2001] ICJ Rep 40, 100 [197]. See also *Sovereignty over Pulau Ligitan and Pulau Sipadan (Indonesia/Malaysia)* (Merits) [2002] ICJ Rep 625, 685 [147].

[158] For the view that low-tide elevations are 'territory', see also Prosper Weil, 'Les hauts fonds découvrants dans la délimitation maritime. À propos des paragraphes 200–209 de l'arrêt de la Cour internationale de Justice du 16 mars 2001 en l'affaire de la *Délimitation maritime et questions territoriales entre Qatar et Bahreïn*' in Nisuke Ando and others (eds), *Liber*

which 'has received general international recognition',[159] or on the continued display of sovereign authority (*effectivités*) as manifested in the construction and operation of lighthouses, navigational aids, artificial islands, installations or other structures which are permanently above sea level.

Alternatively, sovereignty over individual low-tide elevations could be based on historic title over the island group of which they form a part.[160] In this context it is to be remembered that China does not claim sovereignty over individual islands or insular features in the Spratlys, but over the 'Spratly [Nansha] Islands' as a whole. In a statement of the Chinese Ministry of Foreign Affairs it says that the 'Nansha Islands belong to the Chinese territory. China has indisputable sovereignty over these islands and their adjacent waters'.[161] Geographically, the Nansha Islands consist of numerous natural features. According to a Chinese source, they consist of 14 islands/islets, 6 banks, 113 submerged reefs, 35 underwater banks, 21 underwater shoals.[162] In its Note Verbale to the United Nations Secretary-General of 14 April 2011, China stated:

> Since the 1930s, the Chinese Government has given publicity several times the geographical scope of China's Nansha Islands and the names of its components. China's Nansha Islands is therefore clearly defined. In addition, under the relevant provisions of the *1982 United Nations Convention on the Law of the Sea*, as well as the *Law of the People's Republic of China on the Territorial Sea and the Contiguous Zone (1992)* and the *Law on the Exclusive Economic Zone and the Continental Shelf of the People's Republic of China (1998)*, China's Nansha

---

Amicorum Judge Shigeru Oda, vol I (The Hague, Kluwer, 2002) 307, 319. See further Roberto Lavalle, 'Not Quite a Sure Thing: The Maritime Areas of Rocks and Low-Tide Elevations Under the UN Law of the Sea Convention' (2004) 19 *International Journal of Marine and Coastal Law* 43, 49.

[159] *cf* UNCLOS, art 7(4). See also the Statement of Mr Pinto (Ceylon [today Sri Lanka]) (2 December 1971) UN Doc A/AC.138/SC.II/SR.4-23, 188: 'From the earliest times, his country's historic rights to certain pearl banks in the Indian Ocean beyond the territorial sea had been universally acknowledged'.

[160] On the question of historic title, see text at section III.1.a.(2)(b).

[161] PRC MFA, 'Statement of the Ministry of Foreign Affairs of the People's Republic of China' (21 June 2012) www.mfa.gov.cn. See also Law of the People's Republic of China on the Territorial Sea and the Contiguous Zone (25 February 1992) art 2 ('The land territory of the People's Republic of China includes ... the Nansha Islands') and the Declaration of the Government of the People's Republic of China on China's Territorial Sea (4 September 1958) para 1 ('all territories of the People's Republic of China, including ... the Nansha Islands'); see Annex I, Docs A.31 and A.33, respectively.

[162] Zeng Zhaoxuan (ed), *Islands in the South China Sea* (Guandong People's Publishing House, 1986) 3 (in Chinese); quoted in Zou Keyuan, 'How Coastal States Claim Maritime Geographic Features: Legal Clarity or Conundrum?' (2012) 11 *Chinese Journal of International Law* 749, 759. According to another Chinese source the Nansha Islands consist of over 230 islands, islets, rocks, banks, and shoals, among which 25 are islands; see China Institute of Marine Affairs, State Oceanic Administration, *Zhong Guo Hai Yang Fa Zhan Bao Gao* [China's Ocean Development Report] (Beijing, Hai Yang Chu Ban She [Oceans Press], 2011) 24. See also Notification and Statement of Claim, para 10 ('The Spratly Islands are a group of approximately 150 small features, many of which are submerged reefs, banks and low-tide elevations').

Islands is fully entitled to Territorial Sea, Exclusive Economic Zone (EEZ) and Continental Shelf.[163]

China treats the 'Nansha Islands' as a single territorial entity which is shown by the use of the verb 'is', rather than 'are', with regard to the plural term 'Islands'. Thus, the whole entity, including any interconnecting waters and low-tide elevations forming part of that entity, are considered by China to be under its territorial sovereignty. This is also confirmed by the fact that reference is sometimes made to the 'Nansha Archipelago'.[164] The term 'archipelago' is used here in a geographical sense referring to a 'group of islands, including parts of islands, interconnecting waters and other natural features which are so closely interrelated that such islands, waters and other natural features form an intrinsic geographical, economic and political entity, or which historically have been regarded as such'.[165] In a Working Paper submitted to the United Nations Seabed Committee in 1973, China stated that an 'archipelago or an island chain consisting of islands close to each other may be taken as *an integral whole* in defining the limits of the territorial sea around it'.[166] If Chinese practice with regard to the 'Xisha Archipelago'[167] [Paracel Islands] is anything to go by, China seems to consider the waters as well as any natural land features included within 'straight lines' joining the outermost islands and drying reefs of the island groups in the South China Sea to be part of its sovereign territory.[168] The drawing of 'straight lines' in this case should not be confused with the drawing of 'straight archipelagic baselines' within the meaning of Article 47(1) UNCLOS. The concept of 'straight lines' connecting base-points on the outermost islands of an island group predates by several years the concepts of 'straight archipelagic baselines' and 'archipelagic State' under UNCLOS. As early as 1958, the PRC claimed a 12nm territorial sea for all

territories of the People's Republic of China, including ... the Penghu Islands [Pescadores], the Dongsha [Pratas] Islands, the Xisha [Paracel] Islands, the Zhongsha Islands [Macclesfield Bank, including Scarborough Shoal (Huangyan Island)], the Nansha [Spratly] Islands which are separated from the mainland

[163] Note Verbale CML/8/2011 (14 April 2011) (n 150).

[164] See Zou Keyuan, 'How Coastal States Claim Maritime Geographic Features' 755.

[165] UNCLOS, art 46(b).

[166] Working Paper on Sea Area within the Limits of National Jurisdiction, submitted by the Chinese Delegation (16 July 1973) UN Doc A/AC.138/SC.II/L.34, reprinted in Jeanette Greenfield, *China's Practice in the Law of the Sea* (Oxford, Clarendon Press, 1992) 230.

[167] See Chinese Government's Official Web Portal, 'Legislative Conference Held in Newly Established City in South China Sea' (23 July 2012) www.gov.cn.

[168] In the case of the Xisha Islands, the PRC drew 'straight lines' joining the outermost islands of the group; see s II of the Declaration of the Government of the People's Republic of China on the Baselines of the Territorial Sea of the People's Republic of China (15 May 1996), Annex I, Doc A.30. The Declaration ends with the proviso that the PRC Government 'will announce the remaining baselines of the territorial sea of the People's Republic of China at another time'. This Declaration was made prior the PRC becoming a party to UNCLOS on 7 June 1996.

and its coastal islands by the high seas and all the other islands belonging to China.[169]

The scope of the 'land territory of the People's Republic of China' in the South China Sea was confirmed in 1992 in Article 2(2) of the Law of the People's Republic of China on the Territorial Sea and the Contiguous Zone.[170] The territorial sea along these islands was to take 'as its baseline the line composed of the straight lines' connecting base-points on the outermost islands of these island groups. The water areas inside the baseline 'are Chinese inland [internal] waters',[171] ie subject to Chinese sovereignty. In this connection, it is of interest to note that the PRC, when ratifying the UNCLOS, expressly reaffirmed 'its sovereignty over all its archipelagos and islands as listed in Article 2 of the Law of the People's Republic of China on the territorial sea and the contiguous zone, which was promulgated on 25 February 1992'.[172] It could thus be argued that China's historic title to the Nansha Islands as a geographical unit, as well as to the other island groups in the South China Sea, remained unaffected by the UNCLOS.

At the end of the day, however, the question is not whether China has acquired, by way of historic title, sovereignty over the four low-tide elevations either individually or as part of an island group, or whether low-tide elevations in general qualify as land territory and as such can and have been acquired through appropriation, but whether these questions are governed by UNCLOS, ie whether they concern 'the interpretation or application of this Convention'. The short answer is 'no'. After having examined the 1958 Convention on the Territorial Sea and Contiguous Zone and the 1982 United Nations Convention on the Law of the Sea, the ICJ in *Qatar v Bahrain* concluded that '[i]international treaty law is silent on the question of whether low-tide elevations can be considered to be "territory"'.[173] In its summary of the ICJ's decision, the *World Court Digest* states that the 'law of the sea does not provide any rules in this context so that it was not clear whether low-tide elevations are "territory" and can be compared to islands with regard to possible appropriation'.[174] Questions concerning the acquisition, transfer or loss of sovereignty or other rights over continental or insular land territory are governed by

---

[169] Declaration of the Government of the People's Republic of China on China's Territorial Sea (4 September 1958) (n 161) s 1.

[170] Law of the People's Republic of China on the Territorial Sea and the Contiguous Zone (25 February 1992) (n 161). On the method of 'straight lines', see ibid, art 3(2).

[171] Declaration of the Government of the People's Republic of China on China's Territorial Sea (4 September 1958) (n 161) ss 4 and 2. See also Law of the People's Republic of China on the Territorial Sea and the Contiguous Zone (25 February 1992) (n 161) art 3(2).

[172] United Nations, Division for Ocean Affairs and the Law of the Sea, *Law of the Sea Bulletin* No 31 (1996) 8. The full declaration is reprinted in Annex I, Doc A.29.

[173] *Maritime Delimitation and Territorial Questions between Qatar and Bahrain (Qatar v Bahrain)* (Merits) [2001] ICJ Rep 40, 101 [205].

[174] Max Planck Institute for International Law (ed), *World Court Digest*, vol 4: 2001–2005 (Berlin, Springer, 2009) 860.

general or customary international law,[175] and as such remain outside the compulsory jurisdiction of UNCLOS arbitral tribunals. The same is true for the question of historic titles and historic waters.[176]

Disputes which are only related to the sea but which are not governed by the Convention, such as disputes concerning sovereignty or other rights over land territory, are removed from the jurisdiction of UNCLOS arbitral tribunals. That the Convention is not a comprehensive instrument governing all sea-related issues is confirmed by its preamble which affirms that 'matters not regulated by this Convention continue to be governed by the rules and principles of general international law'.[177] This, however, does not mean that all disputes requiring the identification, application or interpretation of rules and principles of general or customary international law are beyond the subject-matter jurisdiction of UNCLOS arbitral tribunals.[178] Article 293 UNCLOS provides that a 'tribunal *having jurisdiction under this section* [2 of Part XV] shall apply this Convention and other rules of international law not incompatible with this Convention'.[179] While UNCLOS arbitral tribunals do not have original compulsory jurisdiction over disputes governed by customary international law, they may consider rules of customary international law in disputes concerning the application or interpretation of the Convention. A precondition for the application of customary international law is, however, that the arbitral tribunal has jurisdiction over the subject-matter of the dispute in the first instance. There must be a genuine link between the relevant rule of customary international law and the Convention.[180] The utilization of customary international law rules must be indispensable for the application or interpretation of the Convention in the sense that the Convention cannot be meaningfully applied or interpreted without recourse to customary international law.

The auxiliary application of rules of customary international law in a dispute concerning the interpretation or application of the Convention

---

[175] *cf* UNCLOS, art 298(1)(a)(i). See also eg Marcelo G Kohen and Mamadou Hébié, 'Territory, Acquisition' in Rüdiger Wolfrum (ed), *Max Planck Encyclopedia of Public International Law*, vol IX (Oxford, OUP, 2012) 897 MN 55; Beckman, 'The Philippines v. China Case and the South China Sea Disputes' 2.

[176] See text at section III.1.a.(2)(b).

[177] UNCLOS, preamble, para 8.

[178] But see Rosalyn Higgins, 'The Reformation in International Law' in Richard Rawlings (ed), *Law, Society, and Economy: Centenary Essays for the London School of Economics and Political Science, 1895–1995* (Oxford, Clarendon Press, 1997) 220, who considers the 'identification of customary norms [to be] formally beyond the subject matter jurisdiction of the Law of the Sea Tribunal'.

[179] Emphasis added.

[180] For example, in *Guyana v Suriname* (2007) 139 ILR 566, 683 [406] and 709 [484] the general international law rules on the threat or use of force were considered in the context of whether the threat of force was violating the obligation under UNCLOS, arts 74(3) and 83(3) to 'make every effort…not to jeopardize or hamper the reaching of the final [delimitation] agreement'. See also *M/V 'SAIGA' (No 2) (Saint Vincent and the Grenadines v Guinea)* (Judgment) [1999] ITLOS Rep 10, 61–63 [153]–[159] where the question of the use of force arose in the context of whether the arrest of a ship was in accordance with UNCLOS.

must be distinguished from the concurrent consideration of two disputes — one governed by the Convention and the other governed by customary international law. The fact that disputes concerning sovereignty or other rights over land territory are in practice often 'closely linked or ancillary' to sea boundary delimitation disputes which concern the interpretation or application of Articles 15, 74 and 83 UNCLOS, does not automatically bring these territorial disputes within the compulsory jurisdiction of UNCLOS arbitral tribunals.[181] The Convention is silent on these so-called 'mixed disputes'.[182]

Article 298(1)(a)(i) UNCLOS provides that if a State excludes sea boundary delimitation disputes from the compulsory jurisdiction of an arbitral tribunal under section 2 of Part XV of UNCLOS the State shall accept submission of such disputes to compulsory conciliation provided that they do not necessarily require 'the concurrent consideration of any unsettled dispute concerning sovereignty or other rights over continental or insular land territory'. The express removal of land territory disputes from compulsory conciliation does not necessarily mean that they are, in general, subject to compulsory arbitration if they are connected to any sea boundary delimitation dispute.[183] Indeed, the subject-matters of sovereignty and other rights over land territory are actually misplaced in Article 298 UNCLOS. They are not optional exceptions, but rather part of the general limitations on the compulsory jurisdiction under section 2 of Part XV of UNCLOS.[184] Questions of sovereignty or other rights over land territory do not concern the interpretation or application of the Convention in the first instance, as they are not dealt with in the Convention. Compulsory conciliation is aimed at facilitating an amicable settlement of the dispute by the parties themselves.[185] Unlike the compulsory procedures under section 2 of Part XV conciliation does not produce a final and binding decision by a court or tribunal but a non-binding report with conclusions

---

[181] *cf* Igor V Karaman, *Dispute Resolution in the Law of the Sea* (Leiden, Martinus Nijhoff, 2012) 209 and n 212. But for the view that territorial sovereignty issues closely linked to maritime delimitation are subject to compulsory jurisdiction, see ITLOS, 'Statements of President Wolfrum', Statement Given to the Informal Meeting of Legal Advisers of Ministries of Foreign Affairs (New York, 23 October 2006) 6, www.itlos.org; Tullio Treves, 'What have the United Nations Convention and the International Tribunal for the Law of the Sea to Offer as Regards Maritime Delimitation Disputes?' in Rainer Lagoni and Daniel Vignes (eds), *Maritime Delimitation* (Leiden, Martinus Nijhoff, 2006) 63, 77. The question did not have to be decided in *Guyana v Suriname* (2007) 139 ILR 566, 609 [175] and 643 [280].

[182] On 'mixed disputes' see Irina Buga, 'Territorial Sovereignty Issues in Maritime Disputes: A Jurisdictional Dilemma for Law of the Sea Tribunals' (2012) 27 *International Journal of Marine and Coastal Law* 59.

[183] But see ITLOS, 'Statements of President Wolfrum' (n 181) 6.

[184] See '158th meeting', Official Records of the Third United Nations Conference on the Law of the Sea, vol XVI (Summary Records, Plenary, First and Second Committees, as well as Documents of the Conference, Eleventh Session) (30 March 1982) UN Doc A/CONF.62/SR.158, 15 [13] (Venezuela). See also Bernard H Oxman, 'The Third United Nations Conference on the Law of the Sea: The Ninth Session' (1981) 75 *American Journal of International Law* 211, 233 fn 109.

[185] *cf* UNCLOS Annex V, art 5.

and recommendations to the parties.[186] Article 298(1)(a)(i) UNCLOS simply clarifies that not even in case of compulsory conciliation, which is much less intrusive on State sovereignty than compulsory arbitration, disputes concerning territorial sovereignty must not be considered concurrently with any sea boundary delimitation dispute.

Rather than constructing an argument *a contrario*,[187] it may be argued *a fortiori* that if States are not obliged to submit a dispute to compulsory conciliation if it necessarily involves the concurrent consideration of an unsettled dispute concerning sovereignty or other rights over land territory, this must be true even more so in case of compulsory arbitration. Considering the strong opposition to compulsory means of dispute settlement of about half the States taking part in the Third United Nations Conference on the Law of the Sea (UNCLOS III),[188] including China,[189] and the serious implications of compulsory dispute settlement for State sovereignty,[190] it seems difficult to imagine that States Parties to the Convention intended to expand the limited compulsory jurisdiction under section 2 of Part XV of UNCLOS, somehow through the back door, to any other dispute linked or ancillary to a dispute concerning the interpretation or application of the Convention. For example, could it really be argued that the unresolved dispute between Guatemala and Belize over the land and insular territory of Belize was subject to the compulsory jurisdiction of an arbitral tribunal instituted under Annex VII of UNCLOS because it was linked to a maritime boundary delimitation dispute between the two countries?[191] In reply to a declaration that approval of the Convention by

---

[186] *cf* UNCLOS, art 296 and Annex V, arts 14, 7.

[187] See ITLOS, 'Statements of President Wolfrum' (n 181) 6, who bases his argument on 'a reading *a contrario* of article 298, paragraph 1(a)' of UNCLOS.

[188] See 'Memorandum by the President of the Conference on Document A/CONF.62/WP.10', Official Records of the Third United Nations Conference on the Law of the Sea, vol VIII (Informal Composite Negotiating Text, Sixth Session) (22 July 1977) UN Doc A/CONF.62/WP.10, 70; Myron H Nordquist, Shabtai Rosenne and Louis B Sohn (eds), *United Nations Convention on the Law of the Sea 1982: A Commentary*, vol V (Dordrecht, Martinus Nijhoff, 1989) 112 MN 298.9 and 117 MN 298.20.

[189] The Chinese delegate Wang Tieya had declared: 'any compulsory and binding third-party settlement of a dispute concerning sea boundary delimitations must have the consent of all parties to the dispute. Otherwise such a form of settlement would not be acceptable to the Chinese delegation' ('112th Meeting', Official Records of the Third United Nations Conference on the Law of the Sea, vol XI (Summary Records, Plenary, General Committee, First, Second and Third Committees, as well as Documents of the Conference, Eighth Session) (25 April 1979) UN Doc A/CONF.62/SR.112 14 [49]).

[190] It must be recalled that art 298 UNCLOS with its optional exceptions was the result of a compromise to make the compulsory dispute settlement system more palatable to States opposed to compulsory jurisdiction over boundary and other disputes.

[191] Guatemala has claimed Belizean territory for more than 150 years, ever since the colonial era. On 8 December 2008, Guatemala and Belize concluded a Special Agreement to submit Guatemala's territorial, insular and maritime claim against Belize to the International Court of Justice. The submission of the case is subject to a referendum in both countries that was to be held on 6 October 2013. On 1 May 2013, it was announced that Guatemala had unilaterally withdrawn from holding the referendum on the agreed date. On the dispute see Montserrat Gorina-Ysern, 'OAS Mediates in Belize-Guatemala Border Dispute' (December

Guatemala 'shall under no circumstances affect the rights of Guatemala over the territory of Belize',[192] the Government of Belize clearly stated that 'any alleged *"rights" over land territory* referred to in [Guatemala`s] declaration are outside the scope of the Convention'[193] and thus also outside its compulsory dispute settlement mechanisms. Similarly, one could ask whether Argentina could have its territorial sovereignty dispute with the United Kingdom over the Falkland Islands/Malvinas compulsorily settled by an arbitral tribunal instituted under Annex VII of UNCLOS by unilaterally instituting proceedings in respect of a dispute concerning the delimitation of the continental shelf between the two countries in the area of the Falkland Islands/Malvinas.[194] The answer must surely be no.[195]

In any case, the question of jurisdiction over mixed disputes is of no practical relevance to the South China Sea Arbitration as China has excluded boundary delimitation disputes by its declaration under Article 298(1) UNCLOS, which means that there is nothing for the territorial dispute to piggyback on.[196]

(b) Historic Titles and Historic Rights

The Philippines states that it has instituted the arbitration proceedings in order to challenge China's 'claim to "sovereignty" and "sovereign rights" over a vast maritime area lying within a so-called "nine-dash line" that encompasses virtually the entire South China Sea'.[197] One possible legal basis for China's claim to 'indisputable sovereignty over the islands in

2000) *ASIL Insights*, www.asil.org. Neither State has made a declaration under UNCLOS, art 298(1)(a)(i) so each State could unilaterally bring a sea boundary delimitation before an arbitral tribunal at any time.

[192] Declaration Made Upon Ratification (11 February 1997) United Nations, Division for Ocean Affairs and the Law of the Sea, *Law of the Sea Bulletin* No 35 (1997) 12.

[193] Objection to the Declaration Made by Guatemala Upon Ratification of the Convention (11 September 1997) United Nations, Division for Ocean Affairs and the Law of the Sea, *Law of the Sea Bulletin* No 35 (1997) 8.

[194] For such a case to be brought, Argentina would have to withdraw its declaration with regard to the optional exceptions under art 298, dated 18 October 1995, which excludes sea boundary delimitations from the compulsory jurisdiction under section 2 of Part XV. On 26 October 2012, Argentina withdrew its declaration under art 298 with regard to 'military activities by government vessels and aircraft engaged in non-commercial service'. On 21 April 2009, Argentina made a submission to the Commission on the Limits of the Continental Shelf which includes the Falkland Islands/Malvinas. On 6 August 2009 and 23 August 2012, the United Kingdom objected to Argentina's submission with regard to areas appurtenant to the Falkland Islands/Malvinas; see www.un.org/Depts/los/clcs_new/submissions_files/submission_arg_25_2009.htm.

[195] *cf* Nordquist, Rosenne and Sohn (eds), *United Nations Convention on the Law of the Sea 1982*, vol V (1986) 117 MN 298.20.

[196] It seems generally accepted that the question of jurisdiction over mixed disputes can only arise if the tribunal has jurisdiction over sea boundary disputes, ie if a declaration under UNCLOS, art 298(1)(a)(i) has *not* been made; see eg Buga, 'Territorial Sovereignty Issues in Maritime Disputes' 67, 71, 91; Boyle, 'Dispute Settlement and the Law of the Sea Convention' 44, 49; Treves, 'What Have the United Nations Convention and the International Tribunal for the Law of the Sea to Offer' 77.

[197] Notification and Statement of Claim, para 2.

the South China Sea and the adjacent waters'[198] within the 'nine-dash line' or 'U-shaped line' is historic title.[199] In particular, the claim to territorial sovereignty over the island groups or archipelagos in the South China Sea may be based on historic title.[200] The concept of historic title 'is well-known in international law'[201] and allows States to claim, on a historical basis, sovereignty or sovereign rights over both insular land territory and maritime areas.[202] It has its root in the fact that States through the ages have claimed and maintained sovereignty over the territory or maritime areas in question. With regard to maritime areas, reference is usually made to 'historic waters'. In this connection, it should be recalled that the Philippines was a champion of the concept of historic waters at the First and Third United Nations Conference on the Law of the Sea.[203] The term 'historic waters' is wider in scope that the term 'historic bays'. Historic title can apply to 'waters other than bays, i.e., to straits, archipelagos and generally to all those waters which can be included in the maritime domain of a State'.[204] Historic waters can cover very large sea areas. For example, Hudson Bay, which is claimed as a historic bay by Canada, encompasses some 1.23 million square kilometres,[205] and the archipelagic waters of the Philippines originally claimed as historic waters comprise some 444,000 square kilometres.[206] In comparison, the area enclosed by the nine-dash

---

[198] Note Verbale CML/17/2009 to the Secretary-General of the United Nations from the People's Republic of China with regard to the joint submission made by Malaysia and Viet Nam to the Commission on the Limits of the Continental Shelf (7 May 2009) www.un.org/depts/los (Note Verbale CML/17/2009 (7 May 2009)). See also PRC MFA, 'Statement of the Ministry of Foreign Affairs of the People's Republic of China' (21 June 2012) (n 161).

[199] See Oude Elferink (n 94) 172; Zou Keyuan, 'Historic Rights in International Law and in China's Practice' (2001) 32 *Ocean Development and International Law* 149, 160–64; Beckman (n 126) 6, 10. See also Florian Dupuy and Pierre-Marie Dupuy, 'A Legal Analysis of China's Historic Rights Claim in the South China Sea' (2013) 107 *American Journal of International Law* 124, 124, 128 and 139.

[200] See text at section III.1.a.(2)(a). See also Beckman, 'International Law, UNCLOS and the South China Sea' 62 ('It is undeniable that China has a historic claim to sovereignty over all of the islands, reefs and banks in the South China Sea').

[201] *Eritrea v Yemen* (First Stage – Territorial Sovereignty and Scope of the Dispute) (1998) 22 RIAA 209, 239 [106]. See also ibid, [123] ('There can be no doubt that the concept of historic title has special resonance in situations that may exist even in the contemporary world').

[202] *cf* Andrea Gioia, 'Historic Titles' in Rüdiger Wolfrum (ed), *Max Planck Encyclopedia of Public International Law*, vol IV (Oxford, OUP, 2012) 819 MN 17. See also Antunes, *Towards the Conceptualisation of Maritime Delimitation* (2003) 37.

[203] 'Summary Records of the Meetings of the Second Committee, 6th Meeting Official Records of the United Nations Conference on the Law of the Sea, vol IV (Second Committee (High Seas: General Regime)) (7 March 1958) UN Doc A/Conf.13/C.2/SR.6-10, 7 [15]; Summary Records of Meetings of the Second Committee, 5th Meeting (16 July 1974), 36th Meeting (12 August 1974) and 45th Meeting (28 August 1974), Official Records of the Third United Nations Conference on the Law of the Sea, vol II (Summary of Meetings of the First, Second and Third Committees, Second Session) 111 [30], 264 [57], and 299 [13]–[14], respectively.

[204] 'Juridical Regime of Historic Waters, Including Historic Bays: Study Prepared by the Secretariat' (9 March 1962) UN Doc A/CN.4/143, (1962) 2 *ILC Yearbook* 6 [34].

[205] See Leo J Bouchez, *The Regime of Bays in International Law* (Leyden, AW Sythoff, 1964) 229–30.

[206] See *Magallona v Ermita*, GR No 187167 (Supreme Court of the Philippines, 2011) www.lawphil.net.

line covers some 1.94 million square kilometres,[207] and the area which makes up the Spratly Islands extends to some 425,000 square kilometres.

The PRC itself has not expressly relied on 'historic title' with regard to the South China Sea but Article 14 of the Law on the Exclusive Economic Zone and the Continental Shelf of the People's Republic of China contains the proviso that '[t]he provisions in this Law shall not affect the historical rights that the People's Republic of China has been enjoying ever since the days of the past'.[208] In its Note Verbale to the United Nations Secretary-General of 14 April 2011, the PRC stated that 'China's sovereignty and related rights and jurisdiction in the South China Sea are supported by abundant historical and legal evidence'.[209] The nine-dash line has been interpreted by scholars from the PRC as having become synonymous with a claim based on historic title to sovereignty over the island groups and to historical rights of fishing, navigation and other marine activities including the exploration and exploitation of the mineral resources in the sea area enclosed by the line.[210] The Taiwan Authorities have been more outspoken on the question of historic title. It must be recalled that in 1947, the then Chinese Government published the first official map showing the U-shaped (or, then, eleven-dash) line. The then Chinese Government 'regarded the South China Sea as a region of geostrategic interest and a part of China's "historic waters"'.[211] On 10 March 1993, the Taiwan Authorities adopted 'Policy Guidelines for the South China Sea' which read in part as follows:

> On the basis of history, geography, international law and the facts, the Spratly Islands, the Paracel Islands, Macclesfield Bank and the Pratas Islands, have always been a part of the inherent territory of the Republic of China. The sovereignty of the Republic of China over them is beyond doubt.
> The South China Sea area within the historic water limit is the maritime area under the jurisdiction of the Republic of China, in which the Republic of China possesses all rights and interests.[212]

In April 1995, the Authorities in Taiwan reemphasised that position by stating: 'Undoubtedly, our government has sovereignty over the historic

---

[207] See Notification and Statement of Claim, para 11.

[208] Law on the Exclusive Economic Zone and the Continental Shelf of the People's Republic of China (26 June 1998), Annex I, Doc A.28.

[209] Note Verbale CML/8/2011 (14 April 2011) (n 150).

[210] See Zhiguo Gao and Bing Bing Jia, 'The Nine-Dash Line in the South China Sea: History, Status, and Implications' (2013) 107 *American Journal of International Law* 98, 108, 113–14, 121, 123. See also Li Jinming and Li Dexia, 'The Dotted Line on the Chinese Map of the South China Sea: A Note' (2003) 34 *Ocean Development and International Law* 287, 291–93.

[211] United States, Office of the Secretary of Defense, Annual Report to Congress: Military and Security Developments Involving the People's Republic of China 2011, 39, www.defense. gov.

[212] 'Policy Guidelines for the South China Sea', republished in Kuan-Ming Sun, 'Policy of the Republic of China towards the South China Sea: Recent Developments' (1995) 19 *Marine Policy* 401, 408. For a critical evaluation of the 'historic waters' argument, see ibid, 401–07; Yann-huei Song and Peter Kien-hong Yu, 'China's "Historic Waters" in the South China Sea: An Analysis from Taiwan, R.O.C.' (1994) 12/4 *American Asian Review* 83.

U-shaped territory, including the Spratly Islands'.[213] Arguments of 'historic title' have also been adopted by scholars from Taiwan.[214]

The concept of historic title and that of the maritime zones under UNCLOS are governed by 'distinct legal régimes'.[215] The concept of historic title allows for derogation from otherwise applicable rules of international law.[216] In particular, historic title can 'affect the application of many of the articles on the law of the sea'.[217] Thus, the regime of historic waters has not been superseded by UNCLOS.[218] On the contrary, it may lead to the inapplicability, in whole or in part, of the rules of UNCLOS with regard to the regime of maritime zones and boundary delimitation. The rules on historic legal title and historic rights are quasi-superimposed as a separate layer of normativity over UNCLOS.[219] That the maritime disputes in the South China Sea are not governed exclusively by UNCLOS is also confirmed by the Association of Southeast Asian Nations (ASEAN)-China Declaration on the Conduct of Parties in the South China Sea (DOC) where the parties concerned 'undertake to resolve their territorial and jurisdictional disputes by peaceful means ... in accordance with universally recognized principles of international law, *including* the 1982 UN Convention on the Law of the Sea'.[220]

---

[213] FBIS-CHI-95-066 (6 April 1995), quoted in Jon M Van Dyke, 'Disputes Over Islands and Maritime Boundaries in East Asia' in Seoung Yong Hong and Jon M Van Dyke (eds), *Maritime Boundary Disputes, Settlement Processes, and the Law of the Sea* (Leiden, Martinus Nijhoff, 2009) 65. See also Nong Hong (n 100) 68, 130.

[214] See eg Nien-Tsu Alfred Hu, 'South China Sea: Troubled Waters or a Sea of Opportunity?' (2010) 41 *Ocean Development and International Law* 203, 204.

[215] *Continental Shelf (Tunisia/Libyan Arab Jamahiriya)* (Merits) [1982] ICJ Rep 18, 74 [100].

[216] See Gioia, 'Historic Titles' 816–17 MN 8, 10. See also *Eritrea v Yemen* (First Stage – Territorial Sovereignty and Scope of the Dispute) (1998) 22 RIAA 209, 239 [106].

[217] 'Summary Records of the 61st Meeting of the First Committee', Official Records of the United Nations Conference on the Law of the Sea, vol III (First Committee (Territorial Sea and Contiguous Zone)) (22 April 1958) UN Doc A/CONF.13/C.1/SR.61-66, 190 [46] (Norway).

[218] *cf* Rudolf Bernhardt, 'Rechtsfragen historischer Buchten' in Dieter Blumenwitz and Albrecht Randelzhofer (eds), *Festschrift für Friedrich Berber zum 75. Geburtstag* (Munich, Beck, 1973) 47–48; 'Juridical Regime of Historic Waters, Including Historic Bays: Study Prepared by the Secretariat' (9 March 1962) (n 204) 7 [38] ('It was felt that States could not be expected to accept rules which would deprive them of considerable maritime areas over which they had hitherto had sovereignty'); Congressional Research Service, 'Maritime Territorial Disputes in East Asia' 6 ('UNCLOS submissions are not the only manner in which countries make claims'); Zou Keyuan, *Law of the Sea in East Asia: Issues and Prospects*, Routledge Studies in International Law (London, Routledge, 2005) 174.

[219] *cf* Antunes (n 148) 99. See also *Eritrea v Yemen* (Second Stage – Maritime Delimitation) (1999) 22 RIAA 335, 361 [109] ('the traditional fishing regime ... is not qualified by the maritime zones specified by the United Nations Convention on the Law of the Sea').

[220] 'ASEAN-China Declaration on the Conduct of Parties in the South China Sea, signed during the 8th ASEAN Summit in Phnom Penh' (4 November 2002) para 4 (emphasis added); reproduced in Vaughan Lowe and Stefan Talmon (eds), *The Legal Order of the Oceans: Basic Documents on the Law of the Sea* (Oxford, Hart, 2009) Doc 69, 771–72. See also 'Australia-United States Ministerial Consultations (AUSMIN) 2011 Joint Communiqué' (15 September 2011) www.state.gov, in which the two States 'call on governments to clarify and pursue their territorial claims and accompanying maritime rights [in the South China Sea] in accordance with international law, including the Law of the Sea Convention'; and ASEAN's 'Six Point Principles on the South China Sea', principle 4 (20 July 2013) www.asean.org.

The Philippines asks the Tribunal to declare that 'China's rights in regard to maritime areas in the South China Sea … are those that are established by UNCLOS' only,[221] that 'China's maritime claims in the South China Sea based on its so-called "nine-dash line" are contrary to UNCLOS and invalid',[222] that 'China's occupation of and construction activities' on Mischief Reef, McKennan Reef, Gaven Reef and Subi Reef 'are unlawful',[223] that 'China has unlawfully claimed maritime entitlements beyond 12 M from' Scarborough Shoal, Johnson Reef, Cuarteron Reef and Fiery Cross Reef,[224] and that 'China has unlawfully interfered with the exercise by the Philippines of its rights to navigation and other rights under the Convention in areas within and beyond 200 M of the Philippines' archipelagic baselines'.[225] As a consequence, it requests the Tribunal to require 'China to bring its domestic legislation into conformity with its obligations under UNCLOS',[226] to terminate 'its occupation of and activities on' these reefs,[227] to 'refrain from preventing Philippine vessels from exploiting in a sustainable manner the living resources in the waters adjacent to Scarborough Shoal and Johnson Reef',[228] and to 'desist from' the unlawful interference with the exercise by the Philippines of its right of navigation.[229] Each of these points of the 'Relief Sought' by the Philippines necessarily requires the Tribunal to determine both whether China enjoys historic title to the island groups in the South China Sea, such as the Spratly Islands and Scarborough Shoal, including the maritime area, low-tide elevations and other insular features forming part of these island groups,[230] and whether China has historic sovereign rights (eg to exclusive fishing) in the maritime areas within the nine-dash line. If, for example, China could, on the basis of historic title, claim the island groups, including their water area, as sovereign territory and the maritime areas within the nine-dash line as being subject to its sovereign rights, China's claims would not be 'invalid' and its actions would not be 'unlawful'. The same would be true if the island groups, as historic territorial units, were entitled to, and surrounded by a single belt of territorial sea, contiguous zone, EEZ and continental shelf under UNCLOS which overlaps with the area enclosed by the nine-dash line.[231]

---

[221] Relief Sought, bullet point 1; see also Claims, bullet point 1.

[222] Relief Sought, bullet point 2; see also Claims, bullet point 2.

[223] Relief Sought, bullet points 4 and 6; see also Claims, bullet point 4.

[224] Relief Sought, bullet point 8; see also Claims, bullet point 6. See also Notification and Statement of Claim, para 20.

[225] Relief Sought, bullet point 12; see also Claims, bullet point 10. The interference with the right to navigation concerns the areas of the Spratly Islands and Scarborough Shoal; see Notification and Statement of Claim, paras 12, 17, 20, 28, 29.

[226] Relief Sought, bullet point 3.

[227] Relief Sought, bullet points 5 and 7; see also Claims, bullet point 4.

[228] Relief Sought, bullet point 9; see also Claims, bullet point 7.

[229] Relief Sought, bullet point 13.

[230] On a possible claim to historic title over the island groups, see n 197–n 204 above.

[231] This seems to be the position taken by the PRC. The Law of the People's Republic of China on the Territorial Sea and the Contiguous Zone (25 February 1992) (n 161) provides in art 2(2) that the land territory of the PRC includes, inter alia, the Zhongsha Islands and the

The Philippines portrays those points in its 'Relief Sought' as being governed exclusively by UNCLOS. This is not surprising as questions of historic title, historic rights and historic waters, as a rule, are not covered by the Convention,[232] and any dispute concerning these questions is thus outside the compulsory jurisdiction under section 2 of Part XV of UNCLOS. The Convention, for example, has nothing to say about how historic waters are defined, how historic titles or rights are acquired, how they are proven and what they entail. The reference to disputes involving 'historic … titles' in Article 298(1)(a)(i) UNCLOS does not mean that all disputes involving 'historic titles' are generally within the jurisdiction of UNCLOS arbitral tribunals. Compulsory jurisdiction is limited to the extent that the concept of 'historic titles' is dealt with in the Convention; that means compulsory jurisdiction is limited to the interpretation and application of Article 15 UNCLOS.[233] Otherwise, the question of historic titles continues to be governed by the rules and principles of customary international law.[234] This was confirmed by the ICJ which stated:

> Nor does the draft convention of the Third Conference on the Law of the Sea contain any detailed provisions on the 'régime' of historic waters: there is neither a definition of the concept nor an elaboration of the juridical régime of 'historic waters' or 'historic bays'. There are, however, references to 'historic bays' or 'historic titles' or historic reasons in a way amounting to a reservation to the rules set forth therein. It seems clear that *the matter continues to be governed by general international law* which does not provide for a single 'régime' for 'historic waters' or 'historic bays', but only for a particular régime for each of the concrete, recognized cases of 'historic waters' or 'historic bays'.[235]

The Chinese claim to sovereignty over the islands in the South China Sea and the adjacent waters could be regarded as such a 'particular regime'.[236]

In the present case, however, the question is not which 'particular regime' of historic title applies or whether the requirements to establish historic titles or historic rights have been met by China, but whether the Tribunal is competent to decide upon these questions in the first instance.

Nansha Islands. Scarborough Shoal (Huangyan Island) is considered a part of the Zhongsha Islands. The PRC claims full maritime zones around its islands in the South China Sea; see eg the statement above at n 167 and the working paper at n 164.

[232] See eg Antunes (n 148) 98–99; Oude Elferink (n 94) 172.

[233] See Tullio Treves, 'The Jurisdiction of the International Tribunal for the Law of the Sea' in Patibandla Chandrasekhara Rao and Rahmatullah Khan (eds), *International Tribunal for the Law of the Sea: Law and Practice* (The Hague, Kluwer, 2001) 121. ITLOS considered the question of 'historic title' in the context of UNCLOS, art 15 in *Delimitation of the Maritime Boundary between Bangladesh and Myanmar in the Bay of Bengal (Bangladesh/Myanmar)* (Judgment) [2012] ITLOS Rep [130].

[234] See eg Epsey Cooke Farrell, *The Socialist Republic of Vietnam and the Law of the Sea: An Analysis of Vietnamese Behaviour Within the Emerging International Oceans Regime* (The Hague, Martinus Nijhoff, 1998) 68–69.

[235] *Continental Shelf (Tunisia/Libyan Arab Jamahiriya)* (Merits) [1982] ICJ Rep 18, 73–74 [100] (emphasis added). See also *Barbados v Trinidad and Tobago* (2006) 27 RIAA 147, 224-25 [279] ('range in the content of historic titles').

[236] *cf* Zou Keyuan, *Law of the Sea in East Asia: Issues and Prospects* 174.

The first two are questions of substantive law, while the last one concerns the law relating to jurisdiction. As historic titles and rights do not concern the 'application or interpretation of this Convention' in terms of Articles 286, 288(1) UNCLOS, they are not subject to the compulsory jurisdiction of Annex VII arbitral tribunals.[237] To the extent that the question of whether China's claims to maritime areas in the South China Sea are 'invalid' and its actions 'unlawful' cannot be answered without deciding upon historic titles and rights, the dispute is outside the jurisdiction of the Tribunal.

b. Ipso Jure Limitations on Jurisdiction

The compulsory jurisdiction of arbitral tribunals instituted under Annex VII to UNCLOS is subject to far-reaching limitations.[238] Article 286 UNCLOS states that the apparently broad provision that 'any dispute concerning the interpretation or application of this Convention shall ... be submitted at the request of any party to the dispute to the [competent] court or tribunal' is 'subject to section 3' of Part XV. Article 297 UNCLOS — one of the provisions comprising section 3 — generally excludes from compulsory dispute settlement all 'disputes ... with regard to the exercise by a coastal State of its sovereign rights or jurisdiction provided for in this Convention' (ipso jure limitations). In several Notes Verbales to the UN Secretary-General, the PRC has stated that it 'enjoys sovereign rights and jurisdiction' over the waters as well as the seabed and subsoil thereof within the water area enclosed by the nine-dash line, thereby indicating that it considers itself to be a 'coastal State'.[239] Of particular importance in the present case is the limitation of the subject-matter jurisdiction with regard to disputes relating to the sovereign rights of coastal States, or their exercise, with respect to the living resources in their EEZ[240] and disputes concerning the exercise by coastal States of their jurisdiction with regard to the establishment and use of artificial islands, installations and structures in their EEZ or on their continental shelf.[241]

The Philippines requests the Tribunal to require China to 'refrain from preventing Philippine vessels from exploiting in a sustainable manner the living resources in the waters adjacent to Scarborough Shoal and Johnson

---

[237] Contra Robert C Beckman and Leonardo Bernard, 'Disputed Areas in the South China Sea: Prospects for Arbitration or Advisory Opinion' (Third International Workshop, The South China Sea: Cooperation for Regional Security and Development, Hanoi, November 2011) 15–16, cil.nus.edu.sg/wp.

[238] See *Southern Bluefin Tuna Case (Australia and New Zealand v Japan)* (Award on Jurisdiction and Admissibility) (2000) 119 ILR 508, 526 [60]. See also Patibandla Chandrasekhara Rao, 'Law of the Sea, Settlement of Disputes' in Rüdiger Wolfrum (ed), *Max Planck Encyclopedia of Public International Law*, vol VI (Oxford, OUP, 2012) 738, 746 MN 34.

[239] Note Verbale CML/17/2009 (7 May 2009) (n 198), Note Verbale CML/8/2011 (14 April 2011) (n 150), and Note Verbale CML/18/2009 to the Secretary-General of the United Nations from the People's Republic of China with regard to the submission made by Viet Nam to the Commission on the Limits of the Continental Shelf (7 May 2009) www.un.org/depts/los.

[240] UNCLOS, arts 297(3)(a), 56(1)(a).

[241] UNCLOS, arts 297(1), 56(1)(b)(i), 60, 80.

Reef'.[242] Coastal States, however, have sovereign rights for the purposes of exploiting, conserving and managing the natural living resources in their EEZ.[243] They may, under certain circumstances, totally exclude other States from exploiting the natural resources in their EEZ.[244] Thus, if the waters adjacent to Scarborough Shoal and Johnson Reef are part of China's EEZ, any dispute over China excluding Philippine vessels from fishing in this zone will be outside the compulsory jurisdiction of the Tribunal.[245]

The Philippines also asks the Tribunal to declare that 'China's occupation of and construction activities' on Mischief Reef, McKennan Reef, Gaven Reef and Subi Reef are 'unlawful' and to require China 'to end its occupation of and activities on' these reefs.[246] The establishment of buildings and other facilities on stilts and concrete platforms on these reefs is considered by the Philippines to amount to the construction of 'artificial "islands" on them'.[247] If, indeed, the dispute concerns the construction of artificial islands it will be excluded from the compulsory jurisdiction of the Tribunal, provided that the artificial islands have been constructed within China's EEZ or on its continental shelf.

In both cases, the question of whether the dispute is excluded from the compulsory jurisdiction of the Tribunal depends on whether China qualifies as 'a coastal State' in the South China Sea and whether these land features and the waters in their vicinity are located within China's EEZ or continental shelf. The Philippines' Notification and Statement of Claim is based on the misleading assumptions that in the South China Sea there are no islands in terms of Article 121(2) UNCLOS which generate their own maritime zones, that China does not, or cannot lay claim to any of these islands and that, consequently, China cannot be a coastal State with an EEZ or continental shelf in the South China Sea.[248] This is not surprising as the question of China being a 'coastal State' with its own maritime zones cannot be answered without a determination as to territorial sovereignty over islands or island groups in the South China Sea — subject matters that are outside the compulsory jurisdiction under the Convention.[249] In addition, considering the geographical situation and the multiple claimants to the islands or island groups in the South China Sea, any ruling on the extent of China's EEZ or continental shelf necessarily requires that the Tribunal engage in boundary delimitations,

[242] Relief Sought, bullet point 9; see also Claims, bullet point 7. See also Notification and Statement of Claim, para 21.

[243] UNCLOS, arts 56(1)(a), 61, 62.

[244] *cf* UNCLOS, art 62.

[245] For the exclusion of the Tribunal's jurisdiction with regard to enforcement measures, see text at section III.1.c.

[246] See Relief Sought, bullet points 4, 5, 6 and 7; see also Claims, bullet points 4 and 5.

[247] Notification and Statement of Claim, para 14.

[248] See Notification and Statement of Claim, para 1 ('China's claims to areas of the South China Sea and the underlying seabed as far as 870 nautical miles *from the nearest Chinese coast*'(emphasis added)).

[249] See text at section III.1.a.(2)(a).

a subject-matter removed from the Tribunal's jurisdiction by China's declaration of August 2006.[250]

c. Optional Exceptions to Jurisdiction

The compulsory jurisdiction of Annex VII arbitral tribunals is subject not only to the ipso jure limitations in Article 297 UNCLOS but also to a number of optional exceptions. Article 298(1) UNCLOS provides that a State Party to the Convention may at any time (prior to the dispute) make a declaration excepting from the compulsory jurisdiction under section 2 of Part XV 'disputes ... relating to sea boundary delimitations, or those involving historic bays or titles' (para 1(a)), 'disputes concerning military activities [or] law enforcement activities' (para 1(b)), and 'disputes in respect of which the Security Council of the United Nations is exercising the functions assigned to it by the Charter of the United Nations' (para 1(c)). The PRC made use of this opportunity when, on 25 August 2006, it deposited the following declaration with the Secretary-General of the United Nations:

> The Government of the People's Republic of China does not accept any of the procedures provided for in Section 2 of Part XV of the Convention with respect to all the categories of disputes referred to in paragraph 1 (a) (b) and (c) of Article 298 of the Convention.[251]

The PRC has expressly relied on its declaration in pursuance of Article 298 UNCLOS when commenting on the Philippines' institution of arbitration proceedings[252] and scholars have identified this declaration as one of the major obstacles to the Tribunal's exercise of jurisdiction.[253]

The Philippines stated that it 'is conscious of China's Declaration under Article 298 of UNCLOS, and has avoided raising subjects or making claims that China has, by virtue of that Declaration, excluded from arbitral jurisdiction'.[254] However, this statement is difficult to reconcile with its actual claims. In a press briefing on 7 February 2013, Philippines Foreign Affairs Secretary Albert F del Rosario spoke about a 'territorial dispute with China' and said that his country had initiated arbitral proceedings 'to clearly establish the sovereign rights and jurisdiction over its maritime

---

[250] See text at section III.1.c.

[251] United Nations, Division for Ocean Affairs and the Law of the Sea, *Law of the Sea Bulletin* No 62 (2006) 14.

[252] PRC MFA, 'Foreign Ministry Spokesperson Hua Chunying's Remarks on the Philippines' Efforts in Pushing for the Establishment of the Arbitral Tribunal in Relation to the Disputes between China and the Philippines in the South China Sea' (26 April 2013), Annex I, Doc A.14. See also the statement of the Director-General of the Treaty and Law Department of the MFA: 'This declaration is legitimate, public and effective, which deserves due respect' ('China's Refusal of Arbitration Request by Philippines Meets International Law: Senior Diplomat' (30 August 2013) (n 3)).

[253] See eg Naomi Burke, 'UNCLOS Annex VII Arbitration – Who, What, Where, When?' (25 March 2013) *Cambridge Journal of International and Comparative Law Blog*, www.cjicl.org.uk.

[254] Notification and Statement of Claim, para 7. See also ibid, para 40.

entitlements in the West Philippine Sea'.[255] The establishment of maritime entitlements in areas of conflicting and overlapping claims, however, necessarily entails delimitation of maritime areas. The question of sea boundary delimitations runs like a red thread through the Philippines' Notification and Statement of Claim. In fact, the Philippines gives the impression that the sea boundaries in the South China Sea have all been delimited and are final and binding on the parties. Thus, the Philippines requests the Tribunal to declare that 'Mischief Reef and McKennan Reef ... form part of the Continental Shelf of the Philippines',[256] that 'Gaven Reef and Subi Reef ... are not located on China's Continental Shelf',[257] and that 'China has unlawfully claimed, and has unlawfully exploited, the living and non-living resources in the Philippines' Exclusive Economic Zone and Continental Shelf, and has unlawfully prevented the Philippines from exploiting living and non-living resources within its Exclusive Economic Zone and Continental Shelf'.[258] All these claims require the Tribunal to determine the extent of the EEZ and continental shelf of the parties (as well as other States). Considering the competing claims in the South China Sea of China, the Philippines, Vietnam, Malaysia and Brunei, this will not be possible without engaging in sea boundary delimitations — a subject-matter excluded from the Tribunal's jurisdiction. In addition, sea boundaries cannot be delimited before the question of territorial sovereignty over the islands or island groups in the South China Sea is resolved.

The Philippines also stated that its claims do not fall under the 'military activities or law enforcement' exemption in Article 298(1)(b) UNCLOS.[259] The Convention does not provide a definition of 'military activities' but there is widespread agreement that, considering the highly political nature of military activities, the term must be interpreted widely.[260] Military activities are not limited to actions taken by warships and military aircraft

---

[255] 'Statement of Foreign Affairs Secretary Albert F del Rosario for the Joint Press Briefing with Federal Foreign Minister Dr Guido Westerwelle of Germany' (7 February 2013) www.dfa.gov.ph. See also the statement of Foreign Secretary del Rosario: 'For China, an arbitral award, will finally clarify for the Chinese people its lawful maritime entitlements under UNCLOS in the South China Sea. This will enable China to provide responsible leadership towards fostering stability in the region. For the Philippines, it will clearly define what is ours, specifically its maritime entitlements under UNCLOS with regards to our fishing rights, rights to resources and rights to enforce our laws within our Exclusive Economic Zone'. Secretary del Rosario expressly spoke about 'the delimitation of sea areas' with regard to China's unilateral 'Nine-Dash Line' claim and that 'the validity of the delimitation with regard to other States [ie the Philippines] depends upon international law' ('Managing the South China Sea and Other Regional Security Issues, Hon. Secretary Albert F. del Rosario, Secretary of Foreign Affairs, On the Occasion of Experts' Roundtable on Regional Approaches to Maritime Security in the West Philippine Sea/South China Sea' (Brussels, Belgium, 9 July 2013) www.dfa.gov.ph).

[256] Relief Sought, bullet point 4; see also Claims, bullet point 5.

[257] Relief Sought, bullet point 6; see also Claims, bullet point 4.

[258] Relief Sought, bullet point 11; see also Claims, bullet point 9.

[259] Notification and Statement of Claim, para 40.

[260] Natalie Klein, *Dispute Settlement in the UN Convention on the Law of the Sea* (Cambridge, CUP, 2005) 291–92 and 286; John King Gamble Jr, 'The Law of the Sea Conference: Dispute Settlement in Perspective' (1976) 9 *Vanderbilt Journal of International Law* 323, 331.

or governmental vessels and aircraft engaged in non-commercial service. Whether an activity is a military activity or not ultimately depends on the purpose and intent of the activity. The occupation of insular land territory by a State's armed forces and the establishment of artificial islands, installations or structures for military purposes thus qualify as military activities.[261]

The Philippines requests the Tribunal to declare that 'China's occupation of and construction activities' on Mischief Reef, McKennan Reef, Gaven Reef and Subi Reef are unlawful and to require China to 'end its occupation of and activities on' these reefs.[262] However, it is the Philippines itself that has accused China of erecting 'military structures and facilities', including anti-aircraft artillery, helicopter pads, docking facilities for warships, sophisticated radar and communications equipment and housing for troops, on several reefs in the Spratly Islands, including the ones named above.[263] As military activities, these construction activities as well as the operation and use of these structures by the PLA are excluded from the jurisdiction of the Tribunal by way of China's August 2006 declaration. The same is true for the occupation of at least some of these reefs which were previously held by Vietnam and were captured by the PLA after Chinese and Vietnamese naval forces clashed in the Spratly Islands on 14 March 1988.[264]

The Philippines further petitions the Tribunal to require China to 'refrain from preventing Philippine vessels from exploiting in a sustainable manner the living resources in the waters adjacent to Scarborough Shoal and Johnson Reef'.[265] In other words, China is to refrain from preventing 'the Philippines from fishing at Scarborough Shoal or in its vicinity'.[266] Through its August 2006 declaration, China has excluded from the Tribunal's jurisdiction all disputes concerning law enforcement activities in regard to the exercise of sovereign rights or jurisdiction removed

---

[261] *cf* '67th Plenary meeting' (23 April 1976) and '68th Plenary meeting' (26 April 1976), Official Records of the Third United Nations Conference on the Law of the Sea, vol V (Summary Records, Plenary, General Committee, First, Second and Third Committees, as well as Documents of the Conference, Fourth Session) 56 [2] (Ecuador), 59 [44] (Iraq), 65 [24] (Iran). See also Klein, *Dispute Settlement* (2005) 290, and, generally, Tullio Treves, 'Military Installations, Structures, and Devices on the Seabed' (1980) 74 *American Journal of International Law* 808.

[262] Relief Sought, bullet points 4, 5, 6 and 7; see also Claims, bullet point 4.

[263] See eg 'Mischief Reef a Major Chinese Fortress, Says Philippine Navy' *The Straits Times* (*Singapore*) (25 January 1999) 19; 'Philippine Official Says China Installs Powerful Radar Near Disputed Islet' *BBC Monitoring Asia Pacific – Political* (13 July 2012); 'Philippines Military Aware of Chinese Activities in Disputed Sea – Official' *BBC Monitoring Asia Pacific – Political* (18 July 2012); 'Philippines, China Not on "Brink of Armed Conflict" – Official' *BBC Monitoring Asia Pacific – Political* (26 July 2012); 'Philippines Navy Pictures Show China Boosting Presence on Disputed Reef – Report' *BBC Monitoring Asia Pacific – Political* (2 August 2012). For the view that Mischief Reef is occupied by the PLA, see also James Kraska and Raul Pedrozo, *International Maritime Security Law* (Leiden, Martinus Nijhoff, 2013) 326.

[264] 'Chinese Forces Occupy Two More Islands, Says Vietnam; China' *Sydney Morning Herald* (8 April 1988) 10.

[265] Relief Sought, bullet point 9; see also Claims, bullet point 7.

[266] Notification and Statement of Claim, para 21.

from the jurisdiction of the Tribunal under Article 297(3) UNCLOS. That provision expressly excludes disputes relating to the exercise of the sovereign rights of a coastal State with regard to the living resources in its EEZ.[267] In the exercise of its sovereign rights to explore, exploit, conserve and manage the living resources in that zone, a coastal State may take such enforcement measures, including boarding, inspection, arrest and judicial proceedings, as may be necessary to ensure compliance with its laws and regulations adopted in conformity with UNCLOS.[268] If China prevented the Philippine vessels from fishing in order to ensure compliance with its fisheries laws and regulations, the dispute would be excluded under the law enforcement exemption.[269] The application of that exemption would depend on whether the measures were taken in China's EEZ which, in turn, would require the determination of territorial sovereignty over the island groups in the South China Sea and sea boundary delimitations.

Article 299(1) UNCLOS summarises the legal effect of the limitations and exceptions to the compulsory dispute settlement procedures under section 2 of Part XV by providing that disputes 'excluded under article 297 or excepted by a declaration made under article 298 ... may be submitted to such procedures only by agreement of the parties to the dispute'. Such an agreement is clearly lacking in the present case.

2. Inadmissibility of the Claims

Annex VII arbitral tribunals must satisfy themselves not only that they have jurisdiction over the dispute, but also that the claims brought before them are admissible. The compulsory jurisdiction of the arbitral tribunal under section 2 of Part XV of the Convention can only be invoked 'where no settlement has been reached by recourse to section 1'.[270] It is thus a precondition for the admissibility of any claim that the parties have fulfilled their obligation to exchange views regarding the settlement of the dispute (UNCLOS, Article 283), and that they have not agreed to settle their dispute exclusively by other means of their own choice (UNCLOS, Article 281).[271]

a. Obligation to Exchange Views

UNCLOS, Article 283(1) obliges parties to a dispute concerning the interpretation or application of the Convention to 'proceed expeditiously

---

[267] UNCLOS, art 297(3)(a). See also Beckman and Bernard, 'Disputed Areas in the South China Sea' 16.

[268] UNCLOS, art 73(1).

[269] *cf* Karaman, *Dispute Resolution in the Law of the Sea* (2012) 73 in fn 225, 163 in fn 398.

[270] UNCLOS, art 286.

[271] For negotiations as a condition of admissibility, see eg *M/V 'Louisa' (Saint Vincent and the Grenadines v Kingdom of Spain)* (Provisional Measures, Order of 23 December 2010) [2008–2010] ITLOS Rep 58, 90 [9] and 92 [14] (diss op Treves); *M/V 'Louisa' (Saint Vincent and the Grenadines v Kingdom of Spain)* (Judgment) [2013] ITLOS Rep [152]–[153].

to an exchange of views regarding its settlement by negotiation or other peaceful means'. The exchange of views serves to delimit 'the scope of the dispute and its subject-matter'.[272] The obligation is in practice an obligation of the parties to seek to settle their dispute by recourse to negotiations.[273] The provision is the result of the insistence of certain delegations at the UNCLOS III that the primary obligation of the parties to a dispute should be to make every effort to settle the dispute through negotiation or other peaceful means without recourse to the mechanisms set out in section 2 of Part XV of the Convention.[274] The obligation to exchange views prior to the institution of proceedings as set out in Article 283(1) constitutes a departure from the procedural rules under general international law which do not know of a requirement to exhaust diplomatic negotiations prior to instituting judicial or arbitral proceedings.[275] A previous 'exchange of views' is thus a necessary precondition for submitting a dispute to an arbitral tribunal constituted in accordance with UNCLOS Annex VII.

The obligation to exchange views applies equally to both parties to the dispute,[276] and must be taken seriously. As pointed out by Judge Chandrasekhara Rao, the obligation to exchange views 'is not an empty formality, to be dispensed with at the whims of a disputant. The obligation in this regard must be discharged in good faith, and it is the duty of the Tribunal to examine whether this is being done'.[277] An exchange of views regarding the settlement of the dispute by negotiation is distinct from mere protests or disputations, or a simple request for information. The ICJ summarised the requirement of negotiations as follows:

> Negotiations entail more than the plain opposition of legal views or interests between two parties, or the existence of a series of accusations and rebuttals, or even the exchange of claims and directly opposed counter-claims. As such,

---

[272] *Application of the International Convention on the Elimination of All Forms of Racial Discrimination (Georgia v Russian Federation)* (Preliminary Objections) [2011] ICJ Rep 70, 124 [131].

[273] See *Barbados v Trinidad and Tobago* (2006) 27 RIAA 147, 203 [191], 207 [206]. See also *M/V 'Louisa' (Saint Vincent and the Grenadines v Kingdom of Spain)* (Provisional Measures, Order of 23 December 2010) [2008–2010] ITLOS Rep 58, 85 [27] (diss op Wolfrum) and Malcolm Shaw, *International Law*, 6th edn (Cambridge, CUP, 2008) 1015.

[274] See Nordquist, Rosenne and Sohn (eds), *United Nations Convention on the Law of the Sea 1982*, vol V (1989) 29 MN 283.1. See also *M/V 'Louisa' (Saint Vincent and the Grenadines v Kingdom of Spain)* (Provisional Measures, Order of 23 December 2010) [2008–2010] ITLOS Rep 58, 85 [27] (diss op Wolfrum).

[275] See *Land and Maritime Boundary between Cameroon and Nigeria (Cameroon v Nigeria)* (Preliminary Objections) [1998] ICJ Rep 275, 321–22 [108], [109]. See also ibid, 303 [56].

[276] *M/V 'Louisa' (Saint Vincent and the Grenadines v Kingdom of Spain)* (Provisional Measures, Order of 23 December 2010) [2008–2010] ITLOS Rep 58, 67 [58]; *Land Reclamation in and around the Straits of Johor (Malaysia v Singapore)* (Provisional Measures, Order of 8 October 2003) [2003] ITLOS Rep 10, 19 [38].

[277] *Land Reclamation in and around the Straits of Johor (Malaysia v Singapore)* (Provisional Measures, Order of 8 October 2003) [2003] ITLOS Rep 10, 39 [11] (sep op Rao). See also *M/V 'Louisa' (Saint Vincent and the Grenadines v Kingdom of Spain)* (Provisional Measures, Order of 23 December 2010) [2008–2010] ITLOS Rep 58, 85 [27], [28] (diss op Wolfrum); ibid, 90 [10] (diss op Treves).

the concept of 'negotiations' differs from the concept of 'dispute', and requires — at the very least — a genuine attempt by one of the disputing parties to engage in discussions with the other disputing party, with a view to resolving the dispute. ... the obligation to negotiate [is] an obligation 'not only to enter into negotiations, but also to pursue them as far as possible, with a view to concluding agreements [even if] an obligation to negotiate does not imply an obligation to reach agreement ...'. Manifestly, in the absence of evidence of a genuine attempt to negotiate, the precondition of negotiation is not met.[278]

Whether or not the obligation to exchange views has been met is not a matter for subjective decision by the parties, but is to be determined by the arbitral tribunal.[279] Thus, the Philippines' statement that it 'has complied with the requirements of Article 279 and Article 283(1) fully and in good faith' is not determinative.[280] Even though the ITLOS has held that 'a State Party is not obliged to pursue procedures under Part XV, section 1, of the Convention when it concludes that the possibilities of settlement have been exhausted',[281] and that 'a State Party is not obliged to continue with an exchange of views when it concludes that the possibilities of reaching agreement have been exhausted'[282] the standard for satisfying UNCLOS, Article 283(1) is not a purely subjective one. If the applicant could simply claim that the possibilities of reaching a settlement of the dispute by way of exchanging views have been exhausted, the provision would have no substance.[283] Instead, it is for the applicant to prove, and for the Tribunal to determine, that an exchange of views was held or, at least, that it invited the other party to an exchange of views which was open to the possibility of a settlement of the dispute by negotiations or other peaceful means.[284] This seems to be accepted by the Philippines, which in its Notification and Statement of Claim devotes seven out of 41 paragraphs to 'Exchanges of Views' between the parties.[285] At paragraph 30, it concludes that the 'diplomatic record leaves no doubt that the requirement in Article 283 that

---

[278] *Application of the International Convention on the Elimination of All Forms of Racial Discrimination (Georgia v Russian Federation)* (Preliminary Objections) [2011] ICJ Rep 70, 132–33 [157]–[159] (references omitted). On negotiations on the subject-matter of the dispute, see also ibid, 135–39 [167]–[181]. See also *North Sea Continental Shelf (Germany v Denmark)* (Merits) [1969] ICJ Rep 3, 47 [85].

[279] ibid, 135 [169]. See also John G Merrills, *International Dispute Settlement*, 5th edn (Cambridge, CUP, 2011) 19.

[280] See Notification and Statement of Claim, para 33.

[281] *Southern Bluefin Tuna (New Zealand v Japan; Australia v Japan)* (Provisional Measures, Order of 27 August 1999) [1999] ITLOS Rep 280, 295 [60].

[282] *MOX Plant (Ireland v United Kingdom)* (Provisional Measures, Order of 3 December 2001) [2001] ITLOS Rep 95, 107 [60].

[283] It should be mentioned that in all four cases in which the ITLOS discussed art 283(1) it noted that negotiations had taken place or that diplomatic notes had been exchanged; see *Southern Bluefin Tuna Case* (n 48), *MOX Plant* (n 282), *Land Reclamation in and around the Straits of Johor* (n 276), and *M/V 'Louisa'* (n 91).

[284] *Land Reclamation in and around the Straits of Johor (Malaysia v Singapore)* (Provisional Measures, Order of 8 October 2003) [2003] ITLOS Rep 10, 20 [48] ('in the view of the Tribunal'). See also Karaman (n 181) 129–30.

[285] Notification and Statement of Claim, paras 8, 25–30.

the "parties to the dispute shall proceed expeditiously to an exchange of views regarding its settlement by negotiations or other peaceful means" has been satisfied'.[286] Indeed, the Philippines claims that over 'the past 17 years of such exchanges of views, all possibilities of a negotiated settlement have been explored and exhausted'.[287] This was called into question by China.[288]

The parties need not necessarily expressly refer to the provisions of the Convention at issue in the dispute in their exchanges of views. However, to meet the pre-condition of negotiations, the subject-matter of the negotiations must be identical with the subject-matter of the dispute.[289] As pointed out by the Arbitral Tribunal in *Barbados v Trinidad and Tobago*, the record of the negotiations must show that the subject-matter of the dispute before the Tribunal 'was part of the subject-matter on the table during those negotiations'.[290] In addition, the subject-matter of the negotiations must concern the interpretation or application of the Convention.[291] Negotiations invoking the Convention in general are not sufficient. Whether the conditions of Article 283(1) have been fulfilled is a matter of fact and, as stated by the Philippines, the diplomatic record. The latter will have to be presented to the Tribunal at the pleadings stage. The Notification and Statement of Claim so far remains at the level of generalities. It is not sufficient to show that there were exchanges between the parties with regard to the parties' maritime entitlements in the South China Sea or the legality of China's 'nine-dash line' in general. For example, the Joint Statement of the Republic of the Philippines and the People's Republic of China of 1 September 2011, which records that the leaders of the two countries 'exchanged views on the maritime disputes', will not suffice to meet the requirement under Article 283.[292] The Philippines will have to show that there were 'meaningful' negotiations which covered the 13 specific subject-matters for which it seeks relief.[293] For example, the Philippines will have to demonstrate that the negotiations actually concerned the question of the legal status of the land features named in the Notification and Statement

---

[286] ibid, para 30.

[287] ibid, para 27.

[288] PRC MFA, 'Foreign Ministry Spokesperson Hua Chunying's Regular Press Conference' (12 July 2013), Annex I, Doc A.5 ('The Philippines' claim that "it had exhausted almost all political and diplomatic avenues for a peaceful settlement of the dispute" is completely not true'). But see also the eight-point 'Response of the DFA Spokesperson to the Recent Statement of the Chinese Ministry of Foreign Affairs on the West Philippine Sea Issue' (15 July 2013) www.dfa.gov.ph.

[289] *cf Application of the International Convention on the Elimination of All Forms of Racial Discrimination (Georgia v Russian Federation)* (Preliminary Objections) [2011] ICJ Rep 70, 133 [161].

[290] *Barbados v Trinidad and Tobago* (2006) 27 RIAA 147, 208-09 [213].

[291] On the extent to which the subject-matter of the dispute concerns the interpretation and application of UNCLOS, see text at section IV.1.a(2).

[292] 2011 Joint Statement (n 83).

[293] See *North Sea Continental Shelf (Germany v Denmark)* (Merits) [1969] ICJ Rep 3, 47 [85].

of Claim as islands, rocks or low-tide elevations,[294] and that they covered the question of whether States can acquire territorial sovereignty over low-tide elevations and other submerged land features.[295] While it could be argued that all these subject-matters are merely 'incidental to the real dispute between the Parties' and, therefore, 'can be considered as being subsumed within the [negotiations on the] main dispute',[296] it must be recalled that the main or real disputes, namely the disputes over territorial sovereignty and maritime boundary delimitations, are not before the Tribunal.

In addition, the Philippines will have to show that it engaged or genuinely attempted to engage in discussions with the PRC with a view to resolving the dispute and that the two sides did not just exchange claims and counter-claims or trade protests. The Notification and Statement of Claims seems to suggest the latter. Thus, the Philippines states that 'it has consistently expressed the view to China' and that 'China has repeatedly expressed the conflicting view',[297] and that it 'has repeatedly protested Chinese activities' and that 'China has consistently rejected the Philippines' protests'.[298] This does not suggest that the parties were contemplating any modification of their position.[299] While Article 283(1) does not require the parties to negotiate indefinitely,[300] it does require them actually to negotiate or, at least, genuinely attempt to negotiate with a view to resolving their dispute. Judging by past decisions of the ITLOS, however, the threshold to meet the negotiation requirement does not seem to be particularly high.

b. Commitment to Other Means of Dispute Settlement

The Convention 'falls significantly short of establishing a truly comprehensive regime of compulsory jurisdiction entailing binding decisions'.[301] This is confirmed by Article 281(1) which allows States Parties to preclude subjection of their disputes to the compulsory procedures of section 2 of Part XV of the Convention by agreeing 'to seek settlement of

---

[294] See Notification and Statement of Claim, para 41, bullet points 4, 6 and 8.

[295] ibid, para 41, bullet points 4 and 6.

[296] *Guyana v Suriname* (2007) 139 ILR 566, 684 [410]. In that case, the dispute had 'as its principal concern the determination of the course of the maritime boundary between the two Parties' (ibid).

[297] Notification and Statement of Claim, para 27.

[298] ibid, para 28. See also the statement of the Philippines Foreign Minister: 'When the Philippines protested these [Chinese] intrusions [into areas where the Philippines claim to have sovereign rights], the response was a denial that no [sic] such intrusions occurred', ('"Philippine Policy Response and Action" by Hon. Albert F del Rosario, Secretary of Foreign Affairs' (5 August 2011) www.philippine-embassy.org.il).

[299] cf *North Sea Continental Shelf (Germany v Denmark)* (Merits) [1969] ICJ Rep 3, 47 [85].

[300] *Southern Bluefin Tuna Case (Australia and New Zealand v Japan)* (Award on Jurisdiction and Admissibility) (2000) 119 ILR 508, 526 [55].

[301] ibid, para 62. See also Gamble, 'The Law of the Sea Conference' 331; Klein (n 260) 26–27, 120.

the dispute by a peaceful means of their own choice'. Where the parties have done so, a claim is only admissible if (a) no settlement has been reached by recourse to such means and (b) the agreement between the parties does not exclude any further procedure. While it is evident in the present case that no settlement has been reached, the question of whether the parties have agreed on an exclusive means of dispute settlement is more difficult to answer. The term 'agreement' refers to a legally binding commitment.[302] On 4 November 2002, the PRC and the Philippines, together with other ASEAN Member States, signed the DOC in which the parties undertook 'to resolve their territorial and jurisdictional disputes by peaceful means ... through friendly consultations and negotiations by sovereign states directly concerned'.[303] This commitment was affirmed in a Joint Statement of the Philippines and China in September 2011, when the Presidents of the two countries 'reiterated their commitment to addressing the [maritime] disputes through peaceful dialogue' and 'reaffirmed their commitments to respect and abide by the Declaration on the Conduct of Parties in the South China Sea signed by China and the ASEAN member countries in 2002'.[304]

China objected to the institution of arbitral proceedings, inter alia, on the ground that both 'the Philippines and China are signatories to the Declaration on the Conduct of Parties in South China Sea (DOC) and have made commitments on comprehensive and earnest implementation of the DOC'.[305] The question is whether the DOC constitutes an 'agreement' by the Philippines and China to seek settlement of their maritime disputes in the South China Sea by 'friendly consultations and negotiations' only, to the exclusion of any other means of dispute settlement, especially those under section 2 of Part XV of UNCLOS. The exclusion of further procedures need not necessarily be express. It can also be effected by requiring disputes to be resolved by mutually agreed procedures,[306] or by expressly setting out a limited number of procedures available.

---

[302] cf *Delimitation of the Maritime Boundary between Bangladesh and Myanmar in the Bay of Bengal (Bangladesh/Myanmar)* (Judgment) [2012] ITLOS Rep [89] (with regard to the term 'agreement' in UNCLOS, art 15).

[303] DOC (n 220) para 4.

[304] 2011 Joint Statement (n 83). See also the statement of the Philippines Chief of Staff, General Ricardo David Jr, who stressed that the Philippines is deeply committed to the principles embodied in the 2002 Declaration of Conduct of Parties in the South China Sea (DOC), which calls for cooperation and peaceful negotiations between ASEAN members and China in the South China Sea (RP DFA, 'AFP Chief of Staff, Chinese Military Officials Reaffirm Peaceful Resolution of South China Sea Disputes' (9 December 2010) www.dfa.gov. ph).

[305] PRC MFA, 'Foreign Ministry Spokesperson Hong Lei's Regular Press Conference' (20 February 2013) Annex I, Doc A.16. See also, ibid, 'Foreign Ministry Spokesperson Hong Lei's Regular Press Conference' (19 February 2013) www.fmprc.gov.cn ('It is also the consensus reached by ASEAN countries and China in the Declaration on the Conduct of Parties in the South China Sea (DOC) to resolve disputes through negotiations between directly concerned sovereign states. The Philippines' note and its attached notice ... violate the consensus').

[306] *Southern Bluefin Tuna Case (Australia and New Zealand v Japan)* (Award on Jurisdiction and Admissibility) (2000) 119 ILR 508, 526 [56], 551 [57], 553-54 [63].

It could thus be argued that by undertaking to resolve their disputes 'through friendly consultations and negotiations', the parties intended to exclude all other means of dispute settlement. However, this is not how the Philippines (and other ASEAN Member States) have interpreted the DOC.[307]

International agreements may take a number of forms and be given a diversity of names.[308] For example, documents entitled 'joint communiqués',[309] 'agreed minutes'[310] and 'declarations' have been found to constitute international agreements.[311] The designation as 'Declaration of Conduct' thus does not automatically exclude the DOC from being a binding international agreement. The majority in the literature seems to accept that it is 'a political declaration rather than a binding agreement'.[312] There is some support for this view in the fact that the DOC itself foresees the adoption of a legally binding 'code of conduct in the South China Sea' in the future.[313] In the end, however, it will be for the Tribunal to ascertain whether the DOC or any subsequent act of the parties constitutes an agreement, having 'regard above all to its actual terms and to the particular circumstances in which it was drawn up'.[314] As shown by Bing Big Jia, a good case can be made for the DOC to constitute an agreement that validly excludes any further procedures and, in particular, the compulsory procedures of section 2 of Part XV.[315]

---

[307] See the statement of the Philippine President: 'The Philippines considers the peaceful resolution of the disputes in the West Philippine Sea through a rules-based approach under relevant dispute-settlement mechanisms of the United Nations Convention on the Law of the Sea (UNCLOS) as paramount to regional peace, stability, and progress' (RP DFA, 'President Aquino's Statement on the Declaration on the Conduct of Parties in the South China Sea' (4 April 2012) www.gov.ph).

[308] See *Maritime Delimitation and Territorial Questions between Qatar and Bahrain (Qatar v Bahrain)* (Jurisdiction and Admissibility) [1994] ICJ Rep 112, 120 [23]; *Aegean Sea Continental Shelf (Greece v Turkey)* (Jurisdiction) [1978] ICJ Rep 3, 39 [96].

[309] See *Aegean Sea Continental Shelf (Greece v Turkey)* (Jurisdiction) [1978] ICJ Rep 3, 39 [96].

[310] See *Delimitation of the Maritime Boundary between Bangladesh and Myanmar in the Bay of Bengal (Bangladesh/Myanmar)* (Judgment) [2012] ITLOS Rep [90]; *'Hoshinmaru' (Japan v Russian Federation)* (Prompt Release, Judgment) [2005–2007] ITLOS Rep 18, 46 [86].

[311] See *Land and Maritime Boundary between Cameroon and Nigeria (Cameroon v Nigeria: Equatorial Guinea intervening)* (Merits) [2002] ICJ Rep 303, 429 [263].

[312] Rodolfo C Severino, *Southeast Asia in Search of an ASEAN Community: Insights from the Former ASEAN Secretary-General* (Singapore, Institute of Southeast Asian Studies, 2006) 186. On the non-binding legal nature of the DOC, see also Strupp, 'Spratly Islands' 450 MN 8; Nguyen Hong Thao, 'The 2002 Declaration on the Conduct of Parties in the South China Sea: A Note' (2003) 34 *Ocean Development & International Law* 279, 281; Carlyle A Thayer, 'ASEAN'S Code of Conduct in the South China Sea: A Litmus Test for Community-Building?', *The Asia-Pacific Journal*, vol 10, issue 34, no 4, 20 August 2012, www.japanfocus.org.

[313] DOC (n 220) para 11.

[314] *Maritime Delimitation and Territorial Questions between Qatar and Bahrain (Qatar v Bahrain)* (Jurisdiction and Admissibility) [1994] ICJ Rep 112, 121 [23]; *Aegean Sea Continental Shelf (Greece v Turkey)* (Jurisdiction) [1978] ICJ Rep 3, 39 [96].

[315] See ch 4 below.

3. Other Objections of a Preliminary Character

In addition to preliminary objections based on lack of jurisdiction or inadmissibility of the application, China's rejection of the Philippines' request for arbitration may be based on any other objection of a preliminary character. This is confirmed in Article 294(3) UNCLOS which safeguards the 'right of any party to the dispute to make preliminary objections in accordance with the applicable rules of procedure'. Courts and tribunals do not always make a clear distinction between the three grounds for preliminary objections. The third ground usually serves as a catch-all provision and leaves the Tribunal broad discretion to dispose of a case before any other proceedings on the merits.[316] In the present case, China could argue, for example, that the Philippines has not cited before the Tribunal certain third parties whose presence is indispensable,[317] or that the claims brought by the Philippines constitute an abuse of legal process.

a. Indispensable Third Parties

It is a well-established principle of international law that an international court or tribunal can exercise jurisdiction over a State only with its consent.[318] The doctrine of the absent or indispensable third party precludes a court or tribunal from adjudicating the merits of a case that would compromise the legal position of third States not party to the proceedings. But, the mere fact that a State not party to the proceedings might be affected by a decision is not enough. The decisive factor is that the State's 'legal interests would not only be affected by a decision, but would form the very subject matter of the decision'.[319] The third State's legal interest will, as a matter of principle, be protected, irrespective of whether the third State is intervening in the proceedings or not.[320]

---

[316] See Stefan Talmon, 'Article 43' in Andreas Zimmermann and others (eds), *The Statute of the International Court of Justice: A Commentary*, Oxford Commentaries on International Law, 2nd edn (Oxford, OUP, 2012) 1088, 1161 MN 179.

[317] For the indispensable third party rule as 'some other ground' for putting an end to the proceedings, see ICJ (ed), *The International Court of Justice*, 4th edn (The Hague, ICJ, 1996) 58.

[318] *cf Monetary Gold Removed from Rome in 1943 (Italy v United Kingdom and United States of America)* (Preliminary Question) [1954] ICJ Rep 19, 32.

[319] ibid, 32. This test has been repeated by the ICJ in subsequent decisions such as *Military and Paramilitary Activities in and against Nicaragua (Nicaragua v United States of America)* (Jurisdiction and Admissibility) [1984] ICJ Rep 392, 431 [88]; *Land, Island and Maritime Frontier Dispute (El Salvador/ Honduras)* (Application by Nicaragua for Permission to Intervene) [1990] ICJ Rep 92, 116 [56] and 122 [73]; *Certain Phosphate Lands in Nauru (Nauru v Australia)* (Preliminary Objections) [1992] ICJ Rep 240, 258–62 [48]–[55]; *East Timor (Portugal v Australia)* (Merits) [1995] ICJ Rep 90, 102–05 [28]–[35]; *Armed Activities on the Territory of the Congo (Democratic Republic of the Congo v Uganda)* (Merits) [2005] ICJ Rep 168, 236–38 [197]–[204].

[320] *Territorial and Maritime Dispute (Nicaragua v Colombia)* (Application by Costa Rica for Permission to Intervene) [2011] ICJ Rep 348, 372 [86]. See also *Land and Maritime Boundary between Cameroon and Nigeria (Cameroon v Nigeria: Equatorial Guinea intervening)* (Merits) [2002] ICJ Rep 303, 421 [238].

It has been questioned whether the indispensable third party rule, which was developed by the ICJ, was equally applicable to arbitral proceedings. To this the Arbitral Tribunal in *Larsen v Hawaiian Kingdom* replied:

> That rule applies with at least as much force to the exercise of jurisdiction in international arbitral proceedings. While it is the consent of the parties which brings the arbitration tribunal into existence, such a tribunal, particularly one conducted under the auspices of the Permanent Court of Arbitration, operates within the general confines of public international law and, like the International Court, cannot exercise jurisdiction over a State which is not a party to its proceedings.[321]

Maritime boundary disputes constitute a special category of disputes where a pronouncement on the issues may prejudice the rights of third States.[322] Normally, third States will be protected by the rule set forth in Article 296(2) UNCLOS that any decision rendered by an arbitral tribunal established under the Convention 'shall have no binding force except between the parties and in respect to that particular dispute'. In the case of maritime delimitations, however, where the maritime areas of several States are involved, the protection afforded by Article 296(2) UNCLOS may not always be sufficient.[323] International courts and tribunals have, as a rule, refused to delimit areas which are, or can reasonably be, claimed by third States. In cases where a boundary line reaches an area claimed by other States, courts and tribunals have avoided fixing any endpoint of the boundary line and simply ended the delimitation with a directional line with an arrow at the end, indicating the general direction of the boundary line until it meets the (yet to be determined) maritime area belonging to third States.[324] As the ICJ stated: 'it is usual in a judicial delimitation for the precise endpoint to be left undefined in order to refrain from prejudicing the rights of third States'.[325]

Although the Philippines purports that it does not 'request delimitation of any maritime boundaries', it does exactly that.[326] In fact, the Philippines even

---

[321] *Larsen v Hawaiian Kingdom* (2001) 119 ILR 566, 590 [11.17].

[322] See Christian Tomuschat, 'Article 36' in Andreas Zimmermann and others (eds), *The Statute of the International Court of Justice: A Commentary*, Oxford Commentaries on International Law, 2nd edn (Oxford, OUP, 2012) 633, 650 MN 23, 24.

[323] *cf* with regard to the almost identical art 59 ICJ Statute: *Land and Maritime Boundary between Cameroon and Nigeria (Cameroon v Nigeria: Equatorial Guinea intervening)* (Merits) [2002] ICJ Rep 303, 421 [238]; *Territorial and Maritime Dispute (Nicaragua v Colombia)* (Application by Costa Rica for Permission to Intervene) [2011] ICJ Rep 348, 371 [85].

[324] See eg *Land and Maritime Boundary between Cameroon and Nigeria (Cameroon v Nigeria: Equatorial Guinea intervening)* (Merits) [2002] ICJ Rep 303, 421 [238], 424 [245], 448 [307]; *Barbados v Trinidad and Tobago* (2006) 27 RIAA 147, 210 [218] and 244–45 [381]–[382]; *Territorial and Maritime Dispute between Nicaragua and Honduras in the Caribbean Sea (Nicaragua v Honduras)* (Merits) [2007] ICJ Rep 659, 755–59 [312]–[318]; *Maritime Delimitation in the Black Sea (Romania v Ukraine)* (Merits) [2009] ICJ Rep 61, 100 [112]; 131 [218]; *Territorial and Maritime Dispute (Nicaragua v Colombia)* (Application by Costa Rica for Permission to Intervene) [2011] ICJ Rep 348, 372 [89]; *Delimitation of the Maritime Boundary between Bangladesh and Myanmar in the Bay of Bengal (Bangladesh/Myanmar)* (Judgment) [2012] ITLOS Rep [462].

[325] *Territorial and Maritime Dispute between Nicaragua and Honduras in the Caribbean Sea (Nicaragua v Honduras)* (Merits) [2007] ICJ Rep 659, 756 [312].

[326] See text to n 252.

goes one step further and asks the Tribunal for an abstract determination *erga omnes* that certain maritime areas around Mischief Reef and McKennan Reef 'form part of the Continental Shelf of the Philippines'.[327] In addition, it requests the Tribunal to declare that 'the Philippines is entitled under UNCLOS to ... a 200 M Exclusive Economic Zone, and a Continental Shelf under Parts II, V and VI of UNCLOS, measured from its archipelagic baselines'.[328] The archipelagic baselines are set out in Republic Act No 9522 of 10 March 2009.[329] Any positive ruling on the Philippines' claim would thus confirm in an abstract and absolute way the Philippines' assertion of an EEZ extending 200nm from its archipelagic baselines.

In both cases, the Tribunal is called upon not just to determine which of the two States — China or the Philippines — has a superior claim vis-à-vis the other to a certain maritime area, but to decide in the absolute that certain maritime areas constitute the Philippines' EEZ and continental shelf. To the extent that other States claim the same maritime areas, their legal interests, ie their sovereign rights and jurisdiction over those areas, are not only affected, but form the very subject-matter of the dispute.[330] The PCIJ stated in *Legal Status of Eastern Greenland* that '[a]nother circumstance which must be taken into account by any tribunal which has to adjudicate upon a claim to sovereignty over a particular territory, is the extent to which the sovereignty is also claimed by some other Power'.[331] In the *Libya/Malta Continental Shelf* case, the ICJ held that 'this observation ... is no less true when what is in question is the extent of the respective areas of continental shelf over which different States enjoy "sovereign rights"'.[332] And, it may be added, the same can be said for areas of EEZ over which different States enjoy 'sovereign rights' and 'jurisdiction'.[333] The ICJ ruled:

> If therefore the decision is to be stated in absolute terms, in the sense of permitting the delimitation of the areas of shelf which 'appertain' to the Parties, as distinct from the areas to which one of the Parties has shown a better title than the other, but which might nevertheless prove to 'appertain' to a third State if the Court had jurisdiction to enquire into the entitlement of that third State, the decision must be limited to a geographical area in which no such claims exist.[334]

---

[327] Relief Sought, bullet point 4; see also Claims, bullet point 5.

[328] Relief Sought, bullet point 10; see also Claims, bullet point 8.

[329] Republic Act No 9522 – An Act to Amend Certain Provisions of Republic Act No 3046, as amended by Republic Act No 5446, to Define the Archipelagic Baselines of the Philippines, and for Other Purposes (10 March 2009), reprinted in United Nations, Division for Ocean Affairs and the Law of the Sea, *Law of the Sea Bulletin* No 70 (2009) 32.

[330] *cf Sovereignty over Pulau Ligitan and Pulau Sipadan (Indonesia/Malaysia)* (Application by the Philippines for Permission to Intervene) [2001] ICJ Rep 575, 596 [49] ('very subject-matter of the dispute or the territory in which a delimitation is to be effected').

[331] *Legal Status of Eastern Greenland (Denmark v Norway)* (Judgment of 5 April 1933) PCIJ Rep Series A/B No 53, 46.

[332] *Continental Shelf (Libyan Arab Jamahiriya/Malta)* (Application by Italy for Permission to Intervene) [1984] ICJ Rep 3, 26 [43].

[333] See UNCLOS, art 56(1).

[334] *Continental Shelf (Libyan Arab Jamahiriya/Malta)* (Merits) [1985] ICJ Rep 13, 25 [21]. See also *Frontier Dispute (Burkina Faso/Republic of Mali)* (Merits) [1986] ICJ Rep 554, 578 [47] ('a

Consequently, the ICJ refused to decide on areas of continental shelf claimed by other States. If the ICJ's ruling is applied to the present case, the Tribunal will have to decline to decide on the maritime areas claimed by other States. The existence of other States' claims in the South China Sea has to be taken into account by the Tribunal 'as a fact'.[335]

The Philippines itself admits that '[p]ortions or the entire South China Sea are being claimed by several countries like the Philippines, China, Taiwan, Vietnam and other ASEAN-member countries [ie Brunei and Malaysia]'.[336] The Spratly Islands, including Mischief Reef and McKennan Reef and their adjacent waters, are claimed by China (both the mainland and Taiwan), Philippines and Vietnam. In several diplomatic Notes to the UN Secretary-General, Vietnam stated that the 'Hoang Sa (Paracels) and Truong Sa (Spratlys) archipelagoes are parts of Viet Nam's territory'.[337] In a statement on the arbitral proceedings instituted by the Philippines against China, the spokesman for the Vietnamese Foreign Ministry declared:

> As a coastal State enjoying lawful and legitimate national rights and interests in the East Sea (South China Sea), Viet Nam is interested in and closely follows the development of these arbitral proceedings. … Viet Nam reaffirms its sovereignty over the two archipelagos of Hoang Sa (Paracel) and Truong Sa (Spratly) as well as its sovereignty, sovereign rights and jurisdiction in its own internal waters, territorial sea, contiguous zone, exclusive economic zone and continental shelf in the East Sea (South China Sea).[338]

Leaving aside the intractable question of the legal status of the Taiwan Authorities,[339] the maritime areas claimed by the Philippines as forming 'part of its Continental Shelf' are thus claimed by at least one other State that is not a party to the proceedings. The question is not whether Vietnam has indeed a valid claim to the areas in question. This would

court dealing with a request for the delimitation of a continental shelf must decline, even if so authorized by the disputant parties, to rule upon rights relating to areas in which third States have such claims as may contradict the legal considerations — especially in regard to equitable principles — which would have formed the basis of its decision').

[335] *Continental Shelf (Libyan Arab Jamahiriya/Malta)* (Application by Italy for Permission to Intervene) [1984] ICJ Rep 3, 26 [43]; *Continental Shelf (Libyan Arab Jamahiriya/Malta)* (Merits) [1985] ICJ Rep 13, 24 [20].

[336] 'Malacanang Hopes Other South China Sea Claimants Respect Aquino's Administrative Order No 29 Otherwise Known as "Naming the West Philippine Sea of the Republic of the Philippines"' (20 September 2012) www.pcoo.gov.ph.

[337] See Notes Verbales to the Secretary-General of the United Nations from the Permanent Mission of the Socialist Republic of Viet Nam to the United Nations, No 86/HC-2009 (8 May 2009), No 240/HC-2009 (18 August 2009) and No 77/HC-2011 (3 May 2011), all available at www.un.org/depts/los. See also Law of the Sea of Viet Nam (n 143) arts 1, 19(2). Vietnam holds the largest number of islands and insular features in the Spratly Islands, several of which are located within 200nm of the archipelagic baselines of the Philippines. On a number of these features it has, like China, erected artificial islands, installations and structures. See Strupp (n 101) 449 MN 3.

[338] 'Remark by Foreign Ministry Spokesman Luong Thanh Nghi on the Arbitral Proceedings Instituted by the Philippines Under the Annex VII to the UNCLOS' (26 April 2013) biengioilanhtho.gov.vn.

[339] The Philippines has adopted the 'one China policy', see n 83 above.

confuse the substantive law with the law relating to jurisdiction. The question is only whether the Tribunal can decide on Vietnam's claim. In the present case, the Tribunal cannot render a decision in absolute terms as requested by the Philippines without ruling on the interests of Vietnam — a State not a party to the proceedings.[340] It therefore cannot decide on these issues without violating 'the sacrosanct principle of consent to jurisdiction'.[341]

Similarly, the Tribunal cannot rule on the Philippines' absolute claim that it 'is entitled under UNCLOS to ... a 200 M Exclusive Economic Zone ... measured from its archipelagic baselines'. Such a 200nm EEZ would necessarily impact not only on the overlapping EEZ claims by China (both the mainland and Taiwan) but also by Vietnam, Malaysia, Brunei and Indonesia, which all qualify as indispensable third parties.

b. Abuse of Legal Process

Article 294(1) UNCLOS provides that an Annex VII arbitral tribunal shall take no further action in a case if it determines that the claim constitutes an 'abuse of legal process'. The provision both recognises a special substantive preliminary objection and provides for special preliminary proceedings to deal with that objection. The tribunal may make a determination of 'abuse of legal process' either at the request of a party or *proprio motu* if, for example, the respondent decides not to appear in the case.[342] The purpose of the provision is to protect coastal States against harassment through frivolous or vexatious claims with regard to the exercise of their sovereign rights and jurisdiction in the EEZ and the continental shelf.[343] As pointed out by Tullio Treves, the

> assessment as to whether the claim constitutes an 'abuse of legal process' requires a prudent examination of the specific case taking into account ... that 'the perception of what is vexatious ... may be in the eye of the beholder' ....
> In the light of the above, it would seem that only the most blatant cases of abuse ... are likely to be stopped by the preliminary filter of claims set out in Article 294.[344]

---

[340] This has also been acknowledged by Philippine scholars; see Jay L Batongbacal, 'The Impossible Dream and the West Philippine Sea' (28 January 2013) www.imoa.ph ('Although an arbitration cannot affect the rights of non-parties, obviously if the result of this process is a legal characterization of the maritime zones in the WPS, the logic of any favorable findings could also work against Vietnam's current position').

[341] Alain Pellet, 'Land and Maritime Tripoints in International Jurisprudence' in Holger P Hestermeyer and others (eds), *Coexistence, Cooperation and Solidarity: Liber Amicorum Rüdiger Wolfrum*, vol I (Leiden, Martinus Nijhoff, 2012) 263.

[342] See Nordquist, Rosenne and Sohn (eds), *United Nations Convention on the Law of the Sea 1982*, vol V (1989) 77 MN 294.5.

[343] ibid, 76 MN 294.1.

[344] Tullio Treves, 'Preliminary Proceedings in the Settlement of Disputes under the United Nations Law of the Sea Convention: Some Observations' in Nisuke Ando and others (eds), *Liber Amicorum Judge Shigeru Oda*, vol I (The Hague, Kluwer, 2002) 749, 751, 752.

No tribunal has yet found an abuse of legal process.[345]

In any case, the preliminary objection of 'abuse of legal process' is available only in respect of disputes 'referred to in article 297',[346] ie disputes with regard to the exercise by a coastal State of sovereign rights or jurisdiction in its EEZ or continental shelf. The claims brought by the Philippines against China do not concern the exercise by China, as a coastal State, of its sovereign rights and jurisdiction but, on the contrary, are implicitly based on a denial of China's status as a coastal State and of it enjoying any sovereign rights or jurisdiction in the relevant areas of the South China Sea.[347]

V. THE POLITICS OF ARBITRATION

The Philippines first floated the idea of submitting its dispute with China over entitlements in the South China Sea to adjudication in July 2011. In a Note Verbale, dated 26 April 2012, the Philippines then formally invited the PRC to submit the issue to ITLOS or another dispute settlement mechanism under UNCLOS.[348] The PRC, however, made it clear from the start that it considered the issue of territorial sovereignty over Scarborough Shoal and other island groups in the South China Sea 'not a problem for international arbitration' and as not falling under the UNCLOS dispute settlement mechanisms.[349] On 28 April 2012, the Director-General of the Department of Boundary and Ocean Affairs of the Chinese Ministry of Foreign Affairs summoned the Philippine *chargé d'affaires* 'to lodge solemn representations on the intention of the Philippines to bring the dispute over the territorial sovereignty of Huangyan Island [Scarborough Shoal] to international arbitration'.[350]

Against this background, the prospects of China participating in the arbitral proceedings were slim from the start. In fact, the Philippines never seemed to expect China to take part in the proceedings. In his statement announcing the initiation of arbitral proceedings Philippines

---

[345] In *Southern Bluefin Tuna Case (Australia and New Zealand v Japan)* (Award on Jurisdiction and Admissibility) (2000) 119 ILR 508, 526 [65], the tribunal did 'not find the proceedings brought before ITLOS and before this Tribunal to be an abuse of process, on the contrary ... the proceedings have been constructive'. See also the statement of Barbados that 'a State's invocation of its right to arbitrate under a treaty after it exhausts the potential for a negotiated resolution' is not an abuse of right (*Barbados v Trinidad and Tobago* (2006) 27 RIAA 147, 178 [100]).

[346] UNCLOS, art 294(1).

[347] See text to n 249.

[348] RP DFA, 'Response of the DFA Spokesperson to the Recent Statement of the Chinese Ministry of Foreign Affairs on the West Philippine Sea Issue'(15 July 2013) (n 288).

[349] PRC MFA, 'Foreign Ministry Spokesperson Liu Weimin's Regular Press Conference' (26 April 2012) www.fmprc.gov.cn. See also, eg, the press conferences on 8 September 2011, 27 April 2012 and 8 May 2012; ibid.

[350] 'The MFA Department of Boundary and Ocean Affairs Lodges Representations to the Philippines on the Intention of the Philippines to Bring the Dispute over Huangyan Island Territorial Sovereignty to International Arbitration' (29 April 2012) www.fmprc.gov.cn.

Foreign Affairs Secretary, Albert del Rosario, immediately addressed the requirements of an award made in the absence of one of the parties:

> The Philippines asserts that the Arbitral Tribunal *has jurisdiction* to hear and make an award based on its Notification and Statement of Claim because the dispute is about the interpretation and application by States Parties of their obligations under the UNCLOS. ... The Philippines further asserts *that the claim is well founded in fact and law* based on the Notification and Statement of Claims and supplementary documents that will be submitted in the course of the arbitral proceedings.[351]

The language used in the statement parallels that of UNCLOS Annex VII, Article 9 dealing with the failure of one of the parties to defend its case. This Article states that '[b]efore making its award, the arbitral tribunal must satisfy itself not only that it has jurisdiction over the dispute but also that the claim is well founded in fact and law'.

The Philippines does not seem to have been too concerned about the PRC's non-participation in the proceedings. On 21 May 2013, Foreign Affairs Secretary del Rosario said: 'As far as we are concerned, the train has left the station. Either China is on board or they are not. But as I said this is a compulsory arbitration. The award will come down whether or not China is with us'.[352]

This leaves the question of why the Philippines adopted such a confrontational approach, especially when considering that there is little prospect for the merits of the case ever to be decided by the Tribunal.[353] For the Philippines, the proceedings appear to be an end in themselves. More important than winning the case seems the opportunity for the Philippine Government to publicise its case against China to the world. It has tried to generate support for its position both at home and abroad through a four-prong public relations strategy.[354]

First, it portrayed itself as a champion of 'the rule of law' and 'the peaceful settlement of disputes' by initiating the arbitral proceedings. Foreign Affairs Secretary del Rosario hardly ever missed an opportunity to refer to the 'rule of law' in his speeches and statements on the South China Sea Arbitration, stressing, for example, that the Philippines' 'recourse to arbitration ... promotes the primacy of the rule of law in inter-state relations'.[355]

---

[351] RP DFA, 'SFA Statement on the UNCLOS Arbitral Proceedings against China' (22 January 2013) www.dfa.gov.ph (emphasis added).

[352] 'China Sends Ships to Another Phl Shoal' (22 May 2013) www.philstar.com.

[353] See text at section III.

[354] *cf* RP DFA, 'Department of Foreign Affairs, Q & A on the UNCLOS Arbitral Proceedings against China to Achieve a Peaceful and Durable Solution to the Dispute in the West Philippine Sea' (23 January 2013) question 9, www.dfa.gov.ph. See also 'Del Rosario: UN Arbitration on Sea Row Upholds Rule of Law' (11 April 2013) www.philstar.com, and the publicity leaflet issued by the Philippines Government 'The West Philippine Sea Arbitration, May 2013' (1 June 2013) www.philippineembassy-usa.org.

[355] RP DFA, 'Secretary Del Rosario Expresses Concern Over "Militarization" of the South China Sea' (30 June 2013) www.dfa.gov.ph. See also Bensurto, 'Role of International Law in Managing Disputes in the South China Sea' 16–17.

Arbitration was presented as a 'lawful, non-coercive, and transparent means [of peaceful dispute settlement] that promotes the healthy functioning of an equitable and rules-based international system'.[356] This was contrasted with China's 'increasingly aggressive assertion [of its claims in the South China Sea] based on the threat of use of force'.[357] The question of whether or not China accepted arbitration was elevated to a question of general importance for the international community. Thus, del Rosario stated on 25 May 2013: 'Our arbitration case against China's over-extended claim represents a choice the world needs to ponder as regards the future order it seeks for itself — either an international system that is largely dominated by force, or one that is significantly characterized by the rule of law'.[358] While pledging its 'fullest cooperation' with the Arbitral Tribunal, the Philippines highlighted the PRC's non-participation.[359] On 9 July 2013, Foreign Affairs Secretary del Rosario said: 'It is unfortunate that despite several invitations, China declined to join us in this peaceful endeavor'.[360] The image the Philippines tried to create was that of a China opposed to the rule of law and a rules-based international society. On several occasions, del Rosario stated that 'the recourse to arbitration is firmly rooted in the tradition of good global citizenship',[361] thereby implying that China, because of its apparent rejection of the arbitral proceedings, was not a 'good global citizen'. The 'shaming China' strategy culminated in a statement by Department of Foreign Affairs spokesman Raul Hernandez who said:

> To be accepted as a responsible nation, China has no choice. It must show to the international community its respect for the rule of law, including the mechanism of arbitration which is being pursued by the Philippines to clearly define respective maritime entitlements in the South China Sea.[362]

Second, the Philippines attempted to represent its dispute with China as a battle of David against Goliath with arbitration taking on the role of the slingshot and international law that of the pebbles. Arbitration was portrayed as a means to meet with mighty China 'on equal terms and in a level playing field'.[363] When announcing the institution of arbitral proceedings on 22 January 2013, Foreign Affairs Secretary del Rosario

---

[356] 'Del Rosario: UN Arbitration on Sea Row Upholds Rule of Law' (11 April 2013) (n 354).

[357] Albert F del Rosario, 'Shaping the Future of Asia' (19th Nikkei Future of Asia Conference, Tokyo, 23 May 2013) www.ugnayan.com.

[358] ibid.

[359] See eg 'Phl Arbitral Proceedings against China Now Officially Under Way' (16 July 2013) www.dfa.gov.ph, and 'PHL Ignores China's Three-Way Proposal to Address Sea Disputes' (6 August 2013) www.gmanetwork.com.

[360] 'Managing the South China Sea and other Regional Security Issues' (9 July 2013) (n 255).

[361] 'Del Rosario: UN Arbitration on Sea Row Upholds Rule of Law' (11 April 2013) (n 354); 'EU Backs Philippines in Sea Dispute' (25 April 2013) www.thefreelibrary.com; 'UN Arbitral Panel Member with Pinay Wife Resigns' (7 June 2013) www.abs-cbnnews.com.

[362] 'Philippines Urges China: Be a "Responsible Nation"' (18 July 2013) www.philstar.com; 'China Must Follow the Law – DFA' (18 July 2013) www.mb.com.ph.

[363] 'DFA: PH Arbitration Case Grounded on Rule of Law' (25 May 2013) www.mb.com.ph.

said: 'The Philippines has always asserted that international law including UNCLOS will be the great equalizer in resolving this dispute over the West Philippine Sea'.[364] He tried to insinuate that China favoured using its 'military and economic might' to resolve the dispute, while the Philippines was putting its trust in the rule of law. China was associated with 'might' while the Philippines represented 'right'. This led del Rosario to conclude that '[r]ather than being forced to accept that might is right, we want to show [by going to arbitration] that right is might'.[365]

Third, the Philippines created the impression that arbitration was a measure of 'last resort', having 'exhausted almost all political and diplomatic avenues for a peaceful negotiated settlement of its maritime dispute with China'. The Philippines put the blame for the failure to reach a negotiated settlement squarely at the door of China which it accused of taking a 'hard line position of "indisputable sovereignty" over the South China Sea'.[366] At the same time, arbitration provided an easy excuse for not continuing with bilateral negotiations. On 14 August 2013, the spokesman for the Philippine President said: 'Our concern with the West Philippine Sea is already being handled in the UNCLOS (United Nations Convention on the Law of the Sea) arbitral tribunal. So the discussion on that area with respect to our situation on the West Philippine Sea has been reserved to the arbitral tribunal to decide'.[367]

Finally, the Philippines tried to portray the institution of arbitral proceedings against China as an action that 'benefits all nations' and through which the Philippines is 'able to reinforce unimpeded commerce and ... to do away with the threat to freedom of navigation from the region',[368] thereby indirectly implying that China was impeding freedom of navigation and lawful commerce in the South China Sea.[369] At a meeting in Brussels, Foreign Affairs Secretary del Rosario declared with regard to the arbitration proceedings: 'For ASEAN and the rest of the global community, the clarification of maritime entitlements under UNCLOS would assure peace, security, stability and freedom of navigation in the South China Sea'.[370]

---

[364] RP DFA, 'SFA Statement on the UNCLOS Arbitral Proceedings Against China' (22 January 2013) (n 351). See also Albert F del Rosario, 'Shaping the Future of Asia' (n 357).

[365] 'DFA: PH Arbitration Case Grounded on Rule of Law' (25 May 2013) (n 363).

[366] See 'Managing the South China Sea and other Regional Security Issues' (9 July 2013) (n 255), and 'Response of the DFA Spokesperson to the Recent Statement of the Chinese Ministry of Foreign Affairs on the West Philippine Sea Issue' (15 July 2013) (n 288).

[367] 'Noy Ponders Visit to China for September Expo' (15 August 2013) www.philstar.com.

[368] 'DFA Promotes PHL Foreign Policy to Cebu Youth, Highlights Value of Rule of Law in Resolving Disputes in the WPS' (15 July 2013) www.dfa.gov.ph.

[369] But see PRC MFA, 'Foreign Ministry Spokesperson Hong Lei's Regular Press Conference' (21 June 2011) www.fmprc.gov.cn ('China safeguards its sovereignty and maritime rights and interests in the South China Sea, which does not affect freedom of navigation in the South China Sea enjoyed by countries according to international law. In fact, freedom of navigation in the South China Sea is out of question').

[370] 'Managing the South China Sea and other Regional Security Issues' (9 July 2013) (n 255). See also the statement of the Philippine ambassador to Washington: 'it is important for the US that freedom of navigation, unimpeded lawful commerce, and the observance

It is perhaps not surprising that this strategy was not well received in China, which considered the Philippines' 'willful act of pushing for international arbitration'[371] an act of lawfare rather than an exercise in the rule of law. It may be questioned whether the act will really contribute to achieving peace, security and regional stability.

VI. CONCLUSION

In its 'Relief Sought' the Philippines has asked the arbitral tribunal to issue an award on 13 points. In the following these points will be set out together with the possible preliminary objections that may be raised against them:

> [1] Declares that China's rights in regard to maritime areas in the South China Sea, like those of the Philippines, are those that are established by UNCLOS, and consist of a Territorial Sea and Contiguous Zone under Part II of the Convention, to an Exclusive Economic Zone under Part V, and to a Continental Shelf under Part VI

• There is no dispute between the parties over such a general and abstract declaration.[372]
• A declaration to the effect that China's rights are established by UNCLOS 'only and exclusively' on the other hand will depend on whether China's rights in regard to maritime areas can also be based on grounds outside UNCLOS, such as the concepts of historic title and historic rights.[373]

> [2] Declares that China's maritime claims in the South China Sea based on its so-called 'nine-dash line' are contrary to UNCLOS and invalid;
> [3] Requires China to bring its domestic legislation into conformity with its obligations under UNCLOS

• Whether or not China's claims are contrary to UNCLOS, as asserted by the Philippines, will depend on China's maritime entitlements generated by land territory under its sovereignty which, in turn, will require a determination of territorial sovereignty over land territory in the South China Sea and, in cases of overlapping entitlements, sea boundary delimitations.[374]
• Any declaration of invalidity will depend on whether China's maritime claims and its corresponding domestic legislation can have a basis other than UNCLOS, such as the concepts of historic title and historic rights.[375]

---

of international laws are guaranteed' ('PH Welcomes US Senate Resolution on Sea Row' (2 August 2013) www.sunstar.com.ph).

[371] PRC MFA, 'Foreign Ministry Spokesperson Hua Chunying's Remarks on the Philippines' Statement on the South China Sea' (16 July 2013) Annex I, Doc A.4.
[372] See text at section III.1.a.(1).
[373] See text at section III.1.a.(2)(b).
[374] See text at section III.1.a.(2)(a).
[375] See text at section III.1.a.

[4] Declares that Mischief Reef and McKennan Reef are submerged features that form part of the Continental Shelf of the Philippines under Part VI of the Convention, and that China's occupation and construction activities on them violate the sovereign rights of the Philippines;

[5] Requires that China end its occupation of and activities on Mischief Reef and McKennan Reef;

[6] Declares that Gaven Reef and Subi Reef are submerged features in the South China Sea that are not above sea level at high tide, are not islands under the Convention, and are not located on China's Continental Shelf, and that China's occupation of and construction activities on these features are unlawful;

[7] Requires China to terminate its occupation of and activities on Gaven Reef and Subi Reef.

• The declarations and requests are all inextricably linked with the question of sovereignty over land territory, either over the reefs themselves, proper islands in the vicinity of these reefs, or the Spratly Islands as an island group.[376] The same linkage exists between the declarations and requests on the one hand and the question of maritime delimitation on the other.[377]

• Any declaration of unlawfulness of the occupation of and construction on these reefs will depend on whether China enjoys historic title or historic rights over the reefs in question.[378]

• If China's construction activities on these reefs qualify as construction of 'artificial islands', as claimed by the Philippines, these activities will be excluded from the compulsory jurisdiction of the Tribunal under Article 297(1) UNCLOS provided that the artificial islands have been constructed by China as a coastal State within its EEZ or on its continental shelf.[379] The question of whether these reefs are located within China's EEZ or on its continental shelf, in turn, will depend on territorial sovereignty over islands or island groups in the South China Sea and, in case of overlapping claims, sea boundary delimitations.[380]

• If the reefs have been occupied by the PLA, and the structures erected by China on these reefs are 'military structures and facilities', as claimed by the Philippines, the occupation of and construction activities on them will be subject to the 'military activities' exception under Article 298(1)(b) UNCLOS.[381]

• Any general and abstract declaration that Mischief Reef and McKennan Reef 'form part of the Continental Shelf of the Philippines' will prejudice the rights of third States not party to the proceedings.[382]

[8] Declares that Scarborough Shoal, Johnson Reef, Cuarteron Reef and Fiery Cross Reef are submerged features that are below sea level at high tide, except

---

[376] See text at section III.1.a.(2)(a).
[377] See text at section III.1.c.
[378] See text at section III.1.a.(2)(b).
[379] See text at section III.1.b.
[380] See text at section III.1.a(2) and III.1.c.
[381] See text at section III.1.c.
[382] See text at section III.3.a.

that each has small protrusions that remain above water at high tide, which are "rocks" under Article 121(3) of the Convention and which therefore generate entitlements only to a Territorial Sea no broader than 12 M; and that China has unlawfully claimed maritime entitlements beyond 12 M from these features;

[9] Requires that China refrain from preventing Philippine vessels from exploiting in a sustainable manner the living resources in the waters adjacent to Scarborough Shoal and Johnson Reef, and from undertaking other activities inconsistent with the Convention at or in the vicinity of these features.

• A declaration that China has unlawfully claimed maritime entitlements beyond 12nm from certain land features forming part of Johnson Reef, Cuarteron Reef and Fiery Cross Reef is inextricably linked with the question of territorial sovereignty over proper islands in the vicinity of these reefs and the Spratly Islands as an island group, which each possess their own maritime entitlements.[383]

• Any declaration that China has unlawfully claimed maritime entitlements beyond 12nm from certain land features forming part of Scarborough Shoal will depend on whether China enjoys historic title over the Shoal as a territorial entity, which would give rise to full maritime entitlements in the vicinity of those land features.[384]

• Such declarations are also inextricably linked with the question of maritime delimitation, given the overlapping claims in the South China Sea.[385]

• Any declaration that China refrain from preventing Philippine vessels from fishing in the waters adjacent to Scarborough Shoal and Johnson Reef depends on whether China enjoys historic title over these features (or, in case of Johnson Reef, the Spratly Islands as a whole) which gives rise to sovereign rights and jurisdiction in the adjacent waters, or whether China enjoys historic rights, including sovereign rights over the living resources and jurisdiction with regard to other activities, in the waters adjacent to these features.[386]

• If the waters adjacent to Scarborough Shoal and Johnson Reef are part of China's EEZ, any dispute over China excluding Philippine vessels from fishing in this zone will be exempted from the compulsory jurisdiction of the Tribunal under Articles 297(3)(a) and 298(1)(b) UNCLOS.[387] Whether this is the case will depend on China's status as 'a coastal State' in the South China Sea and whether these land features are located within China's EEZ or on its continental shelf. These questions, in turn, will depend on territorial sovereignty over islands or island groups in the South China Sea and, in case of overlapping entitlements, sea boundary delimitations.[388]

---

[383] See text at section III.1.a.(2)(a).
[384] See text at section III.1.a.(2)(b).
[385] See text at section III.1.c.
[386] See text at section III.1.a.(2)(b).
[387] See text at section III.1.b. and section III.1.c.
[388] See text at section III.1.a.(2) and section III.1.c.

• Finally, there is no dispute between the parties over the general and abstract request that China refrain from activities inconsistent with UNCLOS in the vicinity of Scarborough Shoal and Johnson Reef.[389]

> [10] Declares that the Philippines is entitled under UNCLOS to a 12 M Territorial Sea, a 200 M Exclusive Economic Zone, and a Continental Shelf under Parts II, V and VI of UNCLOS, measured from its archipelagic baselines.

• There is no dispute between the parties over a declaration in such general and abstract terms.[390]
• A declaration *erga omnes* in such general and abstract terms would, if taken at face value, prejudice the rights of third States not parties to the proceedings.[391]

> [11] Declares that China has unlawfully claimed, and has unlawfully exploited, the living and non-living resources in the Philippines' Exclusive Economic Zone and Continental Shelf, and has unlawfully prevented the Philippines from exploiting living and non-living resources within its Exclusive Economic Zone and Continental Shelf.

• The question of whether or not China claimed or acted '*in* the Philippines' Exclusive Economic Zone and Continental Shelf' cannot be answered without determining the extent of the Philippines' maritime entitlements. This will not be possible without determining the territorial sovereignty over the islands and island groups in the South China Sea and, in light of the competing claims, without engaging in sea boundary delimitations.[392]

> [12] Declares that China has unlawfully interfered with the exercise by the Philippines of its rights to navigation and other rights under the Convention in areas within and beyond 200 M of the Philippines' archipelagic baselines;
> [13] Requires that China desist from these unlawful activities.

• The question of unlawfulness of the alleged interference with navigation will depend on the status of the maritime areas in question. If the areas constitute Chinese internal or historic waters, China will be competent to regulate navigation. Whether this is the case will depend on whether China enjoys historic title over the island groups in the South China Sea or historic rights over the waters in their vicinity.[393]

In conclusion, none of the 13 points of the 'Relief Sought' either gives rise to a dispute concerning the interpretation or application of the Convention or can be addressed without considering matters which are or have been validly removed from the jurisdiction of the Tribunal.

---

[389] See text at section III.1.a.(1).
[390] See text at section III.1.a.(1).
[391] See text at section III.3.a.
[392] See text at section III.1.a.(2) and section III.1.c.
[393] See text at section III.1.a.(2)(b).

This would not be the first time that an arbitral tribunal established under Annex VII to UNCLOS has decided that it is without jurisdiction to rule on the merits of the dispute.[394] The Tribunal established to hear the case brought by the Philippines against China would be well advised to do the same.[395]

---

[394] See *Southern Bluefin Tuna Case (Australia and New Zealand v Japan)* (Award on Jurisdiction and Admissibility) (2000) 119 ILR 508, 527 [72(1)].

[395] For the sake of completeness it may be added that there is also no prospect of compulsory conciliation under UNCLOS, art 289(1)(a)(i) which is applicable only in case of disputes 'arising subsequent to the entry into force of this Convention', ie after 16 November 1994. As aptly pointed out by Philippines Foreign Affairs Secretary del Rosario: 'The South China Sea disputes have been around for decades' ('Managing the South China Sea and other Regional Security Issues' (9 July 2013) (n 255)). See also Notification and Statement of Claims, para 25 ('dating back at least to 1995, the Philippines and China have exchanged views regarding the settlement of their disputes').

3

Issues of Jurisdiction in Cases of Default of Appearance

MICHAEL SHENG-TI GAU

I. INTRODUCTION

O N 22 JANUARY 2013, the Government of the Philippines presented China with a Notification and Statement of Claim under Article 287 and Annex VII of the United Nations Convention on the Law of the Sea (UNCLOS or the Convention).[1] The document was aimed at initiating arbitral proceedings to challenge China's territorial and maritime entitlements in the South China Sea (SCS) and the underlying seabed, which the Philippines requests the Arbitral Tribunal to declare as its exclusive economic zone (EEZ) and continental shelf. Based on the 'Philippines' Claims', as set out in section III of the Notification and Statement of Claim,[2] the following five groups of claims may be identified:

- First, China's rights concerning maritime areas in the South China Sea are those established by UNCLOS only, and consist of a territorial sea, contiguous zone, EEZ and continental shelf. China's maritime claims based on the 'nine-dash line' contravene UNCLOS and are invalid.[3]
- Second, Mischief Reef, McKennan Reef, Gaven Reef and Subi Reef are submerged features which are not above sea level at high tide and thus do not qualify as islands or rocks in terms of Article 121 UNCLOS. None of them are located on China's continental shelf, while Mischief Reef and McKennan Reef are part of the continental shelf of the Philippines. China's occupation of and construction

---

[1] See Republic of the Philippines (RP), Department of Foreign Affairs (DFA), Notification and Statement of Claim (22 January 2013) Annex I, Doc B.2 (Notification and Statement of Claim).

[2] See ibid, para 31. The Philippines' Claims comprises 10 bullet points. These 'claims' are largely identical with the 13 bullet points set out in para 41 of the Notification and Statement of Claim which presents the 'Relief Sought' by the Philippines. In the following reference is made to the bullet points of both the 'Claims' and the 'Relief Sought'.

[3] Claims, bullet points 1, 2; see also Relief Sought, bullet points 1–3.

activities on these four maritime features are unlawful and shall be terminated.[4]

- Third, Scarborough Shoal, Johnson Reef, Cuarteron Reef, and Fiery Cross Reef shall be considered as rocks under Article 121(3) UNCLOS, and may only generate entitlement to a territorial sea. Having unlawfully claimed maritime entitlements beyond 12 nautical miles (nm) from these features, China shall refrain from preventing Philippine vessels from exploiting the living resources in the waters adjacent to Scarborough Shoal and Johnson Reef, and from undertaking other activities inconsistent with UNCLOS at or in the vicinity of these features.[5]
- Fourth, the Philippines is entitled under UNCLOS to a 12nm territorial sea, a 200nm EEZ, and a continental shelf measured from its archipelagic baselines. China has unlawfully claimed and exploited the living and non-living resources in that those areas, and has prevented the Philippines from exploiting living and non-living resources therein.[6]
- Fifth, China has unlawfully interfered with the exercise by the Philippines of its rights to navigation and other rights under UNCLOS within and beyond the Philippines' EEZ. China shall desist from these unlawful activities.[7]

On 19 February 2013 China officially refused to participate in the arbitral proceedings.[8] One reason for the refusal is that China considers the 'claims for arbitration as raised by the Philippines' as not falling 'under the compulsory dispute settlement procedures as contained in UNCLOS'.[9] Since there appears to be a dispute between the two countries over whether the Arbitral Tribunal has jurisdiction to entertain the case, the Arbitral Tribunal is obliged by Article 288(4) UNCLOS to decide such an issue as a preliminary matter.

It has also been made clear that China will neither appear nor present written and oral arguments as respondent in this arbitration. Such a default of appearance makes special procedural rules applicable. Most importantly, according to Article 9 of UNCLOS Annex VII, the Arbitral Tribunal is obliged to satisfy itself, inter alia, that it has jurisdiction over the dispute before making its Award. The present chapter will focus on the question of the Tribunal's jurisdiction but, before doing so, will briefly

---

[4] Claims, bullet points 3–5; see also Relief Sought, bullet points 4–7.

[5] Claims, bullet points 6, 7; see also Relief Sought, bullet points 8, 9.

[6] Claims, bullet points 8, 9; see also Relief Sought, bullet points 10, 11.

[7] Claims, bullet point 10; see also Relief Sought, bullet points 12, 13.

[8] See PRC MFA, 'Chinese Spokesperson Hong Lei's remarks on China returned the Philippines' Notification on the Submission of South China Sea Issue to International Arbitration' (19 February 2013) Annex I, Doc A.17.

[9] See PRC MFA, 'Foreign Ministry Spokesperson Hua Chunying's Remarks on the Philippines' Efforts in Pushing for the Establishment of the Arbitral Tribunal in Relation to the Disputes between China and the Philippines in the South China Sea' (26 April 2013) Annex I, Doc A.14.

address the question of whether the parties have even 'accepted' the Tribunal, being an Annex VII Arbitral Tribunal, as the procedure for the settlement of the disputes in question.[10]

China and the Philippines are parties to UNCLOS.[11] Accordingly, both parties are bound by the dispute resolution procedures provided for in Part XV of UNCLOS in respect of any dispute between them concerning the interpretation or application of the Convention. Article 287 UNCLOS allows parties a choice of binding procedures for the settlement of their disputes, but neither party has made a written declaration choosing one of the particular means of dispute settlement set out in Article 287(1). Accordingly, both Parties are deemed to have 'accepted' arbitration in accordance with Annex VII to UNCLOS.[12] Article 298 UNCLOS makes provision for States to make written declarations to the effect that they do 'not accept any one or more' of the compulsory dispute settlement procedures provided for in section 2 of Part XV of UNCLOS with respect to certain categories of disputes. China has expressly declared that it 'does not accept any of the procedures provided for in Section 2 of Part XV', including Annex VII arbitral tribunals, with respect to all categories of disputes that can be excluded under Article 298. The Philippines has also made a declaration referring to Article 298. The question of the 'acceptance' of an Annex VII arbitral tribunal as a procedure for the settlement of disputes is closely linked to the question of its jurisdiction and will be examined below in the context of the Arbitral Tribunal's jurisdiction.[13] To the extent that the Tribunal is lacking jurisdiction over disputes because of an Article 298 declaration it is also not an accepted procedure for the settlement of those disputes.

II. DEFAULT OF APPEARANCE AND ENSUING DUTIES OF THE TRIBUNAL

China's default of appearance brings into play UNCLOS, Article 9 of Annex VII, which provides that:

> If one of the parties to the dispute does not appear before the arbitral tribunal or fails to defend its case, the other party may request the tribunal to continue the proceedings and to make its award. Absence of a party or failure of a party to defend its case shall not constitute a bar to the proceedings. *Before making its award, the arbitral tribunal must satisfy itself* not only *that it has jurisdiction over the dispute* but also that the claim is well founded in fact and law.[14]

---

[10] This question is usually addressed by arbitral tribunals at the outset; see eg *Barbados v Trinidad and Tobago* (2006) 27 RIAA 147, 203–04 [191]–[92]; *Land Reclamation in and around the Straits of Johor (Malaysia v Singapore)* (Arbitral Award on Agreed Terms) (2005) 27 RIAA 136, 137 [2–3].

[11] The Philippines became a party to UNCLOS on 8 May 1984 and China on 7 June 1996.

[12] See UNCLOS, art 287(3). See also Notification and Statement of Claim, para 36.

[13] See section V. below.

[14] UNCLOS Annex VII, art 9 (emphasis added).

The drafting history of the provision shows that the final decision in choosing the term 'claim' (instead of 'award') in the last sentence of Article 9 was to bring the provision in line with Article 53 of the Statute of the International Court of Justice (ICJ or the Court).[15] Therefore, it seems justified to take the commentary on Article 53[16] as guidance when interpreting the last sentence of Article 9 of Annex VII. It follows that, in the event of default of appearance, the 'default' award of the Arbitral Tribunal is not necessarily in favour of the appearing party. The Tribunal cannot automatically find that it has jurisdiction, that the case is admissible, or that the underlying claim is well founded. Rather, the Tribunal can only decide in favour of that appearing party if such an award is justified on both procedural and substantive grounds.[17]

Given China's well-known opposition to the present case, the Tribunal must not reach its decision on such preliminary matters like jurisdiction lightly, just because China is absent from the proceedings and is not submitting legal argument. If the judgments of the ICJ in the two *Icelandic Fisheries* cases are anything to go by, the Arbitral Tribunal must consider any objections which might, in its view, be raised by China against its jurisdiction.[18] While China has made it clear that it will not participate in the proceedings, it has publicly raised, and could further raise, objections to the jurisdiction of the Tribunal.[19] All such objections are, however, informal and not submitted in the form of preliminary objections or in any other way requested by Part XV of and Annex VII to UNCLOS. Again, if the Tribunal adopted the practice of the ICJ, it would have to consider such informal objections as relevant.[20]

Article 9 of Annex VII imposes an obligation upon the Tribunal to investigate whether it has jurisdiction or not. This raises the question as to what extent the Tribunal is obliged to search for possible jurisdictional problems and to discuss every conceivable objection to the Tribunal's

---

[15] See Myron H Nordquist, Shabtai Rosenne and Louis B Sohn (eds), *United Nations Convention on the Law of the Sea 1982: A Commentary*, vol V (Dordrecht, Martinus Nijhoff, 1989) 433–34 MN A.VII.15, 389–90 MN A.VI.145.

[16] See eg Hans von Mangoldt and Andreas Zimmermann, 'Article 53' in Andreas Zimmermann and others (eds), *The Statute of the International Court of Justice: A Commentary*, Oxford Commentaries on International Law, 2nd edn (Oxford, OUP, 2012) 1324–54.

[17] ibid, 1159–60.

[18] See *Fisheries Jurisdiction (United Kingdom v Iceland)* (Jurisdiction) [1973] ICJ Rep 3, 7 [12]: 'It is to be regretted that the Government of Iceland has failed to appear in order to plead the objections to the Court's jurisdiction which it is understood to entertain. Nevertheless, the Court, in accordance with its Statute and its settled jurisprudence, must examine *proprio motu* the question of its own jurisdiction to consider the Application of the United Kingdom. … the Court, in examining its own jurisdiction, will consider those objections which might, in its view, be raised against its jurisdiction'. See also *Fisheries Jurisdiction (Federal Republic of Germany v Iceland)* (Jurisdiction) [1973] ICJ Rep 49, 54 [13].

[19] See eg PRC MFA, 'Foreign Ministry Spokesperson Hua Chunying's Remarks on the Philippines' Efforts in Pushing for the Establishment of the Arbitral Tribunal in Relation to the Disputes between China and the Philippines in the South China Sea' (26 April 2013) Annex I, Doc A.14.

[20] von Mangoldt and Zimmermann, 'Article 53' 1344 MN 54.

jurisdiction that a creative party like China might raise. Again, the commentary on Article 53 ICJ Statute provides insightful guidance.[21] The obligation for the ICJ under Article 53(2) is much higher than that for establishing *prima facie* jurisdiction, which is required by Article 41 ICJ Statute governing provisional measures.[22] This is because Article 53(2) allows for final and binding judgments on jurisdiction and ultimately also on the merits of the case.[23] Applying this differentiation to the UNCLOS regime, the level of investigatory obligation incumbent upon the Tribunal under Article 9 of Annex VII (dealing with final and binding awards)[24] is thus much higher than that under Article 290 UNCLOS (governing provisional measures and expressly providing for a *prima facie* test). Thus, the Tribunal must not only establish prima facie jurisdiction, but it must 'satisfy' itself that it has jurisdiction. The ICJ stated in the *Nicaragua* case:

> The use of the term 'satisfy itself' [...] implies that the Court *must attain the same degree of certainty as in any other case that the claim of the party appearing is sound in law, and so far as the nature of the case permits, that the facts on which it is based are supported by convincing evidence.* For the purpose of deciding whether the claim is well founded in law, the principle *jura novit curia* signifies that the Court is not solely dependent on the argument of the parties before it with respect to the applicable law, so that the absence of one party has less impact. [...] As to the facts of the case, in principle the Court is not bound to confine its consideration to the material formally submitted to it by the parties. Nevertheless, the Court cannot by its own enquiries entirely make up for the absence of one of the Parties; that absence, in a case of this kind involving extensive question of fact, must necessarily limit the extent to which the court is informed of the facts'.[25]

Given the principle of *jura novit curia*, issues of burden of proof do not arise as to whether the claim is well founded in law.[26] As the ICJ put it: 'It being the duty of the Court itself to ascertain and apply the relevant law in the given circumstances of the case, the burden of establishing or proving rules of international law cannot be imposed upon any of the parties, for the law lies within the judicial knowledge of the Court'.[27] Applying this jurisprudence to the present case, it is for the Tribunal to *attain the same degree of certainty as in any other case* that it has jurisdiction.

The jurisdiction of Annex VII arbitral tribunals is not unlimited. On the contrary, Article 286 provides that the compulsory jurisdiction under section 2 of Part XV of UNCLOS is subject to a threefold limitation:

---

[21] ibid, 1345 MN 55.

[22] However, the *prima facie* test is not part of the wording of the Statute of the ICJ, art 41.

[23] von Mangoldt and Zimmermann (n 16) 1345 MN 55.

[24] See UNCLOS Annex VII, art 11.

[25] *Military and Paramilitary Activities in and against Nicaragua (Nicaragua v United States of America)* (Merits) [1986] ICJ Rep 14, 24–25 [29–30] (emphasis added).

[26] von Mangoldt and Zimmermann (n 16) 1346 MN 57.

[27] *Fisheries Jurisdiction (United Kingdom v Iceland)* (Merits) [1974] ICJ Rep 3, 9–10 [17]; *Fisheries Jurisdiction (Federal Republic of Germany v Iceland)* (Merits) [1974] ICJ Rep 175, 181 [18].

first, jurisdiction is limited to 'any dispute concerning the interpretation or application of this Convention'.[28] Second, jurisdiction exists only 'where no settlement has been reached by recourse to section 1'. Third, jurisdiction is generally subject to the limitations and exceptions set out in section 3.

The question of whether there is a dispute between the parties, and its nature and scope is thus central to any decision on jurisdiction. If there is no dispute, because the subject-matters raised are hypothetical, non-contentious or unreal, the Tribunal will be without jurisdiction. The same is true if the dispute submitted to the Tribunal for compulsory settlement under section 2 of UNCLOS is not identical with the dispute for which no settlement has been reached by recourse to section 1, or if the dispute falls under the category of disputes removed from the Tribunal's jurisdiction under section 3.

III. THE REQUIREMENT OF A DISPUTE BETWEEN THE PARTIES

It is for the Tribunal to determine the nature and scope of the dispute or disputes between the parties.[29] The Tribunal is not bound by the view of the Philippines as expressed in its Notification and Statement of Claim. Taking the criteria developed by the arbitral tribunal in *Barbados v Trinidad and Tobago* as guidance, the Tribunal should take into consideration whether a subject-matter 'either forms part of, or is sufficiently closely related to, the dispute submitted', whether 'the record of the negotiations shows that it was part of the subject-matter on the table during those negotiations', and whether the subject-matters in question are treated in law as a single question.[30]

1. Determination of the Disputes

In the judgment of the *Mavrommatis* case, the Permanent Court of International Justice (PCIJ) defined a dispute as 'a disagreement on a point of law or fact, a conflict of legal views or of interests between two persons'.[31] Seen as an elaboration of this definition, Merrills said that a 'dispute may be defined as a specific disagreement concerning a matter of fact, law or policy in which a claim or assertion of one party is met with refusal, counter-claim or denial by another'.[32] Lowe and Collier also describe a dispute as 'a specific disagreement relating to a question

---

[28] See also UNCLOS, art 288(1).

[29] *Barbados v Trinidad and Tobago* (2006) 27 RIAA 147, 204–05 [198]; 208–09 [213].

[30] ibid, [213].

[31] *Mavrommatis Palestine Concessions (Greece v United Kingdom)* (Objection to the Jurisdiction of the Court) 1924 PCIJ Rep Series A No 2, 11.

[32] John G Merrills, *International Dispute Settlement*, 5th ed (Cambridge, CUP, 2011) 1.

of rights or interests in which the parties proceed by way of claims, counter-claims, denials and so on'.[33] One of the hallmarks of a dispute is thus a combination of claim and counter-claim. In the following the actual claims and counter-claims made by the parties will be examined in order to determine whether any disputes exist between the parties and, if so, what their nature and scope are. Only then is it possible to examine whether they concern the application or interpretation of the Convention, or whether they have been removed from the jurisdiction of the Tribunal by way of Article 298 UNCLOS.

a. The First Group of Claims Concerning China's Maritime Areas in the South China Sea

The first group of claims, as identified above, relates to China's rights concerning maritime areas in the South China Sea.[34] China's rights in regard to maritime areas in the South China Sea are to be those established by UNCLOS and are to consist of rights to a territorial sea, contiguous zone, EEZ and continental shelf. In particular, the Philippines claims that 'China's maritime claims in the South China Sea *based on* its so-called "nine dash line" are contrary to UNCLOS and invalid.'[35] The words 'based on' are used by the Philippines interchangeably with 'within'[36] or 'encompassed by'.[37] For example, the Philippines claims that:

> China claims almost the entirety of the South China Sea, and all of the maritime features, *as its own*. [...] According to China, it is *sovereign* over all the waters, all of the seabed, and all the maritime features within this 'nine dash line'.[38]

The Philippines creates the impression that China is claiming sovereignty over the maritime areas in the South China Sea lying 'within' or 'encompassed' by the nine-dash line and that this claim to sovereignty over the waters, seabed and features is 'based on' the nine-dash line. However, this is far from what China really claims.

The Philippines states that 'China first officially depicted the "nine dash line" in a letter of 7 May 2009 to the United Nations Secretary General'.[39] The history of the nine-dash line is, however, much older.[40] The Chinese letter (or, more correctly, the Note Verbale) sent to the Secretary-General was a response to the Joint Submission by Malaysia and Viet Nam to the Commission on the Limits of the Continental Shelf concerning the outer

[33] John Collier and Vaughan Lowe, *The Settlement of Disputes in International Law: Institutions and Procedures* (Oxford, OUP, 1999) 1.

[34] See text accompanying n 4.

[35] Claims, bullet point 2 (emphasis added); see also Relief Sought, bullet point 2.

[36] Notification and Statement of Claim, paras 2, 11.

[37] ibid, paras 3, 12.

[38] ibid, para 11 (emphasis added).

[39] ibid.

[40] See Zhiguo Gao and Bing Bing Jia, 'The Nine-Dash Line in the South China Sea: History, Status, and Implications' (2013) 107 *American Journal of International Law* 98, 100–08.

limits of the continental shelf beyond 200nm.[41] With that Note Verbale China protested an infringement of its 'sovereignty, sovereign rights and jurisdiction in the South China Sea'. China declared that:

> [it] has indisputable sovereignty over the islands in the South China Sea and the adjacent waters, and enjoys sovereign rights and jurisdiction over the relevant waters as well as the seabed and subsoil thereof *(see attached map)*.[42]

While the attached map depicted a nine-dash line in the South China Sea, the term 'nine-dash line' was not used in the text of the Note Verbale. More importantly, China did not claim in the Note that it was 'sovereign over all the waters, all of the seabed and all the maritime features' within the nine-dash line, as claimed by the Philippines. What China did claim was sovereignty over the four groups of islands in the South China Sea enclosed by the nine-dash line depicted on the map,[43] namely the Dongsha [Pratas], Xisha [Paracel], Zhongsha [Macclesfield Bank, including Scarborough Shoal] and Nansha [Spratly] Archipelagos.[44] The 'attached map' referred to the four groups of islands or archipelagos, not to the waters, enclosed by the nine-dash line. Based on its territorial sovereignty over the archipelagos, China claims 'sovereignty' over their adjacent waters and 'sovereign rights and jurisdiction' over the relevant waters surrounding them. The claim to adjacent waters is to be understood as a claim to the territorial sea over which the coastal State enjoys sovereignty,[45] while the claim to relevant waters relates to the EEZ and the continental shelf over which the coastal State enjoys sovereign rights and jurisdiction.[46]

This understanding is confirmed by another Note Verbale, dated 14 April 2011, sent by China to the UN Secretary-General. Surprisingly, there is no mention of this Note Verbale in the Philippines' Notification and Statement of Claim despite the fact that it was sent in direct response to an earlier Note Verbale by the Philippines.[47] That Note reads in the relevant part as follows:

---

[41] Note Verbale CML/17/2009 from the Permanent Mission of the People's Republic of China to the UN Secretary-General with regard to the joint submission made by Malaysia and Viet Nam to the Commission on the Limits of the Continental Shelf (7 May 2009), Annex I, Doc A.24 (Note Verbale CML/17/2009 (7 May 2009)).

[42] ibid (emphasis added). The map attached is also reproduced in Annex I, Doc A.24.

[43] See Zhiguo Gao, 'The South China Sea: From Conflict to Cooperation?' (1994) 25 *Ocean Development and International Law* 345, 346.

[44] The name used in Chinese is 'Quando' which means 'archipelago'.

[45] See UNCLOS, art 2(1).

[46] See UNCLOS, arts 56(1), 77(1).

[47] Note Verbale CML/8/2011 from the Permanent Mission of the People's Republic of China to the UN Secretary-General with regard to the joint submission made by Malaysia and Viet Nam to the Commission on the Limits of the Continental Shelf (14 April 2011), Annex I, Doc A.23 (Note Verbale CML/8/2011 (14 April 2011)). This Note was sent with reference to the Republic of the Philippines' Note Verbale No 000228 dated 5 April 2011 (Philippines Note Verbale (5 April 2011)). The Philippines' Note Verbale of 5 April 2011 can be found at www.un.org/Depts/los.

China has indisputable *sovereignty over the islands* in the South China Sea and the *adjacent waters*, and enjoys *sovereign rights and jurisdiction over the relevant waters as well as the seabed and subsoil thereof.* … Since 1930s, the Chinese Government has given publicity several times the geographical scope of China's Nansha [Spratly] Islands and the names of its components. China's Nansha Islands is therefore clearly defined. In addition, under the relevant provisions of the 1982 United Nations Convention on the Law of the Sea, as well as the Law of the People's Republic of China on the Territorial Sea and the Contiguous Zone (1992) and the Law of the Exclusive Economic Zone and the Continental Shelf of the People's Republic of China (1998), *China's Nansha Islands is fully entitled to Territorial Sea, Exclusive Economic Zone (EEZ) and Continental Shelf.*[48]

This Note also does not mention any claim to sovereignty over maritime areas 'based on' the nine-dash line. What China does claim in the South China Sea in terms of maritime areas are the zones under UNCLOS, namely, a territorial Sea, EEZ and continental shelf. This is made clear with regard to the Nansha [Spratly] Islands which formed the subject-matter of the Note Verbale in question, but applies equally to the other three island groups in the South China Sea claimed by China. There is thus no conflict, disagreement or dispute between China and the Philippines with regard to the legal basis of their maritime zone claims. Both sides agree that the maritime zones that can be claimed in the South China Sea are the ones established by UNCLOS and comprise a territorial sea, EEZ and continental shelf.

This shows that the disputes between the parties are not about UNCLOS as the legal basis of their claims to maritime zones, but about territorial sovereignty over the island groups in the South China Sea and the extent of the maritime zones generated by these island groups. The Philippines seems to be afraid that the maritime zones that China can claim from these islands under UNCLOS comprise the whole area enclosed by the nine-dash line. That the dispute is about territorial sovereignty over the maritime features in the Nansha [Spratly] and Zhongsha [Macclesfield Bank, including Scarborough Shoal] archipelagos is also shown by the fact that several of the maritime features are claimed by both China and the Philippines. Each party claims and occupies land features in the Nansha [Spratly] Archipelago which are also claimed by the other party. For example, the Philippines, in its Notification and Statement of Claim, identifies seven reefs in the Spratlys claimed and occupied by China to which it also lays claim as part of what it calls the 'Kalayaan Island Group' (KIG).[49] Perhaps not surprisingly, the Philippines does not mention the eight maritime features in the Spratlys which it occupies but which are claimed by China as part of its Nansha Archipelago. The maritime features in the Spratlys illegally occupied by the Philippines are as follows:

---

[48] ibid (emphasis added).
[49] See Claims, bullet points 4–6.

Chinese Name[50]	English Name	Philippine Name	Coordinates	
Beizi Dao	Northeast Cay	Parola	11°27′N	114°22′E
Zhongye Qunjiao	Thitu Island	Pagasa	11°01′–11°06′N	114°11′–114°24′E
Nanyue Dao	Loaita Island	Dugao Kota	10°40′N	114°25′E
Feixin Dao	Flat Island	Patag Flat	10°49′N	115°50′E
Mahuan Dao	Nanshan Island	Lawak	10°44′N	115°48′E
Xiyue Dao	West York Island	Likas	11°05′N	115°02′E
Siling Jiao	Commodore Reef	Rizal Reef	8°22′–8°24′N	115°11′–115°17′E
Shuanghuang Shazhou	Double Egg Yolk Shoal[51]	Panata	10°42′–10°43′N	114°19′–114°20′E

The map on the opposite page shows the maritime features claimed by both the Philippines and China. The features occupied by China are depicted in blue; the features occupied by the Philippines are shown in red.

The territorial disputes between the Philippines and China over these land features are not mentioned in the Notification and Statement of Claim, yet they illustrate that the territorial disputes between the two States are not limited to the ones the Philippines chose to present. But these territorial disputes are the root cause of the present case. Considering that territorial disputes have been removed from the jurisdiction of the Tribunal by way of China's 2006 declaration,[52] it is not surprising that the Philippines tries to present the situation as a dispute over the legal basis of maritime zones in the South China Sea. The question of the parties' maritime zones in the South China Sea, even if based on UNCLOS, cannot be decided without determining the question of territorial sovereignty over the Nansha [Spratly] and Zhongsha [Macclesfield Bank, including Scarborough Shoal] Archipelagos which give rise to these maritime zones.

To conclude, the first group of claims made by the Philippines is based on a misunderstanding or misinterpretation of what China actually claimed in its Notes Verbales of 2009 and 2011. China's claims to maritime zones in the South China Sea are not 'based on its so-called "nine dash line"', but on UNCLOS. There is thus no dispute in this respect. The real dispute is about territorial sovereignty over the Nansha [Spratly] and Zhongsha [Macclesfield Bank, including Scarborough Shoal] Archipelagos, which is not subject to the Tribunal's jurisdiction.[53]

---

[50] The names of the South China Sea islands are those adopted by the PRC National Committee on Geographical Names and published in the People's Daily, 25 April 1983. The list of all names of South China Sea islands may be found at www.unanhai.com/nhzddm. htm.

[51] Double Egg Yolk Shoal is also known as Loaita Nan.

[52] See below section V.

[53] See also Robert Beckman, 'The Philippines v. China Case and the South China Sea Disputes' (Asia Society/LKY SPP Conference, South China Sea: Central to Asia-Pacific Peace and Security, New York, 13–15 March 2013) 1, cil.nus.edu.sg/wp ('The fundamental dispute in the South China Sea concerns sovereignty over off-shore islands').

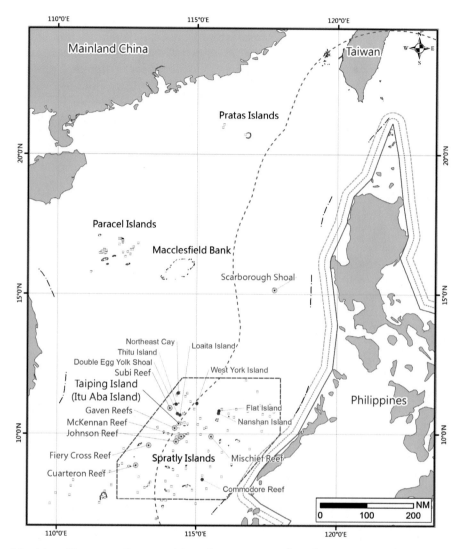

Maritime Features Occupied by China and by the Philippines in the Spratly Islands[54]

b. The Second Group of Claims Concerning the Sovereignty of Certain Reefs

The second group of claims, as identified above,[55] concerns the Philippines' claims that Mischief Reef, McKennan Reef, Gaven Reef and Subi Reef are illegally occupied by China, and that China has declared maritime zones around them, from which it has illegally sought to exclude the Philippines

[54] The author is grateful to Mr Jui-Hsien for preparing this map.
[55] See text accompanying n 4 above.

and other States.[56] According to the Philippines, these reefs are mere low-tide elevations, none of which are located on China's continental shelf, while Mischief Reef and McKennan Reef are part of the continental shelf of the Philippines. Low-tide elevations which are located outside a coastal State's territorial sea are subject to the sovereignty of the State on whose continental shelf they lie, or are part of the international seabed.

In order for there to be a dispute between the parties, China would have to claim that (a) the four reefs are located on China's continental shelf which allows China to acquire sovereignty over these reefs, (b) the four reefs qualify as islands in terms of Article 121(2) UNCLOS which generate a territorial sea, EEZ and continental shelf, (c) the four reefs qualify as rocks under Article 121(3) with their own territorial sea, (d) Mischief Reef and McKennan Reef are not part of the Philippines' continental shelf, or, more generally, that (e) the four reefs are part of the Nansha [Spratly] Archipelago which is subject to China's territorial sovereignty and which generates its own maritime zones.[57]

The four reefs in question are all part of the Nansha [Spratly] Archipelago. In its Note Verbales of 14 April 2011, China claimed that it has 'indisputable sovereignty over the islands in the South China Sea', including the Nansha Islands; that the 'so-called Kalayaan Island Group (KIG) claimed by the Republic of Philippines is in fact part of China's Nansha Islands'; and that 'China's Nansha Islands is fully entitled to Territorial Sea, Exclusive Economic Zone (EEZ) and Continental Shelf'.[58] There is thus clearly a dispute over whether territorial sovereignty over these reefs can be claimed and, if so, by whom. The Chinese claim to territorial sovereignty also necessarily implies a denial of the Philippines' claims that Mischief Reef and McKennan Reef are part of the continental shelf of the Philippines and that China unlawfully occupies and engages in unlawful construction activities on these reefs. At the heart of the dispute is thus, again, the question of territorial sovereignty over land features (either the Nansha Archipelago as a territorial unit or individual maritime features forming part of the Nansha Archipelago) which is excluded from the Tribunal's jurisdiction by way of China's 2006 declaration.[59]

The dispute over territorial sovereignty between the two countries, however, is not limited to these four reefs but extends to all islands, rocks and maritime features of China's Nansha [Spratly] Islands that are also claimed by the Philippines as forming part of its Kalayaan Island Group. The same is true for the land features forming Scarborough Shoal, which is also claimed by both countries. While the Philippines has tried to isolate the question of the legal status of these four reefs, there are numerous other

---

[56] See Notification and Statement of Claim, para 14.

[57] For (e), see text accompanying n 48 above.

[58] Note Verbale CML/8/2011 (14 April 2011) (n 47), Annex I, Doc A.23. See also Note Verbale CML/17/2009 (7 May 2009) (n 41), Annex I, Doc A.24.

[59] See section V. below.

land features in the vicinity of these reefs which are also claimed by China as part of its Nansha [Spratly] Archipelago. Some of these features are proper islands of good size which generate their own continental shelf and EEZ. These islands lie at such distance that the four reefs may well be situated on the continental shelf generated by these islands. Some of these islands are, of course, occupied by the Philippines; some are under the control of Viet Nam. China has challenged this situation of foreign occupation of its territory. However, the fact of foreign occupation cannot blur the picture that China has been claiming territorial sovereignty over all of these islands. Therefore, the question of whether or not the four reefs are part of the Chinese continental shelf cannot be answered without determining the question of whether China enjoys territorial sovereignty over these islands. But, again, this question is removed from the compulsory jurisdiction of the Tribunal. The Tribunal cannot proceed on the premise that China's claims to territorial sovereignty are irrelevant regarding all the maritime features in the Nansha Archipelago (as well as over the Archipelago as a unit), except those mentioned in the Notification and Statement of Claim. As the Philippines is not presenting the whole picture of the territorial disputes in the South China Sea to the Tribunal, the Tribunal could prejudice China's rights to territorial sovereignty in that region.

At the end of the day, it is irrelevant whether the four reefs are islands, rocks or low-tide elevations, or whether they generate any maritime zones of their own, or if they are located on China's continental shelf and within China's EEZ generated by some other proper islands under Chinese territorial sovereignty. Itu Aba [Taiping] Island may serve as an example. Within the Spratly Islands, Taiping Island is located at 10°23′N and 114°22′E, that is less than 200nm from the four reefs in question.[60] It is a proper island in terms of Article 121(2) UNCLOS. The following table shows the relative geographical positions and distances between Taiping Island and each of the four reefs that form part of the second group of claims:

Maritime Feature	Location	Distance from Itu Aba [Taiping] Island
Mischief Reef	9°54′N 115°32′E	74.7nm
McKennan Reef	9°54′N 114°28′E	29nm
Gaven Reef	10°13′N 114°13′E	12.9nm
Subi Reef	10°55′N 114°05′E	36.7nm

Itu Aba [Taiping] Island is claimed by China as part of its land territory and is administered by the authorities in Taiwan. On 9 June 1975, the Governments of the Republic of the Philippines and People's Republic of China signed a Joint Communiqué for the purpose of establishing diplomatic relations between these two Governments which provides in the relevant part:

---

[60] For the location of Itu Aba [Taiping] Island, see also the map reproduced above in section III.1.a.

The Philippine Government recognizes the Government of the People's Republic of China as the sole legal government of China, fully understands and respects the position of the Chinese Government that there is but one China and that Taiwan is an integral part of Chinese territory, and decides to remove all its official representations from Taiwan within one month from the date of signature of this communiqué.[61]

The Philippines is thus under an obligation to accept that the Itu Aba [Taiping] Island, as well as any other islands administered by the Taiwan authorities, are part of the land territory of China which can generate a Chinese EEZ and continental shelf. The fact that the Philippines also claims sovereignty over Itu Aba Island is a separate matter. The question of territorial sovereignty over Itu Aba Island, like the question of territorial sovereignty over the four reefs claimed by China, the Philippines and Viet Nam, are removed from the jurisdiction of the Tribunal.

In conclusion, while there is a dispute between the parties with regard to the second group of claims, the dispute is about territorial sovereignty over land features in the South China Sea and, potentially, the delimitation of maritime zones which they generate. Both questions are, however, excluded from the compulsory jurisdiction of the Tribunal by way of China's 2006 declaration.

c. The Third Group of Claims Concerning the 'Rock'-Status of Certain Reefs

The third group of claims, as identified above,[62] concerns the Philippines' claims that Scarborough Shoal, Johnson Reef, Cuarteron Reef, and Fiery Cross Reef are 'rocks' under Article 121(3) UNCLOS, that 'China has unlawfully claimed maritime entitlements beyond 12 M *from these features*'[63] and that it has unlawfully prevented Philippine vessels from exploiting the living resources in the waters adjacent to Scarborough Shoal and Johnson Reef.

In order for there to be a dispute between the parties, China would have to claim that the four maritime features are islands under Article 121(2) UNCLOS which are capable of generating their own maritime zones beyond a territorial sea of 12nm, and that China has a right to maritime zones, such as an EEZ and continental shelf, measured 'from these features'. However, China has made neither of these claims. On the contrary, China claims territorial sovereignty over the Nansha [Spratly] and Zhongsha [Macclesfield Bank, including Scarborough Shoal] Archipelagos as a whole, which generate a belt of maritime zones surrounding them. In addition, in case of the three maritime features situated in the Nansha [Spratly] Archipelago, namely Johnson Reef, Cuarteron Reef and Fiery

---

[61] PRC MFA, 'Joint Communique of the Government of the People's Republic of China and the Government of the Republic of the Philippines' (9 June 1975) para 6, www.fmprc.gov.cn.

[62] See text accompanying n 5 above.

[63] Claims, bullet point 6; see also Relief Sought, bullet point 8 (emphasis added).

Cross Reef, China would not have to claim any maritime zones 'from these features', as they are located in close vicinity of several islands proper in terms of Article 121(2) UNCLOS which generate an EEZ and continental shelf extending to these reefs and beyond. There is thus no need at all for China to claim island status for these features. Again, Itu Aba [Taiping] Island may serve as an example. All three reefs in the Spratlys are located less than 200nm from Itu Aba as the following table shows:

Maritime Feature	Location	Distance from Itu Aba [Taiping] Island
Johnson Reef	9°42′N 114°22′E	39.7nm
Cuarteron Reef	8°51′N 112°50′E	128.2nm
Fiery Cross Reef	9°33′N 112°54′E	78.8nm

The Philippines' Notification and Statement of Claim thus presents an incomplete and distorted picture to the Tribunal. The same applies to the claim that China unlawfully prevented Philippine vessels from exploiting the living resources in the waters adjacent to Scarborough Shoal and Johnson Reef. At the heart of this subject-matter lies, again, the territorial disputes between the two parties over parts of the Nansha [Spratly] Archipelago (which the Philippines calls the Kalayaan Island Group), and those parts of the Zhongsha Archipelago which are referred to as Scarborough Shoal. These disputes over territorial sovereignty also entail delimitation disputes concerning overlapping maritime zones extending from the two archipelagos claimed by China on the one hand, and from the Philippines archipelago on the other. None of these disputes have been presented to the Tribunal by the Philippines knowing full well that they are removed from the jurisdiction of the Tribunal.

d. The Fourth Group of Claims Concerning the Philippines' Claim to Maritime Zones and Corresponding Rights in the South China Sea

The fourth group of claims, as identified above,[64] concerns the Philippines' claims that it is entitled under UNCLOS to a 12nm territorial sea, a 200nm EEZ along with a continental shelf measured from its archipelagic baselines, that China has unlawfully claimed and exploited the living and non-living resources in that those maritime areas, and has prevented the Philippines from exploiting living and non-living resources therein.

In order for there to be a dispute between the parties, China would have to claim that the Philippines is not entitled under UNCLOS to a 12nm territorial sea, a 200nm EEZ and a continental shelf measured from its archipelagic baselines. It seems highly unlikely that China has made a claim of such absoluteness and generality denying a fellow party to

---

[64] See text accompanying n 6 above.

UNCLOS rights under the Convention to which every party is entitled. At the abstract level of entitlements to maritime zones under UNCLOS, there is thus no dispute between the parties.

With regard to the Philippines' claim that China has unlawfully acted '*in* the Philippines' Exclusive Economic Zone and Continental Shelf',[65] it is difficult to establish a Chinese counter-claim without determining the extent of the Philippines' maritime zones in the South China Sea as well as those of China. This shows that the real dispute between the Philippines and China in the South China Sea concerns maritime boundary delimitation which, in turn, is the result of territorial disputes over the Nansha [Spratly] and Zhongsha [Macclesfield Bank, including Scarborough Shoal] Archipelagos. At the heart of the Philippines' claims lies a complete denial of China's status as a coastal State which, like the Philippines, is entitled to claim a 200nm EEZ and continental shelf from its land territory in the South China Sea. According to the Philippines' Notification and Statement of Claim, all that China could be entitled to, at best, is a 12nm territorial sea around certain rocks within the undiminished 200nm EEZ and continental shelf of the Philippines. This constitutes a complete mischaracterization of both the geographical and legal situation in the South China Sea. The reason that the Philippines chooses not to deal with the questions of China's status as a coastal State and its entitlements to maritime zones in the South China Sea is, of course, that these questions concern the territorial sovereignty over the islands and delimitation of overlapping maritime entitlements – subject-matters that are removed from the compulsory jurisdiction of the Tribunal.

To conclude, there is no dispute between the parties with regard to the Philippines' general and abstract entitlement to maritime zones under UNCLOS. The claim with regard to China's alleged activities *in* the Philippines' EEZ and continental shelf cannot be adjudicated without deciding, as a preliminary question, the disputes between the two countries over territorial sovereignty and maritime boundary delimitation. As the Tribunal lacks jurisdiction over these disputes, it cannot rule on the Philippines' claim that China 'unlawfully' acted inside its maritime zones.

e. The Fifth Group of Claims Concerning the Right to Navigation

The fifth group of claims, as identified above,[66] concerns the Philippines' claim that China has unlawfully interfered with the exercise by the Philippines of its rights to navigation and other rights under UNCLOS within and beyond the Philippines' EEZ.

It must be noted at the outset that a claim of such a level of generality lacks any real substance. The Philippines fails to identify the exact location where the alleged interference took place, fails to specify what

---

[65] See Claims, bullet point 9 (emphasis added).
[66] See text accompanying n 7 above.

that 'interference' looked like, and fails to give the reasons that may have been advanced by China for such interference. One may well perceive a situation in which these so-called 'unlawful activities'[67] turn out to be lawful enforcement measures by Chinese coastguard vessels which enforce Chinese fisheries laws and regulations in the Chinese EEZ in the South China Sea.[68] Again, the Philippines' claim is based on the assumption that China is not a coastal State in the South China Sea and that there can only be the Philippines EEZ or high seas in that region. Any maritime zones (which are claimed by China, Viet Nam and others) are simply painted out of the picture.

This last claim shows again that the dispute, if there is in fact one, cannot be decided without determining the extent of the Philippines' and Chinese maritime zones in the South China Sea and, in case of overlapping zones, delimiting those zone. The question of maritime zones, however, depends on the question of territorial sovereignty over the islands in the South China Sea. Those are the subject-matters at the heart of the disputes between the two countries and both are removed from the Tribunal's jurisdiction.

f. Conclusion

A dispute requires an assertion of one party — in this case China — that is met with refusal, counter-claims or denial by another, in this case the Philippines. A dispute cannot be created unilaterally by simply making a counter-claim against a non-existing or hypothetical claim of the other party. Nor can a dispute be founded on a premise which lacks any factual or legal basis, a misrepresentation of the geographical situation, or the presentation of a partial and incomplete picture of the facts. All these problems exist in the case of the claims advanced by the Philippines. As has been shown, there is no dispute between the parties with regard to the first and fourth group of claims. With regard to the other claims presented by the Philippines the factual situation has been distorted, mischaracterised or presented in an incomplete fashion to avoid anything that could reveal the real disputes between the parties, which concern the question of territorial sovereignty over the Nansha [Spratly] and Zhongsha [Macclesfield Bank, including Scarborough Shoal] Archipelagos and the ensuing question of maritime delimitation of the overlapping maritime zones of China and the Philippines in the South China Sea — questions which have been removed from the Tribunal's jurisdiction by way of China's 2006 declaration.

---

[67] See Relief Sought, bullet point 13.
[68] See UNCLOS, art 73.

2. The Real Disputes between the Parties

The disputes between the Philippines and China over the South China Sea have existed since the 1970s when the Philippines, in violation of the Charter of the United Nations and principles of international law, illegally occupied some islands and reefs of China's Nansha [Spratly] Islands.[69] Over the years countless statements have been made on the disputes by both States. It is helpful to recall the most recent and conclusive exchange of the positions of the two parties in order to ascertain the real disputes underlying the present arbitration and to compare those with the disputes artificially presented to the Tribunal.

In 2009 and 2011, China and the Philippines addressed several Notes Verbales to the UN Secretary-General in the wake of which they set out their conflicting positions on the South China Sea. On 7 May 2009, China sent two almost identical Notes Verbales commenting on the Joint Submission by Malaysia and Viet Nam and the submission of Viet Nam to the Commission on the Limits of the Continental Shelf (CLCS) concerning the outer limits of the continental shelf beyond 200nm.[70] In those Notes, it was stated that:

> China has indisputable *sovereignty over the islands* in the South China Sea *and the adjacent waters*, and enjoys *sovereign rights and jurisdiction over the relevant waters, as well as the seabed and subsoil thereof* (see attached map). The above position is consistently held by the Chinese Government, and is widely known by the international community.[71]

Almost two years later, on 5 April 2011, the Philippines felt obliged to write a direct response to the two Chinese Notes from which it is justified to quote at length. In its Note addressed to the UN Secretary-General, the Philippines wrote:

> On the Islands and other Geological Features
> FIRST, the Kalayaan Island Group (KIG) constitutes an integral part of the Philippines. The Republic of the Philippines has sovereignty and jurisdiction over the geological features in the KIG.
>
> On the 'Water Adjacent' to the Islands and other Geological Features
> SECOND, the Philippines, under the Roman notion of *dominium maris* and the international law principle of *"la terre domine la mer"* which states that the land dominates the sea, necessarily exercises sovereignty and jurisdiction over the waters around or adjacent to each relevant geological feature in the KIG

---

[69] See eg PRC MFA, 'Foreign Ministry Spokesperson Hua Chunying's Remarks on the Philippines' Efforts in Pushing for the Establishment of the Arbitral Tribunal in Relation to the Disputes between China and the Philippines in the South China Sea' (26 April 2013) Annex I, Doc A.14.

[70] Note Verbale CML/17/2009 (7 May 2009) (n 41), Annex I, Doc A.24. See also Note Verbale CML/18/2009 from the Permanent Mission of the People's Republic of China to the UN Secretary-General with Regard to the Submission Made by Viet Nam to the Commission on the Limits of the Continental Shelf (7 May 2009) www.un.org/depts/los.

[71] ibid (emphasis added).

as provided for under the United Nations Convention on the Law of the Sea (UNCLOS).

At any rate, the extent of the waters that are 'adjacent' to the relevant geological features are definite and determinable under UNCLOS, specifically under Article 121 (Regime of Islands) of the said Convention.

On the Other 'Relevant Waters, Seabed and Subsoil' in the SCS

THIRD, since the adjacent waters of the relevant geological features are definite and subject to legal and technical measurement, the claim as well by the People's Republic of China on the '*relevant waters as well as the seabed and subsoil thereof*' (as reflected in the so-called 9-dash line map attached to Noted Verbales CML/17/1009 dated 7 May 2009 and CML/18/2009 dated 7 May 2009) outside of the aforementioned relevant geological features in the KIG and their 'adjacent waters' would have no basis under international law, specifically UNCLOS. With respect to these areas, sovereignty and jurisdiction or sovereign rights, as the case may be, necessarily appertain or belong to the appropriate coastal or archipelagic state – the Philippines – to which these bodies of waters as well as seabed and subsoil are appurtenant, either in the nature of Territorial Sea, or 200 M Exclusive Economic Zone (EEZ), or Continental Shelf (CS) in accordance with Articles 3, 4, 55, 57, and 76 of UNCLOS.[72]

China replied to this Note on 14 April 2011 stating that its contents 'are totally unacceptable to the Chinese Government'.[73] China repeated its position of indisputable sovereignty over the islands in the South China Sea and added that the 'so-called Kalayaan Island Group claimed by the Republic of the Philippines is in fact part of China's Nansha Islands'. It continued:

Since 1970s, the Republic of the Philippines started to invade and occupy some islands and reefs of China's Nansha Islands and made relevant territorial claims, to which China objects strongly. The Republic of the Philippines' occupation of some islands and reefs of China's Nansha Islands as well as other related acts constitutes infringement upon China's territorial sovereignty. Under the legal doctrine of '*ex injuria jus non oritur*', the Republic of the Philippines can in no way invoke such illegal occupation to support its territorial claims. Furthermore, under the legal principle of '*la terre domine la mer*', coastal states' Exclusive Economic Zone (EEZ) and Continental Shelf claims shall not infringe upon the territorial sovereignty of other states.[74]

The substantive part of the Note concluded with the claim that 'under the relevant provisions of the *1982 United Nations Convention on the Law of the Sea*, … China's Nansha Islands is fully entitled to Territorial Sea, Exclusive Economic Zone (EEZ) and Continental Shelf'.[75]

It becomes clear from these Notes that the real Sino-Philippine dispute is threefold. First, there is the territorial dispute over parts of the Nansha [Spratly] Islands which the Philippines calls the Kalayaan Island Group.

---

[72] Philippines Note Verbale (5 April 2011) (n 47).
[73] Note Verbale CML/8/2011 (14 April 2011) (n 47), Annex I, Doc A.23.
[74] ibid.
[75] ibid.

While both parties claim sovereignty, there is an important difference with regard to the object of their claim. China claims sovereignty over 'the islands in the South China Sea'. One of these islands is the 'Nansha Islands'. China treats the Nansha Islands as a territorial unit which becomes clear from the statement that since the '1930s, the Chinese Government has given publicity several times the geographical scope of China's Nansha Islands and the names of its components'.[76] The Philippines on the other hand claims sovereignty not over the Kalayaan Island Group as a whole, but over 'the [individual] geological features *in* the KIG'.[77] Second, there is a dispute over whether the islands in question can generate full maritime entitlements, including an EEZ and continental shelf. China claims that the Nansha Islands as a unit, rather than the individual islands, and other maritime features forming part of it, 'is fully entitled to Territorial Sea, Exclusive Economic Zone (EEZ) and Continental Shelf'.[78] The Philippines on the other hand claims that the maritime entitlements are limited to the exercise of 'sovereignty and jurisdiction over the waters around or adjacent to each relevant geological feature in the KIG'.[79] The maritime entitlements are determined for each geological feature in accordance with Article 121 UNCLOS. All the 'relevant geological features' presented by the Philippines in its Notification and Statement of Claim can, of course, generate a 12nm territorial sea at best. Third, there is a dispute over maritime delimitation. China's claim to a territorial sea, EEZ and continental shelf around the Nansha Islands necessarily overlaps with the Philippines' claim to a territorial sea, 200nm EEZ and continental shelf measured from its archipelagic baselines. The Philippines, however, tries to draw a veil of silence over the delimitation dispute by creating the impression in its Notification and Statement of Claim that the relevant geological features in the KIG are all mere 'rocks or low-tide elevations' which can generate at most a territorial sea of 12nm which is, in any case, surrounded by the Philippines maritime zones. Nothing is, of course, further from the truth as the example of Itu Aba [Taiping] island shows, which qualifies as a proper island in terms of Article 121(2) UNCLOS and thus generates full maritime entitlements, including an EEZ and continental shelf.

What the Tribunal has been asked to resolve is thus a far cry from the real or actual disputes between the parties. The Philippines has artificially tried to re-package the disputes in order not to fall foul of the limitations on and exceptions to the compulsory jurisdiction of the Tribunal. However, none of the claims raised by the Philippines can be addressed by the Tribunal without touching upon, and deciding, the real disputes between the parties. Whether the Philippines or China is entitled to a 200nm EEZ

---

[76] ibid.
[77] See text accompanying n 70 (emphasis added).
[78] Note Verbale CML/8/2011 (14 April 2011) (n 47), Annex I, Doc A.23.
[79] Philippines Note Verbale (5 April 2011) (n 47).

or continental shelf in a certain area of the South China Sea, whether certain reefs are located on the continental shelf of the Philippines or on that of China, whether certain reefs are occupied 'unlawfully', whether China has 'unlawfully' claimed maritime entitlements in a certain area of the South China Sea, or whether it 'unlawfully' prevented Philippine vessels from doing something in a certain area of the South China Sea cannot be answered without deciding the fundamental questions at the heart of all disputes between the two countries, namely the question of territorial sovereignty over the island groups, in particular the Nansha [Spratly] and Zhongsha [Macclesfield Bank, including Scarborough Shoal] Archipelagos, and maritime delimitation. The real disputes and the disputes brought to the Tribunal are inseparable. Any ruling of the Tribunal on the disputes presented would automatically have an effect on, and prejudice the resolution of, the real disputes. This is shown by a brief thought experiment. Assuming the Tribunal would rule in favour of all the Philippines' claims, such a ruling would in effect delimit the maritime boundary between the parties in the South China Sea. The Philippines would be allocated a 12nm territorial sea, 200nm EEZ and a continental shelf measured from its archipelagic baselines with China being at best entitled to four enclaves of a 12nm territorial sea around certain rocks in Scarborough Shoal, Johnson Reef, Cuarteron Reef and Fiery Cross Reef. Whether China was even entitled to a territorial sea around these reefs would, however, remain an open question since the Tribunal does not have jurisdiction to rule on questions of territorial sovereignty over land territory, including rocks. Such a result would be more than artificial, as it would have been reached without regard for China's claims to territorial sovereignty over the four island groups in the South China Sea or its claims to sovereignty over island proper, which form part of these island groups, such as Itu Aba [Taiping] Island.

3. Identity of Disputes under Section 1 and Section 2 of the Convention

Article 286 UNCLOS establishes the jurisdiction of the Tribunal only for such disputes 'where no settlement has been reached by recourse to section 1'. Section 1 of Part XV of UNCLOS requires the parties to a dispute, inter alia, to proceed expeditiously to an exchange of views regarding the settlement of their dispute by negotiation or other peaceful means.[80] The dispute which the parties unsuccessfully tried to settle by negotiation or other peaceful means must be identical with the dispute submitted to the Tribunal. On 9 July 2013, Philippine Secretary of Foreign Affairs Albert F del Rosario stated that the 'Philippines undertook many

---

[80] See UNCLOS, art 283(1).

efforts to peacefully engage China and settle these disputes' and that it 'had exhausted almost all political and diplomatic avenues for a peaceful negotiated settlement of its maritime dispute with China'.[81] Del Rosario himself referred to 'maritime *territorial* disputes' in this context.[82] As revealed by the statements submitted by the Philippines and China to the UN Secretary-General in 2009 and 2011, the real disputes between the parties are territorial and maritime boundary disputes. These disputes differ considerably from the disputes that are now submitted to the Tribunal. It will be for the Tribunal to establish — and for the Philippines to prove — that the disputes that form the subject of negotiations between the parties were the same as the disputes now submitted to the Tribunal. For example, it would have to be shown by the Philippines that there really were negotiations on the question of whether States could acquire sovereignty over low-tide elevations located outside a coastal State's territorial sea.

IV. THE REQUIREMENT THAT THE DISPUTES CONCERN THE INTERPRETATION OR APPLICATION OF THE CONVENTION

Annex VII of UNCLOS does not expressly specify the disputes over which the Tribunal can exercise jurisdiction. UNCLOS Annex VII Article 1, however, subjects proceedings before an arbitral tribunal constituted in accordance with Annex VII to 'the provisions of Part XV' of the Convention, and Article 4 of Annex VII provides that the arbitral tribunal is to function 'in accordance with this Annex and the other provisions of this Convention'. This brings into play Articles 286 and 288(1) UNCLOS which limit the jurisdiction of Annex VII arbitral tribunals to disputes 'concerning the interpretation or application of this Convention'. While it is true, as stated by the Philippines, 'that both Parties have given their advance consent to the regime of settlement of disputes concerning the interpretation and application of the Convention established in Part XV',[83] there are serious doubts as to whether the disputes submitted really concern the 'application or interpretation' of UNCLOS. If this is not the case, the Tribunal will have to decline jurisdiction.

At first sight, the disputes submitted to the Tribunal seem to concern the interpretation or application of UNCLOS. Thus, the Philippines asks the Tribunal, for example, to decide that China's 'rights and obligations in regard to the waters, seabed and maritime features of the South China Sea are governed by UNCLOS',[84] that the nine-dash line is 'in violation of

---

[81] 'Speech of Secretary Albert del Rosario: On the Occasion of Expert's Roundtable on Regional Approaches to Maritime Security in the West Philippine Sea' (9 July 2013) www.gov.ph.

[82] ibid (emphasis added).

[83] Notification and Statement of Claim, para 32.

[84] ibid, para 6. See also ibid, paras 1, 39; and Claims, bullet point 1.

UNCLOS',[85] that China 'has interfered with the exercise by the Philippines of its rights under the Convention ... in violation of UNCLOS',[86] whether, 'under Article 121 of UNCLOS, certain of the maritime features claimed by both China and the Philippines are islands, low tide elevations or submerged banks, and whether they are capable of generating entitlement to maritime zones greater than 12 M',[87] and that the Philippines 'is entitled under UNCLOS to a 12 M Territorial Sea, a 200 M Exclusive Economic Zone, and a Continental Shelf'.[88] The Philippines's Notification and Statement of Claim is, so to speak, soaked with references to 'UNCLOS' and 'the Convention'. But that does not necessarily mean that the disputes presented can all be decided purely on the basis of UNCLOS.

For example, the Philippines' assertion that 'China's maritime claims in the South China Sea based on its so-called "nine dash line" are ... invalid' cannot be decided on the basis of UNCLOS alone. As demonstrated above,[89] the nine-dash line manifests claims to territorial sovereignty over the island groups (including islands proper such as Itu Aba [Taiping] Island) in the South China Sea. The validity of these territorial claims is not a matter of the application or interpretation of UNCLOS, but is governed by general international law. As a consequence, the validity of any maritime zone claims generated by these islands or island groups cannot be decided on the basis of UNCLOS alone, but require, as a precondition, a decision on the validity of the territorial claims.

The real disputes between the parties, as shown above, concern territorial sovereignty over the islands and other maritime features in the South China Sea and the delimitation of overlapping maritime zones generated by these insular land territories and the Philippines archipelago. These real disputes cannot be separated from the disputes artificially cut out of these disputes and presented to the Tribunal. To the extent that the disputes presented cannot be answered without touching upon the question of territorial sovereignty and maritime boundary delimitation they have been removed from the jurisdiction of the Tribunal by virtue of China's 2006 declaration.

V. DISPUTES REMOVED FROM COMPULSORY JURISDICTION UNDER ARTICLE 298 UNCLOS

It has been shown that the real disputes between the parties concern the territorial sovereignty over the islands groups, including individual islands and other maritime features, and the delimitation of overlapping maritime zones generated by the insular land territory in the South China Sea. None of the disputes submitted to the Tribunal can be

---

[85] Notification and Statement of Claim, paras 12, 39. See also Claims, bullet point 2.
[86] Notification and Statement of Claim, para 2. See also ibid, para 13.
[87] ibid, para 6. See also ibid, paras 14, 20, 22, 24, 39.
[88] Claims, bullet point 8.
[89] See above section III.1.a.

decided without first deciding the real disputes. In other words, the Sino-Philippine disputes as presented to the Tribunal are like an onion with different layers. From the inside out, the core or the central disputes are the territorial disputes over the islands and other maritime features in the Nansha [Spratly] and Zhongsha [Macclesfield Bank, including Scarborough Shoal] Archipelagos. Next is the layer of maritime boundary delimitation disputes. The outer layer finally consists of the disputes set out in the Notification and Statement of Claim. By logical necessity, the core or central disputes need to be settled first before the Tribunal can address the middle and outer layer of the disputes. For the tribunal to decide the merits of the case it must thus have jurisdiction over all the disputes, both those presented at the surface and the underlying disputes.

Against this background it must now be examined whether any of the disputes, real or presented, have been excluded from the jurisdiction of the Tribunal by declarations made under Article 298 UNCLOS. Both parties have made declarations with regard to that provision. In its 'Understanding made upon signature and confirmed upon ratification of the Convention', the Philippines declared:

> The agreement of the Republic of the Philippines to the submission for peaceful resolution, under any of the procedures provided in the Convention, of disputes under article 298 shall not be considered as a derogation of Philippines sovereignty.[90]

The Philippines expressly includes any of the disputes under Article 298 UNCLOS in its acceptance of the compulsory dispute settlement procedures established by the Convention. This is confirmed by the fact that the UN Secretariat does not list the Philippines as a State having made use of the opportunity to have made a declaration under Article 298.[91] It is thus not precluded from submitting disputes falling within the excepted category of disputes under that provision.[92]

China, on the other hand, on 25 August 2006 expressly made a declaration under Article 298 UNCLOS which reads as follows:

> The Government of the People's Republic of China does not accept *any of the procedures* provided for in Section 2 of Part XV of the Convention with respect to all the categories of disputes referred to in paragraph 1 (a) (b) and (c) of Article 298 of the Convention.[93]

---

[90] Understanding Made by the Republic of the Philippines upon Signature of the United Nations Convention on the Law of the Sea, 10 December 1982, and Confirmed upon Ratification of the Convention (8 May 1984) point 8, reproduced in Annex I, Doc B.3.

[91] See United Nations, Division for Ocean Affairs and the Law of the Sea, *Law of the Sea Bulletin* No 5 (1985) 60–61. See also United Nations, Division for Ocean Affairs and the Law of the Sea, 'Settlement of disputes mechanism – 1. Settlement of disputes mechanism under the Convention: Choice of procedure under article 287 and optional exceptions to applicability of Part XV, Section 2, of the Convention under article 298 of the Convention', www.un.org/depts/los.

[92] *cf* UNCLOS, art 298(3).

[93] Declaration by the People's Republic of China under Article 298 UNCLOS (25 August 2006) Annex I, Doc A.26 (emphasis added).

China excluded any of the procedures provided for in Section 2 of Part XV, including Annex VII arbitral tribunals. This means that these tribunals are lacking jurisdiction to hear, inter alia, disputes concerning the interpretation or application of Articles 15, 74 and 83 relating to sea boundary delimitations, disputes involving historic bays or titles, as well as disputes concerning military activities and law enforcement activities. In addition, it should be noted that disputes 'concerning sovereignty or other rights over continental and insular land territory', which are also mentioned in Article 298(1)(a)(i), are not excluded from the jurisdiction of the Tribunal because of any declaration under Article 298, but because such disputes do not constitute disputes 'concerning the interpretation or application of this Convention'. This is obvious for the simple reason that such disputes are not governed by UNCLOS, but by general international law rules on the acquisition of territory.

The territorial disputes over the Nansha [Spratly] and Zhongsha [Macclesfield Bank, including Scarborough Shoal] Archipelagos and the disputes concerning the delimitation of overlapping claims of the two parties to territorial sea, EEZ and continental shelf in the South China Sea fall fairly within the categories of disputes excluded from the Tribunal's jurisdiction by China's 2006 declaration.

For the sake of completeness, it might be added that even if the Philippines was right to claim that 'China's maritime claims in the South China Sea [are] based on its so-called "nine dash line"' rather than on the island groups under its sovereignty, these maritime claims could be claims to historic waters based on Chinese historic titles. But, such disputes over historic titles are also removed from the jurisdiction of the Tribunal.

VI. CONCLUSION

Since China has declined to participate in the arbitral proceedings, the Tribunal is required to satisfy itself 'that it has jurisdiction over the dispute',[94] and to state the reasons on which its award on jurisdiction is based.[95] In order to assist the Tribunal in this task, this chapter has exposed several major defects in the Philippines' Notification and Statement of Claim which deprive the Tribunal of jurisdiction to hear the case.

First, with regard to the claims in bullet points 1, 2 and 8 there is no dispute between the parties. These claims are either of such generality or based on a misconception of the Chinese position that they are hypothetical and unreal, and it is difficult to see how they could be opposed by China.

Second, there is a gross mismatch between the real disputes between the parties and the disputes presented to the Tribunal. While the Philippines artificially tries to present claims of a general and abstract nature (or

[94] UNCLOS Annex VII, art 9.
[95] ibid, art 10.

claims related to technical questions of the legal status of geological features), the history of the exchanges between the two parties shows that the real disputes are concerned with territorial sovereignty and maritime boundary delimitations.

Third, this mismatch between the real and presented disputes calls into question whether the disputes submitted are the same as the ones the parties have allegedly been unable to settle by recourse to section 1 of Part XV of UNCLOS. But, if there is no identity between the disputes which the parties tried to settle by way of negotiations or other peaceful means and the disputes presented to the Tribunal, the requirement that 'no settlement has been reached by recourse to section 1' is not fulfilled and the way to the compulsory dispute settlement procedures under section 2 is closed.

Fourth, the dispute regarding territorial sovereignty over the islands in the South China Sea which is underlying all the other disputes presented to the Tribunal, does not concern the interpretation or application of UNCLOS but is governed by general international law.

Fifth, maritime boundary delimitation disputes, as well as disputes over historic titles, are removed from the jurisdiction of the Tribunal by China's 2006 declaration under Article 298 UNCLOS.

Sixth, and finally, the artificial disputes presented to the Tribunal and the real disputes between the parties are inseparable and the disputes presented cannot be decided without dealing with the real disputes.

4

The Issue of Admissibility in Inter-State Arbitration

BING BING JIA*

I. INTRODUCTION

THE NOTIFICATION AND Statement of Claim served on the Chinese Embassy in Manila by the Philippine Department of Foreign Affairs on 22 January 2013 has brought to the fore the complex disputes in the South China Sea in an explosive fashion. Granted, this act by the Philippines is of such a design that it seeks to be based, substantively and procedurally, on the United Nations Convention on the Law of the Sea (UNCLOS or the Convention).[1] It must, however, be pointed out that it is an act that ultimately relies, for its viability, on presumptions that are not relevant to the Convention. This point has been dealt with elsewhere,[2] and will not be considered here. It suffices to say that disputes related to those presumptions were deliberately excluded from the compulsory procedures of Part XV at the beginning of the negotiations of UNCLOS,[3] such as the issue of territorial sovereignty over certain geographical features in the South China Sea. The Arbitral Tribunal seized of this dispute, however, cannot avoid addressing this issue in the present case, that determines the root and extent of maritime entitlement due to the coastal States under UNCLOS. The disputants probably do not expect an award that presumes a shared or undecided ownership of the features in question as referred to in the Notification and Statement of Claim, but exclusive possession in

---

* The author would like to thank Mr Zhongzheng Tan, doctoral candidate at the Law School, Tsinghua University, Beijing, for his assistance.

[1] United Nations Convention on the Law of the Sea (adopted 10 December 1982, entered into force 16 November 1994) 1834 UNTS 387 (UNCLOS).

[2] Bing Bing Jia, 'China and International Law' (2013) *Proceedings of the American Society of International Law* (forthcoming). See also section III.1.a and 2 below.

[3] Myron H Nordquist, Shabtai Rosenne and Louis B Sohn (eds), *United Nations Convention on the Law of the Sea 1982: A Commentary*, vol V (Dordrecht, Martinus Nijhoff, 1989) 88 MN 297.2 (referring to Ambassador Galindo Pohl's statement at the second session of the conference in 1974).

favour of one of them only. This exclusive ownership will define the scope of the overall conclusion of the Arbitral Tribunal on the Philippine claims as a whole.[4]

This chapter considers the admissibility of the Notification and Statement of Claim on the hypothesis that it might actually be concerned with the interpretation or application of UNCLOS — which it is not, of course — and therefore, that the Arbitral Tribunal might have jurisdiction to deal with the claims contained in the Notification and Statement of Claim. The point to be made here is that even based on that hypothesis, the claims contained in the Notification and Statement of Claim are inadmissible, in whole or in part. The admissibility of any international claim, such as those advanced by the Philippines, must be decided before the Arbitral Tribunal proceeds to the merits stage of the case,[5] just like the International Court of Justice (ICJ or the Court) does in its contentious or advisory proceedings.[6] The Court once noted that:

> as a judicial organ, [the Court] is however only concerned to establish, first, that the dispute before it is a legal dispute, in the sense of a dispute capable of being settled by the application of principles and rules of international law, and secondly, that the Court has jurisdiction to deal with it, and that that jurisdiction is not fettered by any circumstance rendering the application inadmissible.[7]

On another occasion, the Court explained that '[o]bjections to admissibility [*recevabilité*] normally take the form of an assertion that, even if the Court has jurisdiction and the facts stated by the applicant State are assumed to be correct, nonetheless there are reasons why the Court should not proceed to an examination of the merits'.[8] Additionally, the Court may decline to exercise its jurisdiction 'in appropriate circumstances',[9] which is sometimes described as a question of 'general admissibility'.[10] It may still be correct, therefore, to see admissibility as a notion that goes to the procedural defects that dissuade a judicial body from formally examining any aspect

---

[4] This feature of the present arbitration distinguishes it from the *Nauru* case: *Certain Phosphate Lands in Nauru (Nauru v Australia)* (Preliminary Objections) [1992] ICJ Rep 240, 261 [55].

[5] The consideration of the issue of admissibility may not stand, in terms of importance to a judicial or arbitral body, on the same footing as that of jurisdiction, which is, however, a rather fine point: Hugh Thirlway, 'The Law and Procedure of the International Court of Justice, 1960–1989 (Part Eleven)' (2000) 71 *British Year Book of International Law* 71, 74.

[6] Christian Tomuschat, 'Article 36' in Andreas Zimmermann and others (eds), *The Statute of the International Court of Justice: A Commentary*, Oxford Commentaries on International Law, 2nd edn (Oxford, OUP, 2012) 698 MN 119. As has been noted, problems like those of admissibility are 'common to all judicial procedures for the settlement of international disputes' (John Collier and Vaughan Lowe, *The Settlement of Disputes in International Law: Institutions and Procedures* (Oxford, OUP, 1999) 190).

[7] *Border and Transborder Armed Actions (Nicaragua v Honduras)* (Jurisdiction and Admissibility) [1988] ICJ Rep 69, 91 [52].

[8] *Oil Platforms (Iran v United States of America)* (Merits) [2003] ICJ Rep 161, 177 [29].

[9] *Military and Paramilitary Activities in and against Nicaragua (Nicaragua v United States of America)* (Jurisdiction and Admissibility) [1984] ICJ Rep 392, 431 [88].

[10] Georges Abi-Saab, *Les Exceptions Préliminaires dans la Procédure de la Cour Internationale* (Paris, Éditions A Pedone, 1967) 97.

of the merits of a dispute brought before it.[11] That is so if only for the sake of judicial propriety. In addition, it covers exceptions which, as specially recognised in international law but not procedural defects as such, prevent the Court from proceeding to the merits stage of the case, if they are present. In a way, the notion of admissibility is difficult to define, except in rather general terms.[12] Despite all of this, the stage at which admissibility is to be considered seems to be beyond dispute. The ICJ stated in *Armed Activities* that 'in accordance with established jurisprudence, the Court will examine the issue of admissibility of the DRC's Application only should it find that it has jurisdiction to entertain that Application'.[13] If the issues raised regarding the admissibility are not bound up with the merits,[14] they fall for decision before the Court moves on to the merits stage of a given case, in the light of the established jurisprudence of the Court.[15]

It may be pointed out that the issue of admissibility may be raised before a judicial or arbitral body by the parties, or the judicial or arbitral body should consider it *proprio motu*. Where procedures of Annex VII of UNCLOS are initiated for the settlement of an inter-State dispute, it is inevitable that the parties will argue about admissibility, especially considering that one of the parties may well have been reluctantly brought into this compulsory mechanism.[16] Moreover, it is felt that, where the issue of admissibility is not raised by the parties (as would be the case when the respondent does not participate in the proceedings), there is a duty for the court or tribunal to consider the issue *proprio motu*.[17] The tribunal must satisfy itself 'in fact and law' that it has jurisdiction before reaching its final award.[18] That reference to jurisdiction must mean not only 'jurisdiction' *stricto sensu*,[19] but also the conditions under which the jurisdiction is to be exercised. In addition, this initiative on the part of a court or tribunal is always necessary, given the fact that some of the established grounds of admissibility are rules of a substantive nature which, duly recognised in UNCLOS, assume precedence even before a court or tribunal can

---

[11] *cf* Thirlway, 'Law and Procedure (Part Eleven)' 71, 73–83.

[12] Abi-Saab, *Les Exceptions Préliminaires* (1967) 92 ('les termes "conditions de recevabilité" sont en général employés pour désigner certaines conditions matérielles—distinctes à la fois de la compétence et du fond main en rapport avec celui-ci—qui doivent être remplies pour permettre l'examen de la prétention').

[13] *Armed Activities on the Territory of the Congo (New Application: 2002) (Democratic Republic of the Congo v Rwanda)* (Jurisdiction and Admissibility) [2006] ICJ Rep 6, 17 [18].

[14] ICJ Rules of Court, art 79(9) anticipates that an objection may not possess an exclusively preliminary character.

[15] Hugh Thirlway, *The Law and Procedure of the International Court of Justice: Fifty Years of Jurisprudence*, vol 2 (Oxford, OUP, 2013) 1710–11.

[16] *Southern Bluefin Tuna Case (Australia and New Zealand v Japan)* (Award on Jurisdiction and Admissibility) (2000) 119 ILR 508, 544 [42]–[43]; *Mauritius v United Kingdom* (Procedural Order No 2, Application to Bifurcate Proceedings) (15 January 2013) www.pca-cpa.org.

[17] See also Abi-Saab (n 10) 205–13.

[18] UNCLOS Annex VII, art 9.

[19] For the term 'jurisdiction' in its narrow and broad senses, see Shabtai Rosenne, *The Law and Practice of the International Court, 1920–2005*, vol 2, 4th edn (Leiden, Martinus Nijhoff, 2006) 523.

consider the issue of jurisdiction. Examples of such rules would include the exhaustion of local remedies, as recognised in Article 295 UNCLOS which appears in section 2 of Part XV. Any dispute between the parties may accordingly be submitted to the compulsory dispute settlement procedures '*only after* local remedies have been exhausted'.[20] Furthermore, it is a feature of any international claim that it deals not only with the jurisdiction of the tribunal before which the claim is filed, but 'all its aspects', such as those of admissibility and the merits.[21] The obligation to give a complete answer to all aspects of a claim or dispute stems from the mandate of an international judicial or arbitral body to effect peaceful settlement of disputes.

That would be the guiding principle for this chapter in examining the issues of admissibility that arise following the Notification and Statement of Claim. There is sense in stating that jurisdiction undermined by inadmissible grounds is not perfect, and, without a perfect jurisdiction, the court or tribunal concerned cannot proceed to deal with the merits of the case at hand.

It is recognised that the arguments presented here would need to be refined or even revised after the Philippine Government files its memorial in later stages of the arbitration proceedings.[22] For that reason, certain parts of the following discussion are not elaborated. However, one could not help noticing that the Notification and Statement of Claim, even in its present form, may give rise to certain grounds of inadmissibility that may not be easily cured by the expected memorial. This chapter will consider the following four grounds of inadmissibility: firstly, Article 281(1) UNCLOS; secondly, defects in certain claims of the Notification, in the form of the mootness or vagueness of those claims; thirdly, Article 300 UNCLOS; and, lastly, contamination of arbitral jurisdiction due to the consequences of an estoppel. There is a caveat that these grounds of inadmissibility may not be exhaustive at this stage of the proceedings, and that new developments may well give rise to new grounds of the same category.

II. PRIMARY OBLIGATION TO NEGOTIATE: ARTICLE 281(1) UNCLOS

Article 281(1) UNCLOS provides that if 'the States Parties which are parties to a dispute concerning the interpretation or application of this Convention have agreed to seek settlement of the dispute by a peaceful means of their own choice, the procedures provided for in this Part apply only where no

[20] UNCLOS, art 295 (emphasis added).

[21] *Nottebohm Case (Liechtenstein v Guatemala)* (Preliminary Objections) [1953] ICJ Rep 111, 123. See PCA 'Arbitration between the Philippines and China, Arbitral Tribunal, First Press Release' (27 August 2013) www.pca-cpa.org (the Tribunal directed the Philippines to fully address all issues, including those of admissibility).

[22] On 27 August 2013 the Tribunal adopted its first Procedural Order. It fixed 30 March 2014 as the deadline for filing the Philippine Memorial; www.pca-cpa.org.

settlement has been reached by recourse to such means and the agreement between the parties does not exclude any further procedure'.

The provision relates to a situation where a body, such as an arbitral tribunal established under Annex VII of UNCLOS, is prevented by the Convention from exercising jurisdiction over any dispute that actually falls within its jurisdiction.[23] The preventive effect of the provision derives from the existence of a means of peaceful settlement with regard to a dispute in question, which has been previously agreed to between the States Parties to the dispute. The requirements for the application of Article 281(1) are the following: (a) there is an agreement to settle the dispute by a peaceful means chosen by the parties to the dispute; (b) no settlement has been reached by recourse to the agreed means; and (c) the agreement does not exclude any further procedure. The three requirements are cumulative and must all be fulfilled before any procedure prescribed in UNCLOS section 2, Part XV — including those provided under Article 287 — becomes applicable. Insofar as the Philippines' Notification and Statement of Claim is concerned, requirement (a) is met by the circumstances of the present case, but requirements (b) and (c) are not. Those requirements will be considered in turn below.

1. Agreement to Seek Settlement by Negotiations

a. Agreement as Evidenced in the 2002 Declaration and Other Official Documents Issued Jointly by China and the Philippines

It is submitted that there has been an agreement between China and the Philippines to deal with the disputes in question through consultations and negotiations between the parties, as stated in paragraph 4 of the Declaration on the Conduct of Parties in the South China Sea (DOC or the Declaration), signed on 4 November 2002, which expressly provides that:

> The Parties concerned undertake to resolve their territorial and jurisdictional disputes by peaceful means, without resorting to the threat or use of force, through friendly consultations and negotiations by sovereign states directly concerned, in accordance with universally recognized principles of international law, including the 1982 UN Convention on the Law of the Sea.[24]

While fully aware of other interpretations of the nature of the DOC, it is felt that its wording is such that, at a minimum, it constitutes

---

[23] UNCLOS obviously differs in this regard from art 33 UN Charter; see *Land and Maritime Boundary between Cameroon and Nigeria (Cameroon v Nigeria)* (Preliminary Objections) [1998] ICJ Rep 275, 302 [56]. Charter of the United Nations (adopted 26 June 1945, entered into force 24 October 1945) 892 UNTS 119.

[24] 'ASEAN-China Declaration on the Conduct of Parties in the South China Sea, signed during the 8th ASEAN Summit in Phnom Penh' (4 November 2002) para 4 (DOC); reproduced in Vaughan Lowe and Stefan Talmon (eds), *The Legal Order of the Oceans: Basic Documents on the Law of the Sea* (Oxford, Hart Publishing, 2009) Doc 69, 771–72.

an agreement among the 'Parties', a term specifically used in the Declaration—as distinct from mere participants to the instrument. In particular, paragraph 4 of the DOC includes an *undertaking* of the Parties to the Declaration to settle their disputes by way of the specific means of consultation and negotiation, and it becomes a double undertaking by virtue of paragraph 8 of the Declaration by which the 'Parties undertake to respect the provisions of this Declaration and take actions consistent therewith'.[25] It goes without saying that a word such as 'undertake' is not lightly used in diplomatic documents,[26] and the specific thrust carried by such wording, a serious promise, is unmistakable.[27] As the ICJ put it in the *Genocide* case:

> The ordinary meaning of the word 'undertake' is to give a formal promise, to bind or engage oneself, to give a pledge or promise, to agree, to accept an obligation. It is a word regularly used in treaties setting out the obligations of the Contracting Parties ... It is not merely hortatory or purposive.[28]

Whether the DOC is a treaty in the sense of Article 2(1)(a) of the Vienna Convention on the Law of Treaties is beside the point, and this author certainly does not argue it as such.[29] The point is that the provision of Article 281(1) has the purpose of enabling the States Parties to settle disputes by peaceful means,[30] rather than to require them to enter into binding agreements analogous to treaties, in order to realise that purpose. Thus, the DOC, supplemented by official documents issued subsequently and reaffirming its content, is sufficient to establish an agreement on the part of the parties to the present disputes. It has been noted by an arbitral tribunal that an agreement in terms of Article 281(1) does not have to be 'formal', but could exist by conduct or through the practice of the parties concerned, and it could well be *ad hoc*.[31]

That there has been an agreement in the sense as defined above between China and the Philippines can further be evidenced in official documents jointly issued by the two governments. Subsequent to the DOC's signature, a joint press statement between China and the Philippines was issued on 3 September 2004 during the state visit of China by Philippine President Macapagal-Arroyo, stating that:

---

[25] ibid. The language of paras 4 and 8 is clearly different from that of paras 6 and 7, for instance. The DOC was signed by Foreign Ministers of the parties.

[26] cf American Law Institute, *Restatement of the Law (Third). The Foreign Relations Law of the United States*, vol 1 (St Paul Minnesota, American Law Institute, 1990) sec 301.

[27] Kelvin Widdows, 'What is an Agreement in International Law?' (1979) 50 *British Year Book of International Law* 117, 121.

[28] *Application of the Convention on the Prevention and Punishment of the Crime of Genocide (Bosnia and Herzegovina v Serbia and Montenegro)* (Merits) [2007] ICJ Rep 43, 111 [162].

[29] cf 'Terms of Reference of the ASEAN-China Joint Working Group on the Implementation of the Declaration on the Conduct of Parties in the South China Sea' (adopted 7 December 2004) www.asean.org.

[30] Nordquist, Rosenne and Sohn (eds), *United Nations Convention on the Law of the Sea 1982*, vol V (1989) 22-23 MN 281.1-5.

[31] *Barbados v Trinidad and Tobago* (2006) 27 RIAA 147, 205 [200 (ii)].

The two sides reaffirmed their commitment to the peace and stability in the South China Sea and their readiness to continue discussions to study cooperative activities like joint development pending the comprehensive and final settlement of territorial disputes and overlapping maritime claims in the area. They agreed to promote the peaceful settlement of disputes in accordance with universally-recognized principles of international law, including the 1982 United Nations Convention on the Law of the Sea. They agreed that the early and vigorous implementation of the 2002 ASEAN-China Declaration on the Conduct of Parties in the South China Sea will pave the way for the transformation of the South China Sea into an area of cooperation.[32]

On 1 September 2011, another joint statement between the Presidents of China and the Philippines was issued during the state visit of China by President Aquino III, stating in particular:

Both leaders exchanged views on the maritime disputes and agreed not to let the maritime disputes affect the broader picture of friendship and cooperation between the two countries. The two leaders reiterated their commitment to addressing the disputes through peaceful dialogue, to maintain continued regional peace, security, stability and an environment conducive to economic progress. Both leaders reaffirmed their commitments to respect and abide by the Declaration on the Conduct of Parties in the South China Sea signed by China and the ASEAN member countries in 2002.[33]

It is beyond doubt that the statements cited above, all drafted with general regard to the disputes now alleged in the Notification and Statement of Claim, could only create the impression that the disputes between the two governments should be taken up on the basis of these statements. The 2011 Joint Statement is particularly relevant, in that it was jointly issued by the Chinese President and the Philippine President, the government of the latter being the one that initiated this arbitration in January 2013.

In light of the documented commitment of the parties to the present disputes, there exists a genuine and, indeed, solemn agreement between them.[34] There is no need to consider the existence or lack of a treaty. In practice, even a memorandum of understanding can be an agreement, notwithstanding its often non-binding nature.[35] The two joint statements, furthermore, do not simply record points of agreement, or state intentions of cooperation and hope, but reaffirm previous commitments undertaken under the DOC.[36]

[32] PRC MFA, 'Joint Press Statement of the Government of the People's Republic of China and the Government of the Republic of the Philippines' (3 September 2004) www.fmprc.gov. cn (2004 Joint Statement).

[33] 'Joint statement of the Republic of the Philippines and the People's Republic of China' (Beijing, 1 September 2011) www.gov.ph, para 15 (2011 Joint Statement).

[34] *Barbados v Trinidad and Tobago* (2006) 27 RIAA 147, 205 [200 (ii)]: 'In the present case the Parties have agreed *in practice*, although not by any formal agreement, to seek to settle their dispute through negotiations' (emphasis added). See also Anthony Aust, *Modern Treaty Law and Practice*, 2nd edn (Cambridge, CUP, 2008) 33.

[35] Aust, *Modern Treaty Law* (2008) 21.

[36] *Maritime Delimitation and Territorial Questions between Qatar and Bahrain (Qatar v Bahrain)* (Jurisdiction and Admissibility) [1994] ICJ Rep 112, 121 [25]: 'they do not merely

In further support of this interpretation, four points are added. First, reference is made to the 'List of Philippine-China Bilateral Agreements', compiled by the Philippine Embassy in Beijing, China, which includes the 2011 Joint Statement, as cited above, among the agreements on political affairs.[37] Secondly, on more than one occasion, the parties to the DOC have expressed that the document was based on 'consensus' between them,[38] which is just another expression of 'agreement'.[39] Thirdly, the commitment to the DOC has been clearly stated time and again by China and the Philippines in official documents issued by them, which are evidence of more than just 'a good argument' that they have agreed to settle their dispute by reference to the DOC.[40] Last but not least, the Notification and Statement of Claim concedes that there has been such an agreement, by stating that 'as the Philippines and China have failed to settle the dispute between them by peaceful means of their own choice, Article 281(1) allows recourse to the proceedings provided for in Part XV'.[41] This acknowledgement is significant, in that it was preceded by the remark that 'the Philippines had complied with the requirements of Article 279 and Article 283(1) fully and in good faith, and has exhausted possibilities of settlement by negotiations'. This calls for a short discussion.

Needless to say, Article 279 is relevant, but it is too general to have any clear impact on the procedural interplay between sections 1 and 2 of Part XV of UNCLOS. Article 283(1), on the other hand, requires that 'the parties to the dispute shall proceed expeditiously to an exchange of views regarding its settlement by negotiation or other peaceful means'. The provision is more specific procedurally, but it requires two conditions for its application. The first is that a dispute arises between two States Parties to UNCLOS regarding the interpretation or application of the Convention. Without attempting to define the exact time when the present disputes crystallised — which is a flaw in presentation — the Notification and Statement of Claim seems to imply that they arose in 2009 when China 'first officially' showed the nine-dash line in a communication to the UN

give an account of discussions and summarize points of agreement and disagreement. They enumerate the commitments to which the Parties have consented. They thus create rights and obligations in international law for the Parties. They constitute an international agreement'.

[37] 'List of Philippines-China Bilateral Agreements, 1975 — 1 September 2011' (published by the Philippines Embassy in China) www.philembassychina.org.

[38] *cf* 'Terms of Reference of the ASEAN-China Joint Working Group on the Implementation of the Declaration on the Conduct of Parties in the South China Sea' (adopted 7 December 2004) (n 29) paras 1–3.

[39] UNCLOS, art 161(8)(e): '"consensus" means the absence of any formal objection'. It is sometimes known as general agreement; see Erik Suy, 'Consensus' in Rudolf Bernhardt (ed), *Encyclopedia of Public International Law*, vol I (Amsterdam, North-Holland Publishing, 1992) 759, 759.

[40] *Southern Bluefin Tuna Case* (*Australia and New Zealand v Japan*) (Award on Jurisdiction and Admissibility) (2000) 119 ILR 508, 558 [5] (sep op Keith).

[41] Republic of the Philippines (RP), Department of Foreign Affairs (DFA), Notification and Statement of Claim (22 January 2013) para 34; reproduced in Annex I, Doc B.2 (Notification and Statement of Claim).

Secretary-General.[42] If so, the claim that bilateral negotiations could be dated back to 1995,[43] could not be correct. Indeed, it is suggested in section 2 below that negotiations regarding the claims alleged in the Notification and Statement of Claim could not have happened earlier than 2002. In fact, the negotiations might have become possible only in 2011. The second condition of Article 283(1) is that the disputants shall proceed to an exchange of views regarding the settlement of the dispute by negotiation or by other peaceful means. In the present case, negotiation has been the means chosen.[44] But the problem of whether those negotiations fulfilled the requirements of Article 281(1) has not been discussed in the Notification and Statement of Claim. It is significant that the document does not deal with Article 281 except for a passing reference, and then deals only briefly with Article 279 and, in slightly more detail, Article 283. It is plain that neither Article 279 nor Article 283(1) is difficult to prove as being fulfilled in the light of existing case-law.[45] By relying on, among others, those two articles in instituting these arbitral proceedings, the Philippines is faced with a rather obvious lacuna in its approach. Those two articles are hardly dominant in the scheme of section 1, Part XV of UNCLOS, because of the general nature of Article 279 and the less stringent requirement of Article 283(1).[46] In comparison, Articles 281 and 282 are much more specific and significant, and if proved, can forestall the application of Part XV as a whole. The Philippines has sidestepped this point completely.

b. Agreement in the Form of the Treaty of Amity and Cooperation of 1976, as Amended

The preceding argument that an agreement in the sense of Article 281(1) UNCLOS exists between China and the Philippines would be incomplete if there was no reference to the 1976 Treaty of Amity and Cooperation in Southeast Asia (TAC or the Treaty).[47] China acceded to the Treaty, as amended by two subsequent protocols of 1987 and 1998, on 8 October 2003.[48] The Treaty became effective between China and the Philippines from

---

[42] Notification and Statement of Claim, para 11.

[43] ibid, para 26.

[44] ibid, para 33.

[45] *cf* above ch 2 section IV.2.a.

[46] *Barbados v Trinidad and Tobago* (2006) 27 RIAA 147, 206 [202]–[03].

[47] Treaty of Amity and Cooperation in Southeast Asia, done at Denpasar, Bali, Indonesia among Indonesia, Singapore, Malaysia, Thailand and the Philippines (signed on 24 February 1976, entry into force 21 June 1976) 1025 UNTS 15063 (TAC). The TAC was initially concluded by Indonesia, Singapore, Malaysia, Thailand and the Philippines. The substantive provisions are only to be found in the TAC proper, as the three subsequently concluded protocols are all concerned with wider participation issues.

[48] For the text of the Chinese instrument of accession, see 'Instrument of Accession to the Treaty of Amity and Cooperation in Southeast Asia' (8 October 2003). China also ratified the third protocol to the TAC (dated 23 July 2010) on 26 August 2011; see Standing Committee of the National People's Congress of the People's Republic of China, *Quan Guo Ren Min Dai Biao Da Hui Chang Wu Wei Yuan Hui Gong Bao [Gazette of the Standing Committee of the National People's Congress]*, 2011, Issue 6, 594. The protocol entered into force on 6 June 2012.

that moment onwards. It is for this reason that the TAC is discussed after the DOC in the present analysis. The significance of the Treaty is shown by the fact that it served as a basis for the drafting of the DOC.[49] But its importance in this context goes beyond that. Article 13 of the TAC provides that:

> The High Contracting Parties shall have the determination and good faith to prevent disputes from arising. In case disputes on matters directly affecting them should arise, especially disputes likely to disturb regional peace and harmony, they shall refrain from the threat or use of force and *shall at all times settle such disputes among themselves through friendly negotiations.*[50]

Two comments are in order. First, Article 13 clearly establishes a legal obligation for the contracting parties to the treaty to settle their disputes in Southeast Asia by negotiations singularly and 'at all times'. Even if the word 'agreement' in Article 281(1) were understood to mean only 'treaty', the TAC squarely fits the bill. This Treaty has no specific period of validity, and will remain permanently in force for the contracting parties after ratification or accession, unless certain situations specifically envisaged in the international law of treaties arise that allow its denunciation. Secondly, under this provision, there is no limit to the categories of disputes that may fall under the obligation to negotiate. The only condition is that disputes must be 'on matters directly affecting them'. The disputes as alleged in the Notification and Statement of Claim are exactly of this type, as they are matters directly affecting China and the Philippines. The fact that these disputes happen to be concerned, in various ways, with the interpretation or application of UNCLOS does not contradict the terms of Article 13 TAC.

c. Conclusion

In conclusion, requirement (a) of Article 281(1) is fulfilled in the present circumstances in more than one way; there are in fact two agreements between China and the Philippines, and they both require the settlement of disputes between these two countries in the South China Sea through negotiation.

2. No Relevant and Conclusive Proof as to the Failure of Negotiations

a. Negotiations Undertaken under the 2002 Declaration and Other Related Official Documents

Since the bilateral negotiations focusing on the issues embodied in the Notification and Statement of Claim have yet to start in the spirit of the

---

[49] *cf* '1992 ASEAN Declaration on the South China Sea' (adopted by foreign ministers at the 25th ASEAN Ministerial Meeting in Manila, Philippines, 22 July 1992) para 4. The Declaration was signed by the Foreign Ministers of Brunei, Indonesia, Malaysia, the Philippines, Singapore and Thailand.
[50] Emphasis added.

DOC and other related official documents, requirement (b) of Article 281(1),[51] regarding the failure to reach a settlement, is far from being met, for three reasons.

First, the 2004 Joint Statement between the Presidents of the two States, as quoted above, shows that the DOC, including the undertaking to negotiate, was to be implemented *early*, and that, therefore, in 2004 the implementation of the document had yet to start. Indeed, the Guidelines for the Implementation of the Declaration on the Conduct of Parties in the South China Sea (DOC Guidelines) were agreed to only in July 2011 between the parties to the DOC.[52] Furthermore, the DOC was meant to establish the principles for the resolution of territorial and jurisdictional disputes, and it was duly followed up by a series of subsequent meetings between the signatory countries which were to provide guidance and details for the negotiations to be held under that document.[53] It is therefore highly unlikely that any pertinent and meaningful negotiations between China and the Philippines in the spirit of the DOC could have taken place prior to 2002. More likely than not, the negotiations could not have happened before 2011. It may be recalled that the DOC Guidelines adopted in July 2011 specifically stated that the 'decision to implement concrete measures or activities of the DOC should be based on consensus among parties concerned'.[54] The initiation of arbitration by the Philippines in this case hardly seems in line with the DOC Guidelines. No consensus has been sought by it before it served the Notification and Statement of Claim on China.

Secondly, the 2011 Joint Statement between the Presidents of China and the Philippines reaffirmed the commitment of both countries to 'addressing the disputes through peaceful dialogue', in addition to their reaffirmation of the commitment 'to respect and abide by' the DOC.[55] Between 2004 and 2011, the direction taken by the two countries in respect of the disputes in the South China Sea had not been altered.

Thirdly, in international law, the relevance and the impossibility for success of the negotiating process must be considered fully before drawing any conclusion as to the exhaustion of the venue of negotiations.

---

[51] See also Notification and Statement of Claim, paras 8 and 33 (an argument was made that the requirement of art 279 was fulfilled).

[52] Guidelines for the Implementation of the Declaration of Conduct of Parties in the South China Sea (adopted 20 July 2011); see 'China Keen to Further Strengthen Bilateral Relations with ASEAN in the New Century Bali, Indonesia' (22 July 2011) www.asean.org. For the draft text, as released to the press, see 'South China Sea Guidelines Agreed' (21 July 2011) www.thejakartapost.com. Only the first six points seem to have been adopted. See also PRC MFA, 'The Senior Officials' Meeting for the Implementation of "the Declaration on Conduct of Parties in the South China Sea" Reaches an Agreement on the Guideline' (20 July 2011) www.fmprc.gov.cn.

[53] See eg 'Joint Statement of the 15th ASEAN-China Summit on the 10th Anniversary of the Declaration on the Conduct of Parties in the South China Sea' (Phnom Penh, Cambodia, 19 November 2012) www.china.org.cn.

[54] Guidelines for the Implementation of the Declaration of Conduct of Parties in the South China Sea (n 52) para 6.

[55] 2011 Joint Statement (n 33).

On the one hand, the relevance of any bilateral negotiations on the issues in question is important, since it is known that such negotiations have certain features, such that 'the subject-matter of the negotiations must relate to the subject-matter of the dispute which, in turn, must concern the substantive obligations contained in the treaty in question'.[56] This was the view of the ICJ expressed at the jurisdiction and admissibility stage of a recent case. The Court further explained on that occasion:

> In the present case, the Court is therefore assessing whether Georgia genuinely attempted to engage in negotiations with the Russian Federation, with a view to resolving their dispute concerning the Russian Federation's compliance with its substantive obligations under CERD. Should it find that Georgia genuinely attempted to engage in such negotiations with the Russian Federation, the Court would examine whether Georgia pursued these negotiations as far as possible with a view to settling the dispute.[57]

It is reasonable to think that negotiations in the sense of Article 279 UNCLOS and other relevant provisions of section 1 of Part XV need to show the same features as the Court required in the passage quoted above, in order to be perceived as fulfilling the requirements of those provisions. General exchanges of views, without actually seeking a settlement, cannot count as 'negotiations' in this connection any more than 'agreeing to disagree' after the exchanges. It may be recalled that the ICJ has made the point that '[n]egotiations entail more than the plain opposition of legal views or interests between two parties, or the existence of a series of accusations and rebuttals, or even the exchange of claims and directly opposed counter-claims'.[58] Even presuming the exchange of views constitutes negotiations, it must be doubted that this exchange is relevant in the present case if it proceeded without reference to UNCLOS, general international law, or the DOC. The 2011 Joint Statement, for instance, did refer to an exchange of views with a reference to the DOC, which in turn refers to UNCLOS. Negotiations of disputes in the area of the law of the sea would require a presentation of the respective positions of the parties to the disputes between themselves, and those positions would each contain, among others, a suitable legal basis. Otherwise, these negotiations may become irrelevant for the purposes of Article 288(1) UNCLOS, due to the fact that the subject-matter of the disputes on which the exchange of views or negotiations have been contemplated is not necessarily one concerning the interpretation or application of UNCLOS.

The preceding argument may be illustrated by using the 'Response of the Philippines Department of Foreign Affairs Spokesperson to the Recent Statement of the Chinese Ministry of Foreign Affairs on the West Philippine

---

[56] *Application of the International Convention on the Elimination of All Forms of Racial Discrimination (Georgia v Russian Federation)* (Preliminary Objections) [2011] ICJ Rep 70, 133 [161].

[57] ibid, [162].

[58] ibid, [157].

Sea Issue' (DFA Response) as an example.[59] The DFA Response of 15 July 2013, which tried to explain the rationale for the institution of the current arbitral proceedings, used the consultations with regard to Scarborough Shoal [Huangyan Island, or Bajo de Masinloc as it is known in the Philippines], as evidence that consultations between the two countries had been held without result. However, the DFA Response made no reference to the legal basis for the consultations. Moreover, Scarborough Shoal [Huangyan Island] is by no means the only claim (or even one of the main claims) put forward by the Philippines in the Notification and Statement of Claim.[60] If the consultations held between the two countries focused on this single issue, they could hardly resolve the rest of the Philippines' claims in the Notification and Statement of Claim. Additionally, it is not entirely clear whether the Philippines' initiatives for talks were merely concerned with bringing the disputes to judicial settlement or toward negotiations properly understood.[61] The relevance of those consultations, as revealed by the DFA Response of 15 July 2013, is rather limited indeed as far as this arbitration case is concerned.

On the other hand, 'the concept of "negotiations"... requires, at the very least, a genuine attempt by one of the disputing parties to engage in discussions with the other disputing party, with a view to resolving the dispute'.[62] The genuineness of the attempt to negotiate must be shown until there is no possibility for a final solution. But given the importance of the matters subject to negotiations in this kind of situation, the exhaustion of possible solutions cannot be assumed lightly. In the history of contact between China and the Philippines in respect of the current disputes, there has never been any indication — the Notification and Statement of Claim's narrative of the factual background included — that 'one of the Parties definitely declares himself unable, or refuses, to give way, and there can therefore be no doubt that *the dispute cannot be settled by diplomatic negotiations*',[63] or that 'there appears to be no prospect of its [ie negotiation] being continued or resumed'.[64]

It is a fact that the bilateral negotiations that may be relevant to the present case have stalled due to inaction on the part of the Philippines, despite the Philippines having been repeatedly invited by China in the past to commence mechanisms of consultation and negotiation on the

---

[59] RP DFA, 'Response of the DFA Spokesperson to the Recent Statement of the Chinese Ministry of Foreign Affairs on the West Philippine Sea Issue' (15 July 2013) www.dfa.gov.ph.

[60] Notification and Statement of Claim, para 31.

[61] RP DFA, 'Response of the DFA Spokesperson to the Recent Statement of the Chinese Ministry of Foreign Affairs on the West Philippine Sea Issue' (15 July 2013) (n 59) paras 5–8.

[62] *Application of the International Convention on the Elimination of All Forms of Racial Discrimination (Georgia v Russian Federation)* (Preliminary Objections) [2011] ICJ Rep 70, 132 [157].

[63] *Mavrommatis Palestine Concessions (Greece v United Kingdom)* (Objection to the Jurisdiction of the Court) 1924 PCIJ Rep Series A No 2, 13 (emphasis added).

[64] *Border and Transborder Armed Actions (Nicaragua v Honduras)* (Jurisdiction and Admissibility) [1988] ICJ Rep 69, 100 [80].

maritime issues between the two countries.[65] The Philippines' response to those calls came in a Note Verbale, dated 26 April 2012, inviting China to submit the issue 'to a dispute settlement mechanism',[66] which hardly reflected a willingness to negotiate the substance of the disputes as undertaken by both countries through a series of commitments since the DOC in 2002. In fact, the only definite proclamation on the impossibility to negotiate, to date, was made by the Philippines' Department of Foreign Affairs Spokesperson in the DFA Response of 15 July 2013.[67]

It follows from the preceding discussion that any previous contact between the two countries, as alleged in the Notification and Statement of Claim to have started as early as 1995,[68] must be assessed against the background of contacts that are outlined above. What happened in 1995 was that, in August of that year, the Deputy Foreign Ministers of China and the Philippines issued a joint statement to declare the principles for the establishment of a code of conduct, which included, among others, non-use or threat of force to settle territorial disputes, eventual settlement by way of negotiation, and settlement to be reached by reference to international law, including UNCLOS.[69] One of the agreed principles of the 1995 Joint Statement was that disputes should be settled by 'consultations' between the two governments. This actually strengthens the view argued earlier in this chapter that the means of negotiation has been selected by the two governments as the solution in respect of the disputes concerned. In addition, there was no solution whatsoever reached by, or foreseen in the 1995 statement, apart from an exchange of opposing views of the two sides on that occasion. In any case, the negotiations envisaged under the 1995 statement were later placed under the framework of the DOC, which provided new terms of reference. It is noteworthy that neither the 2004 nor the 2011 joint statements issued by the Presidents of the two countries made any reference to the 1995 Joint Statement, but instead made reference to the DOC. The bilateral contacts since 1995 as referred to in the Notification and Statement of Claim must be deemed, therefore, to be of questionable relevance for the purposes of Article 281(1) UNCLOS.

---

[65] See PRC MFA, 'Foreign Ministry Spokesperson Hua Chunying's Remarks on the Philippines' Statement on the South China Sea' (16 July 2013) Annex I, Doc A.4 (referring to two approaches made by China to the Philippines in March 2010 and January 2012).

[66] RP DFA, 'Response of the DFA Spokesperson to the Recent Statement of the Chinese Ministry of Foreign Affairs on the West Philippine Sea Issue' (15 July 2013) (n 59) para 5.

[67] ibid, para 8.

[68] Notification and Statement of Claim, para 26.

[69] 'Joint Statement on People's Republic of China and the Republic of the Philippines Consultations on the South China Sea and on Other Areas of Cooperation' (10 August 1995), reprinted in Xinhua News Agency 'China and the Philippines Held Consultations on the Issue of Nansha Islands, Reached General Agreement and Issued Joint Statement' *People's Daily* (12 August 1995) 1 (1995 Joint Statement). See also Ian James Storey, 'Creeping Assertiveness: China, the Philippines and the South China Sea Disputes' (1999) 21 *Contemporary Southeast Asia* 95, 104.

b. Negotiations under the Treaty of Amity and Cooperation in Southeast Asia

The foregoing analysis applies equally in the context of the TAC. The TAC is often mentioned in the part on general principles in relevant official documents that have been issued since the DOC in 2002. Paragraph 1 of the DOC, for instance, juxtaposes the TAC with the UN Charter,[70] UNCLOS, and universally recognised principles of international law, as 'the basic norms governing state-to-state relations'. It is not overstating the case to say that the principles of the TAC are universally recognised by all States,[71] and that the obligation to negotiate in the event of disputes, set forth in Article 13 of the Treaty, is one such universal principle for the contracting States as well as non-parties. This point on negotiations to be held in accordance with the TAC is not pressed further at this juncture, except for one remark that, since negotiations over the issues alleged in the Notification and Statement of Claim have not actually taken place, the question of whether they have been held in accordance with Article 13 of the TAC does not arise in the present case. Consequently, it is not possible to say that no settlement has been reached under the TAC. This means that the relevant requirement of Article 281(1) UNCLOS, is not satisfied.

c. Conclusion

It can be seen, on the whole, that negotiations under Article 281(1) UNCLOS have never properly taken place between China and the Philippines, even though negotiations as a means of dispute settlement has been the clear choice for them to settle their disputes in the South China Sea since 2002, under the DOC, the TAC and other relevant documents. It is therefore premature to conclude — as the Philippines did when rushing to serve the Notification and Statement of Claims on China — that the 'requirements of Article 279 have been satisfied' after 'good faith negotiations between the Parties',[72] or that over 'the past 17 years of such exchanges of views, all possibilities of a negotiated settlement have been explored and exhausted'.[73]

In addition, the negotiations relevant to the issues raised by the Notification and Statement of Claim could not have commenced properly before the DOC was adopted in 2002, to say the least. It is also unlikely

---

[70] See DOC (n 24).

[71] TAC, art 2 provides that 'in their relations with one another, the High Contracting Parties shall be guided by the following fundamental principles: a. Mutual respect for the independence, sovereignty, equality, territorial integrity and national identity of all nations; b. The right of every State to lead its national existence free from external interference, subversion or coercion; c. Non-interference in the internal affairs of one another; d. Settlement of differences or disputes by peaceful means; e. Renunciation of the threat or use of force; f. Effective cooperation among themselves'.

[72] Notification and Statement of Claim, para 8.

[73] ibid, para 27.

that when both parties to the present disputes were still reaffirming their commitment to negotiations in 2011, they were actually mindful at the same time that the negotiations would produce no result. The uncertain terms of reference for any negotiations between the two countries in this respect persisted until July 2011, when the DOC Guidelines were issued by the leaders of the parties to the DOC.

Requirement (b) of Article 281(1) UNCLOS is thus clearly *not* met in the present case.

3. Exclusion of Further Procedures

a. Exclusion under the 2002 Declaration

It is submitted that requirement (c) of Article 281(1) UNCLOS is not met in the circumstances of the present case, since the DOC was drafted in such a way as to exclude other, further procedures for settlement with regard to territorial and maritime disputes in the South China Sea. The DOC reads in its relevant part as follows:

> The Parties concerned undertake to resolve their territorial and jurisdictional disputes by peaceful means, without resorting to the threat or use of force, through friendly consultations and negotiations by sovereign states directly concerned, in accordance with universally recognized principles of international law, including the 1982 UN Convention on the Law of the Sea.[74]

The undertaking is specific regarding the means of settlement that it contemplates. It is neither open-ended nor ambiguous as to any possibility of other procedures that may also be subject to this undertaking. The parties to the Declaration only agreed to the specific means of dispute settlement as stated in the DOC, even though they could have included any other means recognised under Article 33(1) UN Charter. This silence in the text is even more glaring, considering that the above provision is the only part of the DOC that sets forth the agreed means of dispute settlement. This interpretation is strengthened by subsequent documents issued by the parties to the DOC, as referred to in the preceding paragraphs. The exclusion of other procedures of settlement, as contemplated by Article 281(1), is therefore implied in the DOC. It has been said that States Parties to UNCLOS 'are permitted by Article 281(1) to confine the applicability of compulsory procedures of section 2 of Part XV to cases where all parties to the dispute have agreed upon submission of their dispute to such compulsory procedures'.[75] The prior agreement between China and the Philippines has clearly been for consultation and negotiation, and no other agreement exists between them for other procedures.

---

[74] DOC (n 24) para 4.
[75] *Southern Bluefin Tuna Case* (*Australia and New Zealand v Japan*) (Award on Jurisdiction and Admissibility) (2000) 119 ILR 508, 544 [42]–[43]; 553 [62].

b. Exclusion under the Treaty of Amity and Cooperation in Southeast Asia

Under the TAC, there is an alternative procedure in case negotiations envisaged under Article 13 of the Treaty fail to produce a solution to disputes between the contracting parties. This calls for the High Council, as a regional process, to intervene by way of good offices, mediation, inquiry or conciliation.[76] However, the application of this provision is subject to one condition. Under Article 16, seeking recourse to the High Council requires the consent of all parties to a dispute. It is not certain whether the parties to the present arbitration will both give that consent. Supposing one party to the present arbitration withholds consent to recourse to the Article 15 procedure, there is only the means of negotiation under Article 13 that remains available to the parties to the present arbitration. It may be noted that the obligation to negotiate under Article 13 is categorical. Its requirement that the contracting parties 'shall at all times settle such disputes among themselves through friendly negotiations' excludes other alternative means. In addition, when Article 16 does not apply, Article 13 is the only means left for settlement. In that light, one may wonder whether Article 17 contradicts Article 13 by throwing the door open again for recourse to other solutions that belong to the modes of settlement contained in Article 33(1) UN Charter.[77] There is room for the view that recourse to Article 17 can only become possible when negotiations undertaken under Article 13 have failed completely, and when the alternative procedure under Article 15 does not apply. Even then, it would be difficult to avoid the requirement of having negotiations 'at all times' under Article 13. It should also be added that Article 17 itself reaffirms, in the second sentence, the priority of negotiations over other procedures provided for in the UN Charter.

One possible interpretation of this scheme of the TAC is, therefore, that there is a primary obligation on the contracting States to negotiate at all times, over and above all other means of settlement, and that the alternative venue of the High Council and other means of settlement as enumerated in Article 33 UN Charter only come into play when the negotiations fail to resolve the dispute in question. Then, the High Council's involvement is subject to the consent of all the parties to the dispute, and the other means of settlement are subject to conditions that are specific to their invocation. However, another equally possible interpretation is that the effect of Article 13 may simply be exclusionary, as the wording of the Article does not contain any point of ambiguity. It excludes all other means of

---

[76] TAC, art 15. This process is probably not covered by art 282 UNCLOS since it does not lead to a 'binding decision' as required by that article.

[77] TAC, art 17 provides: 'Nothing in this Treaty shall preclude recourse to the modes of peaceful settlement contained in Article 33(1) of the Charter of the United Nations. The High Contracting Parties which are parties to a dispute should be encouraged to take initiatives to solve it by friendly negotiations before resorting to the other procedures provided for in the Charter of the United Nations'.

settlement when a dispute arises. As has been noted above, the categorical nature of the wording of Article 13 may pose difficulty in the application of the TAC's regime for the settlement of disputes.

It should finally be noted that the TAC does not contain a separate mechanism for settling disputes concerning its interpretation or application. It appears possible to apply Article 13 and the subsequent provisions for that purpose. That would again require the parties to a dispute to negotiate a solution. Alternatively, it falls upon the contracting States to the TAC to come up with a supplementary treaty or protocol to address this issue. What this means, at this moment, is that the two interpretations discussed in the preceding paragraph are probably equally acceptable, depending on the difference of views with regard to the admissibility of a dispute like the one that gives rise to the present arbitration between the Philippines and China.

c. Conclusion

It may be recalled that the evidence was supplied in the DFA Response of 15 July 2013 regarding the Philippines' initiatives for talks. That evidence shows exactly the significance of what is being argued in this section, namely, that the exclusion in this case of other means of settlement, including arbitration, by treaty or conduct is not intended to deny their value as peaceful means to settle international disputes, but that international law prioritises prior agreement between parties to a dispute in certain situations. In the present arbitration, the parties are under an obligation to settle their disputes by negotiation.[78] In other words, the view that judicial and diplomatic means can be pursued concurrently for the resolution of a dispute is not being questioned.[79] But they have clearly been assigned different levels of precedence by the regime enacted through UNCLOS, the existence of which constitutes a procedural bar pursuant to Article 281(1) UNCLOS.

4. Summary

Out of the three requirements of Article 281(1), two are not met. The conclusion for this section is therefore that there are important handicaps to the applicability of section 2 of Part XV which must be overcome before the Philippines' case is deemed admissible, and Article 281(1) is one of these. Where the requirements of Article 281(1) are not fulfilled to the extent indicated above, 'the procedures provided for in this Part' (ie Part

---

[78] RP DFA, 'Response of the DFA Spokesperson to the Recent Statement of the Chinese Ministry of Foreign Affairs on the West Philippine Sea Issue' (15 July 2013) (n 59) paras 4–7.

[79] *Land and Maritime Boundary between Cameroon and Nigeria (Cameroon v Nigeria)* (Preliminary Objections) [1998] ICJ Rep 275, 303 [56].

XV of UNCLOS) including the compulsory procedures, cannot apply. The case is consequently inadmissible on this ground.

III. DEFECTS OF CERTAIN CLAIMS

The mootness and vagueness of the 'Philippines' Claims' are presented together in this section, as they are both indicative of the defects of the Notification and Statement of Claim. But in arbitral proceedings, those two aspects should perhaps constitute two separate grounds of inadmissibility for the tribunal to consider.

1. Mootness of Claims

It may be recalled that 'the existence of a dispute is the primary condition for the Court to exercise its judicial function; it is not sufficient for one party to assert that there is a dispute, since "whether there exists an international dispute is a matter for objective determination" by the Court'.[80] It is clear that 'no dispute' is not equivalent to 'no dispute regarding the interpretation or application of UNCLOS', and that the former is meant in this context concerning the admissibility of the present case. Where a dispute is non-existent, there would be no basis for the arbitral tribunal to consider the issue as to whether it has jurisdiction over such a dispute.[81] In addition, it would be quite curious if an arbitral tribunal, such as the one in the present case, proceeded to determine the case as an abstract question of law, or, on a hypothetical state of facts, unless the jurisdiction *ratione materiae* allowed for such an exercise of the judicial function of the tribunal. While the former scenario is not unimaginable as something which the tribunal could indeed examine on some occasions, the latter is simply a situation in which it would be inappropriate for the tribunal to exercise its jurisdiction because the tribunal could not possibly find the claims of the claimant to be well-founded in fact. Several claims of the Notification and Statement of Claim fall within these scenarios.

It is plain that the Claims, bullet point 2 advanced by the Philippines, regarding the nine-dash line,[82] is moot, or without object, as the nine-dash line is primarily concerned with territorial sovereignty in the South China

---

[80] *Nuclear Tests (Australia v France)* (Merits) [1974] ICJ Rep 253, 270–71 [55], referring to the Court's advisory opinion in *Interpretation of Peace Treaties with Bulgaria, Hungary and Romania* (First Phase: Advisory Opinion) [1950] ICJ Rep 65, 74.

[81] *Nuclear Tests (Australia v France)* (Merits) [1974] ICJ Rep 253, 271 [56]. See also *Northern Cameroons (Cameroon v United Kingdom)* (Preliminary Objections) [1963] ICJ Rep 15, 104 (sep op Fitzmaurice).

[82] The Philippines' 'Claims' are set out in para 31 of the Notification and Statement of Claim and comprise 10 bullet points. Hereafter reference is made to the bullet points in the 'Claims' section.

Sea.[83] No dispute otherwise exists in this regard so as to justify the exercise by the Arbitral Tribunal of its jurisdiction under UNCLOS, as bilateral negotiations are still to be held between China and the Philippines.[84] The claim by the Philippines should have been preceded by a query addressed to the Chinese Government as to the nature and extent of the area hemmed in by the nine-dash line. Without an answer by China to that query, it is hardly appropriate to ask the Arbitral Tribunal to, effectively, guess China's answer for the benefit of the claimant in this case.

The Philippines' Claims, bullet point 6 that 'China has unlawfully claimed maritime entitlements beyond 12 M' from Scarborough Shoal [Huangyan Island], Johnson Reef [Chigua Jiao], Cuarteron Reef [Huayang Jiao] and Fiery Cross Reef [Yongshu Jiao]'[85] is moot with regard to the latter three reefs. The reason is that any maritime entitlement generated by them is, geographically speaking, within the exclusive economic zone (and the concomitant continental shelf) measured from the baselines to be drawn from, among others, Itu Aba [Taiping] Island — an island which, in any case, belongs to China. If Philippine fishermen intended to carry out fishing activities in the area of the sea adjacent to the island, they would be subject to Chinese law, including those of an enforcement nature in terms of Article 298(1)(b) UNCLOS. Regardless of the way these reefs, apart from Scarborough Shoal [Huangyan Island], are defined (as rocks or islands), no finding that China has illegally prevented Philippine vessels from exploiting the living resources in their vicinity can be made. In any case, in order to address this claim, evidence from China is necessary. For that reason the above claim clearly concerns a moot question. It should be added that the dispute over Scarborough Shoal [Huangyan Island] is one of territorial sovereignty, as acknowledged in the Notification and Statement of Claim.[86] It thus falls outside the jurisdiction of the Arbitral Tribunal, but for a reason different from this ground of mootness.

In Claims, bullet point 8, the Philippines asks the Arbitral Tribunal to declare that it is entitled to various maritime zones under UNCLOS.[87] The Notification and Statement of Claim contains no indication that China has ever denied, in law or in fact, such entitlement to any State party to UNCLOS. On the contrary, as a party to UNCLOS, China is equally entitled to those zones. There is no conflict of views or interests in this regard, which renders this a moot point.

For the foregoing reasons, Claims, bullet points 2, 8 and part of bullet point 6 are moot and therefore inadmissible.

---

[83] Zhigou Gao and Bing Bing Jia, 'The Nine-Dash Line in the South China Sea: History, Status, and Implications' (2013) 107 *American Journal of International Law* 98, 108.

[84] See section II. above.

[85] Claims, bullet point 6.

[86] Notification and Statement of Claim, para 20.

[87] Claims, bullet point 8.

2. Vagueness of Claims

It is submitted that the vagueness of Claims, bullet points 7, 9, and 10 will also render the Philippines' case inadmissible to the extent of those claims, in that these claims are not precise enough for a respondent to respond effectively.[88] Claims, bullet point 7, for instance, alleges that China has unlawfully prevented Philippine vessels from exploiting the living resources in the waters adjacent to Scarborough Shoal [Huanyang Island] and Johnson Reef [Chigua Jiao], without, however, giving a precise account of the extent of such adjacent waters.[89] But it is obvious that the extent and the legal nature of the adjacent waters are central to the claim, and a claim should be based on 'a sufficiently *precise* statement of the facts',[90] even though the Philippines has reserved 'the right to supplement and/or amend its claims and the relief sought'.[91] If, for example, the alleged incidents took place within China's territorial sea or exclusive economic zone, the claim would become absurd and meaningless. There is no denying of the opportunity afforded to the applicant to supplement its claims and facts in later stages of the proceedings. But given the normal way to proceed in an arbitration,[92] it is inefficient to leave the specifics of a claim unfilled until a later date. It is not argued here that the factual specifics requested in this connection might transform the nature of the original dispute as alleged in the Notification and Statement of Claim, which would probably not be allowed by the Tribunal.[93] Additionally, with regard to the reference to 'waters *adjacent* to Scarborough Shoal',[94] what has been asked for is not so unreasonable a request that the applicant would not have had time or space to oblige in the Notification and Statement of Claim. On the contrary, a few words would have sufficed to delineate the confines of the area clearly, in which the alleged preventive action taken by Chinese vessels took place.

Claims, bullet points 9 and 10 suffer from the same defect of vagueness as Claims, bullet point 7. The plain question would be why China cannot enforce its laws within waters always deemed to be subject to its sovereignty, sovereign rights or jurisdiction, which is in harmony with UNCLOS. Those laws also empower Chinese nationals to claim rights to,

---

[88] *cf Land and Maritime Boundary between Cameroon and Nigeria (Cameroon v Nigeria)* (Preliminary Objections) [1998] ICJ Rep 275, 319 [101]. The Court continued: 'It is the applicant which must bear the consequences of an application that gives an inadequate rendering of the facts and grounds on which the claim is based'.

[89] In its Notification and Statement of Claim, para 21, the Philippines remained vague as to the meaning and extent of 'in its vicinity' and of 'in these waters'.

[90] *Land and Maritime Boundary between Cameroon and Nigeria (Cameroon v Nigeria)* (Preliminary Objections) [1998] ICJ Rep 275, 319 [101].

[91] Notification and Statement of Claim, para 43.

[92] See PCA, 'Arbitration between the Philippines and China, Arbitral Tribunal, First Press Release' (27 August 2013) (n 21).

[93] *Land and Maritime Boundary between Cameroon and Nigeria (Cameroon v Nigeria)* (Preliminary Objections) [1998] ICJ Rep 275, 318 [99].

[94] Claims, bullet point 7 (emphasis added).

and exploit, the living and non-living resources in the waters, subjacent sea-bed and subsoil concerned and to navigate the sea. Moreover, those laws entitle Chinese authorities to enforce them in the relevant areas of the South China Sea. Those three claims are therefore inadmissible.

In any case, whether or not the Philippines clarifies these vague points later in the proceedings, the fundamental flaw in the basis for the three claims will not be remedied. As the Notification and Statement of Claim itself conceded,[95] both China and the Philippines have protested against each other with regard to interference with navigational and exploratory rights. The reason for that exchange of protests is, without question, the disputes over the territorial sovereignty over certain insular features of the Spratly [Nansha] Islands and Macclesfield Bank, including Scarborough Shoal [Zhongsha Islands].[96] That root cause is a matter that goes beyond the scope of UNCLOS.

IV. ABUSE OF RIGHTS/PROCEDURE

As a ground of inadmissibility this section suggests that the filing of the Notification and Statement of Claim also touches upon the principle of good faith. The action taken by the Philippines, namely, the institution of arbitral proceedings despite a prior commitment to resolving the dispute by negotiation, is likely to constitute an act of bad faith. As such, it may constitute an abuse of procedural rights recognised under Article 287(3) UNCLOS. Such an act is in direct contravention of the provision of Article 300 UNCLOS, which states that 'States Parties shall fulfil in good faith the obligations assumed under this Convention and shall exercise the rights, jurisdiction and freedoms recognized in this Convention in a manner which would not constitute an abuse of right'. In regard to the present case, it is suggested that Article 300 may well give rise to an issue of admissibility when it is considered in conjunction with the exercise of the right under Article 287(3).[97] In addition, given the importance of the principle of good faith in international law,[98] it would be judicially inappropriate for the Arbitral Tribunal to admit the Notification and Statement Claim. This abuse of right or procedure argument is not only based in the explicit

---

[95] Notification and Statement of Claim, paras 28 and 29.

[96] See eg ibid, para 20: 'Yet, China, which like the Philippines asserts sovereignty over Scarborough Shoal'.

[97] *Border and Transborder Armed Actions (Nicaragua v Honduras)* (Jurisdiction and Admissibility) [1988] ICJ Rep 69, 105 [94]. See also *M/V 'Louisa' (Saint Vincent and The Grenadines v Kingdom of Spain)* (Judgment of 28 May 2013) [2013] ITLOS Rep [34] (diss op Jesus).

[98] *cf* Declaration on Principles of International Law Concerning Friendly Relations and Co-operation Among States, UNGA Res 2625 (XXV) (24 October 1970) UN Doc A/RES/2625 (XXV), Annex, principle I: 'All States shall comply in good faith with their obligations under the generally recognized principles and rules of international law with respect to the maintenance of international peace and security'.

provision of Article 300 UNCLOS, but is also grounded on the broader view that good faith 'ought to govern international relations'.[99]

The reason for this basis of inadmissibility does not lie with the terms of Article 297 UNCLOS, and therefore does not give rise to a discussion of Article 294(1) which expressly invites an arbitral tribunal to determine *proprio motu* whether the claims made constitute an 'abuse of legal process'. The prerequisites for the application of Article 297 are that there exists a dispute concerning the interpretation or application of UNCLOS and that the dispute concerns a coastal State. However, the present case is concerned neither with the interpretation or application of UNCLOS,[100] nor is it based on an identity of the coastal State as agreed between China and the Philippines. In fact, if either Party to the present case relied on Article 297, this would imply recognition of the other party's sovereignty over relevant insular features in the South China Sea.

Well aware of the limited effects of the principle of good faith in general,[101] it is submitted that it is a legal obligation under UNCLOS by virtue of Article 300. The reason for invoking this ground of (in)admissibility on the basis of the principle of good faith rests on the following considerations.

Firstly, the Notification and Statement of Claim was apparently filed without prior consultation between the countries concerned, due to the unilateral character of the arbitration procedure under Article 287 and Annex VII of UNCLOS.[102] In this respect, it may be recalled that, in the *Land Reclamation* case, Judge José Luis Jesus stated in his separate opinion that:

> In my view, if the parties to a dispute have agreed through a treaty provision or otherwise to settle their disputes through a particular settlement procedure, the determination of whether that procedure has run its course without producing a settlement is to be made by the concurrence of the two parties.[103]

This view is reasonable enough, for it is an eminent act of good faith if one party informs the other in the negotiating process that there seems to be an exhaustion of utility of this method of settlement. The unilateral character of the Annex VII procedure is not challenged here, but that character is obviously subject to the provision of Article 281(1) UNCLOS, among other provisions. To inform the other party to a negotiation process of an intention to break it off is even more necessary in the circumstances of this arbitration, since the Philippines has been under a treaty obligation to negotiate, along with a concurrent obligation to negotiate pursuant to its

---

[99] See *Venezuelan Preferential Case (Germany, Great Britain, Italy v Venezuela et al)* (1904) 9 RIAA 107, 110.

[100] *cf* ch 3, section IV.

[101] The principle 'is not in itself a source of obligation'; see: *Border and Transborder Armed Actions (Nicaragua v Honduras)* (Jurisdiction and Admissibility) [1988] ICJ Rep 69, 105 [94].

[102] *cf Barbados v Trinidad and Tobago* (2006) 27 RIAA 147, 207 [207].

[103] *Land Reclamation in and around the Straits of Johor (Malaysia v Singapore)* (Provisional Measure, Order of 8 October 2003) [2003] ITLOS Rep 52, 54 (sep op Jesus).

conduct. It may also be recalled that the Philippines has formally agreed to seek consensus before implementing the DOC measures or activities.[104]

Secondly, the effect of the filing of the Notification and Statement of Claim is such that it may enable the filing party to avoid its obligation to negotiate under Articles 279 and 281(1), and its obligation to do so in good faith under Article 300.[105] Concomitantly, the act of filing has hindered China's enjoyment of its right to negotiate a settlement to the disputes in question. While peaceful means of dispute settlement are not stipulated in a hierarchical order under general international law, Article 281(1) UNCLOS, drafted in view of the particular conditions of maritime disputes, suggests just such a hierarchy with a degree of exclusivity in favour of the means agreed between the States Parties concerned. Article 295 UNCLOS, another example of this design for the regime of compulsory dispute settlement under UNCLOS, also presupposes an order of precedence between the rules of exhaustion of local remedies and the procedures to bring questions of interpretation or application of UNCLOS to a venue envisaged in section 2 of Part XV of the Convention.

Lastly, there is evidence, as shown above,[106] that pertinent and meaningful negotiations between China and the Philippines are yet to commence in the spirit of the DOC with its Terms of Reference of 2011, or under the TAC.[107] There is simply no possibility of a good faith performance of the commitment or obligation to negotiate. Indeed, without negotiations along those lines, the disputes as presented in the Notification and Statement of Claim are not defined clearly enough for the parties to consider recourse to arbitral or judicial processes.

By initiating arbitral proceedings in these circumstances, even though all States Parties to the DOC and the TAC have undertaken to engage in consultations and negotiations — an undertaking which the Philippines itself has on several occasions reaffirmed in bilateral documents issued jointly with China — the Philippines has abused its right under Part XV of UNCLOS in general, and the procedures of Article 287(3) UNCLOS, in particular. This abuse is a breach of the terms of Article 300. Further, it has produced an adverse effect upon the effective operation of the mechanism of settlement as laid down in Part XV of UNCLOS, depriving the provisions of section 1 of Part XV of all practical effect. The act of filing clearly flows from an interpretation of the scheme of Part XV that should be firmly rejected by the Arbitral Tribunal for the sake of a stable and effective regime such as the one found in UNCLOS.

---

[104] *cf* Guidelines for the Implementation of the Declaration of Conduct of Parties in the South China Sea (n 52); see also accompanying text at n 52 above.

[105] This is the reason why this case differs from the arbitration in *Barbados v Trinidad and Tobago* (2006) 27 RIAA 147, 207–08 [208].

[106] See section II.2.

[107] In comparison, negotiations had actually taken place between Australia and New Zealand, on the one hand, and Japan, on the other, in the *Southern Bluefin Tuna* cases: see *Southern Bluefin Tuna Cases (New Zealand v Japan; Australia v Japan)* (Provisional Measures, Order of 27 August 1999) [1999] ITLOS Rep 280, 294–95 [57]–[60].

V. ESTOPPEL

This section contains an argument based on the effect of the filing of the Notification and Statement of Claim upon China as the recipient and, as such, operates *inter partes*. This is posited as a corollary to the argument based on Article 281(1) UNCLOS, as well as the concept of abuse of right. The thrust of this argument of inadmissibility is that the commitment undertaken by the Philippines under both the DOC and the TAC (which was reaffirmed, inter alia, by the joint statement of China and the Philippines of September 2011), is embodied in a series of official acts, which are by their nature 'an engagement of the State'.[108] It takes the form of a reaffirmation of a prior (and formal) undertaking that binds the Philippines both legally and politically. In this light, the issue of estoppel arises. The argument is that, while the consequences of an estoppel would exist between China and the Philippines, it could still contaminate the exercise of the jurisdiction of the Arbitral Tribunal, were the Tribunal to continue with the proceedings in spite of the prohibitive aspect of estoppel. A breach of the generally recognised rule of estoppel constitutes a violation of substantive international law, [109] to which the Arbitral Tribunal should not lend its hand. The doctrine of estoppel is embedded in, and emblematic of, the general principle of good faith. That principle is the cornerstone of the system of international law.[110] It is submitted that the estoppel of the filing party can only be overcome by initiating, conducting and bringing to a natural conclusion the necessary prior negotiations over the disputes between the two parties. The issue of estoppel is thus considered as one that bears upon the admissibility of the Notification and Statement of Claim. The rules associated with the doctrine of estoppel are to be found in general international law.

As the Permanent Court of International Justice (PCIJ) stated in *Eastern Greenland*, 'Norway reaffirmed that she recognised the whole of Greenland as Danish; and thereby she has debarred herself from contesting Danish sovereignty over the whole of Greenland and, in consequence, from proceeding to occupy any part of it'.[111] In *Temple of Preah Vihear* case, the ICJ

---

[108] *cf Nuclear Tests (Australia v France)* (Merits) [1974] ICJ Rep 253, 266 [37]; 269 [49].

[109] As Judge Sir Percy Spender stated in his dissenting opinion in *Temple of Preah Vihear (Cambodia v Thailand)* (Merits) [1962] ICJ Rep 6, 143: 'The principle of preclusion is a beneficent and powerful instrument of substantive international law. Based as it is upon the necessity for good faith between States in their relations one with another, it is not to be hedged in by artificial rules'. See also Jörg Paul Müller and Thomas Cottier, 'Estoppel' in Rudolf Bernhardt (ed), *Encyclopedia of Public International Law*, vol II (Amsterdam, North Holland Publishing, 1995) 116, 118.

[110] *Nuclear Tests (Australia v France)* (Merits) [1974] ICJ Rep 253, 268 [46]: 'One of the basic principles governing the creation and performance of legal obligations, whatever their source, is the principle of good faith. Trust and confidence are inherent in international co-operation, in particular in an age when this cooperation in many fields is becoming increasingly essential'.

[111] *Legal Status of Eastern Greenland (Denmark v Norway)* (Judgment of 5 April 1933) PCIJ Rep Series A/B No 53, 22, 68–69.

considered Thailand as being estopped from raising issues of sovereignty, through various types of official conduct that precluded it from contesting the validity of a frontier that was known to it, and which its officials had reaffirmed by conduct on separate occasions.[112] As Judge Sir Gerald Fitzmaurice held in his separate opinion in that case:

> The real field of operation, therefore, of the rule of preclusion or estoppel, stricto sensu, in the present context, is where it is possible that the party concerned did not give the undertaking or accept the obligation in question (or there is room for doubt whether it did), but where that party's subsequent conduct has been such, and has had such consequences, that it cannot be allowed to deny the existence of an undertaking, or that it is bound.[113]

Or, in Judge Sir Percy Spender's view expressed in the same case, an estoppel prevents a State from contesting 'a situation contrary to a clear and unequivocal representation previously made by it to another State, either expressly or implicitly, on which representation the other State was, in the circumstances, entitled to rely and in fact did rely, and as a result that other State has been prejudiced or the State making it has secured some benefit or advantage for itself'.[114]

For the present purposes, it may be said that an estoppel may arise from a previous fact stated, or conduct undertaken by a State, on which another State relies to its detriment, or to the advantage of the former State. In this context, no distinction is to be made between reliance upon a representation of fact and reliance upon conduct.[115] As the preceding cases show, recognition of a certain state of fact alone can give rise to an estoppel in international disputes.

Estoppel clearly operates in the present case, given the course of the evolution of the disputes since the DOC in 2002. China, like the other parties to the DOC, is entitled to rely on, and has indeed relied on, the undertakings contained in the Declaration. There has since been a succession of official documents issued by China and the ASEAN countries to promote the full and effective implementation of the DOC.[116] There is a previous state of fact established by activities imputable to the Philippine Government, that the latter undertook under the DOC to pursue consultation and negotiation in the settlement of territorial and maritime disputes with other States in the South China Sea. That undertaking has been reaffirmed by subsequent

---

[112] *Temple of Preah Vihear (Cambodia v Thailand)* (Merits) [1962] ICJ Rep 6, 27–28; 30; 32–33.
[113] ibid, 63.
[114] ibid, 143–44 (diss op Spender).
[115] Derek William Bowett, 'Estoppel before International Tribunals and its Relation to Acquiescence' (1957) 33 *British Year Book of International Law* 176, 189; Ian Brownlie, *Principles of Public International Law*, 7th edn (Oxford, OUP, 2008) 644.
[116] See eg 'Joint Statement of the 15th ASEAN-China Summit on the 10th Anniversary of the Declaration on the Conduct of Parties in the South China Sea' (Phnom Penh, Cambodia, 19 November 2012) (n 53); ASEAN Secretariat News, '19th ASEAN-China Senior Officials' Consultation' (4 April 2013) www.asean.org; ASEAN Secretariat News, 'Foreign Minister of The People's Republic of China Visits ASEAN Secretariat' (2 May 2013) www.asean.org.

activity by the Philippines in documents issued by the ASEAN countries and China, and issued jointly by China and itself.

Before the consultation and negotiation as required under the DOC or the TAC commenced, however, China was surprised by a drastic change of course initiated unilaterally by the Philippines in serving China with the Notification and Statement of Claim in January 2013. The detriment to China is plain, since China has never had the opportunity to engage the Philippines in pertinent consultations and negotiations in accordance with the DOC, the attendant DOC Guidelines or the TAC.[117] Its lawful right to seek a settlement by negotiation has been pre-empted by the Philippines' action. Needless to say, the detriment it may have suffered can take other forms, which will transpire with the development of the arbitral proceedings.

In consequence, there is a presumption of estoppel against the Philippines in the present circumstances.[118] The conduct or representation of fact relied on by China is, above all, the undertaking by the Philippines only to pursue consultation and negotiation in the settlement of territorial and jurisdictional disputes in the South China Sea. That conduct has been reinforced and reaffirmed by the joint statements issued between China and the Philippines in 2004 and 2011, respectively, as well as through the TAC.[119] By recourse to Annex VII of UNCLOS, the Philippines has disowned the undertakings it assumed between 2002–2011, despite the fact that China has been seeking negotiations in accordance with UNCLOS and in the spirit of the DOC.

Even supposing the DOC and the joint statements of 2004 and 2011 are not binding on the parties to this arbitration, they may still result in legal consequences that, while being different from those arising from a binding treaty, can bring estoppel into play.[120] For such documents, with a clear degree of consistency, bring forth 'an expectation of, and reliance on, compliance by the parties',[121] and nothing stops the States that have adopted them from regarding the documents as controlling their relationships, with or without legal responsibility.[122]

In addition, by official acts of the Philippine President in joining, in particular, the 2011 Joint Statement with China, the State of the Philippines literally reaffirmed the undertakings of the DOC, and is further bound to it as a result. It may be recalled that, in case of a unilateral act, the President of a State is a person 'competent to formulate' unilateral declarations that are binding upon his or her country,[123] as long as the declarations are made

---

[117] See also accompanying text at n 51 and n 53 above.

[118] See *Land and Maritime Boundary between Cameroon and Nigeria (Cameroon v Nigeria)* (Preliminary Objections) [1998] ICJ Rep 275, 319 [100].

[119] See above section II.1.

[120] Oscar Schachter, 'The Twilight Existence of Nonbinding Agreements' (1971) 71 *American Journal of International Law* 296, 301.

[121] ibid, 299.

[122] ibid, 300.

[123] See ILC, 'Guiding Principles Applicable to Unilateral Declarations of States Capable of Creating Legal Obligations' *Yearbook of the International Law Commission*, vol 2 (2006) 164 (principle 4).

publicly and 'manifesting the will to be bound'[124] without being intended as a 'witticism of the kind regularly uttered as press conferences'.[125] The nature of the act of the Philippine President in relation to the 2011 Joint Statement is more than just a unilateral act, as the issuance of the statement consisted in bilateral, official acts resulting in an official document that recorded a joint commitment of the Presidents of the two countries to implement or abide by the DOC. It is thus all the more perplexing that the Philippine Government instituted arbitral proceedings only slightly more than a year after the 2011 Joint Statement — with both documents being issued by the same President as Head of State and Government of the Philippines.

An alternative expression of this argument is that the Philippines has violated the terms of the TAC. It is not denied that, on this point, opinions differ in regard to whether this is an estoppel or simply a clear breach of treaty obligations.[126] But there is room for the view that a breach of a treaty obligation also falls foul of the prior conduct in accepting a treaty obligation, thereby raising the possibility of estoppel by conduct. Ultimately, the basis for the doctrine of estoppel and the obligation to comply with one's treaty obligations is the same: good faith.[127]

At this stage of the arbitration, the Arbitral Tribunal should find that this is a basis of inadmissibility that impacts upon judicial propriety, and it is not really a matter that may be joined to the merits of the case. After all, this issue of estoppel flows from the Philippines' failure to meet Article 281(1) UNCLOS which precedes the Annex VII procedures. It could not therefore concern the merits of the present case. Furthermore, estoppel as a substantive rule of international law rests upon the general principle of good faith. That principle is one that anchors the system of international law,[128] and failure to deal with it, when it directly concerns the appropriateness of the initiation of the arbitration proceedings in this case, could cast doubt upon the judicial role of this Tribunal.

Where estoppel is ignored by a State subject to its effect, like the Philippines in this case, China as the other party is entitled to reserve the right to seek reparation with regard to the consequences of this wrongful act of the Philippines—including a breach of the TAC by the same act.[129]

---

[124] ibid, 162 (principle 1).

[125] *Frontier Dispute (Burkina Faso/Republic of Mali)* (Merits) [1986] ICJ Rep 554, 572 [38].

[126] *Temple of Preah Vihear (Cambodia v Thailand)* (Merits) [1962] ICJ Rep 6, 63 (sep op Fitzmaurice).

[127] ibid, 143 (diss op Spender). See also Bin Cheng, *General Principles of Law as Applied by International Courts and Tribunals* (Cambridge, CUP, 1953 [1994 reprint]) 144; Bowett, 'Estoppel before International Tribunals' 176.

[128] *Border and Transborder Armed Actions (Nicaragua v Honduras)* (Jurisdiction and Admissibility) [1988] ICJ Rep 69, 105 [94]: 'one of the basic principles governing the creation and performance of legal obligations'.

[129] See ILC Articles on Responsibility of States for Internationally Wrongful Acts, art 31(1): 'The responsible State is under an obligation to make full reparation for the injury caused by the internationally wrongful act'; art 31(2): 'Injury includes any damage, whether material or moral, caused by the internationally wrongful act of a State' (UNGA Res 56/83 (28 January 2002) UN Doc A/RES/56/83, Annex).

VI. CONCLUSION

This chapter uses the Philippines' Notification and Statement of Claim as a case study of the issue of admissibility in inter-State arbitrations. There is, it is felt, no distinction between grounds of this category arising in arbitral proceedings and in judicial proceedings on the international plane. They are, however, not necessarily identical since each case, arbitral or judicial, may give rise to grounds of inadmissibility that defy attempts at generalization.

The chief consequence of applying the reasoning developed in this chapter to the arbitral proceedings instituted by the Philippines is as what the ICJ concluded in *Georgia v Russia*:

> Considering the Court's conclusion ... that under Article 22 of CERD, negotiations and the procedures expressly provided for in CERD constitute preconditions to the exercise of its jurisdiction, and considering the factual finding that neither of these two modes of dispute settlement was attempted by Georgia.[130]

The Court accordingly concluded that neither requirement contained in Article 22 CERD had been satisfied. Therefore, Article 22 of CERD could not serve as a basis of the Court's jurisdiction in that case.

There is of course the hair-splitting question as to whether that statement determined an issue of jurisdiction or one of admissibility. But admissibility clearly affects the *exercise* of the jurisdiction of an arbitral or judicial body and is therefore closely related to the context of jurisdiction. It is in that sense *jurisdictional*. Thus, the statement quoted above is not unsuitable to further illustrate the way in which the theme of this present chapter operates in a concrete case.

The claims as set out in the Notification and Statement of Claim are therefore inadmissible on account of the four grounds set out above, and the most obvious precondition out of them — for the purposes of the application of Part XV of UNCLOS — is the fulfilment of the conditions laid down in Article 281(1). A parallel thus exists between the present arbitration and the ICJ case quoted above. But the grounds of inadmissibility in respect of the present arbitration are more than just the one of negotiation. The tentative conclusion, however, remains that, because the claims meet all four grounds of inadmissibility discussed here, they should be declared inadmissible and rejected in their entirety by the Arbitral Tribunal.

---

[130] *Application of the International Convention on the Elimination of All Forms of Racial Discrimination (Georgia v Russian Federation)* (Preliminary Objections) [2011] ICJ Rep 70, 140 [183]–[84].

5

Jurisprudential Tenability of the Philippines v China Arbitration on South China Sea Disputes?

HAIWEN ZHANG AND CHENXI MI

I. INTRODUCTION

O N 22 JANUARY 2013, the Philippines sent a written notification informing China of its submission of the maritime jurisdiction disputes in the South China Sea between the two countries to an arbitral tribunal to be constituted according to Annex VII of the United Nations Convention on the Law of the Sea (UNCLOS or the Convention).[1] Meanwhile, the official website of the Philippines Department of Foreign Affairs (DFA) explained in a Q&A form this unilateral move to initiate compulsory arbitral proceedings. Interestingly, the webpage stressed that the US and Japan did not influence the Philippines' decision to take this independent action, which only serves to invite curiosity about the driving forces behind it.[2]

The Philippines initiated compulsory arbitration proceedings against China on maritime disputes between the two countries in the South China Sea, attracting widespread and sustained international attention. Containing multiple legal loopholes and inaccurate statements, the Philippines' Notification and Statement of Claim, which circumvents the Chinese declaration submitted to the United Nations under Article 298 of UNCLOS on 25 August 2006,[3] specifically states that the Philippines 'has avoided raising subjects or making claims that China has, by virtue

---

[1] Republic of the Philippines (RP), Department of Foreign Affairs (DFA), Notification and Statement of Claim (22 January 2013), reproduced in Annex I, Doc B.2 (Notification and Statement of Claim).

[2] RP DFA, 'Q & A on the UNCLOS Arbitral Proceedings against China to Achieve a Peaceful and Durable Solution to the Dispute in the West Philippine Sea' (23 January 2013) question 18, www.dfa.gov.ph.

[3] Declaration by the People's Republic of China under Article 298 UNCLOS (25 August 2006) Annex I, Doc A.26.

of that Declaration, excluded from arbitral jurisdiction'.[4] However, the ten claims which the Philippines presents are all, from content to nature, closely linked to issues concerning the sovereignty over the islands, rocks and other features in the South China Sea and the delimitation of overlapping maritime zone claims.[5]

On 19 February 2013, China officially rejected and returned the Philippine Notification and Statement of Claim, reiterated its principled stance and stressed that China has always insisted that the South China Sea disputes be settled through consultations and negotiations between the parties directly concerned, which is also the consensus reached by parties which have signed the ASEAN-China Declaration on the Conduct of Parties in the South China Sea (DOC).[6]

II. WHAT ARE THE PHILIPPINES' CLAIMS AGAINST CHINA?

The Philippine Note Verbale to China is very brief, with detailed reasons and litigation claims for the compulsory arbitration included in an attachment referred to as 'Notification and Statement of Claim'.[7] The latter document includes seven sections which cover such topics as the 'factual background' as perceived by the Philippines, the Philippines' claims in the South China Sea, the jurisdiction of the arbitral tribunal, relief sought, the appointment of arbitrators and the reservation of rights.[8] The 'Philippines' Claims' in the Notification and Statement of Claim can be summarised as follows:

1. China and the Philippines' rights in regard to maritime areas in the South China Sea are those that are established by UNCLOS, and consist of rights to the territorial sea, contiguous zone, exclusive economic zone (EEZ), and continental shelf;
2. China's maritime claims in the South China Sea based on the 'nine-dash line' are contrary to UNCLOS and invalid;
3. Submerged features in the South China Sea that are not above sea level at high tide, and are not located in a coastal State's territorial sea, are part of the seabed and cannot be acquired by a State, or subjected to its sovereignty, unless they form part of that State's continental shelf under Part VI of UNCLOS;

---

[4] Notification and Statement of Claim, para 7.

[5] For the 'Philippines' Claims', see Notification and Statement of Claim, para 31.

[6] See PRC MFA, 'Chinese Spokesperson Hong Lei's Remarks on China Returned the Philippines' Notification on the Submission of South China Sea Issue to International Arbitration' (19 February 2013) and 'Foreign Ministry Spokesperson Hua Chunying's Remarks on the Philippines' Efforts in Pushing for the Establishment of the Arbitral Tribunal in Relation to the Disputes between China and the Philippines in the South China Sea' (26 April 2013) Annex I, Docs A.17 and A.14, respectively.

[7] Note Verbale No 13-0211 from the Department of Foreign Affairs of the Republic of the Philippines to the Embassy of the People's Republic of China in Manila (22 January 2013) Annex I, Doc B.1.

[8] See Notification and Statement of Claim.

4. Mischief Reef [Meiji Jiao], McKennan Reef [Ximen Jiao], Gaven Reef [Nanxun Jiao] and Subi Reef [Zhubi Jiao] are submerged features that are not above sea level at high tide, are not islands under UNCLOS, are not located on China's continental shelf; and China has unlawfully occupied and engaged in unlawful construction activities on these features;

5. Mischief Reef [Meiji Jiao] and McKennan Reef [Ximen Jiao] are part of the Philippines' continental shelf under Part VI of UNCLOS;

6. Scarborough Reef [Huangyan Dao], Johnson Reef [Chigua Jiao], Cuarteron Reef [Huayang Jiao] and Fiery Cross Reef [Yongshu Jiao] are submerged features that are below sea level at high tide, except that each has small protrusions that remain above water at high tide, which qualify as 'rocks' under Article 121(3) of UNCLOS, and generate an entitlement only to a territorial sea no broader than 12 nautical miles (nm); and China has unlawfully claimed maritime entitlements beyond 12nm from these features;

7. China has unlawfully prevented Philippine vessels from exploiting the living resources in the waters adjacent to Scarborough Reef [Huangyan Dao] and Johnson Reef [Chigua Jiao];

8. The Philippines is entitled under UNCLOS to a 12nm territorial sea, a 200nm EEZ, and a continental shelf, measured from its archipelagic baselines;

9. China has unlawfully claimed rights to, and has unlawfully exploited, the living and non-living resources in the Philippines' EEZ and continental shelf, and has unlawfully prevented the Philippines from exploiting the living and non-living resources within its EEZ and continental Shelf; and

10. China has unlawfully interfered with the exercise by the Philippines of its rights to navigation under UNCLOS.

The claims call for some observations. It is essential to say that the Philippines made an obvious factual error mistaking Hughes Reef [Dongmen Jiao] for McKennan Reef [Ximen Jiao], on which China has never built any installation.

In the section 'Relief Sought',[9] the Philippines then requests, '[i]n light of the above, and the evidence to be submitted in the course of this arbitration', that the arbitral tribunal issue an award that makes certain declarations and orders which can be summarized as follows:

1. Declares that China's rights in regard to maritime areas in the South China Sea are limited to those that are established by UNCLOS;

2. Declares that China's maritime claims in the South China Sea based on the 'nine-dash line' are contrary to UNCLOS and invalid;

3. Requires China to bring its domestic legislation into conformity with its obligations under UNCLOS;

---

[9] Notification and Statement of Claim, para 41.

4. Declares that Mischief Reef [Meiji Jiao] and McKennan Reef [Ximen Jiao] are submerged features that form part of the continental shelf of the Philippines, and that China's occupation of and construction activities on them violate the sovereign rights of the Philippines;

5. Requires that China end its occupation of and activities on Mischief Reef [Meiji Jiao] and McKennan Reef [Ximen Jiao];

6. Declares that Gaven Reef [Nanxun Jiao] and Subi Reef [Zhubi Jiao] are not islands under UNCLOS, and are not located on China's continental shelf, and that China's occupation of and construction activities on these features are unlawful;

7. Requires China to terminate its occupation of and activities on Gaven Reef [Nanxun Jiao] and Subi Reef [Zhubi Jiao];

8. Declares that Scarborough Reef [Huangyan Dao], Johnson Reef [Chigua Jiao], Cuarteron Reef [Huayang Jiao] and Fiery Cross Reef [Yongshu Jiao] are rocks under Article 121(3) of UNCLOS which generate only a territorial sea no broader than 12nm;

9. Requires that China refrain from preventing Philippine vessels from exploiting in a sustainable manner the living resources in the waters adjacent to Scarborough Reef [Huangyan Dao] and Johnson Reef [Chigua Jiao];

10. Declares that the Philippines is entitled under UNCLOS to a 12nm territorial sea, a 200nm EEZ and a continental shelf;

11. Declares that China has unlawfully claimed, and has unlawfully exploited, the living and non-living resources in the Philippines' EEZ and continental shelf, and has unlawfully prevented the Philippines from exploiting living and non-living resources within its EEZ and continental shelf;

12. Declares that China has unlawfully interfered with the exercise by the Philippines of its rights to navigation and other rights under UNCLOS in areas within and beyond 200nm of the Philippines' archipelagic baselines; and

13. Requires that China desist from these unlawful activities.

As a party to UNCLOS, China has accepted the dispute settlement system of Part XV of the Convention. It places importance on upholding the principles and purposes of the Convention.[10] So why is it that China refused to accept the Philippines' arbitration request?

---

[10] See 'Foreign Minister Yang Jiechi on the South China Sea Issue' (13 July 2012) Annex I, Doc A.21.

III. CHINA'S REASONS FOR REFUSING THE PHILIPPINES' ARBITRATION
REQUEST

1. Failure to Fulfil in Good Faith Legal Obligations under UNCLOS

The Philippines has failed to fulfil relevant legal obligations as its submission of these disputes between China and the Philippines in the South China Sea to compulsory arbitral procedures established under Annex VII of UNCLOS constitutes an abuse of legal proceedings. It is the State Parties' legal obligation under UNCLOS to comply with UNCLOS in good faith and to avoid such abuses. As is provided in Article 300 UNCLOS, 'States Parties shall fulfil in good faith the obligations assumed under this Convention and shall exercise the rights, jurisdiction and freedoms recognised in this Convention in a manner which would not constitute an abuse of right'. There are serious problems in the Philippines' Notification and Statement of Claim including fabricated information and misrepresentation of material facts, as well as legal and political errors. The Philippines may thereby intend to mislead international public opinion and the Arbitral Tribunal. By submitting the disputes to international arbitration, the Philippines tries once again to exaggerate the so-called South China Sea Disputes and put more pressure of international public opinion on China.

According to UNCLOS, any submission of a dispute to arbitration requires that the parties previously proceeded expeditiously to an 'exchange of views regarding its settlement by negotiations or other peaceful means'.[11] In other words, a dispute may be submitted to the arbitral tribunal only after due consultations have been conducted between the parties without an appropriate settlement having been reached. Has the Philippines fulfilled its obligations under UNCLOS and carried out due consultation with China regarding the disputes it submitted to the compulsory arbitral procedures?

There exist multiple problems in the Philippines' Notification and Statement of Claim. For example, in the section entitled 'factual background', the Philippines falsely claimed that '[t]he Parties have been exchanging views on these disputes in attempts to achieve negotiated solutions since the first "Philippines-China Bilateral Consultations on the South China Sea Issue" were held in August 1995',[12] and that '[w]ith respect to the status of maritime features in the Spratly Islands and adjacent waters, and rights to navigate and exploit the living resources in these waters, the Parties have exchanged views since at least August 1995, and as recently as July 2012'.[13]

---

[11] UNCLOS, art 283.
[12] Notification and Statement of Claim, para 26.
[13] ibid, para 28.

In fact, the Philippines has never launched formal consultations with China on the issues set out in its Notification and Statement of Claim. The purpose of initiating the South China Sea arbitration is to distort the truth by means of deliberate misrepresentation. It is important to put the record straight and to point out that there are deliberate cover-ups and distortions of important facts in the Notification and Statement of Claim of the Philippines, which, inter alia, conceal the following facts:

First, at the invitation of President Hu Jintao, Philippine President Benigno S Aquino III had undertaken a State Visit to China from 30 August to 3 September 2011. On 31 August 2011, Chinese President Hu Jintao met with Philippine President Benigno Aquino at the Great Hall of the People in Beijing where Hu declared that the 'South China Sea disputes should be resolved peacefully through consultation and negotiation between the two countries concerned'.[14] On 1 September 2011, the two countries issued a Joint Statement which reads in the relevant parts as follows:

> *Both leaders exchanged views on the maritime disputes* and agreed not to let the maritime disputes affect the broader picture of friendship and cooperation between the two countries. *The two leaders reiterated their commitment to addressing the disputes through peaceful dialogue*, to maintain continued regional peace, security, stability and an environment conducive to economic progress. *Both leaders reaffirmed their commitments to respect and abide by the Declaration on the Conduct of Parties in the South China Sea signed by China and the ASEAN member countries in 2002.*[15]

Second, in March 2010 and January 2012, respectively, China suggested through formal diplomatic channels to establish the Sino-Philippine regular consultation mechanism on maritime issues and to resume the Sino-Philippine mechanism on trust-building measures.[16] The Philippines has not given any response to China's above mentioned suggestions.

Third, there is no mention in the Notification and Statement of Claim of the tripartite agreement reached by China, the Philippines and Vietnam. On 14 March 2005, the China National Offshore Oil Corporation, Philippine National Oil Company, and Vietnam Oil and Gas Corporation under the respective authorities of their governments signed a 'Tripartite Agreement for Joint Marine Seismic Undertaking in the Agreement Area in the South China Sea', in which 'the parties expressed desire to engage in a joint research of petroleum resource potential of a certain area of the South China Sea as a pre-exploration activity'.[17] The joint activities covered

---

[14] See 'China, the Philippines Agree to Downplay Maritime Disputes, Enhance Economic Ties' (31 August 2011) news.xinhuanet.com.

[15] 'Joint Statement of the Republic of the Philippines and the People's Republic of China' (Beijing, 1 September 2011) para 15, www.gov.ph (emphasis added) (2011 Joint Statement).

[16] See PRC MFA, 'Foreign Ministry Spokesperson Hua Chunying's Remarks on the Philippines' Statement on the South China Sea' (16 July 2013) Annex I, Doc A.4.

[17] Tripartite Agreement for Joint Marine Seismic Undertaking in the Agreement Area in the South China Sea by and among China National Offshore Oil Corporation and Vietnam Oil and Gas Corporation and Philippine National Oil Company (14 March 2005) (copy on file with the authors) (Tripartite Agreement).

a disputed area of 142,886 square km in the Nansha [Spratly] Archipelago which is defined by specific geographic coordinates. The agreement area is shown on the following map.[18]

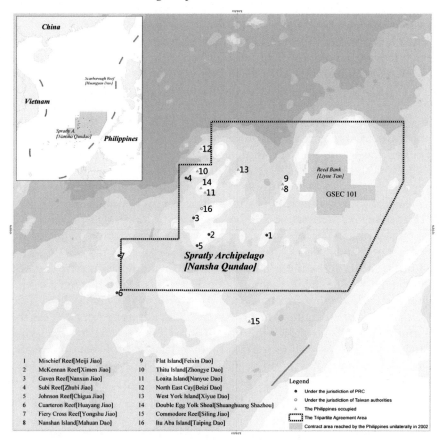

The Tripartite Agreement shows that the parties recognised that the agreement area was subject to overlapping EEZ and continental shelf claims. The three parties expressly affirmed that the signing of the agreement will not undermine the basic positions held by their respective governments on the South China Sea issue and will contribute to the transformation of the South China Sea into an area of peace, stability, cooperation, and development.[19] Philippine President Gloria Macapagal Arroyo met the delegates from the three countries and spoke highly of the historic significance of the Agreement.[20] The three parties' cooperation had been

[18] The authors are grateful to Dr Jun Qiu and Mr Mingjie Li, Research Fellows of the China Institute of Marine Affairs, for preparing this map.

[19] Tripartite Agreement (n 17).

[20] 'Vietnam, China, Philippines Firms Sign Oil Survey Deal' (14 March 2005) talkvietnam. com. See also PRC MFA, 'Oil Companies of China, the Philippines and Vietnam Signed Agreement on South China Sea Cooperation' (15 March 2005) www.fmprc.gov.cn.

implemented well in the first phase which made a positive contribution to stability, cooperation and development of the South China Sea.[21] However, the second phase was cancelled by the Philippines for internal political reasons.[22] If the Philippines had the sincerity to solve the maritime dispute, once the agreement expired in 2008, China and the Philippines could have reached an agreement through diplomatic channels to shelve disputes and carry out joint development of natural resources in such disputed areas. However, the Philippines arbitrarily reached an agreement with UK Forum Energy PLC in February 2010 to explore oil and gas in Reed Bank [Liyue Tan],[23] a part of the contract area under the 2005 Tripartite Agreement. This shows the Philippines' attempt to unilaterally change the facts on the ground and treat the area as its own.[24]

Fourth, the Philippines promulgated a new Act in 2009 to define its archipelagic baselines, which actually violated China's sovereignty and was opposed by the Chinese government. The Philippines defined its baselines for measuring the breadth of the territorial sea by Republic Act No 3046 of 17 June 1961.[25] On 18 September 1968, the Philippines promulgated Republic Act No 5446 to correct certain typographical errors with regard to the geographical coordinates defining and describing the baselines for the territorial sea of the Philippines.[26] In 2009, the Philippines promulgated Republic Act No 9522 again to amend the provision of Republic Act No 3046 defining and describing the 'baselines of the Philippines archipelago', and making certain other changes to Act No 3046.[27] In Republic Act No 9522, the Philippines illegally claimed Scarborough Shoal [Huangyan Island (referred as 'Bajo de Masinloc' in the Act)] and some islands and reefs of Spratly [Nansha] Archipelago (referred as 'The Kalayaan Island Group' in the Act), both of which form part of Chinese territory. According to the Act, these

---

[21] 'First Phase of Joint Marine Survey Complete' (17 November 2005) www.chinadaily.com. cn. See also 'Joint exploration project in South China Sea Finishes 1st phase' (17 November 2005) english.gov.cn.

[22] 'China Proposes Joint Development Formula in South China Sea' (22 September 2009) www.china.org.cn.

[23] Deng Yingying and Liu Feng, 'Disputing Nations Should Side with China for Joint Development of Oil and Gas in South China Sea' (22 September 2011) www.chinausfocus. com.

[24] In June 2002, the Philippines had unilaterally reached a Geophysical Survey and Exploration Contract (GSEC) with Sterling Energy PLC in Reed Bank [Liyue Tan] which was referred to as block 101. That contract expired in December 2003. With its new contract with UK Forum Energy PLC, concluded in February 2010, the Philippines again tried unilaterally to exploit the resources of block 101 in Reed Bank [Liyue Tan].

[25] Republic Act No 3046 – An Act to Define the Baselines of the Territorial Sea of the Philippines (17 June 1961) www.un.org.

[26] Republic Act No 5446 – An Act to Amend Section One of the Republic Act Numbered Thirty Hundred and Forty-Six, Entitled 'An Act to Define the Baselines of the Territorial Sea of the Philippines' (18 September 1968) www.un.org.

[27] Republic Act No 9522 – An Act to Amend Certain Provisions of Republic Act No 3046, as Amended by Republic Act No 5446, to Define the Archipelagic Baselines of the Philippines, and for Other Purposes (10 March 2009): United Nations, Division for Ocean Affairs and the Law of the Sea, *Law of the Sea Bulletin* No 70 (2009) 32.

islands and reefs constituted 'areas over which the Philippines likewise exercises sovereignty and jurisdiction'.[28] In a Note Verbale addressed to the Secretary-General of the United Nations, the Chinese government reiterated its well-known position that 'Huangyan Island and Nansha Islands have been part of the territory of China since ancient time', and requested the Secretary-General to communicate China's position to all States Parties to UNCLOS and all member States of the United Nations.[29] In other words, the Philippines' claim to an EEZ and continental shelf in the South China Sea infringes on China's territory, ie Huangyan Island [Scarborough Shoal] and some islands or reefs of the Nansha [Spratly] Islands, and thus are null and void. In spite of this illegal and invalid claim, the Philippines now accuses China of interfering with the exercise by the Philippines of its rights in its EEZ. Such an accusation obviously lacks any reasonable legal basis.

Fifth, the Philippines' Notification and Statement of Claim very selectively mentioned a few islands of the Nansha [Spratly] Archipelago, but other islands in the Archipelago that are unlawfully occupied by the Philippines, such as Nanshan Island [Mahuan Dao], Flat Island [Feixin Dao], Thitu Island [Zhongye Dao], Loaita Island [Nanyue Dao], Northeast Cay [Beizi Dao], West York Island [Xiyue Dao], Double Egg Yolk Shoal [Shuanghuang Shazhou] and Commodore Reef [Siling Jiao], are ignored.[30] In addition, no reference is made to those islands of the Spratly [Nansha] Archipelago in nearby maritime areas that are occupied by Vietnam[31] and Malaysia,[32] and the claims of these States to maritime areas overlapping with those by the Philippines.

Last but not least, another factual misrepresentation may be found in the section of the Notification and Statement of Claim entitled 'Factual Background', where the Philippines claims that 'China first officially depicted the "nine dash line" in a letter of 7 May 2009 to the United Nations Secretary General'.[33] As is widely known, the Chinese government internally circulated an atlas on which the dotted line was drawn to indicate the geographical scope of its authority over the South China Sea in 1947.[34] In February 1948, the Chinese government published an atlas of national administrative districts through the Commerce Press, Beijing, which reflected the dotted line in the 1947 atlas.[35]

---

[28] ibid, section 2.

[29] See Note Verbale CML/12/2009 from the Permanent Mission of the People's Republic of China to the UN Secretary-General (13 April 2009) Annex I, Doc A.25.

[30] See PRC MFA, 'Foreign Ministry Spokesperson Hua Chunying's Remarks on the Philippines' Efforts in Pushing for the Establishment of the Arbitral Tribunal' (26 April 2013) (n 6).

[31] Wu Shicun, *Nan Sha Zheng Duan De Qi Yuan Yu Fa Zhan [The Origin and Development of the Nansha Disputes]* (Beijing, Zhong Guo Jing Ji Chu Ban She [China Economic Publishing House], 2010) 80–93.

[32] ibid, 144–45.

[33] Notification and Statement of Claim, para 11.

[34] See Zhiguo Gao and Bing Bing Jia, 'The Nine-Dash Line in the South China Sea: History, Status, and Implications' (2013) 107 *American Journal of International Law* 98, 102.

[35] ibid, 103.

Based on such misinformation, the Philippines, in the section on the 'Jurisdiction of the Tribunal', further falsely claims that '[t]he Philippines has complied with the requirements of Article 279 and Article 283(1) fully and in good faith, and has exhausted possibilities of settlement by negotiation'.[36] Furthermore, it is stated that 'the Philippines and China have failed to settle the dispute between them by peaceful means of their own choice'.[37] Thus a conclusion is drawn by the Philippines that it has 'fully and in good faith' fulfilled its related legal obligations and the tribunal should accept its request for arbitration. If China accepted the Philippines' Notification and Statement of Claim based on factual misrepresentations and a distorted legal basis, it would make itself an accomplice to the Philippines' abuse and undermining of UNCLOS Annex VII arbitration.

2. Serious Legal Flaws in the Notification and Statement of Claim

The Philippine request also contains serious legal flaws. Arbitration in accordance with Annex VII, as one of the four means of compulsory dispute settlement under UNCLOS,[38] is available only for disputes 'concerning the interpretation or application of this Convention'.[39] Significantly, disputes involving questions of territorial sovereignty cannot be submitted to such arbitral proceedings as they do not concern the 'interpretation or application' of UNCLOS. Furthermore, if one of the parties has made a declaration under Article 298 UNCLOS excluding sea boundary delimitation disputes, such disputes can no longer be submitted to arbitration. The Philippines' claims are essentially covered by China's 2006 declaration and therefore do not fall under the jurisdiction of an Annex VII arbitral tribunal.

On the day the Philippines notified China of the institution of arbitral proceedings, the Philippines Foreign Minister explained that his country had instituted the proceedings in order to 'achieve a peaceful and durable solution to the dispute over the West Philippine Sea'.[40] This raises the question of what is actually in dispute between China and the Philippines. In its true nature, the dispute between China and the Philippines in the South China Sea is one over territorial sovereignty and sea boundary delimitations.

---

[36] Notification and Statement of Claim, para 33. UNCLOS, art 279 requires States Parties to seek a solution by peaceful means in accordance with the Charter of the United Nations, and UNCLOS, art 283(1) requires them to proceed expeditiously to an exchange of views regarding a settlement by negotiation or other peaceful means.

[37] Notification and Statement of Claim, para 34.

[38] See UNCLOS, art 287(1)(c).

[39] See UNCLOS, Annex VII, art 1 read together with UNCLOS, art 286.

[40] RP MFA, 'SFA Statement on the UNCLOS Arbitral Proceedings against China' (22 January 2013) www.dfa.gov.ph.

As early as 25 August 2006, the Chinese government submitted to the United Nations Secretariat a written declaration under Article 298 UNCLOS explicitly stating that:

> The Government of the People's Republic of China does not accept any of the procedures provided for in Section 2 of Part XV of the Convention with respect to all the categories of disputes referred to in paragraph 1 (a) (b) and (c) of Article 298 of UNCLOS.[41]

In accordance with Article 298(1) UNCLOS, a State may declare in writing that it does not accept any one or more of the procedures provided for in Section 2, Part XV of UNCLOS with respect to one or more of the following categories of disputes:

(a) disputes concerning the interpretation or application of Articles 15, 74 and 83 relating to sea boundary delimitations, or those involving historic bays or titles;
(b) disputes concerning military activities and disputes concerning law enforcement activities in regard to the exercise of sovereign rights or jurisdiction excluded from the jurisdiction of a court or tribunal under Article 297(2) or (3);
(c) disputes in respect of which the Security Council of the United Nations is exercising the functions assigned to it by the Charter of the United Nations.

As for the first category, when such a dispute arises subsequent to the entry into force of UNCLOS and where no agreement within a reasonable period of time is reached by negotiation between the parties, the State having made the declaration under Article 298 shall, at the request of any party to the dispute, accept submission of the matter to conciliation under Annex V, section 2. However it is further provided that 'any dispute that necessarily involves the concurrent consideration of any unsettled dispute concerning sovereignty or other rights over continental or insular land territory shall be excluded from such submission'.[42]

Reading the Philippines Notification and Statement of Claim, it is obvious that the 10 claims and 13 points of the 'Relief Sought' either concern or affect China's territorial sovereignty or the delimitation of the EEZ or continental shelf between the Philippines and China in the South China Sea. These issues are excluded by China's 2006 declaration and as such are not subject to compulsory arbitration. Well aware of this fact, the Philippines, like a person whistling in the dark, simply stated that 'the Philippines' claims do not fall within China's Declaration of 25 August 2006',[43] so as to cover its real intention and the true nature of the disputes.

---

[41] Declaration by the People's Republic of China under Art 298 UNCLOS (25 August 2006) Annex I, Doc A.26.

[42] UNCLOS, art 298(1)(a)(i).

[43] Notification and Statement of Claim, para 40.

The Philippines explained that it 'does not seek in this arbitration a determination of which Party enjoys sovereignty over the islands claimed by both of them. Nor does it request a delimitation of any maritime boundaries'.[44] Following this logic, if the proceedings yielded an award, disputes between the two countries over islands and maritime boundary delimitation in the South China Sea would still remain unsettled. How then could the goal of the international arbitration be 'to achieve a peaceful and durable solution to the dispute over the West Philippine Sea',[45] as claimed by the Philippines' Secretary of Foreign Affairs? Clearly, there is an inconsistency between what the Philippines stated in its Notification and Statement of Claim and its true intentions. With the Tribunal and the international community thus misled, the Philippines then continues to completely deny the validity of the nine-dash line and the legal status of the Chinese islands and reefs and China's related rights in the South China Sea, in order to seek and establish its rights to an excessive EEZ and continental shelf in the so-called 'West Philippine Sea', in disregard of China's territorial sovereignty over the Spratly [Nansha] Archipelago and Scarborough Shoal [Huangyan Island]. This move on the part of the Philippines defies the right conferred upon the State Parties under Article 298 UNCLOS to make a declaration with respect to such significant matters as territorial sovereignty and sea boundary delimitations.

3. Breach of Numerous Declarations and Bilateral Agreements

In addition, there are serious political problems with the Notification and Statement of Claim. The Philippines' unilateral initiation of arbitral procedures is a serious breach of the DOC, which was signed by the Philippines and China, as well as other members of ASEAN.[46] In the DOC, '[t]he Parties concerned undertake to resolve their territorial and jurisdictional disputes by peaceful means ... through friendly consultations and negotiations by sovereign states directly concerned, in accordance with universally recognized principles of international law, including the 1982 UN Convention on the Law of the Sea;'[47] and, '[p]ending the peaceful settlement of territorial and jurisdictional dispute ... to intensify efforts to seek ways, in the spirit of cooperation and understanding,

---

[44] ibid, para 7.

[45] See text accompanying n 40. See also the Philippines' Note Verbale No 13-0211 from the Department of Foreign Affairs of the Republic of the Philippines to the Embassy of the People's Republic of China in Manila (22 January 2013) Annex I, Doc B.1, where the aim of the arbitral proceedings is set out as clearly establishing 'the sovereign rights and jurisdiction of the Philippines over its maritime entitlements in the West Philippine Sea'.

[46] ASEAN-China Declaration on the Conduct of Parties in the South China Sea (signed during the 8th ASEAN Summit in Phnom Penh, 4 November 2002), reproduced in Vaughan Lowe and Stefan Talmon (eds), *The Legal Order of the Oceans: Basic Documents on the Law of the Sea* (Oxford, Hart, 2009) Doc 69, 771–2 (DOC).

[47] ibid, para 4.

to build trust and confidence between and among them'.[48] China has always been committed to these undertakings, while the Philippines is now backtracking on these solemn commitments, repeatedly breaking the consensus achieved between ASEAN States and China, frequently provoking incidents and seriously impacting the stability and peace in the South China Sea region. On 9 May 2013, a Philippine vessel fired at a Taiwanese fishing boat killing one fisherman.[49] Moreover, in its Notification and Statement of Claim, the Philippines has reviewed each of the islands and reefs in the South China Sea under actual administration of the People's Republic of China, but has completely omitted the largest island of the Nansha [Spratly] Archipelago, Taiping Dao [Itu Aba Island], which is under the control of the Taiwan authorities. The Philippines only lists seven of the islands which are under China's jurisdiction and control, but not Taiping Dao [Itu Aba Island]. This could imply that, from the Philippines' perspective, Taiwan-controlled Taiping Island is not part of Chinese territory — a position that seriously compromises its 'one-China policy',[50] and as such is unacceptable to China.

IV. CHINESE POLICY TOWARD RESOLUTION OF THE SOUTH CHINA SEA DISPUTES

1. The Essence of the South China Sea Disputes

The essence of the South China Sea disputes between China and the Philippines falls into two categories: those caused by the Philippines' illegal occupation of some islands/reefs of the Nansha [Spratly] Archipelago of China, and those caused by overlapping claims of China and the Philippines to un-delimited waters.

China established territorial sovereignty over the South China Sea islands in ancient times and thus much earlier than other countries surrounding the South China Sea. All Chinese governments, despite a succession of several different dynasties, have maintained effective jurisdiction over the South China Sea islands, constantly reaffirming and consolidating sovereignty over them and never expressing any intention

---

[48] ibid, para 5 (mistakenly numbered para 6 in Lowe and Talmon).

[49] See 'Philippine Coast Guard Admits Killing of Taiwan Fisherman' (10 May 2013) and 'Philippine Coast Guard Members Face Homicide Charges for Taiwanese Fisherman Killing' (7 August 2013) both at news.xinhuanet.com.

[50] On 9 June 1975, both countries issued a Joint Communique which declared that 'the Philippine Government recognizes the Government of the People's Republic of China as the sole legal government of China, fully understands and respects the position of the Chinese Government that there is but one China and that Taiwan is an integral part of Chinese territory, and decides to remove all its official representations from Taiwan within one month from the date of signature of this communique' ('Joint Communique of the Government of the People's Republic of China and the Government of the Republic of the Philippines' (9 June 1975) para 6, www.fmprc.gov.cn). That position was recently reaffirmed in the 2011 Joint Statement (n 15).

to relinquish such sovereignty.[51] It is well-known that during World War II parts of China's territory were occupied by Japan. The occupied territory, including the Xisha [Paracel] and Nansha [Spratly] Archipelagos, was restored to China after the war in accordance with the Cairo Communiqué. The Communiqué stated that it was the 'purpose' of the 'Three Great Allies' that:

> Japan shall be stripped of all the islands in the Pacific which she has seized or occupied since the beginning of the First World War in 1914, and that all the territories Japan has stolen from the Chinese, such as Manchuria, Formosa, and the Pescadores, shall be restored to the Republic of China. Japan will also be expelled from all other territories which she has taken by violence and greed.[52]

This was confirmed in the Potsdam Declaration.[53] For a long time after World War II, there was no such a thing as the 'South China Sea Issue' or 'South China Sea Dispute'. Although beginning in the 1970s various countries began to send troops to occupy some islands and reefs and claim rights in the region, the South China Sea did not become a hotspot until this century. This only changed with some countries exaggerating the situation and some others getting involved in the situation from outside.

The disputes between China and the Philippines in the South China Sea can be divided into three categories: (1) territorial sovereignty disputes caused by the Philippines' unlawful occupation of some islands and reefs in China's Nansha [Spratly] Archipelago; (2) maritime boundary delimitation disputes concerning overlapping EEZ and continental shelf claims; and (3) disputes with regard to the exploitation of living and non-living resources and other issues caused by unsettled maritime boundaries. The rules of international law applicable to solve these types of disputes are different. The settlement of territorial disputes over the Nansha Archipelago should be based on general international law, including, among others, rules concerning territorial acquisition, the doctrine of intertemporal law, the doctrine of estoppel, the principle of non-retroactivity, rules concerning historical title and rights, rules concerning the determination of critical dates and the law of treaties. China takes the view that UNCLOS, which is for settling 'all issues relating to the law of the sea',[54] should be complied with by all States Parties to the Convention. However, it should not be used in a simplistic manner to replace or negate other rules and principles of international law. In its preamble, UNCLOS affirms that 'matters not

---

[51] Wu, *Nan Sha Zheng Duan De Qi Yuan Yu Fa Zhan [The Origin and Development of the Nansha Disputes]* (2010) 15–39.

[52] See 'Conference of President Roosevelt, Generalissimo Chiang Kai-Shek, and Prime Minister Churchill in North Africa, 1 December 1943', United Sates, Department of State Bulletin, vol IX, no 232 (4 December 1943) 393.

[53] See 'Proclamation Defining the Terms for the Japanese Surrender, 26 July 1945', ibid, vol XIII, no 318 (29 July 1945) 137–38 [8] ('The terms of the Cairo Declaration shall be carried out and Japanese sovereignty shall be limited to the islands of Honshu, Hokkaido, Kyushu, Shikoku and such minor islands as we determine').

[54] UNCLOS, preamble, para 1.

regulated by this Convention continue to be governed by the rules and principles of general international law'.[55] UNCLOS does not provide rules for either the determination of territorial sovereignty over islands and reefs or the assessment of claims to territorial sovereignty. The same is true for rules for the settlement of disputes over those questions. It constitutes neither the basis of any country's denial of China's sovereignty over the South China Sea islands, nor the basis of any new territorial claims by countries bordering the South China Sea. Therefore, it cannot be used as a pretext to call into question the historical and legal fact that China has enjoyed territorial sovereignty over the South China Sea islands since ancient times. From the perspective of general international law, the manner in which China obtained territorial sovereignty over, and its continuous administration of, the South China Sea islands is in full compliance with the rules of international law and therefore valid under international law.

2. Integrity of the Dispute Settlement System under UNCLOS

The three sections of Part XV constitute an integrated system of dispute settlement under UNCLOS. The rights and obligations set out in section 1, headed 'General Provisions', reflect the priority given to peaceful means of dispute settlement freely chosen by the parties. According to Article 36 of the Statute of the International Court of Justice (ICJ), the jurisdiction of the ICJ is based on the consent of the parties to the dispute. In the same spirit, UNCLOS explicitly provides for the right of States Parties to settle their disputes by 'any peaceful means of their own choice';[56] their obligation to settle disputes according to a special procedure if they have 'agreed' to do so 'through a general, regional or bilateral agreement or otherwise';[57] and their obligation 'to proceed expeditiously to an exchange views'.[58] Besides this, section 3 regulates 'limitations and exceptions to application of section 2'. Therefore, application of section 2, headed 'compulsory procedures entailing binding decisions' should be constrained by section 1 and section 3. Article 286 UNCLOS explicitly regulates that 'subject to section 3', the disputes concerning the interpretation or application of UNCLOS shall, 'where no settlement has been reached by recourse to section 1', be submitted at the request of any party to 'the court or tribunal having jurisdiction' under section 2.

As mentioned above,[59] Article 298, one of the provisions of section 3, provides that a State Party may, by means of a written declaration, exclude

---

[55] UNCLOS, preamble, para 8.
[56] UNCLOS, art 280.
[57] UNCLOS, art 282.
[58] UNCLOS, art 283(1).
[59] See section III.2.

disputes concerning territorial sovereignty and maritime delimitation from the application of the compulsory dispute settlement procedures in section 2. Since China has submitted such a declaration, it is under no obligation to accept the Philippines' request to submit the disputes over territorial sovereignty and maritime delimitation in the South China Sea to arbitration. The submission of these disputes to arbitration breaches Article 300 UNCLOS and constitutes an abuse of legal proceedings. The essence of the Philippines' strategy is to submit issues based on fabricated facts, concealment and misrepresentations to compulsory arbitration under Annex VII of UNCLOS, put pressure on China, internationalise the South China Sea disputes and try to gain support for its position from the international community.

3. Peaceful Settlement of the Disputes through Negotiations

The Chinese government has iterated that the disputes should be resolved through direct negotiations between the parties directly concerned in accordance with international law and historical facts.[60] Considering the nature of the disputes in question, their regionalisation and internationalisation can only result in a more complicated regional situation.

China has always believed that international relations should be handled in accordance with the Five Principles of Peaceful Co-Existence, namely, mutual respect for each other's sovereignty and territorial integrity, mutual non-aggression, non-interference in each other's internal affairs, equality and mutual benefit and peaceful co-existence.[61] China takes the view that all countries, big or small, should be treated as equals. It is opposed to the practice of the big and strong bullying the small and weak, and calls for the peaceful resolution of international disputes and conflicts through consultation and negotiation. China rejects the arbitrary use or threat of force, the violation of other countries' sovereignty and interference in their internal affairs against their will. A peaceful and harmonious environment in the South China Sea is in line with the common interest of all coastal countries in the area. During the past 60 years, China has gained experience in successfully resolving boundary questions in a peaceful and friendly manner by way of bilateral negotiations, which can serve as a good model

---

[60] See eg PRC MFA, 'Foreign Ministry Spokesperson Hua Chunying's Regular Press Conference' (12 July 2013); 'Wang Yi Stressed that the South China Sea Issue Should Be Resolved by Parties Directly Concerned Through Negotiation' (2 July 2013); 'Foreign Ministry Spokesperson Hua Chunying's Regular Press Conference' (1 July 2013); 'Foreign Minister Wang Yi: Confrontation Leads Nowhere' (27 June 2013) Annex I, Docs A.6, A.8, A.9 and A.10, respectively.

[61] See PRC MFA, 'China's Initiation of the Five Principles of Peaceful Co-Existence' (17 November 2000) www.fmprc.gov.cn. The parties to the DOC have reaffirmed their commitment to, inter alia, the Five Principles of Peaceful Coexistence. See DOC (n 46) para 1.

for the world. To date, it has successfully settled land boundary questions left over from history with 12 of its 14 neighbours,[62] totalling some 20,000 km of borderlines.

This approach and policy is also applied by the Chinese Government to solve the South China Sea disputes. For example, in December 2000 China and Vietnam successfully signed the Agreement on the Delimitation of Maritime Zones in the Beibu Gulf,[63] and in October 2011, China and Vietnam signed the Agreement on the Basic Principles Guiding the Settlement of Sea-related Issues, in which the two countries reaffirm to solve their sea-related disputes 'through friendly talks and negotiations'.[64] The Chinese Government has also put forward the proposition of 'shelving disputes and going in for joint development' with regard to disputes that cannot be resolved in the short-term.[65] Settling disputes peacefully through friendly bilateral consultations is the proper and realistic means for resolving the complex issues in the South China Sea. In the DOC, the countries in the region have undertaken to 'exercise self-restraint in the conduct of activities that would complicate or escalate disputes and affect peace and stability'.[66] Intensification and internationalisation of the South China Sea disputes will only disturb peace and stability in the South China Sea.

V. FUTURE OF THE ARBITRATION

1. Possibility of the Philippines Revising Its Claims or Introducing New Ones

There is no doubt that it is for the Philippines, in its Notification and Statement of Claim, to present to the Tribunal the disputes with which it wishes to seize the Tribunal and to set out the claims which it is submitting to it.[67] This means that the 'subject-matter' of the dispute must be set out in the Notification and Statement of Claim. In section VII of its Notification and Statement of Claim, entitled 'Reservation of Rights', the Philippines explicitly declared that it 'reserves the right to supplement and/or amend its claims and the relief sought as necessary'.[68] On 5 September 2013,

---

[62] See PRC Embassy in the Philippines, 'China in Pinoy's Eyes, Renaissance' (26 March 2013) ph.china-embassy.org.

[63] Agreement between the People's Republic of China and the Socialist Republic of Viet Nam on the Delimitation of the Territorial Seas, Exclusive Economic Zones and Continental Shelves of the Two Countries in Beibu Gulf/Bac Bo Gulf (signed in Beijing, 25 December 2000) 2336 UNTS 179.

[64] Agreement on Basic Principles Guiding the Settlement of Sea-related Issues (signed in Beijing, 11 October 2011) para 3, reprinted at 'VN-China Basic Principles on Settlement of Sea Issues' (12 October 2011) en.vietnamplus.vn.

[65] See eg PRC MFA, 'Position Paper of the People's Republic of China on the Issue of the South China Sea' (17 November 2000) Annex I, Doc A.27.

[66] DOC (n 46) para 5.

[67] UNCLOS Annex VII, art 1.

[68] Notification and Statement of Claim, para 43.

following 'sightings'[69] of Chinese concrete blocks in the Scarborough Shoal [Huang Yan Dao], Philippine Foreign Affairs Secretary Albert del Rosario said that 'that's a substantive piece of information that we can tag on to our arbitration case and have it worked positively for us'.[70] It seems that the Philippines' claims will be full of variables.

Such a reservation is incompatible with the principles of legal security and the good administration of justice and is without validity in international law. In a number of instances, the ICJ has held that new claims, formulated during the course of proceedings, which would transform the subject of the dispute originally brought before it under the terms of the application, are inadmissible.[71] This was confirmed most recently by the International Tribunal for the Law of the Sea (ITLOS).[72] Any new claim or any amendment of existing claims by the Philippines must have its origin in the Notification and Statement of Claim, ie it must 'arise directly out of or be implicit in it'. It follows that while the Philippines may clarify its claims in the subsequent pleadings and in oral argument, it may not go beyond the 'Claims' and the 'Relief Sought' as set out in the Statement and Notification of Claim. In short, the tribunal may not allow the Philippines to transform the dispute in the course of proceedings into another dispute which is different in character. It is, after all, the unfounded claims in the Notification and Statement of Claim which prompted China not to take part in the arbitral proceedings.

2. Attitude of Vietnam toward the Case

Annex VII of UNCLOS does not provide for third-party participation in arbitration proceedings. The Socialist Republic of Vietnam also claims parts of the South China Sea. On 21 June 2012, Vietnam adopted its own 'Law of the Sea' which declared China's Paracel [Xisha] and Spratly [Nansha] Archipelagos part of 'Vietnam's territory'.[73] Therefore, based on Vietnam's claim, those Chinese islands and reefs identified by the Philippines in the present case are also 'territory' claimed by Vietnam.

On 1 August 2013, Vietnam and the Philippines held their 7th Meeting of the Joint Commission for Bilateral Cooperation (JCBC) in Manila.

---

[69] Later, 'President Benigno "Noy Noy" Aquino said previous accusations that Chinese ships had brought concrete blocks to Scarborough Shoal ... for construction were wrong' ('Philippines Retracts China Claims over Contested Reef' (28 October 2013) www.intellasia.net).

[70] 'Phl to File Diplomatic Protest Anew vs China' (5 September 2013) www.philstar.com.

[71] See eg *Fisheries Jurisdiction (Spain v Canada)* (Jurisdiction) [1998] ICJ Rep 432, 448 [29]; *Certain Phosphate Lands in Nauru (Nauru v Australia)* (Preliminary Objections) [1992] ICJ Rep 240, 266–67 [67]–[70]. See also *Prince von Pless Administration (Germany v Poland)* (Preliminary Objection, Order of 4 February 1933) PCIJ Rep Series A/B No 52, 14.

[72] *M/V 'Louisa' (Saint Vincent and the Grenadines v Kingdom of Spain)* (Judgment) [2013] ITLOS Rep [95], [142]–[143].

[73] See Law of the Sea of Viet Nam (adopted 21 June 2012) arts 1, 19(2), reprinted at vietnamnews.vn.

During the meeting the two sides 'agreed to cooperate in ensuring the rule of law in the West Philippine Sea/East Sea, peaceful settlement of disputes in accordance with international law including UNCLOS, implementing the ... DOC, and expediting the early conclusion of a regional Code of Conduct ("COC")'.[74] In contrast, despite its commitments made in the DOC, the Philippines unilaterally initiated compulsory arbitration proceedings against China. The JCBC shows that the Philippines attempts to draw Vietnam over to its side. Former Chief of the Ministry of Public Security's Strategy Institute, Le Van Cuong, was quoted by Vietnamese website Dan Tri Online as saying that Vietnam should maintain the status quo irrespective of the Philippines' case and not join with other countries against China, and also that it was not the right time for Vietnam to institute such kind of proceedings.[75] In the past decades, dialogue and negotiation between China and Vietnam on resolving the South China Sea disputes have been making good progress. It will have to be seen whether Vietnam will continue to maintain a sound friendship with China or follow the Philippines in bringing a case against China.

3. Attitude of Taiwan Authorities toward the Case

Both sides across the Taiwan Strait share the same claims and concerns over the South China Sea's islands and reefs, as well as over maritime rights in the region. As mentioned above,[76] the U-shaped line claim in the South China Sea was first publicly promulgated by the Government of the Republic of China in 1948 and both sides across the Taiwan Strait have insisted on the claim since 1949. On 10 February 1999, the Taiwan authorities promulgated 'The First Part of the Baselines of the Territorial Sea of Taiwan' which covered four areas: Taiwan and its appurtenant islands, Dongsha [Pratas] Archipelago, Zhongsha [Macclesfield] Archipelago, and Nansha [Spratly] Archipelago.[77] The Taiwan authorities reaffirmed the territorial sovereignty over the islands and reefs of the Nansha [Spratly] Archipelago surrounded by the traditional 'U-shaped line' and adopted normal baselines for the Zhongsha [Macclesfield] Archipelago (including Scarborough Shoal), while reserving the announcement of the baselines

---

[74] 'PHL, Viet Nam Successfully Conclude 7th Meeting of PHL-Viet Nam Joint Commission for Bilateral Cooperation' (1 August 2013) www.gov.ph; 'Philippines, Vietnam Hold 7th Joint Commission Meeting' (1 August 2013) www.philstar.com.

[75] 'Yue Nan Qian Guan Yuan Cheng Jue Bu Hui Lian Shou Qi Ta Guo Jia Zhi Heng Zhong Guo' [Vietnam Former Official Said that Vietnam Would Not Join With Other Countries Against China] (31 January 2013) world.huanqiu.com.

[76] See above section III.1.

[77] See Decree No Tai 88 Nei Tze #06161 (10 February 1999), reproduced in Coast Guard Administration (Taiwan, China), *Hai Yang Shi Wu Fa Gui Hui Bian [Collection of Laws relating to Marine Affairs]*, 2nd edn (Taipei, Xing Zheng Yuan Hai Xun Shu [Coast Guard Administration Executive Yuan of Taiwan], 2008) 106.

for the Nansha [Spratly] Archipelago for later.[78] On 18 November 2009, Taiwan's 'Executive Yuan' Gazette published a revision to 'The First Part of the Baselines of the Territorial Sea and Outer Limit Lines of the Territorial Sea and Contiguous Zone', which also covered the Zhongsha [Macclesfield] Archipelago (including Scarborough Shoal). [79] Currently, a detachment of the Coast Guard Administration of Taiwan is stationed on Taiping Dao [Itu Aba Island], the largest island of the Nansha [Spratly] Archipelago and the only one with freshwater reserves. Against this background, the Taiwan authorities might find it inappropriate to turn a deaf ear to a Philippine suit challenging the U-shaped line, Chinese sovereignty over the South China Sea's islands and reefs, as well as Chinese maritime rights.[80]

VI. CONCLUSION

To date, there have been nine arbitration cases submitted in accordance with section 2 of Part XV of UNCLOS and its Annex VII.[81] None of these cases involved a dispute excluded by a declaration under Article 298 UNCLOS, except the arbitration pending between the Philippines and China on South China Sea disputes, which is also the very first case in which the initiating party participates in the arbitral procedures alone. Indeed, in all documented modern cases of arbitration involving international territorial and maritime disputes, a tribunal giving an award with only one party participating in compulsory procedures, and the other party being absent, is a rarity. This rarity underscores a fundamental difference between inter-state arbitrations and ordinary commercial arbitrations. In inter-state arbitrations the State's consent and free will is always considered the decisive factor when evaluating obligations under international treaties and dispute settlement mechanisms. As international treaties are based on the premise of State consent, a State Party's obligations under a treaty are limited by its declarations and reservations. Declarations or reservations made by a State Party as provided for by a treaty precisely mark the State Party's understanding of the treaty and define the limits of its obligation and compliance.

In international law, it is a general principle that States are required to resolve disputes by peaceful means, including negotiation, enquiry,

---

[78] ibid. See also United States Department of State, Bureau of Oceans and International Environmental and Scientific Affairs, Limits in the Seas, No 127: Taiwan's Maritime Claims (15 November 2005) 25.

[79] Li Mingje, *Tai Wan Di Qu Hai Yang Wen Ti Yan Jiu [A Study on the Maritime Issues of the Taiwan Region]* (Beijing, Zhong Guo She Ke Chu Ban She [China Social Sciences Press], 2011) 246–48.

[80] Both sides across the Taiwan Strait have the same stance on the South China Sea. Therefore, the initiation of the South China Sea arbitration by the Philippines is substantially challenging Taipei's position as well.

[81] For a list of UNCLOS Annex VII arbitrations see the 'UNCLOS' tab at www.pca-cpa.org. To this list of eight cases the *Southern Bluefin Tuna Case* must be added.

mediation, conciliation, arbitration, judicial settlement, resort to regional agencies or arrangements or other peaceful means of the States' own choice.[82] UNCLOS respects the States Parties' right to settle their disputes by peaceful means of their own choice, explicitly providing that nothing in Part XV of UNCLOS 'impairs the right of any States Parties to agree at any time to settle a dispute between them concerning the interpretation or application of UNCLOS by any peaceful means of their own choice'.[83] This indicates that the dispute settlement mechanism devised by UNCLOS embodies to the fullest extent the principle of State sovereignty. On the one hand, compulsory procedures entailing binding decisions can only be instigated after States Parties have exhausted all peaceful means of dispute settlement provided for in section 1 of Part XV without reaching a settlement.[84] On the other hand, Article 298 UNCLOS explicitly permits States Parties to make a declaration excluding the application of compulsory procedures entailing binding decisions to disputes concerning critical issues such as State sovereignty and security, sea boundary delimitations, historic title and military interests. Simply put, a State enjoys the right not to be hauled before an arbitral tribunal with respect to disputes concerning such critical issues as sovereignty.

Provisions on arbitration in Article 287 and Annex VII of UNCLOS should be applied by States Parties in 'good faith'.[85] If territorial sovereignty and maritime delimitation issues could easily be submitted in disguise to compulsory arbitration under Annex VII, the UNCLOS dispute settlement system would become extremely vulnerable to abuse by States acting in bad faith and Article 298 would be deprived of any meaning. This would not only be a serious departure from the original intention of UNCLOS to establish a legal order for the seas and oceans with due regard for the sovereignty of all States,[86] but would also trample on the right of States Parties to make declarations of exclusion provided for in Article 298.

The South China Sea disputes involve a complex web of claims. They include claims to territorial sovereignty over dozens of islands and reefs by five States[87] and claims to overlapping exclusive economic zones and continental shelves by six States.[88] The situation is characterised by decades of contest among the claimants and other complicated historical processes and facts. How can such disputes fit so readily into the category of 'disputes concerning the interpretation or application of UNCLOS', even under some disguise? Peaceful coexistence, equal consultation, dialogue

---

[82] See Charter of the United Nations (adopted 26 June 1945, entered into force 24 October 1945) 892 UNTS 119, art 33(1); UNCLOS, art 279.

[83] UNCLOS, art 280.

[84] See UNCLOS, arts 286 and 295.

[85] See UNCLOS, art 300, and section III.1 above.

[86] See UNCLOS, preamble, para 4.

[87] China, Vietnam, Philippines, Malaysia and Brunei. To this Taiwan may be added as a sixth side.

[88] China, Vietnam, Philippines, Malaysia, Brunei and Indonesia. To this Taiwan may be added as a seventh side.

and cooperation are the sensible course of action to take in maintaining regional peace and stability and trying to resolve disputes properly. The Philippines should honour history and facts, respect the principles and spirit of international law, including UNCLOS, and recognise that bilateral negotiations in good faith with China are the only path toward achieving a peaceful and definitive settlement of the disputes.

China's advocacy of resolving the South China Sea disputes through bilateral negotiations is not only in accordance with international law, but has also gained broad international support. Asked about the United Nation's response to the Philippines' action to bring the South China Sea disputes before an UNCLOS arbitral tribunal, UN Secretary-General Ban Ki-moon said:

> I have been following this situation carefully. It is important for those countries in the region to resolve all these issues *through dialogue* in a peaceful and amicable way. The United Nations, if necessary, if requested, is ready to provide technical and professional assistance; but primarily, all these issues *should be resolved by the parties concerned.*[89]

The UN Secretary-General thus professed a clear preference for 'dialogue' between the parties concerned, rather than one party trying to force the hand of the other. The Philippines would do well to heed his advice.

---

[89] United Nations, 'Press Conference by Secretary-General Ban Ki-moon at United Nations Headquarters' (22 January 2013) UN Doc SG/SM/14778, www.un.org (emphasis added).

Annex I

Selected Documents Relevant to the South China Sea Arbitration

A. Documents of the People's Republic of China

1. Foreign Ministry Spokesperson Hong Lei's Regular Press Conference, 11 September 2013
2. Foreign Ministry Spokesperson Hong Lei's Remarks on the Huangyan Island Questions, 4 September 2013
3. Ambassador Ma Keqing Addressed UA&P Students on China-ASEAN Relationship, 4 September 2013
4. Foreign Ministry Spokesperson Hua Chunying's Remarks on the Philippines' Statement on the South China Sea, 16 July 2013
5. Foreign Ministry Spokesperson Hua Chunying's Remarks on the South China Sea Issue, 12 July 2013
6. Foreign Ministry Spokesperson Hua Chunying's Regular Press Conference, 12 July 2013
7. Foreign Ministry Spokesperson Hua Chunying's Regular Press Conference, 8 July 2013
8. Wang Yi Stressed that the South China Sea Issue Should Be Resolved by Parties Directly Concerned Through Negotiation, 2 July 2013
9. Foreign Ministry Spokesperson Hua Chunying's Regular Press Conference, 1 July 2013
10. Foreign Minister Wang Yi: Confrontation Leads Nowhere, 27 June 2013
11. Foreign Ministry Spokesperson Hua Chunying's Regular Press Conference, 24 June 2013
12. Chinese Embassy in UK Refutes Accusations against China over South China Sea Issue, 12 June 2013
13. Foreign Ministry Spokesperson Hong Lei's Regular Press Conference, 22 May 2013
14. Foreign Ministry Spokesperson Hua Chunying's Remarks on the Philippines' Efforts in Pushing for the Establishment of the Arbitral Tribunal in Relation to the Disputes between China and the Philippines in the South China Sea, 26 April 2013

15. Foreign Ministry Spokesperson Hong Lei's Regular Press Conference, 26 March 2013
16. Foreign Ministry Spokesperson Hong Lei's Regular Press Conference, 20 February 2013
17. Chinese Spokesperson Hong Lei's Remarks on China Returned the Philippines' Notification on the Submission of South China Sea Issue to International Arbitration, 19 February 2013
18. Foreign Ministry Spokesperson Hong Lei's Regular Press Conference, 28 January 2013
19. Foreign Ministry Spokesperson Hong Lei's Regular Press Conference, 23 January 2013
20. Statement of the Chinese Embassy in the Republic of the Philippines on the Submission of South China Sea Issue to International Arbitration by the Philippine Side, 23 January 2013
21. Foreign Minister Yang Jiechi on the South China Sea Issue, 13 July 2012
22. Some Basic Facts on China's Sovereignty over Huangyan Island, 13 April 2012
23. Note Verbale CML/8/2011 from the Permanent Mission of the People's Republic of China to the UN Secretary-General, 14 April 2011
24. Note Verbale CML/17/2009 from the Permanent Mission of the People's Republic of China to the UN Secretary-General, 7 May 2009
25. Note Verbale CML/12/2009 from the Permanent Mission of the People's Republic of China to the UN Secretary-General, 13 April 2009
26. Declaration by the People's Republic of China under Article 298 UNCLOS, 25 August 2006
27. Position Paper of the People's Republic of China on the Issue of the South China Sea, 17 November 2000
28. Law on the Exclusive Economic Zone and the Continental Shelf of the People's Republic of China, 26 June 1998
29. Declaration Made by the People's Republic of China upon Ratification of the United Nations Convention on the Law of the Sea, 7 June 1996
30. Declaration of the Government of the People's Republic of China on the Baselines of the Territorial Sea of the People's Republic of China, 15 May 1996
31. Law of the People's Republic of China on the Territorial Sea and the Contiguous Zone, 25 February 1992
32. Declaration by the People's Republic of China in Relation to the Declaration Made by the Government of the Philippines upon Signature and Confirmed upon Ratification, 12 June 1985
33. Declaration of the Government of the People's Republic of China on China's Territorial Sea, 4 September 1958

B. Documents of the Republic of the Philippines

1. Note Verbale No 13-0211 from the Department of Foreign Affairs of the Republic of the Philippines to the Embassy of the People's Republic of China in Manila, 22 January 2013
2. Republic of the Philippines, Notification and Statement of Claim, 22 January 2013
3. Understanding Made by the Republic of the Philippines upon Signature of the United Nations Convention on the Law of the Sea, 10 December 1982, and Confirmed upon Ratification of the Convention, 8 May 1984

A. DOCUMENTS OF THE PEOPLE'S REPUBLIC OF CHINA

1. Foreign Ministry Spokesperson Hong Lei's Regular Press Conference, 11 September 2013

Q: The Philippine Vice Admiral Jose Luis Alano reportedly said yesterday that discussions were under way about how to address the block-laying issue on the Huangyan Island and said that whether to remove the blocks would be finally decided by the Philippine government. What is China's comment?

A: China has indisputable sovereignty over the Huangyan Island and its adjacent waters. No one knows the situation on the Huangyan Island better than China. What the Philippines said was completed fabricated. I would like to underline that China's activities on the Huangyan Island and in its adjacent waters fall entirely within the scope of China's sovereignty. China urges the Philippines to stop stirring up new troubles and work together with China to uphold peace and stability in the South China Sea and restore bilateral relations.[1]

2. Foreign Ministry Spokesperson Hong Lei's Remarks on the Huangyan Island Questions, 4 September 2013

Q: The Philippine side reportedly said that China had built concrete facilities on the Huangyan Island. Please confirm.

A: What the Philippines said is untrue. The Huangyan Island is China's inherent territory. Given the current situation, Chinese government ships maintain routine patrol in the waters off the Huangyan Island to safeguard the sovereignty over the Huangyan Island and keep order in relevant waters. It is within China's legitimate rights and interests and beyond dispute.[2]

[1] www.fmprc.gov.cn/eng/xwfw/s2510/2511/t1075618.shtml.
[2] www.fmprc.gov.cn/eng/xwfw/s2510/2511/t1072920.shtml.

3. Ambassador Ma Keqing Addressed UA&P Students on China-ASEAN Relationship, 4 September 2013

On Aug 30, Ambassador Ma Keqing delivered a speech with the theme of China-ASEAN relations to an audience of about 200 students and faculties of University of Asia Pacific in Pasig, at the invitation from Dr Jose Maria Mariano, President of UA&P.[3]

> [...] Talking about the South China Sea issue, Ambassador Ma stressed that China has always advocated to resolve the disputes through negotiations on the basis of the respect for historical facts and international laws, which are equally important. The South China Sea disputes can be solved through three ways which could be processed simultaneously. First is to reach agreement through consultation and negotiation between direct parties concerned. This is the fundamental way and the only way that can lead to final solution. China has always kept the door open to dialogues and consultations. Second is to continue to implement the 'Declaration on Conduct of Parties in the South China Sea' (DOC), while gradually push forward the consultations on a code of conduct of the South China Sea, but with reasonable expectations. Third, to search for ways of joint exploitation.[4]

4. Foreign Ministry Spokesperson Hua Chunying's Remarks on the Philippines' Statement on the South China Sea, 16 July 2013

Q: In response to China's statement that the Philippines' claim of having exhausted almost all political and diplomatic avenues for a peaceful settlement of the dispute is completely not true, the Philippine Foreign Ministry issued an eight-point statement on July 15, saying that the Chinese statement is baseless and China's hard line position makes it impossible to continue bilateral discussions and leads the Philippines to finally resort to international arbitration.[5] What is China's comment?

A: We regret that the Philippines stated that it has become impossible to continue bilateral discussions with China, and are dissatisfied with its refusal to diplomatic negotiation and closure of the door to dialogue. We are firmly opposed to the Philippines' indifference to China's lawful rights and interests and legitimate concerns as well as its willful act of pushing for international arbitration.

The Philippines' illegal occupation of some of the islands and reefs of China's Nansha Islands is the direct cause to the South China Sea dispute between China and the Philippines. China sticks to the longstanding position of safeguarding national territorial sovereignty, which is totally

---

[3] University of Asia and the Pacific, Pasig City, Philippines.
[4] www.fmprc.gov.cn/ce/ceph/eng/sgdt/t1072909.htm.
[5] For the text of the Philippines' 'eight-point statement', see 'Response of the DFA Spokesperson to the Recent Statement of the Chinese Ministry of Foreign Affairs on the West Philippine Sea Issue', 15 July 2013, https://www.dfa.gov.ph/index.php/2013-06-27-21-50-36/dfa-releases/332.

legitimate. Meanwhile, bearing in mind the relations between China and the Philippines as well as regional peace and stability, China stays committed to solving disputes concerning territorial sovereignty and maritime delimitation through bilateral negotiations in accordance with relevant regulations of international law and the spirit of the Declaration on the Conduct of Parties in the South China Sea (DOC). This position remains unchanged.

There has been communication and agreement between China and the Philippines on disputes in the South China Sea. The two sides reached the important consensus of carrying out cooperation in a step by step manner and resolving bilateral disputes through negotiations. There has also been sound cooperation between China and the Philippines. As approved by the two governments, China National Offshore Oil Corporation and Philippine National Oil Company signed an agreement for joint marine seismic undertaking on certain areas of the South China Sea, which later included Vietnam. The three parties have carried out joint marine seismic operations, making positive contribution to stability, cooperation and development of the South China Sea.

However, it is regrettable that over recent years, the Philippines has changed its attitude and approach in handling the issue, gone back on its consensus with China, broken its commitment in the DOC, cast aside the framework of dialogue upheld by a majority of countries, refused to cooperate, aggravated the situation and set off the incident of the Huangyan Island by harassing Chinese civilians with warships, casting a shadow over China-Philippine relations and peace and stability of the South China Sea.

The Philippines publicly criticized China during the recently held ASEAN Foreign Ministers' Meetings, regardless of the consensus among ASEAN countries, and thus was reasonably refuted by China. It is difficult for China to understand how could the Philippines continue to play up the issue of the South China Sea, distort the facts and smear China.

The overall situation of the South China Sea is stable. China and ASEAN countries have consensus on upholding peace and stability of the South China Sea. China will stay committed to safeguarding peace and stability of the South China Sea with maximum good faith and sincerity. China has never closed the door to negotiation and consultation with the Philippines in the hope of improving and developing bilateral relations. China urges the Philippines to correct its erroneous actions, make positive response to China's suggestions in March, 2010 and January, 2012 respectively of establishing the Sino-Philippine regular consultation mechanism on maritime issues and resuming the Sino-Philippine mechanism on trust-building measures, and come back to the correct track of resolving disputes through bilateral negotiations.[6]

---

[6] www.fmprc.gov.cn/eng/xwfw/s2510/2535/t1059343.shtml.

5. Foreign Ministry Spokesperson Hua Chunying's Remarks on the South China Sea Issue, 12 July 2013

Q: Was the South China Sea issue discussed at the fifth round of China-US Strategic and Economic Dialogue? Please brief us on the specifics.

A: China stated its principled position on the South China Sea issue at the fifth round of China-US Strategic and Economic Dialogue. The Chinese side emphasized that China stays committed to solving disputes through negotiations with countries directly concerned while resolutely safeguarding its territorial sovereignty and maritime rights and interests. We hope that relevant countries could make good on its commitment to properly handle and solve relevant dispute through bilateral and friendly consultation. We say it and we do it.

The US said that it does not take sides on the South China Sea issue. China hopes that the US side could respect the facts and live up to what it says.[7]

6. Foreign Ministry Spokesperson Hua Chunying's Regular Press Conference, 12 July 2013

Q: The Philippine Foreign Secretary Albert del Rosario criticized China on the South China Sea issue when addressing an experts' roundtable in Belgium, arguing that the Philippines had exhausted almost all political and diplomatic avenues for a peaceful settlement of its dispute with China and its last resort therefore was to utilize the legal track of international arbitration. What is China's comment?

A: While resolutely safeguarding national territorial sovereignty and maritime rights and interests, China stays committed to solving territorial and maritime disputes through negotiation and consultation. China has repeatedly made clear its position on the Philippines' taking of the South China Sea issue to international arbitration. China's rejection of the Philippines' request for arbitration has a solid basis in international law. The Philippines' claim that "it had exhausted almost all political and diplomatic avenues for a peaceful settlement of the dispute" is completely not true. China has repeatedly suggested to the Philippines that the two sides could resume the existing consultation mechanism or establish new ones. But we have not yet got any response from the Philippine side. The Philippines is keen on attacking China in international settings while unilaterally shutting the door for negotiation and consultation. Such practice is anything but helpful to solve the issue. China urges the Philippine side to change its wrong course, stop misleading public opinion and come back to the right track of solving the dispute through bilateral negotiation and consultation.[8]

[7] www.fmprc.gov.cn/eng/xwfw/s2510/2535/t1058519.shtml.
[8] www.fmprc.gov.cn/eng/xwfw/s2510/2511/t1058584.shtml.

7. Foreign Ministry Spokesperson Hua Chunying's Regular Press Conference, 8 July 2013

Q: The Philippine Department of Foreign Affairs recently distributed foldouts about international arbitration in relation to the South China Sea issue to foreign diplomatic missions in Manila, promoting its position on arbitration and publicizing statements by relevant countries in support of its claim for arbitration. What is China's comment?

A: China has repeatedly expounded on its position regarding the Philippines' request for arbitration on the disputes between China and the Philippines in the South China Sea. I would like to reiterate that China rejects the Philippines' taking of the South China Sea issue to arbitration. This position will remain unchanged.

China's position stands on a solid basis of international law. It is China's lawful rights and interests as a sovereign country and a party to the UN Convention on the Law of the Sea (UNCLOS), which should be respected by other countries.

The Philippines attempted to use the arbitration to mislead the international community and pressure China. China is firmly opposed to that. We once again urge the Philippine side to come back to the right track of solving the disputes through bilateral negotiations. We also hope that other countries could be discreet on the issue of arbitration and do more things that truly contribute to peace and stability in the South China Sea so as to avoid aggravating and complicating the situation.[9]

8. Wang Yi Stressed that the South China Sea Issue Should Be Resolved by Parties Directly Concerned Through Negotiation, 2 July 2013

On 2 July, Foreign Minister Wang Yi expounded on the solemn position of the Chinese government during the ASEAN Regional Forum (ARF) Foreign Ministers' Meeting in Bandar Seri Begawan, Brunei in response to the claim the Philippines made at the meeting that the Huangyan Island and the Ren'ai Reef are "occupied".

Wang Yi said that this meeting is not the proper venue to discuss specific cases in the South China Sea. However, since the Philippines brought it up, I believe it is necessary that we get the facts clear.

Wang Yi reviewed the historical background of the South China Sea issue, emphasizing that China has solid historical and legal evidence supporting its position on the issue. This position has been upheld by successive Chinese governments and is widely supported by the Chinese people. China has an unwavering resolve to uphold its sovereignty and maritime rights and interests. At the same time, we are committed to resolving the disputes through consultation and negotiation with the

[9] www.fmprc.gov.cn/eng/xwfw/s2510/2511/t1057224.shtml.

countries concerned. This is stipulated in the Declaration on the Conduct of Parties in the South China Sea (DOC) and is a commitment jointly made by China and ASEAN.

Wang Yi pointed out that the situation in the South China Sea is generally stable and there is no problem with the freedom of navigation at all. During the foreign ministers' meeting, my ASEAN colleagues and I had an in-depth exchange of views on the South China Sea issue and we increased mutual trust. We are all of the view that China-ASEAN relations are multi-faceted and cannot be defined by a single issue. We must not let a single issue overshadow the friendship and cooperation between the two sides. The South China Sea issue is not an issue between China and ASEAN. It is only an issue between China and a small number of Southeast Asian countries. China and ASEAN countries are fully and effectively implementing the DOC and have the full capacity to ensure peace and stability in the South China Sea.

We agreed to hold the next round of Senior Officials' Meeting and Joint Working Group Meeting on the Implementation of the DOC in China this September to promote full and effective implementation of the DOC, hold consultation on how to advance a code of conduct (COC) within the framework of implementation of the DOC and gradually advance the COC process on the basis of consensus.

Wang Yi cited a large amount of facts and evidence to show that China has indisputable sovereignty over the Huangyan Island and the Ren'ai Reef, and stressed that it is fully justified for China to make necessary reaction to provocative activities.

Wang Yi emphasized that bilateral disputes should be resolved through bilateral consultation. Should one choose to play up the issue on multilateral occasions, it will not help resolve the issue. Rather, it will harm the bilateral relations and this is not in the interests of that country and its people.

Many foreign ministers fully recognized in their remarks the new progress China and ASEAN made in safeguarding stability in the South China Sea and pointed out that disputes in the South China Sea should be resolved through consultation and negotiation between the countries directly concerned. Parties should move forward the process of formulating COC within the framework of full and effective implementation of the DOC. Some countries argued that outside forces and countries outside the region should not intervene in the disputes in the South China Sea and that the South China Sea issue should not be internationalized, otherwise it is not conducive to resolving the issue. ASEAN countries expressed their willingness to work with China to jointly uphold peace and stability in the region.[10]

---

[10] www.fmprc.gov.cn/eng/zxxx/t1055452.shtml.

9. Foreign Ministry Spokesperson Hua Chunying's Regular Press Conference, 1 July 2013

Q: It is reported that the Philippines circulated a statement on day one of the 46th ASEAN Foreign Ministers' Meetings, saying that "it views with serious concern the militarisation of the South China Sea", and the "massive" presence of Chinese military and paramilitary ships at the Huangyan Island and the Ren'ai Reef in the Philippines' exclusive economic zone would be a threat to maritime peace and security of the region. What is China's comment?

A: China has indisputable sovereignty over the Nansha Islands and their adjacent waters and will continue to defend resolutely its national sovereignty, rights and interests. China also steadfastly upholds peace and stability in waters off the Nansha Islands.

Facts have proven that what has happened in the South China Sea over recent years was not caused by China. Last year, the Philippines stirred up the incident of the Huangyan Island by harassing Chinese fishermen with warships in relevant waters. This year, the Philippines attempted to build fixed facilities on the Ren'ai Reef where it illegally "grounded" its warship. I would like to call your attention to the fact that China has made repeated representations with the Philippines since the "grounding" of the Philippine warship on the Ren'ai Reef in 1999, asking it to tow away the ship. The Philippines made it clear to the Chinese side that due to a shortage of component parts, it was unable to drag away the ship for the moment, adding that it did not want to be the first party to violate the Declaration on the Conduct of Parties in the South China Sea (DOC). Therefore, the "grounding" of the Philippine ship does not constitute its occupation of the Ren'ai Reef. Just think about it, if every country could create the so-called "status quo" by grounding a broken-down ship on other's reef, then what rule is there going to be? What honesty and credibility is there going to be? How can we uphold peace and stability of the South China Sea? Therefore, China has every reason to make necessary response to the Philippines' provocative actions that gravely violate China's territorial sovereignty and maritime rights and interests as well as the DOC.

I want to stress once again that China has enough sincerity and patience and stays committed to properly solving relevant disputes through dialogue and negotiation with parties directly concerned in light of the spirit of the DOC. If some individual claimant chooses the course of confrontation, it will lead nowhere.[11]

---

[11] www.fmprc.gov.cn/eng/xwfw/s2510/2511/t1055206.shtml.

10. Foreign Minister Wang Yi: Confrontation Leads Nowhere, 27 June 2013

On June 27, 2013, at the luncheon of the Second World Peace Forum, Foreign Minister Wang Yi answered questions on the issue of South China Sea. Wang Yi said that China holds clear and consistent position on the Nansha islands issue. Successive Governments of China have always adhered to the position and got wide support from the Chinese people. This position will not be and is impossible for any change. We will continue to unswervingly safeguard our national sovereignty, rights and interests. In recent years, a number of disputes have been stirred up in South China Sea. When we look into the facts, none of these disputes were started or caused by China. Some individual country illegally grounded warships and constructed buildings on the reef within China's territorial sovereignty, and unilaterally called for international arbitration in these bilateral disputes. These actions, which expand and complicate the disputes, violate not only the spirit of the United Nations Convention on the Law of the Sea (UNCLOS) but also the Declaration on the Conduct of Parties (DOC) in the South China Sea. To deal with such provocations, China has every reason to make necessary responses.

Wang Yi stressed that, with the most sincerity and patience, China is willing to abide by the rules of DOC and continue to seek proper solutions to related disputes through dialogue and negotiation between the countries directly concerned, so as to maintain peace and stability in the South China Sea. Pending the settlement of disputes, we propose shelving differences and seeking joint development. If some individual country choose the course of confrontation, it will lead nowhere. If they attempt to reinforce their illegitimate claims by relying on outside forces, it is futile and will prove to be a strategic misjudgment that will bring more losses than gains.[12]

11. Foreign Ministry Spokesperson Hua Chunying's Regular Press Conference, 24 June 2013

Q: Comments say that out of humanitarian consideration, China opened a passage for the Philippines to rotate and supply its personnel on the Ren'ai Reef. However, the Philippine Defense Secretary said that the Philippines could take any action without notifying China. What is China's comment?

A: China has indisputable sovereignty over the Nansha Islands including the Ren'ai Reef and their adjacent waters. The Philippines grounded its warship on China's Ren'ai Reef due to a "malfunction" in 1999 and refused to honor its commitment of towing away the ship under the excuse of technical problems despite China's persistent requirement. The

---

[12] www.fmprc.gov.cn/eng/wjdt/wshd/t1054830.shtml.

Philippines' activities violated the Declaration on the Conduct of Parties in the South China Sea (DOC). I want to point out that the Philippine warship's grounding on the Ren'ai Reef does not constitute an actual occupation of it. China will by no means accept the Philippines' illegal occupation of the Ren'ai Reef in any form. We once again urge the Philippine side to earnestly honor its commitment, avoid taking provocative actions that complicate the situation, and make its due efforts to uphold peace, stability and cooperation in the South China Sea.[13]

12. Chinese Embassy in UK Refutes Accusations against China over South China Sea Issue, 12 June 2013

The following is a letter from Mr. He Rulong, Spokesman of the Chinese Embassy in London to Financial Times ' Letters' Editor, which was carried in the print and online editions of Financial Times on 12 June under the title "Bilateral talks are way forward for South China Sea".

Sir,
Your newspaper carried on 30 May an article by David Pilling The Philippines is right to challenge China. I find this article unacceptable.
The essence of the South China Sea issue is the disputes over territorial sovereignty caused by the illegal occupation of China's Nansha Islands by some littoral countries and overlapping claims to some waters in the South China Sea. A close study of the issue will clearly show that China is a victim of this issue, rather than a trouble maker. China has long maintained that the related countries should bear in mind the overall interests of regional peace and stability and find ways to properly manage and resolve the disputes through bilateral negotiation and dialogue while fully respecting historical facts and international law. China also believes that pending a final solution all related parties should refrain from taking any actions to expand and further complicated the disputes.
The China-Philippines dispute over South China Sea is no exception. China is always committed to resolving the dispute through bilateral negotiation and consultation with the Philippines. In fact through bilateral negotiation and consultation, China and Philippines for a long time effectively kept the dispute under control and managed to concentrate on bilateral practical cooperation to the benefit of the people in both countries.
All signatories to the Declaration on the Conduct of the Parties in the South China Sea (DOC) have agreed to resolve disputes over territory and maritime rights and interests through negotiations between directly related sovereign states. This is also the commitment made by the Philippines as one of the signatories. The DOC should be implemented in full and in good faith.
However, in disregard of China's position and its own commitment, the Philippines has put the dispute to international arbitration. This move has breached the consensus established in the DOC by the countries in the region. It also runs counter to the overriding trend of regional peace, development and cooperation. It is neither popular nor valid.

[13] www.fmprc.gov.cn/eng/xwfw/s2510/2511/t1053084.shtml.

It is the shared aspiration of majority countries in the region to achieve lasting stability and common prosperity. Common security and common development through dialogue and cooperation is the only workable way to achieve lasting peace and stability in South China Sea.

Recently China and ASEAN countries held a joint working group meeting in Bangkok on implementing the DOC. Good progress was made at the meeting on strengthening cooperation in the framework of the DOC. It is counterproductive that while countries in the region work together to maintain stability in the South China Sea through closer exchanges and cooperation, someone is writing to openly claim that 'The Philippines is right to challenge China'. We can not but wonder about the purpose of these people. Do they really want safe and secure shipping lanes in the South China Sea? Do they genuinely hope for peace and development in Asia? The instigations in the article will only make the situation more complicated, therefore undesirable.

China is firm in its pursuit of peaceful development. We are also determined to safeguard territorial sovereignty and lawful rights and interests, while maintaining an amicable and stable neighborhood. We hope all related parties will work with us toward the same goal.

He Rulong, Spokesman, Chinese Embassy, London, UK[14]

13. Foreign Ministry Spokesperson Hong Lei's Regular Press Conference, 22 May 2013

Q: Spokesperson of the Philippine Foreign Ministry said on May 21 that the Philippine side had protested to the Chinese side about the recent entry of Chinese warships and maritime surveillance ships into waters off the Ren'ai Reef. The Philippine side claimed that China violated its sovereignty and international law. What is China's comment?

A: The Ren'ai Reef is part of the Nansha Islands. China has indisputable sovereignty over the Nansha Islands and their adjacent waters. It is beyond reproach that Chinese government vessels carry out normal patrol in relevant waters. China urges relevant country to follow through on the Declaration on the Conduct of Parties in the South China Sea (DOC) and refrain from taking actions that complicate and aggravate the dispute and spoil peace and stability of the South China Sea.[15]

14. Foreign Ministry Spokesperson Hua Chunying's Remarks on the Philippines' Efforts in Pushing for the Establishment of the Arbitral Tribunal in Relation to the Disputes between China and the Philippines in the South China Sea, 26 April 2013

Q: At the request of the Philippines, an arbitral tribunal on the South China Sea disputes between China and the Philippines has been composed recently. What is China's comment on this?

---

[14] www.chinese-embassy.org.uk/eng/EmbassyNews/t1050127.htm.
[15] www.fmprc.gov.cn/eng/xwfw/s2510/2511/t1043177.shtml.

A: On 22 January 2013, the Philippines sent China a note verbale, attached with a notification, to initiate arbitration proceedings against China regarding issues of the South China Sea. On 19 February, China stated its rejection of the request for arbitration by the Philippines and returned the latter's note verbale and the attached notification. The position of China, as indicated above, will not change.

Since the 1970s, the Philippines, in violation of the Charter of the United Nations and principles of international law, illegally occupied some islands and reefs of China's Nansha Islands, including Mahuan Dao, Feixin Dao, Zhongye Dao, Nanyao Dao, Beizi Dao, Xiyue Dao, Shuanghuang Shazhou and Siling Jiao. Firmly and consistently opposed to the illegal occupation by the Philippines, China hereby solemnly reiterates its demand that the Philippines withdraw all its nationals and facilities from China's islands and reefs.

The Philippines professed in the notification of 22 January 2013 that it "does not seek...a determination of which Party enjoys sovereignty over the islands claimed by both of them." On 22 January, however, the Philippines publicly stated that the purpose for initiating the arbitration was to bring to "a durable solution" the Philippines-China disputes in the South China Sea. These statements are simply self-contradictory. In addition, by initiating the arbitration on the basis of its illegal occupation of China's islands and reefs, the Philippines has distorted the basic facts underlying the disputes between China and the Philippines. In so doing, the Philippines attempts to deny China's territorial sovereignty and clothes its illegal occupation of China's islands and reefs with a cloak of "legality". The Philippines' attempt to seek a so-called "durable solution" such as this and the means it has employed to that end are absolutely unacceptable to China.

In accordance with international law, and especially the principle of the law of the sea that 'land dominates the sea', determined territorial sovereignty is the precondition for, and basis of maritime delimitation. The claims for arbitration as raised by the Philippines are essentially concerned with maritime delimitation between the two countries in parts of the South China Sea, and thus inevitably involve the territorial sovereignty over certain relevant islands and reefs. However, such issues of territorial sovereignty are not the ones concerning the interpretation or application of the UN Convention on the Law of the Sea (UNCLOS). Therefore, given the fact that the Sino-Philippine territorial disputes still remain unresolved, the compulsory dispute settlement procedures as contained in UNCLOS should not apply to the claims for arbitration as raised by the Philippines. Moreover, in 2006, the Chinese Government made a declaration in pursuance of Article 298 of UNCLOS, excluding disputes regarding such matters as those related to maritime delimitation from the compulsory dispute settlement procedures, including arbitration. Therefore, the request for arbitration by the Philippines is manifestly unfounded. China's rejection of the Philippines' request for arbitration, consequently, has a solid basis in international law.

In the interest of maintaining the Sino-Philippine relations and the peace and stability in the South China Sea, China has been persistent in pursuing bilateral negotiations and consultations with the Philippines to resolve relevant disputes. It is a commitment undertaken by all signatories, the Philippines included, under the Declaration on the Conduct of Parties in the South China Sea (DOC) that disputes relating to territorial and maritime rights and interests be resolved through negotiations by sovereign states directly concerned therewith. The DOC should be implemented in a comprehensive and serious manner. China will adhere to the means of bilateral negotiations to resolve territorial and maritime delimitation disputes both in accordance with applicable rules of international law and in compliance with the spirit of the DOC.[16]

15. Foreign Ministry Spokesperson Hong Lei's Regular Press Conference, 26 March 2013

Q: The Philippine Foreign Ministry recently said that the International Tribunal on the Law of the Sea had appointed another judge as the member of the arbitration panel for Philippines-China dispute on the South China Sea. What is China's comment?

A: The note and its attached notice submitted by the Philippines to arbitration not only violates the consensus reached between ASEAN countries and China in the "Declaration on the Conduct of Parties in the South China Sea" (DOC), but also contains serious errors in fact and law as well as many false accusations against China. We have made clear that China does not accept the note and its attached notice and has returned it.

China hopes the Philippines could honor its commitment, refrain from taking actions that may complicate and aggravate the issue and return to the right track of resolving disputes through bilateral negotiations.[17]

16. Foreign Ministry Spokesperson Hong Lei's Regular Press Conference, 20 February 2013

Q: Philippine Foreign Ministry issued a statement yesterday, saying that it would push forward the arbitration process against China on the South China Sea dispute between the two countries. What is your comment?

A: Both the Philippines and China are signatories to the Declaration on the Conduct of Parties in South China Sea (DOC) and have made commitments on comprehensive and earnest implementation of the DOC.

---

[16] www.fmprc.gov.cn/eng/xwfw/s2510/2535/t1035577.shtml.
[17] www.fmprc.gov.cn/eng/xwfw/s2510/2511/t1025838.shtml.

We disapprove of the Philippine Foreign Ministry's practice of bringing international arbitration and have made clear our opposition stance.

China maintains that the dialogue framework supported by most countries in the region should be upheld. We will continue to make efforts to maintain peace and stability in the South China Sea and unswervingly safeguard national sovereignty and interests.[18]

17. Chinese Spokesperson Hong Lei's Remarks on China Returned the Philippines' Notification on the Submission of South China Sea Issue to International Arbitration, 19 February 2013

Q: It is said that China has returned the Philippines' Notification on the submission of South China Sea issue to international Arbitration, please confirm.

A: China's position on the South China Sea issue is consistent and clear. China's sovereignty over the Nansha Islands and their adjacent waters is supported by abundant historical and legal evidence. Meanwhile, bearing in mind the larger interest of China-Philippines relations and regional peace and stability, China has remained committed to resolving the disputes through bilateral negotiations, and has made every effort to maintain stability and to promote regional cooperation in the South China Sea. To resolve the disputes through negotiations by sovereign states directly concerned is also the consensus between China and ASEAN countries as stipulated in the Declaration on the Conduct of Parties in the South China Sea (DOC). The Philippines' Note Verbale and the attached Notification not only runs counter to the consensus, but also contains many grave errors both in fact and in law, and includes many false accusations against China. China firmly opposes to this.

On Feb. 19, Ambassador of China to the Philippines Ma Keqing met with officials of Department of Foreign Affairs of the Philippines, and stated that the Chinese side rejected and returned the Philippines' Note Verbale and the attached Notification.

The Chinese side hopes that the Philippine side keeps its word, not to take any action that magnifies and complicates the issue, responds positively to China's proposals on establishing a bilateral regular consultation mechanism on maritime issues, resumes the operation of the Confidence Building Measures Mechanism (CBMs) as established between the two countries, and reverts to the right track of settling the disputes through bilateral negotiations.[19]

---

[18] www.fmprc.gov.cn/eng/xwfw/s2510/2511/t1015425.shtml.
[19] ph.china-embassy.org/eng/xwfb/t1014903.htm.

18. Foreign Ministry Spokesperson Hong Lei's Regular Press Conference, 28 January 2013

Q: Philippine President Benigno Aquino III reportedly said on January 26 that Chinese vessels recently prevented Philippine fishing boats from seeking shelter in waters off the Huangyan Island on two occasions, thus the Philippine side had decided to ask for international arbitration on the dispute of the South China Sea. Aquino said he could not allow China to claim effective control over Huangyan Island by this act, as this could encourage China to move into the Philippine-claimed and allegedly resource-rich Liyue Bank. What is China's comment?

A: The Huangyan Island is indisputable Chinese territory. Last year's Huangyan Island incident was caused by Philippine warships' harassment of Chinese fishermen and fishing boats. At present, the situation over the Huangyan Island is mainly stable. The Chinese side does not want to see a setback.

China's position on the Liyue Bank issue is clear. The Liyue Bank is part of Nansha Islands, and China has indisputable sovereignty over Nansha Islands and their adjacent waters. The Chinese government always maintains that the Nansha dispute should be resolved through bilateral negotiation and consultation, which is also the consensus of relevant parties.[20]

19. Foreign Ministry Spokesperson Hong Lei's Regular Press Conference, 23 January 2013

Q: [...] Second, Philippine Foreign Secretary Albert del Rosario reportedly said on January 22 that the Philippines would ask for international arbitration on its dispute with China on the South China Sea. How does China respond?

A: [...] On your second question, China has indisputable sovereignty over the Nansha Islands and their adjacent waters. It is based on full historical and jurisprudential evidence. Territorial sovereignty dispute caused by the Philippines' illegal encroachment on some islets of China's Nansha Islands is the root cause and essence of relevant dispute between China and the Philippines in the South China Sea. China has been firmly opposed to that.

Bearing China-Philippines relations and regional peace and stability in mind, China has been committed to resolving disputes through bilateral consultation and negotiation, which reflects China's good faith and sincerity. To solve relevant disputes through negotiation between directly-concerned sovereign states is also the consensus between China and ASEAN countries as stipulated in the *Declaration on the Conduct of Parties*

[20] www.fmprc.gov.cn/eng/xwfw/s2510/2511/t1008951.shtml.

in the South China Sea (DOC). All the signatories to the DOC should stand by their solemn commitments.

We hope that relevant country would keep its word, earnestly and fully carry out the DOC and refrain from taking actions that could complicate and aggravate this issue.[21]

20. Statement of the Chinese Embassy in the Republic of the Philippines on the Submission of South China Sea Issue to International Arbitration by the Philippine Side, 23 January 2013

On Jan 22nd, Ambassador Ma Keqing met upon request with Assistant Secretary of Department of Foreign Affairs of the Philippines Theresa Lasaro. The latter submitted the Note Verbale that the Philippines will initiate arbitral proceedings of South China Sea issue. Ambassador Ma reiterated the principled position of the Chinese side, that China has indisputable sovereignty over the islands in South China Sea and its adjacent waters. The Chinese side strongly holds the disputes on South China Sea should be settled by parties concerned through negotiations. This is also the consensus reached by parties concerned in the DOC (The Declaration on the Conduct of Parties in the South China Sea).[22]

21. Foreign Minister Yang Jiechi on the South China Sea Issue, 13 July 2012

In response to the remarks by some countries about the South China Sea issue at the ASEAN Regional Forum Foreign Ministers' Meeting, Foreign Minister Yang Jiechi explained China's position on the issue.

Yang pointed out that China's sovereignty over the Nansha Islands and their adjacent waters is supported by ample historical and legal evidence. Yet given the complexity of the South China Sea issue, China has always called for shelving disputes and seeking joint development. China and ASEAN countries had candid discussions and reached broad consensus on the South China Sea issue 20 years ago and signed the Declaration on the Conduct of Parties in the South China Sea (DOC) in Phnom Penh ten years ago. An important principle of the DOC is to let sovereign states directly concerned resolve their territorial and jurisdictional disputes by peaceful means through friendly consultations and negotiations. Parties agreed to work, on the basis of consensus, towards the eventual formulation of a code of conduct in the South China Sea (COC). China is open to launching discussions on COC on the basis of full compliance with the DOC by all parties. What is essential is that all parties exercise self-restraint in keeping with the spirit of the DOC, and refrain from taking moves that will escalate and complicate the disputes and affect peace and stability. China hopes

---

[21] www.fmprc.gov.cn/eng/xwfw/s2510/2511/t1007746.shtml.
[22] ph.china-embassy.org/eng/xwfb/t1007184.htm.

that all parties will do more to enhance mutual trust, promote cooperation, and create necessary conditions for the formulation of COC.

Yang said that China is a party to the United Nations Convention on the Law of the Sea (UNCLOS) and places importance on upholding the principles and purposes of the Convention. The Convention states at the very outset the desirability of "establishing, with due regard for the sovereignty of all States, a legal order for the seas and oceans". This means that the Convention has not given itself the authority to change the territory of countries and that it cannot be cited as the basis for arbitration in territorial disputes between countries. Countries concerned should first resolve their territorial disputes over the Nansha Islands and, on that basis, proceed to resolve the issue of maritime delimitation in the South China Sea in accordance with international law, the UNCLOS included.

Yang said that the South China Sea is an important shipping route. China is a big trading nation, and 60% of China's external trade goes through the South China Sea. Therefore, China attaches great importance to the freedom and safety of navigation in the South China Sea. Last November, China and Indonesia co-hosted in China the Workshop on Maintaining Freedom and Safety of Navigation in the South China Sea. China has taken an active part in the Cooperative Mechanism in the Straits of Malacca and the Regional Cooperation Agreement on Combating Piracy and Armed Robbery Against Ships in Asia and set up the Maritime Consultation Mechanism with ASEAN countries. China will continue to work closely with the littoral countries to ensure smooth sea lanes in the South China Sea. Countries in the region should make better use of the convenience brought about by the freedom of navigation in the South China Sea to strengthen connectivity and facilitate trade and mutually beneficial cooperation between regional countries and countries outside the region.[23]

22. Some Basic Facts on China's Sovereignty over Huangyan Island, 13 April 2012

1. It is China who first discovered Huangyan Island, gave it the name, incorporated it into its territory, and exercised jurisdiction over it.

Huangyan Island was first discovered and drew [sic] into China's map in China's Yuan Dynasty (1271-1368AD). In 1279, Chinese astronomer Guo Shoujing performed surveying of the seas around China for Kublai Khan, and Huangyan Island was chosen as the point in the South China Sea.
In January 1935, Map Verification Committee of China, which consisted of representatives from Ministry of Interior Affairs, Ministry of Foreign Affairs, Ministry of Education, and Navy, declared sovereignty over 132 islands reefs and shoals, Huangyan Island was included as a part of Zhongsha Islands into Chinese territory as the name of Scarborough

---

[23] no.china-embassy.org/eng/zyxw/t951025.htm.

Shoal. In October 1947, Chinese government announced the new namelist of South China Sea Islands, in which Scarborough Shoal was included and renamed as Democratic Reef as a part of Zhongsha Islands. In 1983, China Board on Geographic Names released Geographic Names of Some of South China Sea Islands, which decided to use Huangyan Island as the standard name of the island and Democratic Reef as alternative name. All the official maps published by Chinese governments of different periods marked Huangyan Island as Chinese territory. Huangyan Island has been consistently under administration of China's Guangdong Province first and Hainan Province later. China's sovereignty over Huangyan Island have [sic] been declared in all the government announcements and statements on South China Sea. All of these happened long before the United Nations Convention on the Law of the Sea (UNCLOS) came into force in 1994.

2. China has long been developing and exploiting Huangyan Island.

Huangyan Island and its surrounding waters are traditional fisheries for Chinese fishermen. Since ancient time, the Chinese fishermen have been fishing in Huangyan Island and its surrounding waters. Many scientific expedition activities organized by China's State Bureau of Surveying, National Earthquake Bureau and National Bureau of Oceanography were held in the Island and around this area in various periods.

3. Some Comments on Philippine's claims

The Philippine territory is set by a series of international treaties, no of which involves Huangyan Island. The Treaty of Paris (1898), The Treaty of Washington (1900) and the Treaty with Great Britain (1930) state clearly that west limit of the Philippines territory is 118th degree meridian of longitude east of Greenwich, while the Huangyan Island is obviously outside this limits (15°08'-15°14'N, 117° 44'-117°48'E). The 1935 Constitution of the Republic of the Philippines, the 1946 Treaty of General Relations between the United States of America and the Republic of the Philippines, the 1952 U.S.-Philippines Mutual Defense Treaty, the 1961 Republic Act No. 3046 and the 1968 Republic Act. No. 5446 have reaffirmed the legal effects of the above-mentioned three treaties and once again expressively defined the Philippine territorial limits, the baseline points and baseline of the territorial waters, which had not included the Huangyan Island. The Philippine maps published in 1981 and 1984, just to name a few, also indicated that Huangyan Island is outside the Philippine territorial limits. The above facts fully prove that Huangyan Island is outside the scope of Philippine territory.

Until 1997, the Philippines has never put dispute on China's jurisdiction and development on Huangyan Island, while it repeatedly stated that the Huangyan Island was outside the Philippine territory. Then Philippine Ambassador to Germany indicated clearly in his letter to a Germany radio amateur on 5 February of 1990 that, Huangyan Island was not within the Philippine territory and sovereignty according to the National Mapping and Resource Information Authority of the Philippines. The documents issued by the National Mapping and Resource Information Authority of the Philippines to the American Radio Relay League on 18 October and 18 November 1994 have also confirmed respectively that the Philippine territorial limits and sovereignty was stipulated in the Paragraph 3 of the Treaty of Paris of 1898 and Huangyan Island was outside of the Philippine territory boundaries.

It is the basic principle of the international maritime law that land rules water. UNCLOS allows coastal states to claim a 200-nautical-mile exclusive economic zone (EEZ), but coastal states have no rights to harm the inherent territory and sovereignty of other countries. It is a violation of the principles of international laws, including that of UNCLOS, to change the ownership of the territorial sovereignty through UNCLOS.[24]

23. Note Verbale CML/8/2011 from the Permanent Mission of the People's Republic of China to the UN Secretary-General, 14 April 2011

The Permanent Mission of the People's Republic of China to the United Nations presents its compliments to the Secretary-General of the United Nations and, with reference to the Republic of Philippines' Note Verbale No.000228 dated 5 April 2011[25] addressed to the Secretary-General of the UN, has the honor to state the position as follows:

China has indisputable sovereignty over the islands in the South China Sea and the adjacent waters, and enjoys sovereign rights and jurisdiction over the relevant waters as well as the seabed and subsoil thereof. China's sovereignty and related rights and jurisdiction in the South China Sea are supported by abundant historical and legal evidence. The contents of the Note Verbale No.000228 of the Republic of Philippines are totally unacceptable to the Chinese Government.

The so-called Kalayaan Island Group (KIG) claimed by the Republic of Philippines is in fact part of China's Nansha Islands. In a series of international treaties which define the limits of the territory of the Republic of Philippines and the domestic legislation of the Republic of Philippines prior to 1970s, the Republic of Philippines had never made any claims to Nansha Islands or any of its components. Since 1970s, the Republic of Philippines started to invade and occupy some islands and reefs of China's Nansha Islands and made relevant territorial claims, to which China objects strongly. The Republic of Philippines' occupation of some islands and reefs of China's Nansha Islands as well as other related acts constitutes infringement upon China's territorial sovereignty. Under the

---

[24] www.fmprc.gov.cn/ce/ceph/eng/sgdt/t922594.htm.
[25] The Philippines' Note Verbale No 000228 (5 April 2011) can be found at www.un.org/Depts/los/clcs_new/submissions_files/mysvnm33_09/phl_re_chn_2011.pdf.

legal doctrine of *'ex injuria jus non oritur'*, the Republic of Philippines can in no way invoke such illegal occupation to support its territorial Claims. Furthermore, under the legal principle of *'la terre domine la mer'*, coastal states' Exclusive Economic Zone (EEZ) and Continental Shelf Claims shall not infringe upon the territorial sovereignty of other states.

Since 1930s, the Chinese Government has given publicity several times the geographical scope of China's Nansha Islands and the names of its components. China's Nansha Islands is therefore clearly defined. In addition, under the relevant provisions of the *1982 United Nations Convention on the Law of the Sea,* as well as the *Law of the People's Republic of China on the Territorial Sea and the Contiguous Zone (1992)* and the *Law on the Exclusive Economic Zone and the Continental Shelf of the People's Republic of China (1998)*, China's Nansha Islands is fully entitled to Territorial Sea, Exclusive Economic Zone (EEZ) and Continental Shelf.

The Permanent Mission of the People's Republic of China to the United Nations avails itself of this opportunity to renew to the Secretary-General of the United Nations the assurance of its highest consideration.[26]

24. Note Verbale CML/17/2009 from the Permanent Mission of the People's Republic of China to the UN Secretary-General, 7 May 2009

The Permanent Mission of the People's Republic of China to the United Nations presents its compliments to the Secretary-General of the United Nations and, with reference to the Joint Submission by Malaysia and the Socialist Republic of Viet Nam dated 6 May 2009, to the Commission on the Limits of the Continental Shelf (hereinafter referred to as 'the Commission') concerning the outer limits of the continental shelf beyond 200 nautical miles, has the honor to state the position as follows:

China has indisputable sovereignty over the islands in the South China Sea and the adjacent waters, and enjoys sovereign rights and jurisdiction over the relevant waters as well as the seabed and subsoil thereof (see attached map). The above position is consistently held by the Chinese Government, and is widely known by the international community.

The continental shelf beyond 200 nautical miles as contained in the Joint Submission by Malaysia and the Socialist Republic of Viet Nam has seriously infringed China's sovereignty, sovereign rights and jurisdiction in the South China Sea. In accordance with Article 5(a) of Annex I to the Rules of Procedure of the Commission on the Limits of the Continental Shelf, the Chinese Government seriously requests the Commission not to consider the Joint Submission by Malaysia and the Socialist Republic of Viet Nam. The Chinese Government has informed Malaysia and the Socialist Republic of Viet Nam of the above position.

---

[26] www.un.org/Depts/los/clcs_new/submissions_files/mysvnm33_09/chn_ 2011_ re_ phl_e.pdf.

The Permanent Mission of the People's Republic of China to the United Nations requests that this Note Verbale be circulated to all members of the Commission, all States Parties to the United Nations Convention on the Law of the Sea as well as all Members of the United Nations.

The Permanent Mission of the People's Republic of China to the United Nations avails itself of this opportunity to renew to the Secretary-General of the United Nations the assurances of its highest consideration.[27]

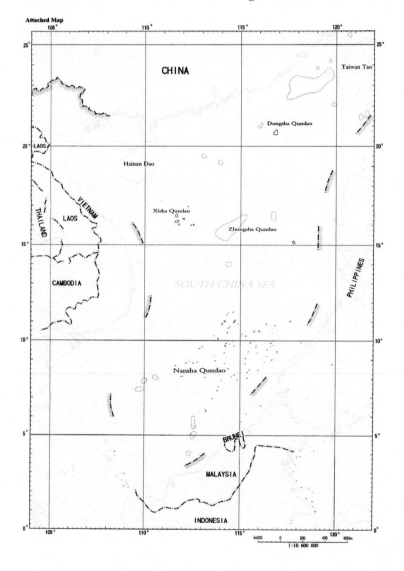

[27] www.un.org/Depts/los/clcs_new/submissions_files/mysvnm33_09/chn_2009re_mys_vnm_e.pdf.

25. Note Verbale CML/12/2009 from the Permanent Mission of the People's Republic of China to the UN Secretary-General, 13 April 2009

The Permanent Mission of the People's Republic of China to the United Nations presents its compliments to the Secretary-General of the United Nations and, with reference to the *Republic Act No. 9522: An Act to amend certain provisions of Republic Act No. 3046, as amended by Republic Act No. 5446, to define the Archipelagic Baselines of the Philippines, and for other purposes* deposited by the Republic of the Philippines with the Secretary-General, the depositary of the United Nations Convention on the Law of the Sea, and posted on the website of the Division for Ocean Affairs and the Law of the Sea (DOALOS) of the Secretariat of the United Nations, has the honor to inform the latter of the position of the Chinese Government as follows:

The above-mentioned Philippine Act illegally claims Huangyan Island (referred as 'Bajo de Masinloc' in the Act) and some islands and reefs of Nansha Islands (referred as 'The Kalayaan Island Group' in the Act) of China as 'areas over which the Philippines likewise exercises sovereignty and jurisdiction'. The Chinese Government hereby reiterates that Huangyan Island and Nansha Islands have been part of the territory of China since ancient time. The People's Republic of China has indisputable sovereignty over Huangyan Island and Nansha Islands and their surrounding maritime areas. Any claim to territorial sovereignty over Huangyan Island and Nansha Islands by any other State is, therefore, null and void.

The Chinese government has the honor to request the Secretary-General to communicate the above-mentioned position to all States Parties to the United Nations Convention on the Law of the Sea and all member States of the United Nations.

The Permanent Mission of the People's Republic of China to the United Nations avails itself of this opportunity to renew to the Secretary-General of the United Nations the assurances of its highest consideration.[28]

26. Declaration by the People's Republic of China under Article 298 UNCLOS, 25 August 2006

The Government of the People's Republic of China does not accept any of the procedures provided for in Section 2 of Part XV of the Convention with respect to all the categories of disputes referred to in paragraph 1 (a) (b) and (c) of Article 298 of the Convention.[29]

---

[28] www.un.org/Depts/los/LEGISLATIONANDTREATIES/PDFFILES/DEPOSIT/communicationsredepo sit/mzn69_2009_chn.pdf.

[29] United Nations, Division for Ocean Affairs and the Law of the Sea, *Law of the Sea Bulletin* No 62 (2006) 14.

27. Position Paper of the People's Republic of China on the Issue of the South China Sea, 17 November 2000

ITS ORIGIN

China has indisputable sovereignty over the Nansha Islands and their adjacent waters. It was the first to discover and name the islands as the Nansha Islands and the first to exercise sovereign jurisdiction over them. We have ample historical and jurisprudential evidence to support this, and the international community has long recognized it. During World War II, Japan launched the war of aggression against China and occupied most of China's territory, including the Nansha Islands. It was explicitly provided in the Cairo Declaration, the Potsdam Proclamation and other international documents that all the territories Japan had stolen from China should be restored to China, and naturally, they included the Nansha Islands. In December 1946, the then Chinese government sent senior officials to the Nansha Islands for their recovery. A take-over ceremony was held on the islands and a monument erected in commemoration of it, and the troops were sent over on garrison duty. In 1952 the Japanese Government officially stated that it renounced all its 'right, title and claim to Taiwan, Penghu Islands as well as Nansha and Xisha islands', thus formally returning the Nansha Islands to China. All countries are very clear about this part of historical background. As a matter of fact, the United States recognized China's sovereignty over the Nansha Islands in a series of subsequent international conferences and international practice.

For quite a long period of time after WWII, there had been no such a thing as the so-called issue of the South China Sea. No country in the area surrounding the South China Sea had challenged China's exercise of sovereignty over the Nansha Islands and their adjacent waters. Prior to 1975, Vietnam had, in explicit terms, recognized China's territorial integrity and sovereignty over the Nansha Islands. Before the 1970s, countries like the Philippines and Malaysia had never referred to their territories as including the Nansha Islands in any of their legal instruments or statements made by their leaders. In the Treaty of Peace signed in Paris in 1898 and the Treaty signed in Washington in 1900 between the United States and Spain, the scope of the Philippines' territory was expressly laid down, which did not include the Nansha Islands. This was further confirmed in the Philippines Constitution of 1935 and the Mutual Defense Treaty Between the Philippines and the United States in 1951. As for Malaysia, it was only in December 1978 that it first marked part of the Nansha Islands, reefs and waters into the territory of Malaysia in its published continental shelf maps.

Moreover, the Nansha Islands are recognized as China's territory by governments of quite a few countries and by resolutions of international conferences. For example, Resolution No. 24 adopted by the ICAO conference on Pacific regional aviation held in Manila in 1955 requested the Taiwan authorities of China to improve meteorological observation on the Nansha Islands, and no representative at the conference made objection to or reservation about it. In maps published in many countries, the Nansha Islands are marked as China's territory. For example, this is clearly done in Japan's Standard World Atlas of 1952, which was recommended by the then Japanese Foreign Minister Katsuo Okazaki in his own handwriting, the World New Atlas published in Japan in 1962, which was recommended by the then Foreign Minister Masayoshi Ohira, the Welt-Atlas published in the Federal Republic of Germany in 1954, the Penguin World Atlas published in the United Kingdom in 1956, and the Larousse Atlas published in France in 1956. Vietnam acknowledged the Nansha Islands as being China's territory in its world maps published in 1960 and 1972 as well as its textbooks published in 1974. The Nansha Islands are recognized as China's territory in many countries' authoritative encyclopedias published since the beginning of the 20th century, such as the Worldmark Encyclopedia of the Nations in the United States in 1963, the Bolshaya Sovietskaya Enciclopediya of 1973 and the Japanese Kyodo World Manual of 1979.

Beginning from the 1970s, countries like Vietnam, the Philippines and Malaysia have by military means occupied part of the islands and reefs of the Nansha Islands, gone in for big-scale resource development in waters adjacent to the Nansha Islands and laid claim to sovereignty over them. In view of this, the Chinese Government has time and again made solemn statements that these acts constitute serious infringement upon China's sovereignty and territorial integrity, and are illegal, null and void. The so-called legal basis provided by those countries is not tenable at all.

HISTORICAL EVIDENCE TO SUPPORT CHINA'S SOVEREIGNTY OVER NANSHA ISLANDS

China was the first to discover, name, develop, conduct economic activities on and exercise jurisdiction of the Nansha Islands.

A. China the First to Discover and Name the Nansha Islands

The earliest discovery by the Chinese people of the Nansha Islands can be traced back to as early as the Han Dynasty. Yang Fu of the East Han Dynasty (23-220 AD) made reference to the Nansha Islands in his book entitled Yiwu Zhi (Records of Rarities), which reads: 'Zhanghai qitou, shui qian er duo cishi' ('There are islets, sand cays, reefs and banks in the South China Sea, the water there is shallow and filled with magnetic rocks or stones'). Chinese people then called the South China Sea Zhanghai and all the islands, reefs, shoals and isles in the South China Sea, including the Nansha and Xisha Islands, Qitou.

General Kang Tai, one of the famous ancient Chinese navigators of the East Wu State of the Three Kingdoms Period (220-280 AD), also mentioned the Nansha Islands in his book entitled Funan Zhuan (or Journeys to and from Phnom) (the name of an ancient state in today's Cambodia). He used the following sentences in describing the islands: 'In the South China Sea, there are coral islands and reefs; below these islands and reefs are rocks upon which the corals were formed.'

In numerous history and geography books published in the Tang and Song Dynasties, the Nansha and Xisha Islands were called Jiuruluo Islands, Shitang (literally meaning atolls surrounding a lagoon), Changsha (literally meaning long ranges of shoals), Qianli Shitang, Qianli Changsha, Wanli Shitang, and Wanli Changsha among others. Reference was made to the Nansha Islands in over one hundred categories of books published in the four dynasties of Song, Yuan, Ming and Qing in the name of Shitang or Changsha.

There were more detailed descriptions of the geographical locations and specific positions of the various islands of the Nansha Islands in the Yuan Dynasty. For instance, Wang Dayuan, a prominent Chinese navigator in the Yuan Dynasty, wrote about the Nansha Islands in his book entitled Abridged Records of Islands and Barbarians in these words: 'The base of Wanli Shitang originates from Chaozhou. It is tortuous as a long snake lying in the sea. Its veins can all be traced. One such vein stretches to Java, one to Boni (or Burni, a kingdom which then existed in what is now Brunei in the vicinity of the Kalimantan) and Gulidimen (another kingdom on the Kalimantan), and one to the west side of the sea toward Kunlun (Con Son Islands, located outside the mouth of the Mekong River some 200 nautical miles away from Saigon) in the distance....' Wanli Shitang here refers to all the islands in the South China Sea, including the Nansha Islands.

In the Consolidated Map of Territories and Geography and Capitals of Past Dynasties published in the Ming Dynasty, we find the words 'Shitang', 'Changsha' and 'Shitang.' Judging from the geographical locations of these places as marked on the Map, the second Shitang denotes today's Nansha Islands.

The Road Map of the Qing Dynasty marks the specific locations of all the islands, reefs, shoals and isles of the Nansha Islands where fishermen of China's Hainan Island used to frequent, including 73 named places of the Nansha Islands.

B. China the First to Develop the Nansha Islands

Chinese people started to develop the Nansha Islands and engage in fishing on the islands as early as in the beginning of the Ming Dynasty. At that time, fishermen from Haikou Port, Puqian Port, Qinglan Port and Wenchang County went to the Nansha Islands to fish sea cucumber and other sea produce.

The 1868 Guide to the South China Sea has accounts of the activities of the Chinese fishermen in the Nansha Islands. According to the Guide, 'fishermen from Hainan Island went to Zhenhe Isles and Reefs and lived on sea cucumber and shells they got there. The footmarks of fishermen could be found in every isle of the Nansha Islands and some of the fishermen would even live there for a long period of time. Every year, there were small boats departing from Hainan Island for the Nansha Islands to exchange rice and other daily necessities for sea cucumber and shells from the fishermen there. The ships used to leave Hainan Island in December or January every year and return when the southwesterly monsoon started.' Since the end of the Qing Dynasty, fishermen from Hainan Island and Leizhou Peninsula of China have kept going for fishing on the Nansha Islands. Most of the fishermen come from Wenchang County and Qionghai County. One or two dozens of fishing boats from these two counties would go to the Nansha Islands every year.

The Road Map is another strong evidence to the development of the islands on the South China Sea by the Chinese people since the Ming and Qing Dynasties. The Road Map served as a navigational guide to the Chinese fishermen for their trips to the Xisha and Nansha Islands for productive activities there. It was a result of the collective work of many people on the basis of their navigational experience. The first Road Map was produced in the Ming Dynasty and it was constantly improved later on. It showed the navigational routes and courses from Qinglan, Wenchang County, Hainan Island or Tanmen Port of Qionghai County to the various isles of the Xisha and Nansha Islands.

The development and productive activities of the Chinese fishermen on the Nansha Islands after the founding of the Republic of China in 1912 have been recorded in both Chinese and foreign history books. Mr. Okura Unosuke of Japan wrote about his expedition trip to Beizi Island in 1918 in his book Stormy Islands, which reads: 'he saw three people from Haikou of Wenchang County when the expedition team he organized arrived in Beizi Island.' In 1933, Miyoshi and Matuo of Japan saw two Chinese people on the Beizi Island and three Chinese people on the Nanzi Island when they made an investigation trip to the Nansha Islands. It is also recorded in A Survey of the New South Islands published in Japan that 'fishermen planted sweet potato on Zhongye Island and that fishermen from the Republic of China resided on the islands and grew coconuts, papaya, sweet potato and vegetables there.'

C. China the First to Exercise Jurisdiction over the Nansha Islands

The Nansha Islands came under the jurisdiction of China from the Yuan Dynasty. Geography Book of the History of the Yuan Dynasty and Map of the Territory of the Yuan Dynasty with Illustration both includes the Nansha Islands within the domain of the Yuan Dynasty. The History of the

Yuan Dynasty has accounts of the patrol and inspection activities by the navy on the Nansha Islands in the Yuan Dynasty.

The inscription on the Memorial Tablet of the Tomb to General Qian Shicai of the Hainan Garrison Command of the Ming Dynasty reads: 'Guangdong is adjacent to the grand South China Sea, and the territories beyond the Sea all internally belong to the Ming State.' 'General Qian led more than ten thousand soldiers and 50 huge ships to patrol tens of thousands of li on the South China Sea.' All these descriptions clearly testify to the ownership by China of the Nansha Islands in the Ming Dynasty. The Hainan Garrison Command of the Ming Dynasty was responsible for inspecting and patrolling as well as exercising jurisdiction over the Xisha, Zhongsha and Nansha Islands.

In the Qing Dynasty, the Chinese Government marked the Nansha Islands on the authoritative maps and exercised administrative jurisdiction over these islands. The Nansha Islands were marked as Chinese territory in many maps drawn in the Qing Dynasty such as A Map of Administrative Divisions of the Whole China of the 1724 Map of Provinces of the Qing Dynasty, A Map of Administrative Divisions of the Whole China of the 1755 Map of Provinces of the Imperial Qing Dynasty, the 1767 Map of Unified China of the Great Qing for Ten Thousand Years, the 1810 Topographical Map of Unified China of the Great Qing for Ten Thousand Years and the 1817 Map of Unified China of the Great Qing for Ten Thousand Years.

Between 1932 and 1935, the Chinese Government set up a Committee for the Review of Maps of Lands and Waters of China, which was composed of officials from the Headquarters of the General Staff, the Ministry of Internal Affairs, the Ministry of Foreign Affairs, the Navy Command, the Ministry of Education and the Mongolian and Tibetan Affairs Commission. This Committee examined and approved 132 names of the islands in the South China Sea, all of which belonged to the Xisha, Zhongsha and Nansha Islands.

In 1933, France invaded and occupied 9 of the Nansha Islands, including Taiping and Zhongye Islands. The Chinese fishermen who lived and worked on the Nansha Islands immediately made a firm resistance against the invasion and the Chinese Government lodged a strong protest with the French Government.

All the names of the islands, isles and reefs on the South China Sea including the Nansha Islands were unmistakably marked on the Map of the Islands in the South China Sea compiled and printed by the Committee for the Review of Maps of Lands and Waters of China in 1935.

In 1939, Japan invaded and occupied the islands on the South China Sea. In line with the Cairo Declaration and the Potsdam Proclamation, the Ministry of Internal Affairs of China, in consultation with the Navy and the government of Guangdong Province, appointed Xiao Ciyi and Mai Yunyu Special Commissioner to the Xisha and Nansha Islands respectively in 1946 to take over the two archipelagos and erect marks of sovereignty on the Islands.

In 1947, the Ministry of Internal Affairs of China renamed 159 islands, reefs, islets and shoals on the South China Sea, including the Nansha Islands. It subsequently publicized all the names for administrative purposes.

In 1983, the Chinese Toponymy Committee was authorized to publicize the approved names of the islands, reefs, islets and shoals on the South China Sea.

In short, a host of historical facts have proved that it was the Chinese people who were the first to discover and develop the Nansha Islands and it was the Chinese Government that has long exercised sovereignty and jurisdiction over these islands. The Nansha Islands have become an inalienable part of Chinese territory since ancient times.

JURISPRUDENTIAL EVIDENCE TO SUPPORT CHINA'S SOVEREIGNTY OVER THE NANSHA ISLANDS

China has indisputable sovereignty over the Nansha Islands and it has ample jurisprudential evidence to support this.

A. Full and accurate historical data, both Chinese and foreign, has provided rich and substantial evidence to show that the Chinese people were the first to discover and name the Nansha Islands. As early as in the Han Dynasty that was more than two thousand years ago, the Chinese people discovered the Nansha Islands through their navigational experience and in the course of their productive activities over the years. All this was amply recorded in the books such as Records of Rarities by Yang Fu of the Eastern Han Dynasty, Records of Rarities in Southern Boundary by Wan Zhen of the Three Kingdoms Period and A History of Phnom by General Kang Tai of the East Wu State. All these historical records represent the Chinese people's cognition and appreciation of the land on which they lived and worked. They are of great importance in the perspective of international law. In view of the development of international law, these records and accounts of the discovery by the ancient Chinese people of the islands on the South China Sea bear abundant evidence to China's indisputable territorial sovereignty over the Nansha Islands. Obviously, the Nansha Islands are not land without owners, but rather they are an inalienable part of Chinese territory. No country in the world has the right to change China's legal status as the owner of the Nansha Islands in any way.

B. The fact that the Chinese people have developed the Nansha Islands and carried out productive activities there and that the Chinese Government has actually exercised jurisdiction over these islands has reinforced China's sovereignty over the Nansha Islands. After discovering the Nansha Islands, the Chinese people started to develop and engage in fishing, planting and other productive activities on the Nansha Islands and their adjacent waters from the Tang and Song Dynasties at the latest. Fei Yuan of the Jin Dynasty (265-420 AD) wrote about the fishing and collecting of coral samples by the fishermen of China on the South China Sea in his article Chronicles of Guangzhou. After the Ming and Qing Dynasties, fishermen from Wenchang County and Qionghai County of Hainan Island used to sail southward with the northeasterly monsoon to the Nansha Islands and their adjacent waters for fishing every winter and come back to Hainan with the southwesterly monsoon before the typhoon season started. The Chinese people lived and engaged in fishing, planting and other productive activities on the Nansha Islands individually at first, but they were later on organized with the approval and support of the Chinese Government. Even when the conditions on the Nansha Islands were not suitable for people to live, some of the Chinese fishermen still lived on the islands for years. For ages, Chinese fishermen would come and go between Hainan Island and Guangdong Province on the one hand and the Nansha Islands on the other for productive activities and they never failed to pay their taxes and fees to the Chinese Government.

C. The exercise of jurisdiction by the Chinese Government over the Nansha Islands is also manifested in a series of continued effective government behavior. After Emperor Zhenyuan of the Tang Dynasty (785-805 AD) came to the throne, China included the Nansha Islands into its administrative map. It did so more conscientiously in the Ming and Qing Dynasties. A wealth of official documents of the Chinese Government, its local history books and official maps have recorded the exercise of jurisdiction by the successive governments of China over the Nansha Islands and recognized these islands as Chinese territory. Up till the beginning of this century, the Chinese Government had exercised peaceful jurisdiction over the Nansha Islands without any disputes.

Since the beginning of this century, the Chinese Government has undauntedly maintained China's sovereignty over the Nansha Islands. In the 1930s, France once invaded and occupied nine of the Nansha Islands, over which the Chinese Government immediately made diplomatic representations with the French Government and against which Chinese fishermen staged an organized resistance. Between 1912 and 1949 when China was a republic, the then Chinese Government took a series of active measures to safeguard its sovereignty. For instance, it furnished the Chinese fishermen and fishing boats that engaged in the fishing on the Nansha Islands and their adjacent waters with China's national flags. It organized trips to the Nansha Islands for a survey of their history and geography. And it authorized a map-printing and toponymic agency to rename and approve the names of all the islands on the South China Sea including the Nansha Islands, individually and collectively.

During World War II, Japan invaded and occupied China's Nansha Islands. China made unremitting efforts for the recovery of these islands from the Japanese occupation. In 1943, China, the United States and the

United Kingdom announced in the Cairo Declaration that all the territories that Japan had stolen from China should be 'restored to China,' including 'Manchuria, Taiwan and the Penghu Islands.' At that time, Japan put the Nansha Islands under the jurisdiction of Taiwan. The territories to be restored to China as identified in the Cairo Declaration naturally included the Nansha Islands. The 1945 Potsdam Proclamation confirmed once again that the stolen territories should be restored to China. According to the Cairo Declaration and Potsdam Proclamation, China recovered the Nansha Island in 1946. At the same time it went through a series of legal procedures and announced to the whole world that China had resumed the exercise of sovereignty over the Nansha Islands. Subsequently, the Chinese Government held a take-over ceremony and sent troops to the islands on garrison duty. An official map of the Nansha Islands was drawn and printed, the Nansha Islands were renamed, collectively and individually, and the earliest book of the physical geography of the Nansha Islands was also compiled and printed.

After the founding of the People's Republic of China, the Nansha Islands were incorporated into Guangdong Province and Hainan Province successively and the Chinese Government has all along maintained China's sovereignty over the Nansha Islands and taken effective actions for that.

In view of all this, the Chinese Government has indisputable sovereignty over the Nansha Islands. Some countries have claimed sovereignty of these islands on the ground that these islands are within their continental shelves or exclusive economic zones. According to international law and the UN Convention on the Law of the Sea, maritime rights and interests should be based on territorial sovereignty for the former derives from the latter. No country should be allowed to extend its maritime jurisdiction to the territories of other countries, still less should it be allowed to invade and occupy other's territory on the ground of exclusive economic zones or the continental shelves. All in all, any action by any country with regard to the islets, islands or reefs of the Nansha Islands, military or otherwise, constitutes encroachment of China's territorial sovereignty. It is illegal and null and void according to international law. It can in no way serve as a basis for a country's territorial claim, nor can it change China's indisputable legal status as having sovereignty over the Nansha Islands.

BASIC STANCE AND POLICY OF THE CHINESE GOVERNMENT IN SOLVING THE SOUTH CHINA SEA ISSUE

The Chinese Government has always stood for negotiated settlement of international disputes through peaceful means. In this spirit, China has solved questions regarding territory and border with some neighboring countries through bilateral consultations and negotiations in an equitable, reasonable and amicable manner. This position also applies to the Nansha

Islands. China is committed to working with the countries concerned for proper settlement of the disputes related to the South China Sea through peaceful negotiations in accordance with the universally-recognized international law and the contemporary law of the sea, including the fundamental principles and legal regimes set forth in the 1982 U.N. Convention on the Law of the Sea (UNCLOS). This was explicitly written into the Joint Statement issued at the China-ASEAN informal summit in 1997. The Chinese Government has also put forward the proposition of 'shelving disputes and going in for joint development'. China is ready to shelve the disputes for the time being and conduct cooperation with the countries concerned pending settlement of the disputes. This is not only what China stands for but also what China does. In Recent years, China has on many occasions had consultations and exchanged views on the question of the South China Sea with the countries concerned, and a broad identity of views has been reached. The bilateral consultation mechanisms between China and the Philippines, Viet Nam and Malaysia respectively are in effective operation, and positive progress has been made to varying degrees in the dialogues. At China-ASEAN Senior Officials Meetings (SOM) and China-ASEAN Post-Ministerial Conferences (PMC), too, the two sides have had candid exchange of views on the South China Sea question, and agreed to seek and appropriate solution to the problem by peaceful means and through friendly consultations.

China maintains that all the parties concerned should adopt a restrained, calm and constructive approach on the question of the Nansha Islands. In recent years, countries like Viet Nam and the Philippines have sent troops to seize some uninhabited islands and reefs of the Nansha Islands, destroyed the marks of sovereignty erected by China there, and arrested, detained or driven away by force Chinese fishermen fishing in the South China Sea. On this question, the Chinese side has always persisted in having discussions and settling relevant problems with the countries concerned through diplomatic channels and by peaceful means. It fully testifies to China's sincerity in preserving regional stability and the overall interests of bilateral friendly relations.

China attaches great importance to the safety and unimpededness of the international water lanes in the South China Sea. Its efforts to safeguard its sovereignty over the Nansha Islands and maritime rights and interests do not affect the freedom of the passage foreign vessels and aircraft enjoy in accordance with international law. In fact, China has never interfered with the freedom of passage of foreign vessels and aircraft in this area, nor will it ever do so in the future. China is ready to work together with the littoral states of the South China Sea to safeguard the safety the international water lanes in the area of the South China Sea.

The question of the South China Sea is a question between China and the relevant countries. The Chinese Government has consistently advocated settlement of the disputes between China and the countries concerned through amicable bilateral consultations. Involvement by any external force is undesirable and will only further complicate the situation. China and the countries concerned are fully capable and confident of handling their disputes appropriately. Peace and tranquillity in the South China Sea area can be maintained on a long-term basis. At present, there is no crisis at all in that area. The kind of tension in the South China Sea which has been played up, even with ulterior motives, is contrary to the facts.

INTERNATIONAL RECOGNITION OF CHINA'S SOVEREIGNTY OVER THE NANSHA ISLANDS

A. Many countries, world public opinions and publications of other countries recognize the Nansha Islands as Chinese territory.

1. The United Kingdom of Great Britain and the Northern Island

a)   China Sea Pilot compiled and printed by the Hydrography Department of the Royal Navy of the United Kingdom in 1912 has accounts of the activities of the Chinese people on the Nansha Islands in a number of places.

b)   The Far Eastern Economic Review (Hong Kong) carried an article on Dec. 31 of 1973 which quotes the British High Commissioner to Singapore as having said in 1970: 'Spratly Island (Nanwei Island in Chinese) was a Chinese dependency, part of Kwangtung Province… and was returned to China after the war. We can not find any indication of its having been acquired by any other country and so can only conclude it is still held by communist China.'

2. France

a)   Le Monde Colonial Illustre mentioned the Nansha Islands in its September 1933 issue. According to that issue, when a French gunboat named Malicieuse surveyed the Nanwei Island of the Nansha Islands in 1930, they saw three Chinese on the island and when France invaded nine of the Nansha Islands by force in April 1933, they found all the people on the islands were Chinese, with 7 Chinese on the Nanzi Reef, 5 on the Zhongye Island, 4 on the Nanwei Island, thatched houses, water wells and holy statues left by Chinese on the Nanyue Island and a signboard with Chinese characters marking a grain storage on the Taiping Island.

b)   Atlas International Larousse published in 1965 in France marks the Xisha, Nansha and Dongsha Islands by their Chinese names and gives clear indication of their ownership as China in brackets.

3. Japan

a)   Yearbook of New China published in Japan in 1966 describes the coastline of China as 11 thousand kilometers long from Liaodong Peninsula in the north to the Nansha Islands in the south, or 20 thousand kilometers if including the coastlines of all the islands along its coast.

b) Yearbook of the World published in Japan in 1972 says that Chinese territory includes not only the mainland, but also Hainan Island, Taiwan, Penghu Islands as well as the Dongsha, Xisha, Zhongsha and Nansha Islands on the South China Sea.

4. The United States

a) Columbia Lippincott World Toponymic Dictionary published in the United States in 1961 states that the Nansha Islands on the South China Sea are part of Guangdong Province and belong to China.

b) The Worldmark Encyclopaedia of the Nations published in the United States in 1963 says that the islands of the People's Republic extend southward to include those isles and coral reefs on the South China Sea at the north latitude 4°.

c) World Administrative Divisions Encyclopaedia published in 1971 says that the People's Republic has a number of archipelagoes, including Hainan Island near the South China Sea, which is the largest, and a few others on the South China Sea extending to as far as the north latitude 4°, such as the Dongsha, Xisha, Zhongsha and Nansha Islands.

5. Viet Nam

a) Vice Foreign Minister Dung Van Khiem of the Democratic Republic of Viet Nam received Mr. Li Zhimin, charge d'affaires ad interim of the Chinese Embassy in Viet Nam and told him that 'according to Vietnamese data, the Xisha and Nansha Islands are historically part of Chinese territory.' Mr. Le Doc, Acting Director of the Asian Department of the Vietnamese Foreign Ministry, who was present then, added that 'judging from history, these islands were already part of China at the time of the Song Dynasty.'

b) Nhan Dan of Viet Nam reported in great detail on September 6, 1958 the Chinese Government's Declaration of September 4, 1958 that the breadth of the territorial sea of the People's Republic of China should be 12 nautical miles and that this provision should apply to all territories of the People's Republic of China, including all islands on the South China Sea. On September 14 the same year, Premier Pham Van Dong of the Vietnamese Government solemnly stated in his note to Premier Zhou Enlai that Viet Nam 'recognizes and supports the Declaration of the Government of the People's Republic of China on China's territorial sea.'

c) It is stated in the lesson The People's Republic of China of a standard Vietnamese school textbook on geography published in 1974 that the islands from the Nansha and Xisha Islands to Hainan Island and Taiwan constitute a great wall for the defense of the mainland of China.

B. The maps printed by other countries in the world that mark the islands on the South China Sea as part of Chinese territory include:

1. The Welt-Atlas published by the Federal Republic of Germany in 1954, 1961 and 1970 respectively;
2. World Atlas published by the Soviet Union in 1954 and 1967 respectively;
3. World Atlas published by Romania in 1957;
4. Oxford Australian Atlas and Philips Record Atlas published by Britain in 1957 and Encyclopaedia Britannica World Atlas published by Britain in 1958;
5. World Atlas drawn and printed by the mapping unit of the Headquarters of the General Staff of the People's Army of Viet Nam in 1960;
6. Haack Welt Atlas published by German Democratic in 1968;
7. Daily Telegraph World Atlas published by Britain in 1968;
8. Atlas International Larousse published by France in 1968 and 1969 respectively;
9. World Map Ordinary published by the Institut Geographique National (IGN) of France in 1968;
10. World Atlas published by the Surveying and Mapping Bureau of the Prime Minister's Office of Viet Nam in 1972; and
11. China Atlas published by Neibonsya of Japan in 1973.

C. China's sovereignty over the Nansha Islands is recognized in numerous international conferences.

1. The 1951 San Francisco Conference on Peace Treaty called on Japan to give up the Xisha and Nansha Islands. Andrei Gromyko, Head of the Delegation of the Soviet Union to the Conference, pointed out in his statement that the Xisha and Nansha Islands were an inalienable part of Chinese territory. It is true that the San Francisco Peace Treaty failed to unambiguously ask Japan to restore the Xisha and Nansha Islands to China. But the Xisha, Nansha, Dongsha and Zhongsha Islands that Japan was asked to abandon by the Peace Agreement of San Francisco Conference were all clearly marked as Chinese territory in the fifteenth map A Map of Southeast Asia of the Standard World Atlas published by Japan in 1952, the second year after the peace conference in San Francisco, which was recommended by the then Japanese Foreign Minister Katsuo Okazaki in his own handwriting.

2. The International Civil Aviation Organization held its first conference on Asia-Pacific regional aviation in Manila of the Philippines on 27 October 1955. Sixteen countries or regions were represented at the conference, including South Viet Nam and the Taiwan authorities, apart from Australia, Canada, Chile, Dominica, Japan, the Laos, the Republic of Korea, the Philippines, Thailand, the United Kingdom, the United States, New Zealand and France. The Chief Representative of the Philippines served as Chairman of the conference and the Chief Representative of

France its first Vice Chairman. It was agreed at the conference that the Dongsha, Xisha and Nansha Islands on the South China Sea were located at the communication hub of the Pacific and therefore the meteorological reports of these islands were vital to world civil aviation service. In this context, the conference adopted Resolution No. 24, asking China's Taiwan authorities to improve meteorological observation on the Nansha Islands, four times a day. When this resolution was put for voting, all the representatives, including those of the Philippines and the South Viet Nam, were for it. No representative at the conference made any objection to or reservation about it.[30]

28. Law on the Exclusive Economic Zone and the Continental Shelf of the People's Republic of China, 26 June 1998

(Adopted at the 3rd Meeting of the Standing Committee of the Ninth National People's Congress on June 26, 1998 and promulgated by Order No 6 of the President of the People's Republic of China on June 26, 1998)

Article 1 This Law is enacted to ensure that the People's Republic of China exercises its sovereign rights and jurisdiction over its exclusive economic zone and its continental shelf and to safeguard its national maritime rights and interests.

Article 2 The exclusive economic zone of the People's Republic of China covers the area beyond and adjacent to the territorial sea of the People's Republic of China, extending to 200 nautical miles from the baselines from which the breadth of the territorial sea is measured.

The continental shelf of the People's Republic of China comprises the sea-bed and subsoil of the submarine areas that extend beyond its territorial sea throughout the natural prolongation of its land territory to the outer edge of the continental margin, or to a distance of 200 nautical miles from the baselines from which the breadth of the territorial sea is measured where the outer edge of the continental margin does not extend up to that distance.

The People's Republic of China shall determine the delimitation of its exclusive economic zone and continental shelf in respect of the overlapping claims by agreement with the states with opposite or adjacent coasts, in accordance with the equitable principle and on the basis of international law.

Article 3 The People's Republic of China exercises its sovereign rights over the exclusive economic zone for the purpose of exploring, exploiting,

---

[30] The Position Paper was published in English on the Website of the Chinese Foreign Ministry at in five parts. In the original Chinese version, published on 22 November 2000, the headings of the five parts are numbered. The paper is here presented in the sequence of the Chinese version. Obvious typos have been corrected. The English version may be found at www.fmprc.gov.cn/eng/topics/3754.

conserving and managing the natural resources of the waters superjacent to the sea-bed and of the sea-bed and its subsoil, and in its other activities for economic exploitation and exploration of the zone, such as production of energy from water, currents and winds.

The People's Republic of China exercises jurisdiction over the establishment and use of artificial islands, installations and structures, marine scientific research, and the protection and preservation of the marine environment in the exclusive economic zone.

The natural resources in the exclusive economic zone referred to in this Law consist of living and non-living resources.

Article 4 The People's Republic of China exercises its sovereign rights over the continental shelf for the purpose of exploring it and exploiting its natural resources.

The People's Republic of China exercises jurisdiction over the establishment and use of artificial islands, installations and structures, marine scientific research, and the protection and preservation of the marine environment on the continental shelf.

The People's Republic of China has the exclusive right to authorize and regulate drilling on the continental shelf for all purposes.

The natural resources of the continental shelf referred to in this Law consists of the mineral and other non-living resources of the sea-bed and subsoil, and the living organisms that belong to sedentary species-organisms which, at the harvestable stage, either are immobile on or under the sea-bed or are unable to move except in constant physical contact with the sea-bed or the subsoil.

Article 5 All international organizations, foreign organizations or individuals that wish to enter the exclusive economic zone of the People's Republic of China for fishing shall be subject to approval of the competent authorities of the People's Republic of China and shall comply with its laws and regulations as well as the accords and agreements it has signed with the states concerned.

The competent authorities of the People's Republic of China shall have the right to take all necessary conservation and management measures to ensure that the living resources in the exclusive economic zone are protected from the danger of over-exploitation.

Article 6 The competent authorities of the People's Republic of China shall have the right to conserve and manage straddling species, highly migratory species, marine mammals, anadromous stocks that originate in the rivers of the People's Republic of China, and catadromous species that spend the greater part of their life cycle in the waters of the People's Republic of China.

The People's Republic of China enjoys the primary interests in the anadromous stocks that originate in its rivers.

Article 7 All international organizations, foreign organizations or individuals that wish to explore the exclusive economic zone of the People's Republic of China or exploit the natural resources on its continental shelf or for any purpose to drill on the continental shelf shall be subject to approval of the competent authorities of the People's Republic of China and shall comply with the laws and regulations of the People's Republic of China.

Article 8 The People's Republic of China has the exclusive right to construct and to authorize and regulate the construction, operation and use of the artificial islands, installations and structures in its exclusive economic zone and on its continental shelf.

The People's Republic of China exercises exclusive jurisdiction over the artificial islands, installations and structures in its exclusive economic zone and on its continental shelf, including jurisdiction with regard to customs, fiscal, sanitation and safety laws and regulations, and laws and regulations governing entry into and exit from the territory of the People's Republic of China.

The competent authorities of the People's Republic of China shall have the right to establish safety belts around the artificial islands, installations and structures in the exclusive economic zone and on the continental shelf and may take appropriate measures in these belts to ensure safety both of navigation and of the artificial island, installations and structures.

Article 9 All international organizations, foreign organizations or individuals that wish to conduct marine scientific research in the exclusive economic zone or on the continental shelf of the People's Republic of China shall be subject to approval of the competent authorities of the People's Republic of China and shall comply with the laws and regulations of the People's Republic of China.

Article 10 The competent authorities of the People's Republic of China shall have the right to take all necessary measures to prevent, reduce and control pollution of the marine environment for the protection and preservation of the marine environment in the exclusive economic zone and on the continental shelf.

Article 11 All states shall, on the premise that they comply with international law and the laws and regulations of the People's Republic of China, enjoy the freedom of navigation in and flight over its exclusive economic zone, the freedom to lay submarine cables and pipelines and the convenience of other lawful uses of the sea related to the freedoms mentioned above in the exclusive economic zone and on the continental shelf of the People's Republic of China. The routes for the submarine cables and pipelines shall be subject to consent of the competent authorities of the People's Republic of China.

Article 12 The People's Republic of China may, in the exercise of its sovereign rights to explore its exclusive economic zone and to exploit, conserve and manage the living resources there, take such necessary measures as visit, inspection, arrest, detention and judicial proceedings in order to ensure that the laws and regulations of the People's Republic of China are complied with.

The People's Republic of China has the right to take necessary measures against violations of its laws and regulations in its exclusive economic zone and on its continental shelf and to investigate for legal responsibility according to law, and may exercise the right of hot pursuit.

Article 13 The People's Republic of China exercises, in accordance with international law and other relevant laws and regulations of the People's Republic of China, the rights in its exclusive economic zone and on its continental shelf that are not provided for in this Law.

Article 14 The provisions in this Law shall not affect the historical rights that the People's Republic of China has been enjoying ever since the days of the past.

Article 15 The Government of the People's Republic of China may formulate relevant regulations on the basis of this Law.

Article 16 This Law shall go into effect as of the date of promulgation.[31]

29. Declaration Made by the People's Republic of China upon Ratification of the United Nations Convention on the Law of the Sea, 7 June 1996

In accordance with the decision of the Standing Committee of the Eighth National People's Congress of the People's Republic of China at its nineteenth session, the President of the People's Republic of China has hereby ratified the United Nations Convention on the Law of the Sea of 10 December 1982 and at the same time made the following statement:

1. In accordance with the provisions of the United Nations Convention on the Law of the Sea, the People's Republic of China shall enjoy sovereign rights and jurisdiction over an exclusive economic zone of 200 nautical miles and the continental shelf.
2. The People's Republic of China will effect, through consultations, the delimitation of the boundary of the maritime jurisdiction with the States with coasts opposite or adjacent to China respectively on the basis of international law and in accordance with the principle of equitability.
3. The People's Republic of China reaffirms its sovereignty over all its archipelagos and islands as listed in article 2 of the Law of the People's

---

[31] Department of Policy, Legislation and Planning, State Oceanic Administration (ed), *Collection of the Sea Laws and Regulations of the People's Republic of China*, 4th edn (Beijing, Ocean Press, 2012) 305-08.

Republic of China on the territorial sea and the contiguous zone, which was promulgated on 25 February 1992.

4. The People's Republic of China reaffirms that the provisions of the United Nations Convention on the Law of the Sea concerning innocent passage through the territorial sea shall not prejudice the right of a coastal State to request, in accordance with its laws and regulations, a foreign State to obtain advance approval from or give prior notification to the coastal State for the passage of its warships through the territorial sea of the coastal State.[32]

30. Declaration of the Government of the People's Republic of China on the Baselines of the Territorial Sea of the People's Republic of China, 15 May 1996

In accordance with the Law of the People's Republic of China on the Territorial Sea and the Contiguous Zone adopted and promulgated on 25 February 1992, the Government of the People's Republic of China hereby announces the baselines of part of its territorial sea adjacent to the mainland and those of the territorial sea adjacent to its Xisha Islands as follows:

I. The baselines of part of the territorial sea adjacent to the mainland are composed of all the straight lines joining the adjacent base points listed below:

1. Shandonggaojiao (1)	37°24.0'N	122°42.3'E
2. Shandonggaojiao (2)	37°23.7'N	122°42.3'E
3. Moyedao (1)	36°57.8'N	122°34.2'E
4. Moyedao (2)	36°55.1'N	122°32.7'E
5. Moyedao (3)	36°53.7'N	122°31.1'E
6. Sushandao	36°44.8'N	122°15.8'E
7. Chaoliandao	35°53.6'N	120°53.1'E
8. Dashandao	35°00.2'N	119°54.2'E
9. Macaiheng	33°21.8'N	121°20.8'E
10. Waikejiao	33°00.9'N	121°38.4'E
11. Sheshandao	31°25.3'N	122°14.6'E
12. Haijiao	30°44.1'N	123°09.4'E
13. Dongnanjiao	30°43.5'N	123°09.7'E
14. Liangxiongdiyu	30°10.1'N	122°56.7'E

[32] Declaration transmitted at the time of ratification by the Permanent Mission of the People's Republic of China to the United Nations; see United Nations, Division for Ocean Affairs and the Law of the Sea, *Law of the Sea Bulletin* No 31 (1996) 8.

15. Yushanliedao	28°53.3′N	122°16.5′E
16. Taizhouliedao (1)	28°23.9′N	121°55.0′E
17. Taizhouliedao (2)	28°23.5′N	121°54.7′E
18. Daotiaoshan	27°27.9′N	121°07.8′E
19. Dongyindao	26°22.6′N	120°30.4′E
20. Dongshadao	26°09.4′N	120°24.3′E
21. Niushandao	25°25.8′N	119°56.3′E
22. Wuqiuyu	24°58.6′N	119°28.7′E
23. Dongdingdao	24°09.7′N	118°14.2′E
24. Daganshan	23°31.9′N	117°41.3′E
25. Nanpengliedao (1)	23°12.9′N	117°14.9′E
26. Nanpengliedao (2)	23°12.3′N	117°13.9′E
27. Shibeishanjiao	22°56.1′N	116°29.7′E
28. Zhentouyan	22°18.9′N	115°07.5′E
29. Jiapengliedao	21°48.5′N	113°58.0′E
30. Weijiadao	21°34.1′N	112°47.9′E
31. Dafanshi	21°27.7′N	112°21.5′E
32. Qizhouliedao	19°58.5′N	111°16.4′E
33. Shuangfan	19°53.0′N	111°12.8′E
34. Dazhoudao (1)	18°39.7′N	110°29.6′E
35. Dazhoudao (2)	18°39.4′N	110°29.1′E
36. Shuangfanshi	18°26.1′N	110°08.4′E
37. Lingshuijiao	18°23.0′N	110°03.0′E
38. Dongzhou (1)	18°11.0′N	109°42.1′E
39. Dongzhou (2)	18°11.0′N	109°41.8′E
40. Jinmujiao	18°09.5′N	109°34.4′E
41. Shenshijiao	18°14.6′N	109°07.6′E
42. Xigudao	18°19.3′N	108°57.1′E
43. Yinggezui (1)	18°30.2′N	108°41.3′E
44. Yinggezui (2)	18°30.4′N	108°41.1′E
45. Yinggezui (3)	18°31.0′N	108°40.6′E
46. Yinggezui (4)	18°31.1′N	108°40.5′E
47. Gan'enjiao	18°50.5′N	108°37.3′E
48. Sigengshajiao	19°11.6′N	108°36.0′E
49. Junbijiao	19°21.1′N	108°38.6′E

II. The baselines of the territorial sea adjacent to the Xisha Islands of the People's Republic of China are composed of all the straight lines joining the adjacent base points listed below:

1. Dongdao (1)	16°40.5′N	112°44.2′E
2. Dongdao (2)	16°40.1′N	112°44.5′E
3. Dongdao (3)	16°39.8′N	112°44.7′E
4. Langhuajiao (1)	16°04.4′N	112°35.8′E
5. Langhuajiao (2)	16°01.9′N	112°32.7′E
6. Langhuajiao (3)	16°01.5′N	112°31.8′E
7. Langhuajiao (4)	16°01.0′N	112°29.8′E
8. Zhongjiandao (1)	15°46.5′N	111°12.6′E
9. Zhongjiandao (2)	15°46.4′N	111°12.1′E
10. Zhongjiandao (3)	15°46.4′N	111°11.8′E
11. Zhongjiandao (4)	15°46.5′N	111°11.6′E
12. Zhongjiandao (5)	15°46.7′N	111°11.4′E
13. Zhongjiandao (6)	15°46.9′N	111°11.3′E
14. Zhongjiandao (7)	15°47.2′N	111°11.4′E
15. Beijiao (1)	17°04.9′N	111°26.9′E
16. Beijiao (2)	17°05.4′N	111°26.9′E
17. Beijiao (3)	17°05.7′N	111°27.2′E
18. Beijiao (4)	17°06.0′N	111°27.8′E
19. Beijiao (5)	17°06.5′N	111°29.2′E
20. Beijiao (6)	17°07.0′N	111°31.0′E
21. Beijiao (7)	17°07.1′N	111°31.6′E
22. Beijiao (8)	17°06.9′N	111°32.0′E
23. Zhaoshudao (1)	16°59.9′N	112°14.7′E
24. Zhaoshudao (2)	16°59.7′N	112°15.6′E
25. Zhaoshudao (3)	16°59.4′N	112°16.6′E
26. Beidao	16°58.4′N	112°18.3′E
27. Zhongdao	16°57.6′N	112°19.6′E
28. Nandao	16°56.9′N	112°20.5′E
1. Dongdao (1)	16°40.5′N	112°44.2′E

The Government of the People's Republic of China will announce the remaining baselines of the territorial sea of the People's Republic of China at another time.[33]

---

[33] ibid, 297-300.

31. Law of the People's Republic of China on the Territorial Sea and the Contiguous Zone, 25 February 1992

(Adopted at the 24th Meeting of the Standing Committee of the Seventh National People's Congress on February 25, 1992, promulgated by Order No 55 of the President of the People's Republic of China on February 25, 1992, and effective as of the same date)

Article 1 This Law is enacted for the People's Republic of China to exercise its sovereignty over its territorial sea and the control over its contiguous zone, and to safeguard its national security and its maritime rights and interests.

Article 2 The territorial sea of the People's Republic of China is the sea belt adjacent to the land territory and the internal waters of the People's Republic of China.

The land territory of the People's Republic of China includes the mainland of the People's Republic of China and its coastal islands; Taiwan and all islands appertaining thereto including the Diaoyu Islands; the Penghu Islands; the Dongsha Islands; the Xisha Islands; the Zhongsha Islands and the Nansha Islands; as well as all the other islands belonging to the People's Republic of China.

The waters on the landward side of the baselines of the territorial sea of the People's Republic of China constitute the internal waters of the People's Republic of China.

Article 3 The breadth of the territorial sea of the People's Republic of China is twelve nautical miles, measured from the baselines of the territorial sea. The method of straight baselines composed of all the straight lines joining the adjacent base points shall be employed in drawing the baselines of the territorial sea of the People's Republic of China.

The outer limit of the territorial sea of the People's Republic of China is the line every point of which is at a distance equal to twelve nautical miles from the nearest point of the baseline of the territorial sea.

Article 4 The contiguous zone of the People's Republic of China is the sea belt adjacent to and beyond the territorial sea. The breadth of the contiguous zone is twelve nautical miles.

The outer limit of the contiguous zone of the People's Republic of China is the line every point of which is at a distance equal to twenty four nautical miles from the nearest point of the baseline of the territorial sea.

Article 5 The sovereignty of the People's Republic of China over its territorial sea extends to the air space over the territorial sea as well as to the sea-bed and subsoil of the territorial sea.

Article 6 Foreign ships for non-military purposes shall enjoy the right of innocent passage through the territorial sea of the People's Republic of China in accordance with the law.

Foreign ships for military purposes shall be subject to approval by the Government of the People's Republic of China for entering the territorial sea of the People's Republic of China.

Article 7 Foreign submarines and other underwater vehicles, when passing through the territorial sea of the People's Republic of China, shall navigate on the surface and show their flag.

Article 8 Foreign ships passing through the territorial sea of the People's Republic of China must comply with the laws and regulations of the People's Republic of China and shall not be prejudicial to the peace, security and good order of the People's Republic of China.

Foreign nuclear-powered ships and ships carrying nuclear, noxious or other dangerous substances, when passing through the territorial sea of the People's Republic of China, must carry relevant documents and take special precautionary measures.

The Government of the People's Republic of China has the right to take all necessary measures to prevent and stop non-innocent passage through its territorial sea.

Cases of foreign ships violating the laws or regulations of the People's Republic of China shall be handled by the relevant organs of the People's Republic of China in accordance with the law.

Article 9 The Government of the People's Republic of China may, for maintaining the safety of navigation or for other special needs, request foreign ships passing through the territorial sea of the People's Republic of China to use the designated sea lanes or to navigate according to the prescribed traffic separation schemes. The specific regulations to this effect shall be promulgated by the Government of the People's Republic of China or its competent authorities concerned.

Article 10 In case of violation of the laws or regulations of the People's Republic of China by a foreign ship for military purposes or a foreign government ship for non-commercial purposes when passing through the territorial sea of the People's Republic of China, the competent authorities of the People's Republic of China shall have the right to order it to leave the territorial sea immediately and the flag State shall bear international responsibility for any loss or damage thus caused.

Article 11 All international organizations, foreign organizations or individuals shall obtain approval from the Government of the People's Republic of China for carrying out scientific research, marine operations or other activities in the territorial sea of the People's Republic of China, and shall comply with the laws and regulations of the People's Republic of China.

All illegal entries into the territorial sea of the People's Republic of China for carrying out scientific research, marine operations or other activities in contravention of the provisions of the preceding paragraph of this Article, shall be dealt with by the relevant organs of the People's Republic of China in accordance with the law.

Article 12 No aircraft of a foreign State may enter the air space over the territorial sea of the People's Republic of China unless there is a relevant protocol or agreement between the Government of that State and the Government of the People's Republic of China, or approval or acceptance by the Government of the People's Republic of China or the competent authorities authorized by it.

Article 13 The People's Republic of China has the right to exercise control in the contiguous zone to prevent and impose penalties for activities infringing the laws or regulations concerning security, the customs, fiscal, sanitation or entry and exit control within its land territory, internal waters or territorial sea.

Article 14 The competent authorities concerned of the People's Republic of China may, when they have good reasons to believe that a foreign ship has violated the laws or regulations of the People's Republic of China, exercise the right of hot pursuit against the foreign ship.

Such pursuit shall be commenced when the foreign ship or one of its boats or other craft engaged in activities by using the ship pursued as a mother ship is within the internal waters, the territorial sea or the contiguous zone of the People's Republic of China.

If the foreign ship is within the contiguous zone of the People's Republic of China, the pursuit may be undertaken only when there has been a violation of the rights as provided for in the relevant laws or regulations listed in Article 13 of this Law.

The pursuit, if not interrupted, may be continued outside the territorial sea or the contiguous zone until the ship pursued enters the territorial sea of its own country or of a third State.

The right of hot pursuit provided for in this Article shall be exercised by ships or aircraft of the People's Republic of China for military purposes, or by ships or aircraft on government service authorized by the Government of the People's Republic of China.

Article 15 The baselines of the territorial sea of the People's Republic of China shall be promulgated by the Government of the People's Republic of China.

Article 16 The Government of the People's Republic of China formulates the relevant regulations in accordance with this Law.

Article 17 This Law shall come into force on the date of promulgation.[34]

---

[34] ibid, 301-04.

32. Declaration by the People's Republic of China in Relation to the Declaration Made by the Government of the Philippines upon Signature and Confirmed upon Ratification, 12 June 1985

The Permanent Representative of the People's Republic of China to the United Nations presents his compliments to the Secretary-General of the United Nations and, with reference to the Depositary Notifications C.N.7.1983.TREATIES-1 (ANNEX B) [of 23 February 1983] and C.N.104.1984.TREATIES-3 [of 22 May 1984] which involve the sovereignty and interests of the People's Republic of China over its territory of the Nansha Islands, has the honour to reiterate as follows:

The so-called Kalayaan Islands are part of the Nansha Islands, which have always been Chinese territory. The Chinese Government has stated on many occasions that China has indisputable sovereignty over the Nansha Islands and the adjacent waters and resources.[35]

33. Declaration of the Government of the People's Republic of China on China's Territorial Sea, 4 September 1958

The Government of the People's Republic of China declares:

1. The breadth of the territorial sea of the People's Republic of China shall be twelve nautical miles. This provision applies to all territories of the People's Republic of China, including the Chinese mainland and its coastal islands, as well as Taiwan and its surrounding islands, the Penghu Islands, the Dongsha Islands, the Xisha Islands, the Zhongsha Islands, the Nansha Islands which are separated from the mainland and its coastal islands by the high seas and all the other islands belonging to China.

2. China's territorial sea along the mainland and its coastal islands takes as its baseline the line composed of the straight lines connecting base-points on the mainland coast and on the outermost of the coastal islands; the water area extending twelve nautical miles outward from this baseline is China's territorial sea. The water areas inside the baseline, including Bohai Bay and the Chiungchow Straits, are Chines inland waters. The islands inside the baseline, including Tungyin Island, Kaoteng Island, the Matsu Islands, the Paichuan Islands, Wuchiu Island, the Greater and Lesser Quemoy Island, Erhtan Island and Tungting Island, are islands of the Chinese inland waters.

3. No foreign vessels for military use and no foreign aircraft may enter China's territorial sea and the air space above it without the permission of the Government of the People's Republic of China.

While navigating Chinese territorial sea, every foreign vessel must observe the relevant laws and regulations laid down by the Government of the People's Republic of China.

---

[35] 1835 UNTS 157; United Nations, Division for Ocean Affairs and the Law of the Sea, *Law of the Sea Bulletin* No 6 (1985), 8.

4. The principles provided in paragraphs(2) and (3)likewise apply to Taiwan and its surrounding Islands, the Penghu Islands, the Dongsha islands, the Xisha Islands, the Zhongsha Islands, the Nansha Islands, and all the other islands belonging to China.

The Taiwan and Penghu areas are still occupied by the United States by armed force. This is an unlawful encroachment on the territorial integrity and sovereignty of the People's Republic of China. Taiwan, Penghu and such other areas are yet to be recovered, and the Government of the People's Republic of China has the right to recover these areas by all suitable means at a suitable time. This is China's internal affair, in which no foreign interference is tolerated.[36]

B. DOCUMENTS OF THE REPUBLIC OF THE PHILIPPINES

1. Note Verbale No 13-0211 from the Department of Foreign Affairs of the Republic of the Philippines to the Embassy of the People's Republic of China in Manila, 22 January 2013

The Department of Foreign Affairs of the Republic of the Philippines presents its compliments to the Embassy of the People's Republic of China and, with respect to the dispute with China over the maritime jurisdiction of the Philippines in the West Philippine Sea, the Government of the Philippines has the honor to submit the attached Notification under Article 287 and Annex VII of the 1982 United Nations Convention on the Law of the Sea (UNCLOS) and the Statement of Claim on which the Notification is based, in order to initiate arbitral proceedings to clearly establish the sovereign rights and jurisdiction of the Philippines over its maritime entitlements in the West Philippine Sea.

The Government of the Philippines has initiated these arbitral proceedings in furtherance of the friendly relations with China, mindful of its Obligation under Article 279 of UNCLOS to seek a peaceful and durable resolution of the dispute in the West Philippine Sea by the means indicated in Article 33 (1) of the Charter of the United Nations.

The Department of Foreign Affairs of the Republic of the Philippines avails itself of this opportunity to renew to the Embassy of the People's Republic of China the assurances of its highest consideration.

Manila, 22 January 2013

[Stamp, Initials]

The Embassy of the People's Republic of China, Manila

Attachments: Notification and Statement of Claims[37]

---

[36] ibid, 295-96.
[37] www.dfa.gov.ph/index.php/component/docman/doc_download/56-notification-and-statement-of-claim-on-west-philippine-sea?Itemid=546.

2. Republic of the Philippines, Notification and Statement of Claim, 22 January 2013

I. INTRODUCTION

1. The Republic of the Philippines brings this arbitration against the People's Republic of China to challenge China's claims to areas of the South China Sea and the underlying seabed as far as 870 nautical miles from the nearest Chinese coast, to which China has no entitlement under the 1982 United Nations Convention on the Law of the Sea ("UNCLOS", or "the Convention"), and which, under the Convention, constitute the Philippines' exclusive economic zone and continental shelf.

2. Despite China's adherence to UNCLOS in June 1996, and the requirement of Article 300 that States Parties fulfill in good faith their obligations under the Convention, China has asserted a claim to "sovereignty" and "sovereign rights" over a vast maritime area lying within a so-called "nine dash line" that encompasses virtually the entire South China Sea. By claiming all of the waters and seabed within the "nine dash line", China has extended its self-proclaimed maritime jurisdiction to within 50 nautical miles ("M") off the coasts of the Philippine islands of Luzon and Palawan, and has interfered with the exercise by the Philippines of its rights under the Convention, including within its own exclusive economic zone and continental shelf, in violation of UNCLOS.

3. Further, within the maritime area encompassed by the "nine dash line", China has laid claim to, occupied and built structures on certain submerged banks, reefs and low tide elevations that do not qualify as islands under the Convention, but are parts of the Philippines' continental shelf, or the international seabed; and China has interfered with the exercise by the Philippines of its rights in regard to these features, and in the waters surrounding them encompassed by China's designated security zones.

4. In addition, China has occupied certain small, uninhabitable coral projections that are barely above water at high tide, and which are "rocks" under Article 121 (3) of UNCLOS. China has claimed maritime zones surrounding these features greater than 12 M, from which it has sought to exclude the Philippines, notwithstanding the encroachment of these zones on the Philippines' exclusive economic zone, or on international waters.

5. In June 2012, China formally created a new administrative unit, under the authority of the Province of Hainan, that included all of the maritime features and waters within the "nine dash line". In November 2012, the provincial government of Hainan Province promulgated a law calling for the inspection, expulsion or detention of vessels "illegally" entering the waters claimed by China within this area. The new law went into effect on 1 January 2013.

6. In response to these and other unlawful acts in contravention of UNCLOS, the Philippines seeks an Award t:hat: (1) declares that the Parties' respective rights and obligations in regard to the waters, seabed and maritime features of the South China Sea are governed by UNCLOS, and that China's claims based on its "nine dash line" are inconsistent with the Convention and therefore invalid; (2) determines whether, under Article 121 of UNCLOS, certain of the maritime features claimed by both China and the Philippines are islands, low tide elevations or submerged banks, and whether they are capable of generating entitlement to maritime zones greater than 12 M; and (3) enables the Philippines to exercise and enjoy the rights within and beyond its exclusive economic zone and continental shelf that are established in the Convention.

7. The Philippines does not seek in this arbitration a determination of which Party enjoys sovereignty over the islands claimed by both of them. Nor does it request a delimitation of any maritime boundaries. The Philippines is conscious of China's Declaration of 25 August 2006 under Article 298 of UNCLOS, and has avoided raising subjects or making claims that China has, by virtue of that Declaration, excluded from arbitral jurisdiction.

8. All of the Philippines' claims in this arbitration have been the subject of good faith negotiations between the Parties. There have been numerous exchanges of views. The requirements of Article 279 have been satisfied. There is, therefore, no bar to the Arbitral Tribunal's exercise of jurisdiction over the claims asserted by the Philippines.

II. FACTUAL BACKGROUND

A. Maritime Areas

9. The South China Sea, part of which is known in the Philippines as the West Philippine Sea, is a semi-enclosed sea in Southeast Asia that covers approximately 2.74 million square kilometers. The Sea is surrounded by six States and Taiwan. To the north are the southern coast of mainland China, and China's Hainan Island. To the northeast lies Taiwan. To the east and southeast is the Philippines. The southern limits of the sea are bounded by Brunei, Malaysia and Indonesia. And to the west is Vietnam.

10. There are many small insular features in the South China Sea. They are 1argely concentrated in three geographically distinct groups: the Paracel Islands in the northwest; Scarborough Shoal in the east; and the Spratly Islands in the southeast. The Paracel Islands are not relevant to this arbitration. Scarborough Shoal, located approximately 120 M west of the Philippines' coast and more than 350M from China, is a submerged coral reef with six small protrusions of rock above sea level at high tide. The Spratly Islands are a group of approximately 150 small features, many of which are submerged reefs, banks and low tide elevations. They

lie between 50 and 350 M from the Philippine island of Palawan, and more than 550M from the Chinese island of Hainan. None of the Spratly features occupied by China is capable of sustaining human habitation or an economic life of its own.

11. Notwithstanding its adherence to UNCLOS, China claims almost the entirety of the South China Sea, and all of the maritime features, as its own. Specifically, China claims "sovereignty" or "sovereign rights" over some 1.94 million square kilometers, or 70% of the Sea's waters and underlying seabed within its so-called "nine dash line." China first officially depicted the "nine dash line" in a letter of 7 May 2009 to the United Nations Secretary General. It is reproduced below. According to China, it is sovereign over all of the waters, all of the seabed, and all of the maritime features within this "nine dash line".

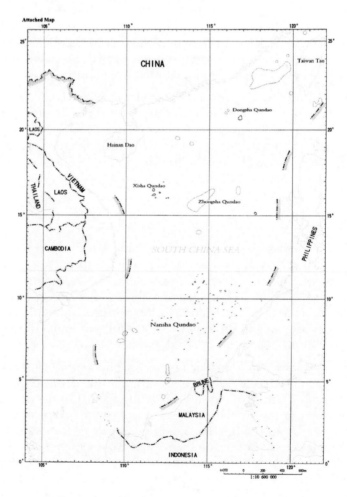

12. In the east, the "nine dash line" depicted in China's letter is less than 50M off the Philippine island of Luzon. In the southeast, it is within 30M from Palawan. In both respects, it cuts through – and cuts off – the Philippines' 200 M exclusive economic zone and continental shelf, in violation of UNCLOS. Within the area encompassed by the "nine dash line", China has engaged in conduct that has unlawfully interfered with the Philippines' right of navigation, notwithstanding that some of the area is in the Philippines' own exclusive economic zone, and the rest is high seas; and China has interfered with the exercise by the Philippines of its rights to the living and non-living resources in its exclusive economic zone and continental shelf extending west from the island of Luzon, and northwest from the island of Palawan. China has also violated the Philippines' rights by exploiting the living resources in the Philippines' exclusive economic zone.

13. China's interference with and violations of the Philippines' rights under UNCLOS have been steadily escalating. In June 2012, China placed the entire maritime area within the "nine dash line" under the authority of the Province of Hainan, which, in November 2012, in the exercise of its administrative authority, promulgated a law that requires foreign vessels to obtain China's permission before entering the waters within the "nine dash line", and provides for inspection, expulsion and detention of vessels that do not obtain such permission. The law went into effect on 1 January 2013.

B. Submerged Features

14. Even before its first official espousal of the "nine dash line", China began to seize physical control of a number of submerged features and protruding rocks in the Spratly Islands, in the southeastern part of the Sea, and to construct artificial "islands" on top of them. Among the submerged features that China occupied and altered in this manner are: Mischief Reef, McKennan Reef, Gaven Reef and Subi Reef. None of these features is an island under Article 121 of UNCLOS. They are all at best low tide elevations, far removed from China's territorial sea, exclusive economic zone and continental shelf. Because they are not above water at high tide, they are part of another State's continental shelf, or the international seabed. Yet, China has not only acted unlawfully by seizing control of these submerged features; it has declared maritime zones around them, from which it has illegally sought to exclude the Philippines and other States.

15. Mischief Reef (Chinese name = Meiji Jiao; known in the Philippines as Panganiban Reef) is a submerged bank that is part of the Philippines' continental shelf, approximately 130 M from Palawan (and more than 600 M southeast of China's Hainan Island, the nearest Chinese land territory). Mischief Reef lies at approximately 9° 54′N – 115° 32′E. Since 1995, China has constructed buildings and other facilities on stilts and concrete

platforms at four different sites atop Mischief Reef, despite repeated protests from the Philippines.

16. McKennan Reef (Chinese name = Ximen Jiao; known in the Philippines as Chigua Reef) is a low tide elevation located at approximately 9°53′5″N – 114° 28′E. It is approximately 180 M west of the Philippine island of Palawan, and is also part of the Philippines' continental shelf. China has constructed buildings and other facilities on stilts and concrete platforms at this feature, as well, despite the Philippines' protests.

17. China has not only unlawfully seized parts of the Philippines' continental shelf, but has also wrongfully sought to prevent Philippine vessels from approaching Mischief Reef and McKennan Reef, even though the surrounding waters are within the Philippines' exclusive economic zone.

18. Gaven Reef (Chinese name = Nanxun Jiao) is a low tide elevation located at approximately 10°13′N – 114°13′E. It lies approximately 205 M northwest of Palawan.

19. Subi Reef (Chinese name = Zhubi Jiao; known in the Philippines as Zamora Reef) is a low tide elevation located at approximately 10°55′N –114°05′E. It lies approximately 230 M west of Palawan.

C. Insular Features

20. In 2012, China seized six small rocks that protrude above sea level within the Philippines' exclusive economic zone, unlawfully claimed an exaggerated maritime zone around these features, and wrongfully prevented the Philippines from navigating, or enjoying access to the living resources within this zone, even though it forms part of the Philippines' EEZ. These half dozen protrusions, which are known collectively as Scarborough Shoal (Bajo de Masinloc in the Philippines; Huang Yan Dao in China), are located approximately 120 M west of the Philippine island of Luzon. They are rocks both literally and under Article 121 of UNCLOS. None is more than 3meters ("m") above sea level at high tide; and none measures more than a few meters in width. None of the rocks, which lie in close proximity to one another, generates entitlement to more than a 12 M territorial sea. Yet, China, which like the Philippines asserts sovereignty over Scarborough Shoal, claims a much larger maritime zone for itself, to the limit of the "nine dash line" approximately 70M to the east.

21. Until April 2012, Philippine fishing vessels routinely fished in this area, which is within the Philippines' 200 M exclusive economic zone. Since then, China has prevented the Philippines from fishing at Scarborough Shoal or in its vicinity, and undertaken other activities inconsistent with the Convention. Only Chinese vessels are now allowed to fish in these waters, and have harvested, inter alia, endangered species such as sea turtles, sharks and giant clams which are protected by both international and Philippine law.

22. To the southwest of Scarborough Shoal, in the Spratly Islands, China has seized similar features. China presently occupies the following features which, though above water at high tide, are uninhabitable and incapable of supporting economic life in their natural state. They are therefore "rocks" within the meaning of Article 121(3) of UNCLOS:

- Johnson Reef (Chinese name = Chigua Jiao; known in the Philippines as Mabini Reef), located at approximately 9°42′N – 114°22′ E and approximately 180 M northwest of Palawan.
- Cuarteron Reef (Chinese name Huayang Jiao; known in the Philippines as Calderon Reef), located at approximately 8°51′N – 112°50′E and approximately 245 M west of Palawan; and
- Fiery Cross Reef (Chinese name = Yongshu Jiao; known in the Philippines as Kagitingan Reef), located at approximately 9°33′N – 112°54′E and approximately 255 M west of Palawan;

23. All of these features are submerged reefs with no more than a few rocks protruding above sea level at high tide. Johnson Reef has a few rocky protrusions rising above water at high tide. Cuarteron Reef is a collection of coral rocks reaching no higher than 1.5 m. Fiery Cross Reef consists of a submerged bank with protruding rocks no more than 1 m above sea level at high tide.

24. Notwithstanding that all of these insular features are "rocks" under Article 121(3) of UNCLOS, China unlawfully claims entitlements to maritime zones greater than 12 M in the waters and seabed surrounding them, and wrongfully excludes the Philippines and other States from these areas. Moreover, in the case of Scarborough Shoal and Johnson Reef, the maritime zones claimed by China unlawfully encroach upon the Philippines' 200 M exclusive economic zone and continental shelf extending from Luzon and Palawan, and prevent the Philippines from enjoying its rights under the Convention within 200 M.

D. Exchanges of Views

25. On numerous occasions, dating back at least to 1995, the Philippines and China have exchanged views regarding the Settlement of their disputes concerning entitlements to maritime areas in the South China Sea, the exercise within those maritime areas of rights pertaining to navigation and the exploitation of living and non-living resources, and the status of maritime features in the Spratly Islands and at Scarborough Shoal.

26. The Parties have been exchanging views on these disputes in attempts to achieve negotiated solutions since the first "Philippines-China Bilateral Consultations on the South China Sea Issue" were held in August 1995. However, despite many bilateral meetings and exchanges of diplomatic correspondence over more than 17 years since those first consultations were held, no settlements have been reached on any of these disputed matters.

27. In regard to entitlements to maritime areas in the South China Sea, the Philippines has consistently expressed the view to China in bilateral meetings and diplomatic correspondence that it is entitled to an exclusive economic zone and continental shelf of 200 M from its archipelagic baselines, and to the exclusive enjoyment of the living and non-living resources in these zones, as well as to the right to navigate without interference by China within and beyond its 200 M limit. In response, China has repeatedly expressed the conflicting view that it is entitled to all the maritime space encompassed by its "nine dash line", to all the living and non-living resources within this limit, and to control navigation within this area. By its diplomatic note dated 21 November 2012, the Philippines declared, as it did on numerous prior occasions, that it cannot accept the validity of the "nine dash line" or China's claims based thereon. Over the past 17 years of such exchanges of views, all possibilities of a negotiated settlement have been explored and exhausted.

28. With respect to the status of maritime features in the Spratly Islands and adjacent waters, and rights to navigate and exploit the living resources in these waters, the Parties have exchanged views since at least August 1995, and as recently as July 2012. The Philippines has repeatedly protested Chinese activities on and adjacent to Subi Reef and Mischief Reef, which form part of the Philippines' continental shelf, as well as China's claims and activities in regard to the other maritime features in the Spratly group occupied or claimed by China. China has consistently rejected the Philippines' protests and maintained its occupation of and activities on these features. Each Party has protested interference by the other with its claimed navigational rights, and with its claimed rights to the living resources, in the waters adjacent to these features. None of the protests, or ensuing meetings or diplomatic correspondence in which views were exchanged, resulted in the settlement of these disputes.

29. With respect to the status of the maritime features at Scarborough Shoal and adjacent waters, and rights to navigate and exploit the living resources in these waters, the Parties have been exchanging views regarding the settlement of their dispute since at least May 1997. Most recently, during a series of meetings in Manila in April 2012, the Parties once again exchanged views on these matters without arriving at a negotiated solution. As a result of the failure of negotiations, the Philippines later that month sent China a diplomatic note in which it invited China to agree to bring the dispute before an appropriate adjudicatory body. China declined the invitation.

30. The diplomatic record leaves no doubt that the requirement in Article 283 that the "parties to the dispute shall proceed expeditiously to an exchange of views regarding its settlement by negotiation or other peaceful means" has been satisfied.

III. THE PHILIPPINES' CLAIMS

31. Based on the foregoing and the evidence to be submitted in the course of this arbitration, the Philippines asserts the following claims:

- [1][38] China's rights in regard to maritime areas in the South China Sea, like the rights of the Philippines, are those that are established by UNCLOS, and consist of its rights to a Territorial Sea and Contiguous Zone under Part II of the Convention, to an Exclusive Economic Zone under Part V, and to a Continental Shelf under Part VI;
- [2] Accordingly, China's maritime claims in the South China Sea based on its so-called "nine dash line" are contrary to UNCLOS and invalid;
- [3] Submerged features in the South China Sea that are not above sea level at high tide, and are not located in a coastal State's territorial sea, are part of the seabed and cannot be acquired by a State, or subjected to its sovereignty, unless they form part of that State's Continental Shelf under Part VI of the Convention;
- [4] Mischief Reef, McKennan Reef, Gaven Reef and Subi Reef are submerged features that are not above sea level at high tide, are not islands under the Convention, are not located on China's Continental Shelf; and China has unlawfully occupied and engaged in unlawful construction activities on these features;
- [5] Mischief Reef and McKennan Reef are part of the Philippines' Continental Shelf under Part VI of the Convention;
- [6] Scarborough Shoal, Johnson Reef, Cuarteron Reef and Fiery Cross Reef are submerged features that are below sea level at high tide, except that each has small protrusions that remain above water at high tide, which qualify as "rocks" under Article 121(3) of the Convention, and generate an entitlement only to a Territorial Sea no broader than 12 M; and China has unlawfully claimed maritime entitlements beyond 12 M from these features;
- [7] China has unlawfully prevented Philippine vessels from exploiting the living resources in the waters adjacent to Scarborough Shoal and Johnson Reef;
- [8] The Philippines is entitled under UNCLOS to a 12 M Territorial Sea, a 200 M Exclusive Economic Zone, and a Continental Shelf under Parts II, V and VI of UNCLOS, measured from its archipelagic baselines;
- [9] China has unlawfully claimed rights to, and has unlawfully exploited, the living and non-living resources in the Philippines' Exclusive Economic Zone and Continental Shelf, and has unlawfully prevented the Philippines from exploiting the living and non-living resources within its Exclusive Economic Zone and Continental Shelf; and
- [10] China has unlawfully interfered with the exercise by the Philippines of its rights to navigation under the Convention.

---

[38] A numbering system to the bullet points has been added by the editors for ease of reference.

IV. JURISDICTION OF THE TRIBUNAL

32. The Philippines and China are both parties to UNCLOS, having ratified the Convention on 8 May 1984 and 7 June 1996, respectively. It follows that both Parties have given their advance consent to the regime of settlement of disputes concerning the interpretation and application of the Convention established in Part XII.

33. Article 279 of the Convention requires States Parties to seek a solution by peaceful means in accordance with the UN Charter. Article 283(1) further requires that when a dispute arises between States Parties, they should proceed expeditiously to an exchange of views regarding a settlement by negotiation or other peaceful means. The Philippines has complied with the requirements of Article 279 and Article 283(1) fully and in good faith, and has exhausted possibilities of settlement by negotiation.

34. As the Philippines and China have failed to settle the dispute between them by peaceful means of their own choice, Article 281(1) allows recourse to the procedures provided for in Part XV, including compulsory procedures entailing binding decisions under Section 2 of Part XV. Article 286 allows these compulsory procedures to be initiated by any State Party in the court or tribunal having jurisdiction under Section 2.

35. The choice of compulsory procedures is governed by Article 287, the first paragraph of which allows a State Party, by means of a written declaration, to choose one or more of the means for settlement of disputes listed therein, including recourse to an arbitral tribunal under Annex VII of the Convention. States Parties to a dispute which have not made declarations pursuant to Article 287(1) are deemed by operation of Article 287(3) to have accepted arbitration in accordance with Annex VII.

36. Since neither the Philippines nor China has made a declaration pursuant to Article 287(1), and since no agreement to the contrary currently exists, it follows that, in accordance with Article 287(5), this dispute may be submitted to arbitration under Annex VII of the Convention.

37. The jurisdiction of an Annex VII tribunal extends to any dispute concerning the interpretation or application of the Convention, subject to the provisions of Section 3 of Part XV.

38. Section 3 of Part XV contains optional exceptions from jurisdiction in Article 298. Such exceptions have been invoked by China in a formal declaration dated 25 August 2006.

39. None of these exceptions is applicable to the Philippines' claims in this arbitration. The present dispute concerns (a) whether, in light of China's repeated assertions of alleged "sovereign rights and jurisdiction" within the so-called "nine dash line", the Parties' respective rights and obligations in regard to the waters, seabed and maritime features of the

South China Sea are governed by the provisions of UNCLOS, including but not limited to Articles 3-14 of Part II, Articles 55 and 57 of Part V, Article 76 of Part VI, Article 121 of Part VIII and Article 300 of Part XVI; (b) whether China's Claims based on the "nine dash line" are inconsistent with those provisions; (c) whether, under Article 121 of UNCLOS, certain of the maritime features in the South China Sea are islands, low tide elevations or submerged banks, and whether they are capable of generating entitlements to maritime zones greater than 12 M; and (d) whether China has violated the right of navigation of the Philippines in the waters of the South China Sea, and the rights of the Philippines in regard to the living and non-living resources within its exclusive economic zone and continental shelf.

40. It follows that the Philippines' claims do not fall within China's Declaration of 25 August 2006, because they do not concern the interpretation or application of Articles 15, 74 and 83 relating to sea boundary delimitations; involve historic bays or titles within the meaning of the relevant provisions of the Convention; concern military activities or law enforcement activities; or concern matters over which the Security Council is exercising functions assigned to it by the UN Charter.

V. RELIEF SOUGHT

41. In light of the above, and the evidence to be submitted in the course of this arbitration, the Philippines respectfully requests that the Arbitral Tribunal issue an Award that:

- [1]³⁹ Declares that China's rights in regard to maritime areas in the South China Sea, like the rights of the Philippines, are those that are established by UNCLOS, and consist of its rights to a Territorial Sea and Contiguous Zone under Part II of the Convention, to an Exclusive Economic Zone under Part V, and to a Continental Shelf under Part VI;
- [2] Declares that China's maritime claims in the South China Sea based on its so-called "nine dash line" are contrary to UNCLOS and invalid;
- [3] Requires China to bring its domestic legislation into conformity with its obligations under UNCLOS;
- [4] Declares that Mischief Reef and McKennan Reef are submerged features that form part of the Continental Shelf of the Philippines under Part VI of the Convention, and that China's occupation of and construction activities on them violate the sovereign rights of the Philippines;
- [5] Requires that China end its occupation of and activities on Mischief Reef and McKennan Reef;
- [6] Declares that Gaven Reef and Subi Reef are submerged features in the South China Sea that are not above sea level at high tide, are not islands

---

³⁹ A numbering system to the bullet points has been added by the editors for ease of reference.

under the Convention, and are not located on China's Continental Shelf, and that China' s occupation of and construction activities on these features are unlawful;

- [7] Requires China to terminate its occupation of and activities on Gaven Reef and Subi Reef;
- [8] Declares that Scarborough Shoal, Johnson Reef, Cuarteron Reef and Fiery Cross Reef are submerged features that are below sea level at high tide, except that each has small protrusions that remain above water at high tide, which are "rocks" under Article 121 (3) of the Convention and which therefore generate entitlements only to a Territorial Sea no broader than 12 M; and that China has unlawfully claimed maritime entitlements beyond 12 M from these features;
- [9] Requires that China refrain from preventing Philippine vessels from exploiting in a sustainable manner the living resources in the waters adjacent to Scarborough Shoal and Johnson Reef, and from undertaking other activities inconsistent with the Convention at or in the vicinity of these features;
- [10] Declares that the Philippines is entitled under UNCLOS to a 12 M Territorial Sea, a 200 M Exclusive Economic Zone, and a Continental Shelf under Parts II, V and VI of UNCLOS, measured from its archipelagic baselines;
- [11] Declares that China has unlawfully claimed, and has unlawfully exploited, the living and non-living resources in the Philippines' Exclusive Economic Zone and Continental Shelf, and has unlawfully prevented the Philippines from exploiting living and non-living resources within its Exclusive Economic Zone and Continental Shelf;
- [12] Declares that China has unlawfully interfered with the exercise by the Philippines of its rights to navigation and other rights under the Convention in areas within and beyond 200 M of the Philippines' archipelagic baselines; and
- [13] Requires that China desist from these unlawful activities.

VI. APPOINTMENT OF ARBITRATOR

42. In accordance with the requirements of UNCLOS Annex VII, Article 3(b), the Philippines hereby appoints Judge Rudiger Wolfrum as a member of the Arbitral Tribunal.

VII. RESERVATION OF RIGHTS

43. The Philippines reserves the right to supplement and/or amend its claims and the relief sought as necessary, and to make such other requests of the Arbitral. Tribunal as may be required, to preserve its rights under UNCLOS, including a request for provisional measures.

Respectfully submitted,

[Signed] Francis H. Jardeleza
Solicitor General
Republic of the Philippines
Agent

22 January 2013[40]

3. Understanding Made by the Republic of the Philippines upon Signature of the United Nations Convention on the Law of the Sea, 10 December 1982, and Confirmed upon Ratification of the Convention, 8 May 1984

The Government of the Republic of the Philippines hereby manifests that in signing the 1982 United Nations Convention on the Law of the Sea, it does so with the understandings embodied in this declaration, made under the provisions of Article 310 of the Convention, to wit:

1. The signing of the Convention by the Government of the Republic of the Philippines shall not in any manner impair or prejudice the sovereign rights of the Republic of the Philippines under and arising from the Constitution of the Philippines;

2. Such signing shall not in any manner affect the sovereign rights of the Republic of the Philippines as successor of the United States of America, under and arising out of the Treaty of Paris between Spain and the United States of America of December 10, 1898, and the Treaty of Washington between the United States of America and Great Britain of January 2, 1930;

3. Such signing shall not diminish or in any manner affect the rights and obligations of the contracting parties under the Mutual Defense Treaty between the Philippines and the United States of America of August 30, 1951, and its related interpretative instruments; nor those under any other pertinent bilateral or multilateral treaty or agreement to which the Philippines is a party;

4. Such signing shall not in any manner impair or prejudice the sovereignty of the Republic of the Philippines over any territory over which it exercises sovereign authority, such as the Kalayaan Islands, and the waters appurtenant thereto;

5. The Convention shall not be construed as amending in any manner any pertinent laws and Presidential Decrees or Proclamations of the Republic of the Philippines; the Government of the Republic of the Philippines maintains and reserves the right and authority to make

[40] www.dfa.gov.ph/index.php/component/docman/doc_download/56-notification-and-statement-of-claim-on-west-philippine-sea?Itemid=546.

any amendments to such laws, decrees or proclamations pursuant to the provisions of the Philippine Constitution;

6. The provisions of the Convention on archipelagic passage through sea lanes do not nullify or impair the sovereignty of the Philippines as an archipelagic State over the sea lanes and do not deprive it of authority to enact legislation to protect its sovereignty, independence, and security;

7. The concept of archipelagic waters is similar to the concept of internal waters under the Constitution of the Philippines, and removes straits connecting these waters with the economic zone or high sea from the rights of foreign vessels to transit passage for international navigation;

8. The agreement of the Republic of the Philippines to the submission for peaceful resolution, under any of the procedures provided in the Convention, of disputes under Article 298 shall not be considered as a derogation of Philippine sovereignty.[41]

---

[41] 1835 UNTS 86-87, 137; United Nations, Division for Ocean Affairs and the Law of the Sea, *Law of the Sea Bulletin* No 5 (1985) 18–19.

Annex II

Select Bibliography on the South China Sea Disputes

1. Alatas, A, 'Managing the Potentials of the South China Sea' (1990) 18 *Indonesian Quarterly* 114

2. Amer, R, 'The Territorial Dispute between China and Vietnam and Regional Stability' (1997) 19 *Contemporary Southeast Asia* 86

3. ——, 'Towards a Declaration on "Navigational Rights" in the Sea-lanes of the Asia-Pacific' (1998) 20 *Contemporary Southeast Asia* 88

4. Arreglado, JM, *Kalayaan: Historical, Legal and Political Background* (Manila, Foreign Service Institute, 1982)

5. ——, 'The Law of the Sea: Its Various Aspects and the Philippine View' (1974) 3 *Philippine Yearbook of International Law* 1

6. Austin, G, *China's Ocean Frontier: International Law, Military Force and National Development* (St Leonards, Allen & Unwin, 1998)

7. Baviera, ASP and Batongbacal, J, *The West Philippine Sea: The Territorial and Maritime Jurisdiction Disputes from a Filipino Perspective (A Primer)* (Quezon City, The Asian Center and the Institute for Maritime Affairs and Law of the Sea, University of the Philippines Diliman, 2013)

8. Beckman, R, 'The UN Convention on the Law of the Sea and the Maritime Disputes in the South China Sea' (2013) 107 *American Journal of International Law* 142

9. Bennett, M, 'The People's Republic of China and the Use of International Law in the Spratly Island Dispute' (1992) 28 *Stanford Journal of International Law* 425

10. Carino, T (ed), *The South China Sea Dispute: Philippine Perspectives* (Manila, Philippine-China Development Resources Centre and Philippine Association for China Studies, 1992)

11. Carpenter, C, 'Legal Aspects of Sino-American Oil Exploration in the South China Sea' (1980) 14 *Journal of International Law and Economics* 443

12. Castro, PA, *The Philippines and the Law of the Sea* (Manila, Foreign Service Institute, 1983)

13. Catley, R and Keliat, M, *Spratlys: The Dispute in the South China Sea* (Singapore, Ashgate, 1997)

14. Chang, PM, 'A New Scramble for the South China Sea Islands' (1990) 12 *Contemporary Southeast Asia* 20

15. Chang, TK, 'Chinas Claim of Sovereignty over Spratly and Paracel Islands. A Historical and Legal Perspective' (1991) 23 *Case Western Reserve Journal of International Law* 399

16. Chao, JKT, 'South China Sea: Boundary Problems Relating to the Nansha and Hsisha Islands' (1990) 9 *Chinese Yearbook of International Law and Affairs* 66

17. ———, 'Analysis of Current Law of the Sea in the Spratly Islands Dispute' (1999) 9 *Asian Review* 17

18. Chemillier-Gendreau, M, *Sovereignty over the Paracel and Spratly Islands* (Dordrecht, Kluwer Law International, 1996)

19. Chen, HY, 'The PRC's South China Sea Policy and Strategies of Occupation in the Paracel and Spratly Islands' (2000) 36 *Issues and Studies* 95

20. Chen, J, 'China's Spratly Policy. With Special reference to the Philippines and Malaysia' (1994) 34 *Asian Survey* 893

21. Chen, DK (ed), *Wo Guo De Nan Hai Zhu Dao [Our Country's Islands in the Southern Sea]* (Beijing, Zhong Guo Qing Nian Chu Ban She [Chinese Youth Publishing House], 1962)

22. Cheng, T, 'The Dispute over the South China Sea Islands' (1975) 10 *Texas International Law Journal* 265

23. Chinese Institute of Marine Affairs, State Oceanic Administration, *Zhong Guo Hai Yang Fa Zhan Bao Gao [China's Ocean Development Report]* (Beijing, Ocean Press, 2001)

24. ———, *Zhong Guo De Ling Tu Huang Yan Dao [Chinese Territory: Huangyan Island]* (Beijing, Ocean Press, 2012)

25. Chiu, HD and Park, CH, 'Legal Status of the Paracel and Spratly Islands' (1975) 3 *Ocean Development and International Law* 1

26. Chiu, HD, 'South China Sea Islands: Implications for Delimiting the Seabed and Future Shipping Routes' (1977) 72 *The China Quarterly* 743

27. ———, 'The PRC's South China Sea Policy and Strategies of Occupation in the Paracel and Spratly Islands' (2000) 36 *Issues & Studies* 95

28. Chung, CP, 'The PRC's Changing Moral and Realist Perceptions Toward Territorial Disputes' (2000) 36 *Issues and Studies* 176

29. Cordner, LG, 'The Spratly Islands Dispute and the Law of the Sea' (1994) 25 *Ocean Development and International Law Journal* 61

30. Davis, EVW, *China and the Law of the Sea Convention. Follow the Sea* (Lewiston, Edwin Mellen Press, 1995)

31. Denécé, E, 'La situation juridique des archipels de mer de Chine méridionale' (1998) 3 *Annuaire du droit de la mer* 273

32. Djalal, H, 'Conflicting Territorial and Jurisdictional Claims in the South China Sea' (1979), reprinted in Djalal, H, *Indonesia and the Law of the Sea* (Jakarta, Center for Strategic and International Studies [CSIS], 1995) 364

33. Drigot, DC, 'Oil Interests and the Law of the Sea: The Case of the Philippines' (1982) 12 *Ocean Development and International Law* 23

34. Dzurek, D, 'The Spratly Islands Dispute: Who's on First?' in Schofield, C (ed), *Maritime Briefing*, vol 2, issue 1 (Durham, International Boundaries Research Unit, 1996)

35. Elferink, AO, 'The Islands in the South China Sea: How Does Their Presence Limit the Extent of the High Seas and the Area and the Maritime Zones of the Mainland Coasts?' (2001) 32 *Ocean Development and International Law* 169

36. Farrell, EC, *The Socialist Republic of Vietnam and the Law of the Sea* (The Hague, Martinus Nijhoff, 1998)

37. Ferrier, JP, 'Le conflit des îles Paracels et le problème de la souveraineté sur les îles inhabitées' (1975) 21 *Annuaire Français de Droit International* 173

38. Fu, KC, *Nan (Zhong Guo) Hai Fa Lü Di Wei Zhi Yan Jiu [Legal Status of the South (China) Sea]* (Tai Bei City, China, 123 Information Ltd, 1995)

39. Fu, Z, *Guan Yu Wo Guo De Ling Hai Wen Ti [Concerning the Issue of Our Country's Territorial Sea]* (Beijing, Knowledge of the World Press, 1959)

40. Furtado, X, 'International Law and the Dispute over the Spratly Islands: Whither UNCLOS?' (1999) 21 *Contemporary Southeast Asia* 386

41. Gao, ZG, 'The South China Sea: From Conflict to Cooperation?' (1994) 25 *Ocean Development and International Law* 345

42. Gao, ZG and Jia, BB, 'The Nine-Dash Line in the South China Sea: History, Status, and Implications' (2013) 107 *American Journal of International Law* 98

43. Garver, JW, 'China Push through the South China Sea: The Interaction of Bureaucratic and National Interests' (1992) 132 *The China Quarterly* 999

44. Gau, MST, 'The U-Shaped Line and a Categorization of the Ocean Disputes in the South China Sea' (2012) 43 *Ocean Development and International Law* 57

45. Geographical Names Commission, Guang Dong Province, China, *Nan Hai Zhu Dao Di Ming Zi Liao Hui Bian [Collection of Materials Regarding the Geographical Names of the Islands in the Southern Sea]* (Guang Zhou, Guang Dong Provincial Press of Maps and Atlases, 1987)

46. Gjetnes, M, 'The Spratlys: Are They Rocks or Islands?' (2001) 32 *Ocean Development and International Law* 191

47. Gomez, ED, 'Marine Scientific Research in the South China Sea and Environmental Security' (2001) 32 *Ocean Development and International Law* 205

48. Greenfield, J, *China and the Law of the Sea, Air and Environment* (Alphen aan den Rijn, Sijthoff and Noordhoff, 1979)

49. ——, *China's Practice in the Law of the Sea* (Oxford, Oxford University Press, 1992)

50. Guo, Y, *Wan Qing Shi Qi Zhong Guo Nan Hai Jiang Yu Yan Jiu [A Study on the Chinese Dominion in the South China Sea in the Late Qing Dynasty]* (Harbin, Hei Long Jiang Jiao Yu Chu Ban She [Hei Long Jiang Education Publishing], 2010)

51. Hamzah, BA, 'The External Maritime Dimension of ASEAN Security' (1995) 18 *Journal of Strategic Studies* 123

52. Han, ZH, 'Yuan Dai "Si Hai Ce Yan" Zhong Zhong Guo Jiang Yu de Nan Hai' [South Sea as Part of the Chinese Dominion during the Four-Sea Survey in the Yuan Dynasty] (1979) *Nan Yang Wen Ti [Southeast Asian Affairs]* 1

53. ——, *Nan Hai Zhu Dao Shi Di Yan Jiu [Study on the History and Geography of the South China Sea Islands]* (Beijing, She Hui Ke Xue Wen Xian Chu Ban She [Social Science Documentation Publishers], 1996)

54. Han, ZH, Lin, JZ and Wu, FQ (eds), *Wo Guo Nan Hai Zhu Dao Shi Liao Hui Bian [Collection of Historical Materials Concerning Our Country's Islands in the South China Sea]* (Beijing, Dongfang [Orient] Press, 1988)

55. Hancox, D and Victor, P, 'A Geographical Description of the Spratly Islands and an Account of Hydrographic Surveys Among Those Islands', *Maritime Briefing*, vol 6, issue 1 (Durham, International Boundaries Research Unit, 1996)

56. Hancox, D and Prescott, V, *Secret Hydrographic Surveys in the Spratly Islands* (Philadelphia, Coronet Books Inc, 1999)

57. Harrison, S, *China, Oil and Asia: Conflict Ahead* (New York, Columbia University Press, 1977)

58. Hearns, GS and Stormont, WG, 'Report: Managing Potential Conflicts in the South China Sea' (1996) 20 *Marine Policy* 177

59. Heinzig, D, *Disputed Islands in the South China Sea: Paracels, Spratlys, Pratas, Macclesfield Bank* (Wiesbaden, Harrassowitz, 1976)

60. Hong, N, *UNCLOS and Ocean Dispute Settlement: Law and Politics in the South China Sea* (Abingdon, Routledge, 2012)

61. Hutchison, CS, *Southeast Asian Oil, Gas, Coal and Mineral Deposits* (Oxford, Clarendon Press, 1996)

62. The Hydrographic Office, Admiralty, UK, *The China Sea Pilot* (London, Admiralty, 1902, 1923, 1937)

63. Hyer, E, 'The South China Sea Disputes: Implications of China's Earlier Territorial Settlements' (1995) 68 *Pacific Affairs* 34

64. International Hydrographic Organization, *Limits of Oceans and Seas*, 3rd edn (Monte-Carlo, Imp Monégasque, 1953)

65. Ji, GX, 'China Versus South China Sea Security' (1998) 29 *Security Dialogue* 101

66. Jia, Y, 'Nan Hai "Duan Xu Xian" De Fa Lü Di Wei' [Legal Status of the "Broken Line" in the South China Sea] (2005) 15 *Zhong Guo Bian Jiang Shi Yan Jiu [China's Borderland History and Geography Studies]* 112

67. Johnson, S, 'Territorial Issues and Conflict Potential in the South China Sea' (1994) 14 *Conflict Quarterly* 26

68. Joyner, CC, 'The Spratly Dispute: Rethinking the Interplay of Law, Diplomacy, and Geo-politics in the South China Sea' (1998) 13 *The International Journal of Marine and Coastal Law* 193

69. Katchen, MH, 'The Spratly Islands and the Law of the Sea: "Dangerous Ground" for Asian Peace' (1977) 17 *Asian Survey* 1177

70. Kittichaisaree, K, *The Law of the Sea and Maritime Boundary Delimitation in Southeast Asia* (New York, Oxford University Press, 1987)

71. ——, 'A Code of Conduct for Human and Regional Security around the South China Sea' (2001) 32 *Ocean Development and International Law* 131

72. Kivimäki, T (ed), *Territorial Disputes in the South China Sea* (a study commissioned by the Finnish Foreign Ministry undertaken by

the Nordic Institute of Asian Studies) (Helsinki, CTS-Conflict Transformation Service, 2001)

73. ——, *War or Peace in the South China Sea* (Copenhagen, NIAS Press, 2002)

74. Lam, PE, 'Japan and the Spratlys Dispute' (1996) 36 *Asian Survey* 995

75. Lee, LT, 'The South China Sea – China and Multilateral Dialogues' (1999) 30 *Security Dialogue* 165

76. ——, *China and the South China Sea Dialogues* (Westport, Praeger, 1999)

77. Leifer, M, 'Chinese Economic Reform and Security Policy: The South China Sea Connection' (1996) 37 *Survival* 44

78. Li, JM, 'Cong Li Shi Yu Guo Ji Fa Kan Huang Yan Dao De Zhu Quan Gui Shu' [Sovereignty over Huang Yan Island from Historical and the International Law of the Sea Perspectives] (2001) 11 *Zhong Guo Bian Jiang Shi Yan Jiu [China's Borderland History and Geography Studies]* 71

79. Li, JM and Li, DX, 'The Dotted Line on the Chinese Map of the South China Sea: A Note' (2003) 34 *Ocean Development and International Law* 287

80. Li, MJ, *Tai Wan Di Qu Hai Yang Wen Ti Yan Jiu [Study on the Maritime Affairs of the Taiwan Region]* (Beijing, Zhong Guo She Hui Ke Xue Chu Ban She [Chinese Social Sciences Publishing], 2011)

81. Lim, BO, 'Tempest over the South China Sea: The Chinese Perspective on the Spratlys' (2000) 36 *Asian Studies* 69

82. Liu, WZ, 'Yue Nan De Wei Zheng Yu Zhong Guo Dui Xi Sha Qun Dao He Nan Sha Qun Dao Zhu Quan De Li Shi He Fa Li Yi Ju' [Forged Evidence of Vietnam vis-à-vis Historical and Legal Grounds for China's Sovereignty over the Xisha and Nansha Islands] [1989] *Zhong Guo Guo Ji Fa Nian Kan [Chinese Yearbook of International Law]* 336

83. Lo, CK, *China's Policy Towards Territorial Disputes. The Case of the South China Sea Islands* (London, Routledge, 1989)

84. Lord Commissioner for the Admiralty, *The China Sea Directory*, vol II, 5th edn (London, Admiralty, 1906)

85. Luu, VL, *The Sino-Vietnamese Difference on the Hoang Sa and Truong Sa Archipelagos* (Hanoi, The Gioi Publishers, 1996)

86. Mak, JN, 'The Chinese Navy and the South China Sea. A Malaysian Assessment' (1991) 4 *The Pacific Review* 150

87. Manguin, PY, 'Trading Ships of the South China Sea' (1993) 36 *Journal of the Economic and Social History of the Orient* 253

88. Marston, G, 'Abandonment of Territorial Claims: The Cases of Bouvet and Spratly Islands' (1986) *British Year Book of International Law* 337

89. McDorman, TL, 'Implementation of the LOS Convention: Options, Impediments and the ASEAN States' (1987) 18 *Ocean Development and International Law* 279

90. ——, 'The South China Sea Island Dispute in the 1990s – A New Multilateral Process and Continuing Friction' (1993) 8 *The International Journal of Marine and Coastal Law* 263

91. Murphy, BK, 'Dangerous Ground: The Spratly Islands and International Law' (1994) 1 *Ocean and Coastal Law Journal* 187

92. Nguyen, HT and Amer, R, 'A New Legal Arrangement for the South China Sea?' (2012) 40 *Ocean Development and International Law* 333

93. Olds, K, Dicken, P and Kelly, P (eds), *Globalisation and the Asia-Pacific: Contested Territories*, Warwick Studies in Globalisation (London, Routledge, 1999)

94. Owen, NA and Schofield, CH, 'Disputed South China Sea Hydocarbons in Perspective' (2011) 36 *Marine Policy* 809

95. Pan, SY, *The Petropolitics of the Nansha Islands. China's Indisputable Legal Case* (in Chinese and English) (Hong Kong, Economic Information and Agency, 1996)

96. Park, CH, 'The South China Sea Disputes: Who Owns the Islands and the Natural Resources?' (1978) 5 *Ocean Development and International Law* 27

97. Rau, R, 'Present and Future Maritime Security Issues in the Southeast Asian and the South China Seas' (1986) 8 *Contemporary Southeast Asia* 37

98. Ridao, LO, 'The Philippine Claims to Internal Waters and Territorial Sea: An Appraisal' (1974) 3 *Philippine Yearbook of International Law* 57

99. Samuels, MS, *Contest for the South China Sea* (New York, Methuen, 1982)

100. Shao, XZ, 'Wo Guo Nan Sha Qun Dao De Zhu Quan Bu Rong Qin Fan' [Inviolability of Our Country's Sovereignty over the Nansha Islands], *Ren Min Ri Bao [People's Daily]*, 5 June 1956, p 3

101. Shee, PK, 'The South China Sea in China's Strategic Thinking' (1998) 19 *Contemporary Southeast Asia* 368

102. Shen, JM, 'China's Sovereignty over the South China Sea Islands: A Historical Perspective' (2002) 1 *Chinese Journal of International Law* 94

103. Shen, KC, *Nan Hai Zhu Dao Zhu Quan Zheng Yi Shu Ping [Commentary on the Sovereign Disputes over the Islands in the South China Sea]* (Taibei City, Xue Sheng Shu Ju [Students' Books], 2009)

104. Shen, PF, *Diao Cha Xi Sha Qun Dao Bao Gao Shu [Report on the Investigation of the Paracel Islands]* (Guang Zhou, Sun Yat-Sen University Press, 1928; reprint of the 1928 edition, Tai Bei City, Xue Sheng Shu Ju [Students' Books], 1975)

105. Smith, R, 'Maritime Delimitation in the South China Sea: Potentiality and Challenges' (2010) 41 *Ocean Development and International Law* 214

106. Song, YH, 'The Application of Article 122 (3) of the Law of the Sea Convention to Five Selected Disputed Islands in the South China Sea' (2011) 27 *Chinese (Taiwan) Yearbook of International Law and Affairs* 43

107. Storey, I, 'Creeping Assertiveness: China, the Philippines and the South China Sea Disputes' (1999) 21 *Contemporary Southeast Asia* 95

108. Tønesson, S, 'The South China Sea in the Age of European Decline' (2006) 40 *Modern Asian Studies* 1

109. ——, 'China and the South China Sea: a Peace Proposal' (2000) 31 *Security Dialogue* 307

110. Townsend-Gault, I, 'Preventive Diplomacy and Pro-activity in the South China Sea' (1998) 20 *Contemporary Southeast Asia* 171

111. Tu, DMT, *Le différend des îles Paracels et Spratleys. Ses problèmes juridiques* (Paris, Memoire, 1976)

112. Valencia, M and Van Dyke, J, 'Comprehensive Solutions to the South China Sea Disputes: Some Options' in Blake, G, Pratt, M, Schofield, C and Allison, J (eds), *Boundaries and Energy: Problem and Prospects* (Dordrecht, Kluwer Law International, 1998) 85

113. Valencia, M, Van Dyke, J and Ludwig, N, *Sharing the Resources of the South China Sea* (The Hague, Martinus Nijhoff, 1997)

114. Valencia, MJ, 'China and the South China Sea Dispute. Conflicting Claims and Potential Solutions in the South China Sea', *Adelphi Paper*, No 298 (Oxford, Oxford University Press, 1995)

115. Van Dyke, J and Brooks, RA, 'Uninhabited Islands: Their Impact on the Ownership of the Ocean's Resources' (1983) 12 *Ocean Development and International Law* 265

116. Wang, GW, *The Nanhai Trade. The Early History of Chinese Trade in the South China Sea* (Singapore, Times Academic Press, 1998, reprint of the 1958 edition)

117. Wang, TY, 'International Law in China: Historical and Contemporary Perspectives' (1990) 221 *Recueil des Cours* 195

118. Whiting, D, 'The Spratly Islands Dispute and the Law of the Sea' (1998) 26 *Denver Journal of International Law and Policy* 879

119. Wu, S and Mesquita, B, 'Assessing the Dispute in the South China Sea: A Model of China's Security Decision Making' (1994) 38 *International Studies Quarterly* 379

120. Wu, SC, Li, XL, Zhong, TX, Wu, Y and Fu, Y (eds), *Nan Hai Wen Ti Wen Xian Hui Bian [Collection of Documents on the Issue of the South China Sea]* (Haikou City, Hainan Press, 2001)

121. Wu, SC, Shen, GC and Li, XL (eds), *Nan Hai Zi Liao Suo Yin [A Bibliography of Research on the South China Sea]* (Hai Kou, Hai Nan Chu Ban She [Hainan Publishing House], 1998)

122. Xia, ZY (ed), *Nan Sha Qun Dao Yu Ye Shi [History of Fisheries in the Nansha Islands]* (Beijing, Hai Yang Chu Ban She [Ocean Publishing], 2011)

123. Yorac, H, 'The Philippine Claim to the Spratly Islands Group' (1983) 58 *Philippine Law Journal* 42

124. Yoshihara, T and Holmes, JR, 'Can China Defend a "Core Interest" in the South China Sea' (2011) 34 *The Washington Quarterly* 45

125. Yu, SKT, 'Who Owns the Paracels and Spratlys? An Analysis of the Nature and Conflicting Territorial Claims' (1989-1990) 9 *Chinese Yearbook of International Law and Affairs* 1

126. Yu, PKH, 'Issues on the South China Sea: A Case Study' (1991-92) 11 *Chinese Yearbook of International Law and Affairs* 138

127. Zhao, LH, 'Guan Yü Nan Hai Zhu Dao De Ruo Gan Fa Lü Wen Ti' [Certain Legal Questions Concerning Islands in the South China Sea] (1995) 4 *Fa Zhi Yu She Hui Fa Zhan [Rule of Law and Societal Development]* 50

128. Zheng, ZY, *Nan Hai Zhu Dao Di Li Zhi Lüe [Gazetteer of the Islands of the Southern Sea]* (Shanghai, Shang Wu Chu Ban She [Commerce Press], 1947)

129. Zou, KY, 'The Chinese Traditional Maritime Boundary Line in the South China Sea and Its Legal Consequences for the Resolution of the Dispute over the Spratly Islands' (1999) 14 *International Journal of Marine and Coastal Law* 27

130. ——, 'Scarborough Reef: A New Flashpoint in Sino-Philippine Relations?', *Boundary and Security Bulletin* (Durham, International Boundaries Research Unit, 1999) 71

131. ——, 'Historic Rights in International Law and in China's Practice' (2001) 32 *Ocean Development and International Law* 149

132. ——, *China's Marine Legal System and the Law of the Sea* (Leiden, Martinus Nijhoff, 2005)

133. ——, 'China's U-Shaped Line in the South China Sea Revisited' (2012) 43 *Ocean Development and International Law* 18

Annex III

Glossary of Place Names

The following Glossary lists all the islands, islets and rocks to which reference is made in the text or the documents Annex. The place names are given in Chinese Pin-yin and English. Under each Pin-yin name is the Chinese equivalent as used in Chinese publications. The translations given in this Glossary are unofficial and included here only for ease of reference.[1]

Chinese Pin-yin	English	Coordinates	
Beizi Dao[2] 北子岛	North East Cay	11°26'N	114°23'E
Chigua Jiao[3] 赤瓜礁	Johnson Reef	9°42'N	114°17'E
Dongmen Jiao 东门礁	Hughes Reef	9°55'N	114°30'E
Dongsha Dao 东沙岛	Pratas Island	20°42'N	116°43'E
Feixin Dao 费信岛	Flat Island	10°49'N	115°50'E
Hongxiu Dao 鸿庥岛	Namyit Island	10°11'N	114°22'E

[1] For a list of islands, islets and rocks, see 'Zhong Guo Di Ming Wei Yuan Hui Shou Quan Gong Bu Wo Guo Nan Hai Zhu Dao Bu Fen Biao Zhun Di Ming' [Chinese Geographical Names Commission Authorized to Publicize Some of the Standard Place Names of Our Southern Sea Islands], *People's Daily* (24 April 1983) 4. The list is also available at www.unanhai.com/nhzddm.htm.

[2] Dao (岛) in Chinese means 'island' or 'islet'.

[3] Jiao (礁) in Chinese means 'rock'.

Huangyan Dao 黄岩岛	Scarborough Reef	15°08'N - 15°14'N	117°44'E - 117°48'E
Huayang Jiao 华阳礁	Cuarteron Reef	80°51'N - 80°52'N	112°50'E - 112°53'E
Jinghong Dao 景宏岛	Sin Cowe Island	9°53'N	114°20'E
Liyue Tan 礼乐滩	Reed Bank	11°06'N - 11°55'N	116°22'E - 117°20'E
Mahuan Dao 马欢岛	Nanshan Island	10°44'N	115°48'E
Meiji Jiao 美济礁	Mischief Reef	9°52'N - 9°56'N	115°30'E - 115°35'E
Nansha Qundao[4] 南沙群岛	Spratly Islands		
Nanwei Dao 南威岛	Spratly Island	8°39'N	111°55'E
Nanxun Jiao 南薰礁	Gaven Reef	10°10'N - 10°13'N	114°13'E - 114°15'E
Nanyue Dao 南钥岛	Loaita Island	10°40'N	114°25'E
Penghu Liedao 澎湖列岛	Pescadores Islands	23°12' - 23°47' N	119°19' - 119°43' E
Ren'ai Jiao 仁爱礁	Second Thomas Reef	9°39'N - 9°48'N	115°51'E - 115°54'E
Shuanghuang Shazhou 双黄沙洲	Double Egg Yolk Shoal[5]	10°42'N - 10°43'N	114°19'E - 114°20'E

[4] Qundao (群岛) in Chinese means 'Archipelago'.
[5] Also known as Loaita Nan.

Siling Jiao 司令礁	Commodore Reef	8°22'N - 8°24'N	115°11'E - 115°17'E
Taiping Dao 太平岛	Itu Aba Island	10°23'N	114°22'E
Ximen Jiao 西门礁	McKennan Reef	9°54'N	114°28'E
Xisha Qundao 西沙群岛	Paracel Islands		
Xiyue Dao 西月岛	West York Island	11°05'N	115°02'E
Yongshu Jiao 永暑礁	Fiery Cross Reef	9°30'N - 9°40'N	112°53'E - 113°04'E
Yongxing Dao 永兴岛	Woody Island	16°50'N	112°20'E
Zengmu Ansha 曾母暗沙	James Shoal	3°58'N	112°17'E
Zhongsha Qundao 中沙群岛	Macclesfield Bank		
Zhongye Qunjiao 中业群礁	Thitu Island	11°01'N - 11°06'N	114°11'E - 114°24'E
Zhubi Jiao 渚碧礁	Subi Reef	10°54'N - 10°56'N	114°04'E - 114°07'E

Bibliography

Abi-Saab, Georges, *Les Exceptions Préliminaires dans la Procédure de la Cour Internationale* (Paris, Editions A Pedone, 1967).

Akande, Dapo, 'Philippines Initiates Arbitration Against China over South China Sea Dispute' (22 January 2013) *EJIL: Talk!*, www.ejiltalk.org.

American Law Institute, *Restatement of the Law (Third). The Foreign Relations Law of the United States* (St Paul, American Law Institute, 1990).

Aust, Anthony, *Modern Treaty Law and Practice*, 2nd edn (Cambridge, Cambridge University Press, 2008).

Batongbacal, Jay L, 'The Impossible Dream and the West Philippine Sea' (28 January 2013) *Institute for Maritime and Ocean Affairs*, www.imoa.ph.

Beckman, Robert C and Bernard, Leonardo, 'Disputed Areas in the South China Sea: Prospects for Arbitration or Advisory Opinion', conference paper (Hanoi, 3–5 November 2011) 15–16, cil.nus.edu.sg/wp/wp-content/uploads/2009/09/Beckman-Bernard-Paper-DAV-Conf-3-5-Nov-2011.pdf.

Beckman, Robert C, 'The Philippines v. China Case and the South China Sea Disputes' (Asia Society/LKY SPP Conference, South China Sea: Central to Asia Pacific Peace and Security, New York, 13–15 March 2013) cil.nus.edu.sg/wp/wp-content/uploads/2013/03/Beckman-Asia-Society-LKY-SPP-March-2013-draft-of-6-March.pdf.

——, 'International Law, UNCLOS and the South China Sea' in Robert C Beckman, Clive Schofield, Ian Townsend-Gault, Tara Davenport and Leonardo Bernard (eds), *Beyond Territorial Disputes in the South China Sea: Legal Framework for the Joint Development of Hydrocarbon Resources* (Cheltenham, Edward Elgar, 2013) 47–92.

Bensurto, Henry, 'Role of International Law in Managing Disputes in the South China Sea' (CSIS Conference, 'Managing Tensions in the South China Sea, 5–6 June 2013) 15, csis.org/files/attachments/130606_Bensurto_ConferencePaper.pdf.

Bernhardt, Rudolf, 'Rechtsfragen historischer Buchten' in Dieter Blumenwitz and Albrecht Randelzhofer (eds), *Festschrift für Friedrich Berber zum 75. Geburtstag* (Munich, Beck, 1973) 47–60.

Borchard, Edwin, *Declaratory Judgments*, 2nd edn (Cleveland, Banks Baldwin Law Publishing, 1941).

Bouchez, Leo J, *The Regime of Historic Waters* (Leyden, AW Sythoff, 1964).

Bowett, Derek William, 'Estoppel before International Tribunals and its Relation to Acquiescence' (1957) 33 *British Year Book of International Law* 176–202.

Boyle, Alan E, 'Dispute Settlement and the Law of the Sea Convention: Problems of Fragmentation and Jurisdiction' (1997) 46 *International and Comparative Law Quarterly* 37–54.

Brownlie, Ian, *Principles of Public International Law*, 7th edn (Oxford, Oxford University Press, 2008).

Buga, Irina, 'Territorial Sovereignty Issues in Maritime Disputes: A Jurisdictional Dilemma for Law of the Sea Tribunals' (2012) 27 *International Journal of Marine and Coastal Law* 59–95.

Burke, Naomi, 'UNCLOS Annex VII Arbitration – Who, What, Where, When?' (25 March 2013) *Cambridge Journal of International and Comparative Law Blog*, www.cjicl.org.uk.

China Institute of Marine Affairs, State Oceanic Administration, *Zhong Guo Hai Yang Fa Zhan Bao Gao [China's Ocean Development Report]* (Beijing, Hai Yang Chu Ban She [Oceans Press], 2011).

Chiu, Hungdah and Park, Choon-Ho, 'Legal Status of the Paracel and Spratly Islands' (1975) 32 *Ocean Development and International Law* 1–28.

Coast Guard Administration (Taiwan, China), *Hai Yang Shi Wu Fa Gui Hui Bian [Collection of Laws relating to Marine Affairs]*, 2nd edn (Taipei, Xing Zheng Yuan Hai Xun Shu [Coast Guard Administration Executive Yuan of Taiwan], 2008).

Collier, John and Lowe, Vaughan, *The Settlement of Disputes in International Law: Institutions and Procedures* (Oxford, Oxford University Press, 1999).

Currie, Duncan EJ, 'The Experience of Greenpeace International' in Tullio Treves, Marco Frigessi di Rattalma, Attila Tanzi, Alessandro Fodella, Cesare Pitea and Chiara Ragni (eds), *Civil Society, International Courts and Compliance Bodies* (The Hague, TMC Asser Press, 2005) 149–66.

Department of Policy, Legislation and Planning, State Oceanic Administration (ed), *Collection of the Sea Laws and Regulations of the People's Republic of China*, 4th edn (Beijing, Ocean Press, 2012).

Dipla, Haritini, 'Islands' in Rüdiger Wolfrum (ed), *Max Planck Encyclopedia of Public International Law*, vol VI (Oxford, Oxford University Press, 2012) 405–14.

Drigot, Diane, 'Oil Interests and the Law of the Sea: The Case of the Philippines' (1982) 12 *Ocean Development and International Law* 23–70.

Dupuy, Florian and Dupuy, Pierre-Marie, 'A Legal Analysis of China's Historic Rights Claim in the South China Sea' (2013) 107 *American Journal of International Law* 124–41.

Eiriksson, Gudmundur, *The International Tribunal for the Law of the Sea* (The Hague, Martinus Nijhoff, 2000).

Farrell, Epsey Cooke, *The Socialist Republic of Vietnam and the Law of the Sea: An Analysis of Vietnamese Behaviour Within the Emerging International Oceans Regime* (The Hague, Martinus Nijhoff, 1998).

Gamble Jr, John King, 'The Law of the Sea Conference: Dispute Settlement in Perspective' (1976) 9 *Vanderbilt Journal of International Law* 323–42.

Gao, Zhiguo, 'The South China Sea: From Conflict to Cooperation?' (1994) 25 *Ocean Development and International Law* 345–59.

Gao, Zhiguo and Jia, Bing Bing, 'The Nine-Dash Line in the South China Sea: History, Status, and Implications' (2013) 107 *American Journal of International Law* 98–124.

Gioia, Andrea, 'Historic Titles' in Rüdiger Wolfrum (ed), *Max Planck Encyclopedia of Public International Law*, vol IV (Oxford, Oxford University Press, 2012) 814–23.

Gjetnes, Marius, 'The Spratlys: Are They Rocks or Islands?' (2001) 32 *Ocean Development and International Law* 191–204.

Goldmann, Matthias, 'International Courts and Tribunals, Non-Appearance' in Rüdiger Wolfrum (ed), *Max Planck Encyclopedia of Public International Law*, vol V (Oxford, Oxford University Press, 2006) 606–12.

Gorina-Ysern, Montserrat, 'OAS Mediates in Belize-Guatemala Border Dispute' (December 2000) *ASIL Insights*, www.asil.org.

Greenfield, Jeanette, *China's Practice in the Law of the Sea* (Oxford, Clarendon Press, 1992).

Greenwood, Christopher, 'Review of Nonappearance before the International Court of Justice by HWA Thirlway' (1985) 44 *Cambridge Law Journal* 311–12.

Guang Dong Provincial Commission of Toponymy, *Nan Hai Zhu Dao Di Ming Zi Liao Hui Bian [Collection of Materials Regarding the Geographical Names of the Islands in the South China Sea]* (Guangzhou, Guang Dong Di Tu Chu Ban She [Provincial Press of Maps and Atlases], 1987).

Han, Zhenhua, Lin, Jinzhi, and Wu, Fengbin (eds), *Wo Guo Nan Hai Zhu Dao Shi Liao Hui Bian [Collection of Historical Materials concerning Our Country's Islands in the South China Sea]* (Beijing, Dong Fang Chu Ban She [Orient Press], 1988).

Heijmans, Albertus MJ, 'Artificial Islands and the Law of Nations' (1974) 21 *Netherlands International Law Review* 139–61.

Higgins, Rosalyn, 'The Reformation in International Law' in Richard Rawlings (ed), *Law, Society and Economy: Centenary Essays for the London School of Economics and Political Science, 1895–1995* (Oxford, Clarendon Press, 1997) 207–24.

Hu, Nien–Tsu Alfred, 'South China Sea: Troubled Waters or a Sea of Opportunity?' (2010) 41 *Ocean Development and International Law* 203–13.

International Court of Justice (ed), *The International Court of Justice*, 4th edn (The Hague, International Court of Justice, 1996).

International Hydrographic Organisation, *Limits of Oceans and Seas*, Special Publication No 23, 3rd edn (Monte-Carlo, Imp Monégasque, 1953).

Irwin, Paul C, 'Settlement of Maritime Boundary Disputes: An Analysis of the Law of the Sea Negotiations' (1980) 8 *Ocean Development and International Law* 105–48.

Jayewardene, Hiran W, *The Regime of Islands in International Law*, Publications on Ocean Development (Dordrecht, Martinus Nijhoff, 1990).

Jesus, José Luis, 'Rocks, New-born Islands, Sea Level Rise and Maritime Space' in Jochen A Frowein, Klaus Scharioth, Ingo Winkelmann and Rüdiger Wolfrum (eds), *Verhandeln für den Frieden/Negotiating for Peace: Liber Amicorum Tono Eitel* (Berlin, Springer, 2003) 579–603.

Jia, Bing Bing, 'China and International Law', *Proceedings of the American Society of International Law* (2013; forthcoming).

Karaman, Igor V, *Dispute Resolution in the Law of the Sea* (Leiden, Martinus Nijhoff, 2012).

Klein, Natalie, *Dispute Settlement in the UN Convention on the Law of the Sea* (Cambridge, Cambridge University Press, 2005).

Kohen, Marcelo G and Hébie, Mamadou, 'Territory, Acquisition' in Rüdiger Wolfrum (ed), *Max Planck Encyclopedia of Public International Law*, vol IX (Oxford, Oxford University Press, 2012) 897–900.

Kolb, Robert, *Case Law on Equitable Maritime Delimitation: Digest and Commentaries* (The Hague, Martinus Nijhoff, 2003).

Kraska, James and Pedrozo, Raul, *International Maritime Security Law* (Leiden, Martinus Nijhoff, 2013).

Lavalle, Robert, 'Not Quite a Sure Thing: The Maritime Areas of Rocks and Low-Tide Elevations Under the UN Law of the Sea Convention' (2004) 19 *International Journal of Marine and Coastal Law* 43–69.

Lee, Lai To, *China and the South China Sea Dialogues* (Westport, Praeger, 1999).

Legislative Affairs Commission of the Standing Committee of the National People's Congress of the People's Republic of China, *The Laws of the People's Republic of China* (1983–1986) (Beijing, Ke Xue Chu Ban She [Science Press], 1987).

——, *The Laws of the People's Republic of China* (1987–1989) (Beijing, Ke Xue Chu Ban She [Science Press], 1990).

Li, Jinming and Li, Dexia, 'The Dotted Line on the Chinese Map of the South China Sea: A Note' (2003) 34 *Ocean Development and International Law* 287–95.

Li, Mingje, *Tai Wan Di Qu Hai Yang Wen Ti Yan Jiu [A Study on the Maritime Issues of the Taiwan Region]* (Beijing, Zhong Guo She Ke Chu Ban She [China Social Sciences Press], 2011).

Lim, Benito O, 'Tempest over the South China Sea: The Chinese Perspective on the Spratlys' (2000) 36 *Asian Studies* 69–132.

Lowe, Vaughan and Talmon, Stefan (eds), *The Legal Order of the Oceans: Basic Documents on the Law of the Sea* (Oxford, Hart Publishing, 2009).

Mangoldt, Hans von and Zimmermann, Andreas, 'Article 53' in Andreas Zimmermann, Karin Oellers-Frahm, Christian Tomuschat and Christian J Tams (eds), *The Statute of the International Court of Justice: A Commentary*, Oxford Commentaries on International Law, 2nd edn (Oxford, Oxford University Press, 2012) 1324–54.

Marques Antunes, Nuno S, *Towards the Conceptualisation of Maritime Delimitation: Legal and Technical Aspects of a Political Process* (Leiden, Martinus Nijhoff, 2003).

Max Planck Institute for International Law (ed), *World Court Digest*, vol 4: 2001–2005 (Berlin, Springer, 2009).

Merrills, John G, *International Dispute Settlement*, 5th edn (Cambridge, Cambridge University Press, 2011).

Mosler, Hermann, 'Nichtteilnahme einer Partei am Verfahren vor dem Internationalen Gerichtshof' in Ingo von Münch (ed), *Staatsrecht, Völkerrecht, Europarecht: Festschrift für Hans-Jürgen Schlochauer zum 75. Geburtstag am 28. März 1981* (Berlin, Walter de Gruyter & Co, 1981) 439–56.

Müller, Jörg Paul and Cottier, Thomas, 'Estoppel' in Rudolf Bernhardt (ed), *Encyclopedia of Public International Law*, vol II (Amsterdam, North Holland Publishing, 1995) 116–19.

Naess,Tom, 'Dangers to the Environment' in Timo Kovomäki (ed), *War or Peace in the South China Sea?* (Copenhagen, NIAS Press, 2002) 43–53.

Nordquist, Myron H, Rosenne, Shabtai and Sohn, Louis B (eds), *United Nations Convention on the Law of the Sea 1982: A Commentary*, vol V (Dordrecht, Martinus Nijhoff, 1989).

Oda, Shigeru, 'Dispute Settlement Prospects in the Law of the Sea' (1995) 44 *International and Comparative Law Quarterly* 863–72.

Oude Elferink, Alex G, 'The Islands in the South China Sea: How Does Their Presence Limit the Extent of the High Seas and the Area and the Maritime Zones of the Mainland Coasts?' (2001) 32 *Ocean Development and International Law* 169–90.

Oxman, Bernard H, 'The Third United Nations Conference on the Law of the Sea: The Ninth Session' (1981) 75 *American Journal of International Law* 211–56.

Pellet, Alain, 'Land and Maritime Tripoints in International Jurisprudence' in Holger P Hestermeyer, Doris König, Nele Matz-Lück, Volker Röben, Anja Seibert-Fohr, Peter-Tobias Stoll and Silja Vöneky (eds), *Coexistence, Cooperation and Solidarity: Liber Amicorum Rüdiger Wolfrum*, vol I (Leiden, Martinus Nijhoff, 2012) 245–63.

People's Republic of China, Ministry of Agriculture, Fisheries Bureau, *Zhong Guo Yu Ye Nian Jian 2012 [China Fisheries Yearbook 2012]* (Beijing, Zhong Guo Nong Ye Chu Ban She [China Agriculture Press], 2012).

——, *Zhong Guo Yu Ye Tong Ji Nian Jian 2013 [China Fisheries Statistics Yearbook 2013]* (Beijing, Zhong Guo Nong Ye Chu Ban She [China Agriculture Press], 2013).

Rahman, Chris and Tsamenyi, Martin, 'A Strategic Perspective on Security and Naval Issues in the South China Sea' (2010) 41 *Ocean Development and International Law* 315–33.

Rao, Patibandla Chandrasekhara, 'Law of the Sea, Settlement of Disputes' in Rüdiger Wolfrum (ed), *Max Planck Encyclopedia of Public International Law*, vol VI (Oxford, Oxford University Press, 2012) 738–47.

Rosenne, Shabtai (with the assistance of Yaël Ronen), *The Law and Practice of the International Court, 1920–2005*, vol 2, 4th edn (Leiden, Martinus Nijhoff, 2006).

Samuels, Marvyn S, *Contest for the South China Sea* (New York, Methuen, 1982).

San Pablo-Baviera, Aileen (ed), *The South China Sea Disputes: Philippine Perspectives* (Quezon City, Philippine China Development Resource Center & Philippine Association for Chinese Studies, 1992).

Schachter, Oscar, 'The Twilight Existence of Nonbinding Agreements' (1971) 71 *American Journal of International Law* 296–304.

Schmalenbach, Kirsten, 'Dispute settlement' in Jan Klabbers and Åsa Wallendahl (eds), *Research Handbook on the Law of International Organizations* (Cheltenham, Edward Elgar, 2011) 251–84.

Schofield, Clive, 'The Trouble with Islands: The Definition and Role of Islands and Rocks in Maritime Boundary Delimitation' in Seoung Yong Hong and Jon M Van Dyke (eds), *Maritime Boundary Disputes, Settlement Processes, and the Law of the Sea* (Leiden, Martinus Nijhoff, 2009) 19–37.

Severino, Rodolfo C, *Southeast Asia in Search of an ASEAN Community: Insights from the Former ASEAN Secretary-General* (Singapore, Institute of Southeast Asian Studies, 2006).

Shaw, Malcolm, *International Law*, 6th edn (Cambridge, Cambridge University Press, 2008).

Shen, Jianming, 'China's Sovereignty over the South China Sea Islands: A Historical Perspective' (2002) 1 *Chinese Journal of International Law* 94–157.

Sinclair, Ian, *The Vienna Convention on the Law of Treaties*, 2nd edn (Manchester, Manchester University Press, 1984).

Song, Yann-huei, 'Article 121(3) of the Law of the Sea Convention and the Disputed Offshore Islands in East Asia: A Tribute to Judge Choon-Ho Park' in Jon M Van Dyke, Sherry P Broder, Seokwoo Lee and Jin-Hyun Paik (eds), *Governing Ocean Resources: New Challenges and Emerging Regimes: A Tribute to Judge Choon-Ho Park* (Leiden, Martinus Nijhoff, 2013) 61–97.

Song, Yann-huei and Yu, Peter Kien-hong, 'China's "Historic Waters" in the South China Sea: An Analysis from Taiwan, ROC' (1994) 12/4 *American Asian Review* 83–101.

Storey, Ian James, 'Creeping Assertiveness: China, the Philippines and the South China Sea Disputes' (1999) 21 *Contemporary Southeast Asia* 95–118.

Strupp, Michael, 'Spratly Islands' in Rüdiger Wolfrum (ed), *Max Planck Encyclopedia of International Law*, vol IX (Oxford, Oxford University Press, 2012) 448–51.

Sun, Kuang-Ming, 'Policy of the Republic of China towards the South China Sea: Recent Developments' (1995) 19 *Marine Policy* 401–08.

Suy, Eric, 'Consensus' in Rudolf Bernhardt (ed), *Encyclopedia of Public International Law*, vol I (Amsterdam, North-Holland Publishing, 1992) 758–61.

Symmons Clive R, *Some Problems Relating to the Definition of Insular Formations in International Law – Islands and Low-Tide Elevations*, Maritime Briefing vol 1, no 5, Clive Schofield and Peter Hocknell (eds) (Durham, International Boundaries Research Unit, 1995).

Talmon, Stefan, 'Article 43' in Andreas Zimmermann, Karin Oellers-Frahm, Christian Tomuschat and Christian J Tams (eds), *The Statute of the International Court of Justice: A Commentary*, Oxford Commentaries on International Law, 2nd edn (Oxford, Oxford University Press, 2012) 1088–171.

Tanaka, Yoshifumi, 'Low-Tide Elevations in International Law of the Sea: Selected Issues' (2006) 20 *Ocean Yearbook* 189–219.

Thao, Nguyen Hong, 'The 2002 Declaration on the Conduct of Parties in the South China Sea: A Note' (2003) 34 *Ocean Development and International Law* 279–85.

Thao, Nguyen Hong and Amer, Ramses, 'A New Legal Arrangement for the South China Sea?' (2009) 40 *Ocean Development and International Law* 333–49.

Thayer, Carlyle A, 'ASEAN'S Code of Conduct in the South China Sea: A Litmus Test for Community-Building?' (20 August 2012) *The Asia Pacific Journal*, vol 10, issue 34, no 4, www.japanfocus.org.

Thirlway, Hugh WA, *Non-appearance before the International Court of Justice*, Cambridge Studies in International and Comparative Law (Cambridge, Cambridge University Press, 1985).

——, 'The Law and Procedure of the International Court of Justice, 1960–1989 (Part Eleven)' (2000) 71 *British Year Book of International Law* 71–180.

——, *The Law and Procedure of the International Court of Justice: Fifty Years of Jurisprudence*, vol 2 (Oxford, Oxford University Press, 2013).

Tomuschat, Christian, 'Article 36' in Andreas Zimmermann, Karin Oellers-Frahm, Christian Tomuschat and Christian J Tams (eds), *The Statute of the International Court of Justice: A Commentary*, Oxford Commentaries on International Law, 2nd edn (Oxford, Oxford University Press, 2012) 633–711.

Tønnesson, Stein, 'The History of the Dispute' in Timo Kovomäki (ed), *War or Peace in the South China Sea?* (Copenhagen, NIAS Press, 2002) 6–23.

Treves, Tullio, 'Military Installations, Structures and Devices on the Seabed' (1980) 74 *American Journal of International Law* 808–57.

——, 'Preliminary Proceedings in the Settlement of Disputes under the United Nations Law of the Sea Convention: Some Observations' in Niuske Ando, Edward McWhinney and Rüdiger Wolfrum (eds), *Liber Amicorum Judge Shigeru Oda*, vol I (The Hague, Kluwer, 2002) 749–61.

——, 'The Jurisdiction of the International Tribunal for the Law of the Sea' in Patibandla Chandrasekhara Rao and Khan Rahmatullah (eds), *International Tribunal for the Law of the Sea: Law and Practice* (The Hague, Kluwer, 2001) 111–31.

——, 'What Have the United Nations Convention and the International Tribunal for the Law of the Sea to Offer as Regards Maritime Delimitation Disputes?' in Rainer Lagoni and Daniel Vignes (eds), *Maritime Delimitation* (Leiden, Martinus Nijhoff, 2006) 63–78.

Valencia, Mark J, Van Dyke, Jon M and Ludwig, Noel A, *Sharing the Resources of the South China Sea* (The Hague, Martinus Nijhoff, 1997).

Van Dyke, Jon M, 'Disputes Over Islands and Maritime Boundaries in East Asia' in Seoung Yong Hong and Jon M Van Dyke (eds), *Maritime Boundary Disputes, Settlement Processes and the Law of the Sea* (Leiden, Martinus Nijhoff, 2009) 39–75.

——, 'The Romania-Ukraine Decision and Its Effect on East Asian Maritime Delimitations' in Jon M Van Dyke, Sherry P Broder, Seokwoo Lee and Jin-Hyun Paik (eds), *Governing Ocean Resources: New Challenges and Emerging Regimes: A Tribute to Judge Choon-Ho Park* (Leiden, Martinus Nijhoff, 2013) 43–60.

Weil, Prosper 'Les hauts fonds découvrants dans la délimitation maritime. À propos des paragraphes 200–209 de l'arrêt de la Cour internationale de Justice du 16 mars 2001 en l'affaire de la *Délimitation maritime et questions territoriales entre Qatar et Bahreïn*' in Nisuke Ando, Edward McWhinney and Rüdiger Wolfrum (eds), *Liber Amicorum Judge Shigeru Oda* (The Hague, Kluwer, 2002) 307–21.

Widdows, Kelvin, 'What is an Agreement in International Law?' (1979) 50 *British Year Book of International Law* 117–49.

Wu, Shicun, *Nan Sha Zheng Duan De Qi Yuan Yu Fa Zhan [The Origin and Development of the Nansha Disputes]* (Beijing, Zhong Guo Jing Ji Chu Ban She [China Economic Publishing House], 2010).

Wu, Shicun, Li, Xiuling, Zhong, Tianxiang, Su, Yan and Fu, Yu (eds.), *Nan Hai Wen Ti Wen Xian Hui Bian [Collection of Documents on the Issue of the South China Sea]* (Hai Kou City, Hai Nan Chu Ban She [Hainan Press], 2001).

Zeng, Zhaoxuan (ed), *Islands in the South China Sea* (in Chinese) (Guangdong, People's Publishing House, 1986).

Zou, Keyuan, 'Historic Rights in International Law and in China's Practice' (2001) 32 *Ocean Development and International Law* 149–68.

——, 'How Coastal States Claim Maritime Geographic Features: Legal Clarity or Conundrum?' (2012) 11 *Chinese Journal of International Law* 749–65.

——, *Law of the Sea in East Asia: Issues and Prospects*, Routledge Studies in International Law (London and New York, Routledge, 2005).

Index